The Governance of Urban Green Spaces in the EU

T0361955

Across European cities the use of urban space is controversial and subject to diverging interests. On the one hand citizens are increasingly aware of the necessity for self-organising to reclaim green spaces. On the other hand local authorities have started to involve citizens in the governance of urban green spaces. While an increased level of citizen participation and conducive conditions for citizens' self-organisation are a desirable development per se, the risk of functionalising civil society actors by the local authority for neoliberal city development must be kept in mind.

Drawing on qualitative and quantitative data collected in 29 European cities from all four European geographic regions, this book examines the governance of urban green spaces and urban food production, focusing on the contribution of citizen-driven activities. Over the course of the book, Schicklinski identifies best practice examples of successful collaboration between citizens and local government. The book concludes with policy recommendations with great practical value for local governance in European cities in times of the growth-turn.

This book will be of great relevance to students, scholars, and policy-makers with an interest in environmental governance, urban geography, and sustainable development.

Judith Schicklinski completed her PhD at the Free University of Bolzano, Italy. Her special interests are civil society's role in the socio-ecological transition, urban development, and EU-migration and development policy. She currently works as a volunteer for a local non-governmental organisation in Quito, Ecuador.

Routledge Explorations in Environmental Studies

The Governance of Urban Green Spaces in the EU

Social Innovation and Civil Society

Judith Schicklinski

Routledge
Taylor & Francis Group

LONDON AND NEW YORK

First published 2017 by Routledge

2 Park Square, Milton Park, Abingdon, Oxfordshire OX14 4RN

711 Third Avenue, New York, NY 10017

Routledge is an imprint of the Taylor & Francis Group, an informa business

First issued in paperback 2018

British Library Cataloguing-in-Publication Data
A catalogue record for this book is available from the British Library

Library of Congress Cataloging-in-Publication Data
A catalog record for this book has been requested

ISBN: 978-1-138-22375-2 (hbk)
ISBN: 978-0-367-03048-3 (pbk)

Typeset in Goudy
by Wearset Ltd, Boldon, Tyne and Wear

'What did you do, (grand)father, when greenhouse gas emissions were allowed to grow out of control in the early 2000s?'

Contents

Figures

Tables

Preface

This book is based on my PhD thesis handed in at the Free University of Bolzano, Italy, in 2016. It could not have been written without the efforts of many people. I would like to thank in the first place an outstanding academic in the field of socio-ecological research, Susanne Elsen, who continuously accompanied the work giving valuable suggestions on literature, advice on thesis structure, and feedback on completed parts. Without her, the work would not have been finished, and a great part of my learning process in the last three years is owed to her. I would equally like to thank Walter Lorenz for his valuable feedback and guidance primarily related to the theoretical part.

Many thanks to the respondents who took their time to be interviewed and/or to fill in the questionnaire. The whole study would have been impossible without their willingness to dedicate their time and share their knowledge. The methodological part could only be written thanks to Thomas Sauer, leader of area five of the WWWforEurope project, who gave his consent for the use of the collected data also for this thesis. I would also like to acknowledge the work of former members of the WWWforEurope project team (cf. 4.1 and 4.2): Benjamin Gloy, Enkeleda Kadriu, Adrien Labaeye, Nadine Marmai, and Kira Reich and to thank the co-field researchers Aleksandra Marta Duda, Alina Brasoveanu, Dalia Campoccia, Etrit Shkreli, Hana Belohoubkova, Isabel Fernández de la Fuente, Joakim Toll, Júlia Colomer Matutano, Juliette Muguet-Guenot, Lea K. Baumbach, Michael Bockhorni, Mikaela Lise Vasström, Renaud Hourcade, Vasileios Latinos, and Vildan Aydin who persistently collected the qualitative and quantitative data and provided the project team with the transcribed and translated English version of the interviews, as well as with a case study report for each city. Furthermore, I would like to express my gratitude to my former colleagues Stephanie Barnebeck and Yannick Kalff for their valuable remarks on contributions to the project that were incorporated into this book. In addition, thanks should be given to them, since Stephanie Barnebeck conducted the quantitative data analysis in the scope of the WWWforEurope project, including the visualisation of the results, and Yannick Kalff created a map of the project's 40 selected cities for the project's final publication (Sauer *et al.* 2016, p. 27) which served as a template for Figure 4.3. I would also like to express my gratitude to Daniel Ross and Hilary Solly for carefully checking the

English, as well as to the friendly and competent staff of the Free University of Bolzano. Especially the people working in the Information and Communication Technology department and the library, which is the best I have ever worked in, have extremely facilitated my working process by responding as quickly as possible to literature requests or PC problems.

Last but not least, I would like to thank Massimo Tommasi for his understanding and continuous support, especially in the phase of writing up the thesis.

Quito, September 2016
Judith Schicklinski

Reference

Sauer, Thomas, Cristina Garzillo, and Susanne Elsen, eds. 2016. *Cities in transition: Social innovation for Europe's urban sustainability*. Abingdon/New York: Routledge.

1   Framing the research

Ulrich Beck, in his book *World Risk Society: On the Search for Lost Security* (2007, own translation) draws attention to the fact that humankind has arrived at a state in which human-produced risks have become global, threatening everyone everywhere. This situation requires an integrated approach from the local to the global level to change the current social and economic system, if the survival of the species human being in a liveable environment wants to be assured:

> From now on the concern for the whole has become the task. This is not an option but the condition. This was not foreseen by anyone, nor wanted nor chosen. However, it evolved from decisions as their unseen sequence of sums and has become the condition humana that no one can elude.
>
> (Beck 2007, 48, own translation)

1.1 Introduction

Worldwide climate change, biodiversity loss, and the end of fossil resources require a paradigmatic shift in direction of sustainable forms of organising society and economy within a limited time frame. Such a shift can be conceptualised with the term 'socio-ecological transition', which first appeared in the title of a European Union (EU) policy document in 2009 (Di Rossetti Valdalbero 2009). Academically, it was only defined later, with the most comprehensive examination of the concept given by Fischer-Kowalski *et al.* (2012, 5):

> Transition is a process starting off from one system state and ending up in another[.] … [a] socio-ecological transition [moves] away from fossil fuels, towards solar and other low carbon energy sources ('new') transition. This transition will inevitably occur, due to the limitations of fossil fuels, but it may be actively accelerated, mainly to avoid catastrophic climate change.

This means on the one hand that the course of this transition can be influenced and even steered by people, whilst on the other it is a comprehensive social process involving all realms of society: 'What is changing is not just the source of energy and technologies, but many other features of society as well: the economy, the demography, the settlement patterns, the social relations and the very make-up of human personalities' (ibid.). Thus, it cannot be achieved by simple technological improvements but entails wider fundamental changes in consumption and production behaviour as well as in the functioning of institutions (Harvey 2012, 127). There is a growing academic and policy discourse about the possibilities of and barriers to the socio-ecological transition. While long-term goals seem to be clear, discussion of how to reach them is controversial. A key assumption of this research is that such a transition is unimaginable without an active contribution from civil society, meaning the involvement, participation, and self-organisation of socially innovative bottom-up actors emerging mostly – but not exclusively – in this societal realm. Previous work confirms the importance of these actors for the transition, for example, Seyfang and Smith's (2007) research on 'grassroots innovations'. The interrelatedness of social, environmental, and economic questions comes to light in quoting Harvey (2012, 127–8) who asks about the influence of urban-based social movements in reaction to three phenomena:

> The first is that of crushing material impoverishment for much of the world's population[.] … The second question derives from the clear and imminent dangers of out-of-control environmental degradations and ecological transformations … [, and] [t]he third … derives from … [an] understanding of the inevitable trajectory of capitalist growth … that exerts such enormous destructive pressure on global social relations and ecosystems.

Finally, yet importantly, Ostrom (e.g. 1990, 2005) shows that a self-organised governance of commons beyond state and market forces is possible, disproving a long-standing economic theorem.

The socio-ecological transition cannot succeed without a shift to sustainable land use. In Europe, land is a finite and shrinking resource because of land use changes that are mostly and increasingly marked by land consumption, due to a rising urbanisation trend with concomitant urban sprawl and soil sealing (Bringezu *et al.* 2014, 50). Therefore, across European cities, the use of urban space is highly controversial and subject to diverging interests, yielding a high conflict potential. A persisting economic growth logic manifests itself in ongoing infrastructure and building development pressure, threatening inner and outer city green spaces, especially in growing cities. Yet, preserving the availability of these spaces is crucial, since apart from offering recreational opportunities for city dwellers, they yield indispensable ecological and further social benefits, such as reducing noise, cleaning the air, providing a habitat for animal and plant species, and mitigating local vulnerability in the face of extreme climate events. In this context, on the one hand citizens are becoming increasingly aware of the necessity for 'commoning'[1] (Helfrich and Bollier 2014, 19), that is, self-organising, to reclaim urban green spaces, for example by taking care of them, in some places also for food production, thereby turning these spaces into common space. On the other hand local authorities have started increasingly to involve citizens in the governance of urban green spaces. While an increased level of citizen participation and conducive conditions for citizens' self-organisation are a desirable development per se, it must be critically examined whether this goes along with public spending cuts and a drawback of the state from core welfare state tasks. Keeping this risk of functionalising civil society actors by the local authority for neoliberal city development in mind, this book examines how civil society's potential and activities can best be supported by the local authority to achieve a triple-win situation of (a) increased citizen participation and self-organisation and (b) civil society's support in the governance of urban green spaces to eventually achieve (c) a sustainable governance of these spaces, contributing to integrated local and regional socio-ecological-economic development and thus to the socio-ecological transition.

1.2   Research context and questions

In the scope of the WWWforEurope project[2] (cf. 4.1 and 4.2), following Ostrom's work on the governance of commons, the role of urban green spaces and particularly the role of citizen participation and self-organisation in their governance was examined (Schicklinski 2016). One of the main findings was that, compared to the other resource systems under scrutiny (water and energy), self-organisation emerges more easily and can be found more often and to a higher degree in the green spaces resource system, up to the point that in some places it has even become a transition driver (Barnebeck *et al.* 2016, 194).

This book connects to these findings by looking at the role of civil society in the post-growth debate, examining its position vis-à-vis state and market players, and exploring the impact of its activities at the local level. To answer the underlying research question *under what local conditions and to which extent civil society can be a transition driver in the green spaces resource system in European cities*, two specific questions are posed:

1   How can citizen groups contribute to maintaining existing green spaces that are available and accessible for all and which should be expanded whilst ensuring biodiversity and providing for a diversity of uses for local needs (recreation, community-based food production, neighbourhood culture, cross-generational, intercultural learning, etc.) at the same time?
2   Which policy framework allows for constructive collaboration between the local authority, economic actors, and citizens, enabling innovative solutions in the governance of urban green spaces, urban food production, and participatory urban development?

Thus, the research, first, aims to provide a deepened analysis of actors, processes, and contributions of citizen-driven activities within the governance of urban green spaces and urban food production across European cities. Second, its goal is to present 'best practice' examples and to identify institutional conditions under which they have evolved in order to prepare replicability elsewhere. Last, its objective is to direct the attention of researchers and policy-makers to civil society actors, recognising their role and potential in contributing to, initiating, and sustaining processes of transition across European cities, in order to create improved framework conditions for their involvement.

The underlying research question suggests two hypotheses. First, the socio-ecological transition requires a fundamental 'new' way of conceiving the relationship between economy and society which does away with the still dominant growth paradigm. Second, without the active involvement and participation of civil society actors, thus with options for citizen participation and self-organisation, the socio-ecological transition is not feasible. Following the second hypothesis, the *socio-ecological transition in the green spaces resource system in European cities* is modelled as dependent variable (Y) which is influenced by the independent explanatory variable (X) *self-organisation and citizen participation in the governance of urban green spaces* (Gerring 2007, 217; cf. Figure 5.1). Thus, it is assumed that the active involvement and participation of civil society actors positively contributes to, and thus 'drives', the transition.

1.3 Structure of the book

The book is structured in ten chapters. After framing the research (Chapter 1), the analysis of current societal and ecological conditions (Chapter 2) shows that taking the way towards a post-growth society and economy is indispensable to ensure the survival of humankind. 'New' approaches for redefining economy and society are presented, starting with Polanyi's 're-embedding' concept, across 'the concept of a new social contract for the transformation towards sustainability' (German Advisory Council on Global Change (WBGU) 2011, 2), to a post-growth society and economy, with social and solidarity economy as one concrete approach of how to implement and organise such an altered relationship between economy and society. Chapter 3 makes reference to the governance of commons, explaining why they are to be considered a special type of goods and how the 'tragedy of the commons' can be countered. To this end it lays out the principles of the governance of commons according to Ostrom, displays the mayor critiques of her theory, and outlines policy implications as deriving from her work. Chapter 4 presents the methodological approach.

Chapters 5–9 introduce further theoretical concepts that are related to the presented empirical results followed by a discussion of the latter. In Chapter 5 the relevance of cities for the socio-ecological transition is depicted as well as the importance of urban green spaces for it, before presenting the actors' view on the observed socio-ecological transition in the city in general and with reference to the green spaces resource system in particular.

In the sixth chapter a theoretical background on the social innovation–civil society nexus is provided, asking how social innovation can be defined and where it occurs before circumscribing *civil society*, depicting it as a corrective power to state and market forces and especially examining the emergence of social movements. Next, it looks into the topic of urban (green) spaces as spaces of civil society action, analysing how space is sociologically created by actors, with commoning being one specific form of space creation. Then, the empirical data on actors, actions, and conflicts is presented, before shedding light on communalities and differences of citizen participation and self-organisation from a theoretical stance and presenting forms and outcomes of citizen participation and self-organisation as emerging from the empirical data.

Chapter 7 deals with the (re)appropriation of urban green spaces and with the topic of urban food production. The interrelationship between power, democracy, and public space is treated. In this context, the disappearance and loss of public space – often linked to privatisation – as well as reactions to these processes, such as citizens (re)appropriating public space and thus defending green spaces, are first described on a theoretical level before empirical evidence is given. Urban food production is then examined from three, often related, angles: as one form of productively reappropriating public space, as an element of a multiple activity society, and as a means to raise awareness for a sustainable global food and agriculture system, again combining theoretical and empirical insights, before lastly shedding light on further trends in urban food production.

In Chapter 8 a theoretical model is devised to elucidate actors' motivations for becoming engaged in sustainability issues which is then applied to shed light on actors' motivations to commit themselves to sustainability issues in general and to produce food in the city in particular.

In Chapter 9 five existing barriers and conducive conditions for citizen participation, self-organisation, and the socio-ecological transition are carved out from the empirical data, and a policy framework with concrete policy recommendations that allows for innovative solutions in the governance of urban green spaces is presented.

Chapter 10 ultimately reflects on civil society's role in the governance of urban green spaces in European cities, and summarises the main findings, linking them to the study's aims and pointing out fields requiring further research.

Notes

1 Translated and reproduced from Helfrich and Bollier 2014.
2 'Welfare, Wealth and Work for Europe', www.foreurope.eu/index.php?id=56 [27 August 2016].

References

Barnebeck, Stephanie, Yannick Kalff, and Thomas Sauer. 2016. 'Institutional diversity'. In *Cities in transition: Social innovation for Europe's urban sustainability*, eds Thomas Sauer, Cristina Garzillo, and Susanne Elsen, 192–203. Abingdon/New York: Routledge.
Beck, Ulrich. 2007. *Weltrisikogesellschaft: Auf der Suche nach der verlorenen Sicherheit*. Frankfurt am Main: Suhrkamp.

Bringezu, Stefan, Helmut Schütz, Walter Pengue, Meghan O'Brian, Fernando Garcia, Ralph Sims, Robert W. Howarth, Lea Kauppi, Mark Swilling, and Jeffrey Herrick. 2014. 'Assessing global land use: Balancing consumption with sustainable supply. A report of the Working Group on Land and Soils of the International Resource Panel'. Nairobi: United Nations Environment Programme. www.unep.org/resourcepanel-old/Portals/24102/PDFs//Full_Report-Assessing_Global_Land_UseEnglish_(PDF).pdf [27 August 2016].

Di Rossetti Valdalbero, Domenico. 2009. 'The world in 2025: Rising Asia and socio-ecological transition'. Luxembourg: Office for Official Publications of the European Communities. https://ec.europa.eu/research/social-sciences/pdf/policy_reviews/the-world-in-2025-report_en.pdf [27 August 2016].

Fischer-Kowalski, Marina, Willi Haas, Dominik Wiedenhofer, Ulli Weisz, Irene Pallua, Nikolaus Possaner, Arno Behrens, Serio Giulia, and Ekke Weis. 2012. 'Socio-ecological transitions: Definitions, dynamics and related global scenarios'. Working Paper of the Neujobs project. http://81.47.175.201/flagship/attachments/Socio_ecological_transitions_and_global_scenarios.pdf [27 August 2016].

German Advisory Council on Global Change (WBGU). 2011. Flagship report. World in transition: A social contract for sustainability. Berlin: WBGU. www.wbgu.de/fileadmin/templates/dateien/veroeffentlichungen/hauptgutachten/jg2011/wbgu_jg2011_en.pdf [27 August 2016].

Gerring, John. 2007. *Case study research: Principles and practices*. New York: Cambridge University Press.

Harvey, David. 2012. *Rebel cities: From the right to the city to the urban revolution*. London: Verso.

Helfrich, Silke and David Bollier. 2014. 'Commons als transformative Kraft: Zur Einführung'. In *Commons: Für eine neue Politik jenseits von Markt und Staat*. 2nd edn, ed. Silke Helfrich, 15–23. Bielefeld: transcript. www.boell.de/sites/default/files/2012-04-buch-2012-04-buch-commons.pdf [27 August 2016].

Ostrom, Elinor. 1990. *Governing the commons: The evolution of institutions for collective action*. New York: Cambridge University Press. www.boell.de/sites/default/files/2012-04-buch-2012-04-buch-commons.pdf [27 July 2016].

Ostrom, Elinor. 2005. *Understanding institutional diversity*. Princeton, NJ: Princeton University Press.

Schicklinski, Judith. 2016. 'Socio-ecological transitions in the green spaces resource system'. In *Cities in transition: Social innovation for Europe's urban sustainability*, eds Thomas Sauer, Cristina Garzillo, and Susanne Elsen, 93–124. Abingdon/New York: Routledge.

Seyfang, Gill and Adrian Smith. 2007. 'Grassroots innovations for sustainable development: Towards a new research and policy agenda'. *Environmental Politics*, 16(4): 584–603. http://community.eldis.org/.5ad5051c/Seyfang%20and%20Smith.pdf [27 August 2016].

2 Towards a post-growth society and economy

Why is a paradigm shift to a post-growth society and economy indispensable? Why can economic growth not be continued to be placed as an overarching aim of economic activity, aligning all societal sectors accordingly with the hope that more growth will bring more well-being for all members of society? Answers to these questions are complex and are tried to be answered in this chapter. The first section is an attempt to analyse current societal conditions of European society, setting the frame in which action is evolving. Section 2.2 delivers the natural-scientific 'hard facts' about the present ecological state of the Earth. Scientists started to deliver proof of humankind's increasing detrimental impact on the world's ecosystems in the early 1970s, and a point has been reached where this impact started to redound on humankind itself with irreversible damage occurring. Section 2.3 returns to a sociological stance, explaining with the help of system theory why a system change is indispensable and how it needs to look as well as show the Janus-faced character of economic growth. In the Section 2.4 the overdue redefinition of the relationship between economy and society, which has been demanded by scholars for more than 70 years, takes shape. What does the re-embedding of economy into society imply for European society and the economy in general and for European cities in particular?

2.1 Analysis of societal conditions: modernisation theory

The theory of reflexive modernisation differentiates between the first (simple) and the second (reflexive) modernity. The first one pictures industrial society which is marked by thinking in national categories and conceived as a stratification of different social classes that are created according to their members belonging to lifelong-held professions in certain sectors (Beck 1993, 72). It is founded on fossil-fuel-driven economic growth and linear technological progress which are believed to lead to wealth for the majority of the population, to solve most of its problems, and even to control and repair any self-created damage (ibid., 84). However, largely unnoticed, the shift to a second modernity becomes manifest (ibid., 76) in which these securities and beliefs vanish. In the second modernity the 'unshakeable belief in planning (in society) and predictability (in science) is long past. ... Gone too is the belief in simple cause–effect relationships often embodying implicit assumptions about their underlying linearity' (Nowotny *et al.* 2013, 5). This major change can be better understood by placing it into a broader historical frame. Another comparably big shift was the one from traditional feudal to industrial society (Beck 1993, 71). The ongoing shift has not, just as the preceding one, been deliberately agreed on, planned, or chosen consciously by the members of society, but is the result of modernisation processes (ibid., 36), which will be described in the next paragraph.

The main thesis of Beck's theory is that

> the transformation of unseen side effects of industrial production into global ecological trouble spots is precisely not a problem of the world surrounding us – not a so-called 'environmental problem' but a profound crisis of institutions of the industrial society itself.
>
> (Ibid., 46, own translation)

This means that the very same institutions incorporating progress and economic growth thinking have to admit that, first, their activities have produced social and environmental externalities of a global all-embracing scale meaning risks for and harm to humankind as a whole and that, second, these institutions have failed in protecting humankind against these self-produced risks. These self-endangering effects of modern civilisation (ibid., 56) in a world of globalised risks which has undermined its own carrying capacity (cf. 2.2) mean that institutions and norms produced by industrial society, such as the principle of insurance, become obsolete and senseless. Risks can no longer be played down as deplorable but inevitable 'latent side effects' (Beck 2009, 13) of a salutary techno-economic growth and progress formula. This is so because the dimension of these side effects has reached too big a scale to be concealed or talked down.

This situation shows that 'a reflexive self-determination and redefinition of the Western model of modernity' (Beck 2007, 173, own translation) has become more than overdue. Reflexivity is here understood in two ways. On the one hand it circumscribes society's attempt to impulsively continue the path of self-endangering modernisation, resembling a hamster not able to exit its wheel, despite increasing knowledge about concomitantly increasing risks. On the other hand, since the produced risks become bigger and more visible and palpable, members of society cannot help but start to reflect on the process of modernisation they are undergoing and to confront the risks produced by it (Beck 1993, 56). They gradually become aware of the fact that industrial society's detrimental impact on nature has turned the global population into a 'world risk community' (Beck 2007, 27, own translation).

Mainstream economic theory, determining the functioning of the economic system, believes in an endless supply of environmental resources and in the infinite possibility of nature to be used as a sink at the end of the production process. This view denies a more systemic one which conceives the world as a unique interrelation between interdependent socio-ecological systems (SES) with limited resources (cf. 2.2 and 2.3). Classical economic theory's habit of externalising social and environmental effects for profit maximisation is short-sighted and falls back, if not already on the current generation, on the subsequent one. Yet, a point of environmental damage and existence of risks has been reached which 'turns the speech about the "option of externalisation" into a joke' (Beck 1993, 83, own translation), since environmental risks have become inescapable (ibid., 235) and incalculable. They can neither be contained in space (Beck 2007, 47–8) or in time nor be charged on only one part of the world's population. Like a boomerang, modern civilisation's detrimental impact on nature strikes back and hits everyone,[1] including those who were not responsible for its creation as well as those who are responsible for it and then feel its impacts not only on their own health but also even on their property and economic interests[2] (Beck 1986, 23, 30, 37; Beck 2007, 78–9).

This analysis describes a society in environmental crisis of which risks have become an integral part and in which the threat of self-destruction has become ubiquitous – the emergency case has become the normal case (Beck 2007, 172). Authorities' insufficient handling of this situation is designated as 'organised irresponsibility' (ibid., own translation). This means that risks are bureaucratised and depicted as manageable, either being ignorant of or disavowing their scale. Powerful actors in administration, politics, economy, and research negotiate security criteria, knowing well that the systems which created the existing threats are no longer able to provide insurance for them, or to prevent a catastrophe. The possibility of catastrophes occurring is eventually accepted. This amounts to a '*systematic violation of fundamental rights*…. Risks are produced industrially, are externalised economically, are individualised juridically, are legitimised scientifically and are downplayed politically'[3] (Beck 1996, 137, own translation). Due to their universality, every human being is exposed to them, no one is spared. This situation constitutes a legitimation crisis of the institutions of the first modernity (Beck 1993, 40–1). Existing political and economic institutions are increasingly incapable of solving risks of the twenty-first century, since solving problems of the second modernity with the means of the first is sheerly impossible (Beck 1986, 225; Beck 2007, 62–3).

The key question of modern times is whether citizens of industrialised and newly industrialising countries will realise that 'an ecological renewal of modernity' (Beck 1993, 25, own translation) is essential for survival and whether they will then be wise enough to reform substantially 'aims, bases, lifestyles and forms of production … [and] conception of … rationality' (ibid., 64, own translation) to achieve this aim. The question is not how to produce ever more economic growth but how to achieve 'smart self-limitation … [and] forms of production, lifestyles and forms of politics that overcome the self-destructive effects of modern industrial society' (ibid., 64, own translation; cf. 2.4.3.4).[4] Then the big question is *how* this can be achieved and what role citizens will play in this transition (cf. 2.4 and Chapter 6). Like every profound societal change, reflexive modernisation contains opportunities and risks at the same time. Transforming industrial society into a sustainable one via a socio-ecological transition simultaneously opens up the possibility of an 'eco-dictatorship' *and* of an 'environmental democracy' to emerge (cf. 6.2.1). Whether the pendulum swings in one or the other direction depends greatly on how democratic values are viewed by people in power but also by the citizens themselves.

At the micro-level, the second modernity is marked by the process of individualisation. Individuals do not choose consciously to become increasingly individualised (Beck 1993, 151–2). This happens due to changing macro- and meso-economic and societal conditions and an altered relationship between the individual and society:

> Biographies become *self-reflexive*; socially prescribed biography is transformed into biography that is self-produced and continues to be produced. Decisions on education, profession, job, place of residence, spouse, number of children and so forth … no longer can be, they must be made.
>
> (Beck 1986, 216, own translation)

This means that individualisation puts a higher burden on the individual. If everything becomes questionable and eligible, if the life course is no longer predetermined by either social class (Beck 1993, 77) or gender, individuals need to make more effort to find their place in society, to decide on their own on their biographies during the whole lifetime. This implies being disembedded from the coordinates of the classical industrial society, assuming more responsibility and becoming more vulnerable at the same time. When family bounds loosen and unemployment becomes a normal part of the life biography, the individual becomes more dependent on statal structures, such as the welfare system where existing and functioning. Individuals have to find ways to cope with this situation of new liberties and choices but also of lost securities and traditions and increased personal risks. On the micro-level of society, the need to reflect on one's own chosen life due to less tight social structures requires more flexible and stronger social agents, agents that have the capacity to shape the social structure.

The individual's anxiety and worries about the future of the Earth and thus about humankind's livelihoods are one driving force behind the personal need for sustainability. Whereas the members of society in the first modernity were driven by the wish to obtain an ever-growing share of the 'wealth pie', achieved via increasing economic growth and a subsequent rise in income levels, in the second modernity members of the risk society, driven by the fear of possible risks and already occurring catastrophes, prioritise their safety needs (Beck 1986, 65): being safe from catastrophic climate change, and from the war on scarce resources, ensuring access to drinking water, to name but a few.

Once understood that human beings have been the source of the Earth's destruction and that a slowing down and reversal can only be achieved by these very same actors, in the age of reflexive modernisation increased global risks and officials' insufficient reactions to them do not remain unanswered by an increasing number of citizens. The global risks, as scary as they are, lead to action, and increasingly citizens have started to demand clarification and transparency from authorities about these self-produced risks. Since risks violate citizens' rights, as described above, and due to being in a 'uniform position of civilization's self-endangering' (Beck 2009, 47), citizens (collectively) become active in the socio-ecological transition to a sustainable future. This is what Beck (2007, 124, own translation) calls the 'cosmopolitical opportunity of the world risk society' consisting of the trial 'to re-forge global risks into realistic utopias for an endangered world, utopias that allow the revitalisation and relegitimisation of state and politics'. Citizens demand democratically controlled institutions and a participatory jointly negotiated path setting for a sustainable future. The second modernity might be scary in many aspects marked by a loss of security and orientation, yet it also involves the opportunity for new actors to enter the stage, for example social movements, to change the way of making politics by arriving at a new culture of participation. This kaleidoscopic diversification of actors, of new actors arriving from the bottom, becoming involved and partly assuming responsibility is made possible by entering the stage of reflexive modernisation. Whereas the simple modernity either offered the options of (a) blinkeredly believing in economic growth and progress or (b) pessimistically believing that the future of humankind is a lost game anyway, with the same result of pursuing the economic growth path, under the terms of reflexive modernisation a society emerges which is stirred up by newly arriving actors. These actors are on the search for new coordinates, values, and securities. The common issue of saving one's own livelihood, thus ensuring the survival of planet Earth, could fill the vacuum produced by the shift from first to second modernity and could be a driving force in a reorientation of society's values and the individual's role in the transition.

2.2 The ecological basis: climate change and further planetary boundaries

In 1992 'sustainability' was defined for the first time by the United Nations.[5] It was conceived as being composed of environmental, social, and economic pillars (World Commission on Environment and Development 1987). This definition has been the best known and most used one to this day. However, this pillar scheme depicts the three parts as standing on an equal footing, concealing that no social or economic system is able to function without its ecological basis. If this basis is threatened, severe irreversible change is to be expected in the other two systems. This section highlights changes in the ecological system which have been caused by human action and can now only be slowed down or reversed by human action. Yet, swift global counter-action is highly difficult to achieve, since the world economy and society are caught in the economic growth trap (cf. 2.3).

Humankind's impact on the Earth system has exponentially grown especially since the middle of the last century. Human beings have influenced Earth system processes to such a great extent that several scientists have suggested speaking of the Anthropocene as a new geological epoch the Earth has entered into, in which the '11,700-year-long Holocene epoch, the only state of the planet that we know for certain can support contemporary human societies, is now being destabilized' (Steffen *et al.* 2015, 1259855-1). This new age is marked by already occurring damage to ecological systems. To estimate its scope and to devise mitigation and adaptation actions, the planetary boundary's framework is a helpful tool.[6] It 'identifies levels of anthropogenic perturbations below which the risk of destabilization of the ES [Earth system] is likely to remain low – a "safe operating space" for global social development'[7] (Steffen *et al.* 2015, 736). This means that if humankind's action remains within this space, life on this planet can continue to exist under conditions human beings are used to, thus 'in a Holocene-like state'[8] (Steffen *et al.* 2015, 1259855-2). The concept delivers two essential findings. First, four of the nine planetary boundaries have already been exceeded. These are climate change, biosphere integrity, biogeochemical flows,[9] and land system change (Steffen *et al.* 2015, 736; cf. Figure 2.1). This means that there is an increasingly high risk 'of a change to the functioning of the Earth system that could potentially be devastating for human societies'[10] (Steffen *et al.* 2015, 1259855-2). Second, the already transgressed boundaries of climate change and biosphere integrity are considered to be the most crucial basic boundaries (Steffen *et al.* 2015, 736). They are fundamentally important for the functioning 'of the Earth System'[11] (Steffen *et al.* 2015, 1259855-2) since substantially and persistently transgressing either of them 'would likely, on their

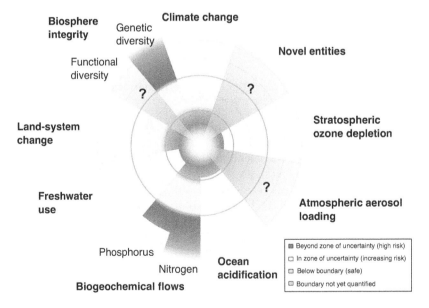

Figure 2.1 The current status of the control variables for seven of the nine planetary boundaries.

Source: Steffen *et al.* 2015, 1259855-6.

own, push the Earth system out of the Holocene state'[12] (Steffen *et al.* 2015, 1259855-8). Earth's history shows that past major transitions were marked by important shifts either in climate change or biosphere integrity or both (ibid.). 'The farther the boundary is transgressed, the higher the risk of regime shifts, destabilized system processes, or erosion of resilience and the fewer the opportunities to prepare for such changes'[13] (Steffen *et al.* 2015, 1259855-2). How far the two major boundaries are transgressed is also influenced by the other boundaries; all boundaries together represent an interconnected mutually influenceable system (Steffen *et al.* 2015, 1259855-8).[14]

That the transgression of the climate change boundary has been largely provoked by human civilisation in the industrialised countries, is no longer a sheer assumption of hard-core environmentalists but has become a mainstream scientific fact.[15] However, despite efforts from the global to the local level since the Earth Summit in Rio de Janeiro in 1992 to reduce greenhouse gas emissions,[16] human-caused emissions are higher than ever before, already now heavily impacting on the world's SES (Intergovernmental Panel on Climate Change (IPCC) 2015, 2). This is because of globally continuing economic and population growth, leading to more CO_2 emissions from industrial processes and fossil fuel combustion, including conventional agriculture (ibid. 2015, 28, 46).[17] The consequences have already been palpable. For example, 'assessment of many studies covering a wide range of regions and crops shows that negative impacts of climate change on crop yields have been more common than positive impacts (*high confidence*)' (ibid., 51, emphasis removed). 'The frequency of heat waves … and the frequency and intensity of heavy precipitation events has *likely* increased … in Europe' (ibid., 53).

The proposed planetary boundaries framework is helpful to understand what room for manoeuvre remains for humankind at the global level on the way to sustainability. Yet, it neither proposes how humankind has to act to remain within the safe operating space in general, nor explains how to cope with the question of causation and equity in particular, considering that the transgression of the four cited boundaries has been provoked primarily by the industrialised countries (Steffen *et al.* 2015, 1259855-8) and thus by the rich part of the world which makes up only about 20 per cent of the world's population (Randers 2012, 19). It must not be concealed that those that have contributed least to the boundary of ongoing climate change will suffer most from it since sea level rise and rising temperatures will cause more damage to poorer countries, first because they are situated mainly in the hotter part of the world and, second, because they have fewer financial means for adaptation measures. Yet, the social consequences of climate change are not only unequally distributed between countries but also within countries. The poor and disadvantaged persons within a country are more vulnerable and have fewer financial means to invest in adaptation measures (IPCC 2015, 13). For example, 'extreme heat events currently result in increases in mortality and morbidity … in Europe with impacts that vary according to people's age, location and socio-economic factors (*high confidence*)' (ibid., 53). With a rising urbanisation and ageing trend in Europe,[18] with increasing social inequalities within European society (cf. 2.4.3.4) as well as an ever-increasing number of highly vulnerable irregular migrants arriving, this tendency is extremely alarming.

Since the beginning of industrialisation, there has been a global average temperature rise of 0.7°C. If the global greenhouse gas emission rate remains unchanged, by 2052 there will be more than 450 ppm[19] carbon dioxide (CO_2) concentration in the atmosphere, which is the calculated critical amount to cross the 2°C threshold (IPCC 2015, 22).[20] Only under 'a stringent mitigation scenario … [will humankind be able] to keep global warming likely below 2°C above pre-industrial temperatures' (ibid., 8). This is the only scenario under which global warming will not go on beyond 2100 (ibid., 16), and the time frame for making this scenario happen is extremely small. According to the German Advisory Council on Global Change (2011, 1) a 'drastic change in direction must be accomplished before the end of the current decade in order to reduce global green house gas emissions to a minimum by 2050, and thereby to maintain the possibility of avoiding dangerous climate change' which leaves 'very little room for manoeuvre … for greenhouse gas emissions intensive development paths in developing and newly industrialising countries' (ibid., 12). The still fossil-fuel-based lifestyle of industrialised countries cannot be transferred to the rest of the world (ibid., 62), since all countries need to decarbonise their economy.[21] If humankind as a whole wants to stay within the 2°C threshold, the mistakes of brown growth[22] of the industrial countries cannot be repeated in the rest of the world.[23]

However, even if humankind is successful in following this scenario, the surface temperature is expected to rise this century.[24] There will be longer and more frequent heat waves, more frequent and intense precipitation events, further sea level rise,[25] and a warming and acidifying ocean (IPCC 2015, 10). Climate change will increase risks for cities, for their 'people, assets, economies and ecosystems, including risks from heat stress, storms and extreme precipitation, inland and coastal flooding, landslides, air pollution, drought, water scarcity, sea level rise and storm surges (*very high confidence*)' (ibid., 69).

The cited impacts are not a future tale but are already happening and can only be confronted by increasing adaptation measures, since choosing the most stringent mitigation scenario will only affect climate change happening from the middle of this century. If humankind manages to choose this scenario, 'the increase of global mean surface temperature by the end of the twenty-first century (2081–2100) relative to 1986–2005 is *likely* to be 0.3°C to 1.7°C' (ibid., 10). Otherwise it will exceed the 2°C threshold leading to 'further warming and long-lasting changes in all components of the climate system, increasing the likelihood of severe, pervasive and irreversible impacts for people and ecosystems' (ibid., 8, emphasis removed) as well as to the societal implications of such an environmental crisis, meaning 'major social, economic and security-political risks' (WBGU 2011, 2).

To implement the stringent mitigation scenario, higher mitigation efforts than those already in place are indispensable (IPCC 2015, 17). With mere adaptation measures with high confidence 'warming by the end of the 21st century will lead to high to very high risk of severe, widespread and irreversible impacts globally (*high confidence*)' (ibid., 17, emphasis removed).

Global anthropogenic greenhouse gas emissions need to be substantially reduced before 2030 to achieve a long-term reduction of 40 to 70 per cent by 2050 relative to 2010 in order to remain below the 2°C threshold (ibid., 20). Due to the delayed consequences of greenhouse gas emissions, 'the greenhouse gas emissions trend must be turned around within the next 10 years as otherwise, compliance with the 2°C guard rail will be unachievable' (WBGU 2011, 63). A major role in this effort is played by the decarbonisation of the global energy systems which has to be mostly achieved by 2050 (ibid., 2). This reduction is technologically feasible and relatively cheap compared to future higher costs for mitigation and adaptation measures in case of current inaction (UNEP 2011; WBGU 2011, 6, 159; Randers 2012, 6; IPCC 2015, 24).[26]

2.3 The economic growth trap: a system theoretical approach

System theory directs the attention to economic growth's detrimental externalities undermining the Earth's carrying capacity. Meadows *et al.* (1972) were the first to deliver a global scenario analysis on this issue in the early 1970s. Three of them presented an updated version of their findings 20 years (Meadows *et al.* 1992) and more than 30 years later (Meadows *et al.* 2005), yet their original main message that the global ecological footprint must be reduced to not undermine the Earth's carrying capacity (ibid., x) remains unchanged, and up to now their initial analysis has turned out to be true (Jackson 2009, 8). The concept of the ecological footprint, developed by Wackernagel (1994) relates the human demand on the biosphere to the globally available bio-capacity, thus designating the amount of land required to be used as a sink and to deliver natural resources. More specifically it can be divided into an energy and nonenergy part. The first refers to the land area needed to absorb anthropogenic CO_2 emissions, the second to the land area required to provide the resources food, meat, fish, wood, and for building cities and infrastructure.

> The ecological footprint in 2010 was some 40% higher than the carrying capacity of the globe. In other words, humanity was, and is, using 1.4 planets to supply its current use of grain, meat, timber, fish, urban space, and energy.[27]

> (Randers 2012, 143)

This situation of overshoot[28] becomes manifest for example in the current level of global greenhouse gas emissions, the continuing cutting down of tropical rain forest, or the overharvesting of global fisheries (Randers 2012, 311).

Whereas in 1972, 1992, and 2005 several scenarios were presented without predicting which one would be likely to come true, in 2012 Randers provided a forecast of world development from 2012 to 2052 elaborating the scenario that he believes will be followed by humankind in these years. This is one of the 2004 overshoot-and-decline scenarios, more specifically scenario three (Meadows *et al.* 2005, 210–11), in which 'both shortage of nonrenewable resources and dangerous pollution are postponed until the middle of the century through the application of technology'[29] (Randers 2012, 304):

> Population will peak at 8.1 billion people just after 2040 and then decline.... Global GDP will reach 2.2 times current levels around 2050.[30] ... Productivity growth will be slower than in the past because economies are maturing, because of increased social strife, and because of negative interference from extreme weather.... The growth rate in global consumption will slow because a greater share of GDP will have to be allocated to investment – in order to solve the problems created by resource depletion, pollution, climate change, biodiversity loss, and inequity. Global consumption of goods and services will peak in 2045.... As a consequence of increased social investment in the decades ahead (albeit often involuntary and in reaction to crisis), resource and climate problems will not become catastrophic before 2052. But there will be much unnecessary suffering from unabated climate damage around the middle of the century.... The lack of a dedicated and forceful human response in the first half of the twenty-first century will put the world on a dangerous track toward self-reinforcing[31] global warming in the second half of the twenty-first century.... Slow growth in per capita consumption in much of the world (and stagnation in the rich world) will lead to increased social tension and conflict which will further reduce orderly productivity growth.... The short-term focus of capitalism and democracy will ensure that the wise decisions needed for long-term well-being will not be made in time.... The global population will be increasingly urban and unwilling to protect nature for its own sake. Biodiversity will suffer.... All – and particularly the poor – will live in an increasingly disorderly and climate-damaged world.[32]
>
> (Ibid., 355–6)

Whereas the 2004 model 'tended to show uncontrolled collapse just after 2052'[33] (ibid., 301), Randers' forecast ends in 2052, however, saying that 'global warming may trigger self-reinforcing climate change in the second half of the twenty-first century' (ibid.), thus matching the 2004 analysis.

Randers extends the 2004 global scenario analysis not only by making a global forecast, but also by adding a differentiated picture for each world region, due to the fact that conditions in the regions will differ greatly (ibid., 56). For Europe this means that the trend of an already stagnating and ageing population will continue until 2025 before then slowly declining, which is 15 years earlier than in the global forecast. The total gross domestic product will slowly grow until reaching its peak in the early 2030s at more or less 15 per cent above its current level (cf. Figure 2.2) which represents a huge difference compared to the global development which will still be growing in 2052 (ibid.,

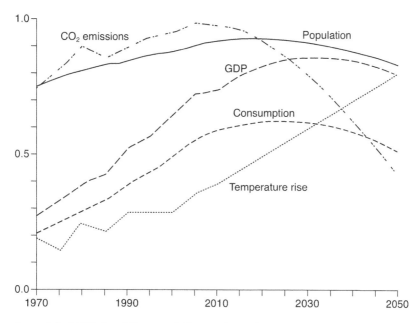

Figure 2.2 OECD-less-US state of affairs, 1970–2050.

Source: Randers 2012, 284; reprinted from *2052*, copyright 2012 by Jørgen Randers, used with permission from Chelsea Green Publishing (www.chelseagreen.com).

Notes
Scale: population (0–800 million people); GDP and consumption ($0–$30 trillion per year); CO_2 emissions (0–7 billion tonnes CO_2 per year); temperature rise (0–2.5°C).

232). The amount of energy used in Europe will not change until 2030, and will then start to decline (cf. Figure 2.3), which is ten years earlier than globally (ibid., 232). Peak oil in the region was already reached in 2010, the share of oil and gas will be further reduced until 2052, with oil then representing one-third of total energy consumption (ibid., 286). Carbon dioxide emissions will be reduced at an ever faster pace between 2012 and 2052 to 55 per cent below the 2012 emission level in 2052 (cf. Figure 2.2),[34] whereas for the whole world a reduction will only start in 2030 (ibid., 232). Finally, European food production will begin to decline from 2040 onwards due to adverse climate change effects, which corresponds to the world development (cf. Figure 2.3; ibid., 232).

2.3.1 Necessary system changes

According to the global forecast, the negative side effects of 'never-ending growth in material consumption and energy use'[35] (Randers 2012, 12) will exceed its short-term benefits, leading to a path of 'managed decline'[36]

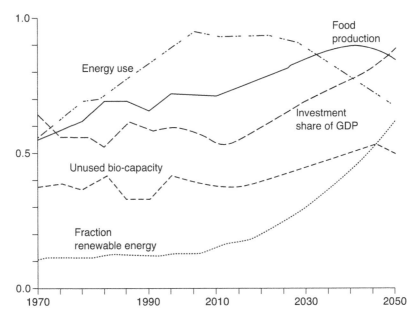

Figure 2.3 OECD-less-US production, 1970–2050.

Source: Randers 2012, 284; reprinted from *2052*, copyright 2012 by Jørgen Randers, used with permission from Chelsea Green Publishing (www.chelseagreen.com).

Notes
Scale: food production (0–1.2 billion tonnes per year); energy use (0–3.2 billion tonnes of oil equivalents per year); proportion of renewable energy (0–70 per cent); investment share of GDP (0–40 per cent); unused bio-capacity (0–50 per cent).

(ibid., 304) with decreasing gross domestic product growth rates between 2030 and 2052 (ibid., 232). This will require profound changes in the way society and economy currently work and can thus be designated as a sustainability 'revolution'[37] (Meadows *et al.* 2005, 12, 266; Randers 2012, 12) in which politics' main objective will not be 'fossil-fueled economic growth'[38] (Randers 2012, 12) any more but 'sustainable well-being' (ibid.) of society's members in the long run. In this transition

> efforts to limit the ecological footprint will continue. Future growth in global population and GDP will be constrained not only by this effort, but also, by rapid fertility decline as a result of urbanization, productivity decline as a result of social unrest, and continuing poverty among the poorest two billion world citizens. At the same time there will be impressive advances in resource efficiency and climate-friendly solutions. There will also be a shift in focus toward human well-being rather than per capita income growth.[39]
>
> (Ibid., 354)

This revolution has already been triggered but is still far from mainstream, and the major question is whether humankind will react fast enough to avoid cata-strophic climate change in the second half of the century (ibid., 13; cf. also 2.1). Randers draws a pessimistic picture, believing that the transition will only be half through by 2052 and that in the second half of this century 'the damage created during overshoot (the climate change, the biodiversity destruction, and the dousing of the global environment with toxics)'[40] (ibid., 162) cannot be reversed even 'through huge instalments of extra investment'[41] (ibid., 163),[42] since humankind will not have managed quickly enough to reduce anthropo-genic greenhouse gas emissions. This means that in the middle of the second half of this century the global temperature will have risen by 2.8°C in compari-son to pre-industrial times, leaving humankind to face self-reinforcing global warming (ibid., 235–6, 255).

This could be a devastating forecast for everyone fighting for the socio-ecological transition. However, the transition has already started, and there is hope that its actors will be able to act in time. Given the scientific facts, the tight time frame and the complicatedness of societal organisation, this is an immense, yet not impossible, endeavour. Here, the difference between optimists and pessimists appears. The current situation can either be viewed as unwinna-ble, leading to resignation and inaction, or it is regarded as a unique opportunity for joint action on all government levels and across countries for a unique cause (cf. 2.1). Meadows *et al.* (2005, 263) consider 'the necessity of taking the indus-trial world to its next stage of evolution … an amazing opportunity'.

Whether humankind manages to operate within the planetary boundaries and to avoid irreversible self-reinforcing climate change, depends on its capacity to understand what is at stake and its willingness to change the way the eco-nomic and political systems work. The challenges humankind faces cannot be coped with by the instruments of the first modernity that all rely desperately on economic growth, but demand 'a fundamental rethinking and reprograming of the prevailing paradigm of modernization' (Beck 2009, 52).

Yet, such a basic reorientation is not easy to implement in a society that has been determined by economic growth since the times of industrialisation (Meadows *et al.* 2005, 5), that expects ever-continuing growth rates, believing that society gains from ongoing economic growth based on fossil fuels and that globalisation and free trade will augment welfare for all (Randers 2012, 9), and in which demanding limits to this kind of growth are politically mostly still out of the question (Meadows *et al.* 2005, 203).

2.3.2 *Refuting the arguments of economic growth defenders*

It is important to state that equating economic growth with progress, develop-ment, or even well-being is not a natural association but one mainly made in countries that have undergone the path of industrialisation and more recently also by parts of the population in still unindustrialised or newly industrialising countries that wish to copy the rich countries' growth path. The argumentation of economic growth defenders is twofold. First, as pointed out by Meadows *et al.* (2005, 6), more economic growth is needed to create the necessary financial basis for taking environmental protection measures. They believe in the force of science and technology as well as of the free market to find solutions to ever-worse environmental damage produced by this very same growth (ibid., 203). Second, they argue that poorer countries need economic growth to get out of the poverty trap to pursue the development path that the highly industrialised countries have already undergone and that denying them economic growth would deprive them of this option (ibid., 6).

Both arguments can be refuted. First, trying to solve the environmental problem with increased economic growth still primarily relying on fossil fuels only leads to the exacerbation of the problem. It constitutes a vicious circle in which the cat bites her tail and is owed to a thinking stuck in the first modernity. Second, although it is true and happened in the past that economic growth can end poverty, the equation is more complicated. In the beginning of industrial society and especially in the decades following the end of the Second World War it was true that economic growth increased productivity, creating employment and increasing income.[43] It thus provided jobs to an ever-increasing proportion of the population which meant the rise out of poverty for many and more options for consumption for an increasing number of people (Randers 2012, 341; Nowotny *et al.* 2013, 6) which led to a more just society. However, this has been more and more achieved at the cost of environmental and social externalities and increasingly, with the process of globalisation accelerating, at the expense of the Global South. As a matter of fact, economic 'growth … has widened the gap between the rich and the poor' (Meadows *et al.* 2005, 43) countries in the world.[44] Whereas 'in 1990 the average American was 38 times richer than the average Tanzanian … [in 2000] the average American … [was] 61 times richer' (Watkins *et al.* 2005, 37). In the same year, 'the richest 20% of the population hold three-quarters of world income … [, whereas] the poorest 20% hold just 1.5%' (ibid., 36) and 'the ratio of the income of the poorest 10% of the population to the richest 10% [was] … 1 to 103' (ibid., 37, 38). This is because growth in general mostly takes place in newly industrialising countries and to a lesser extent, due to saturation effects (cf. 2.4.3.3), in already industrialised countries, whereas the least developed countries are virtually decoupled from the world market.[45] It is implausible that continued economic growth will work in the adverse direction, closing this widening gap (Meadows *et al.* 2005, 42).

Yet, not only has the gap between countries widened but also the gap within a country. Wealth has been concentrated ever more with the rich minority.[46] A further alarming signal is that three-quarters of all people living below the poverty line[47] are to be found in the richer subgroup of countries of the Global South, the so-called newly industrialising countries, which have shown increasing economic growth rates since the 1990s (OECD 2010). Yet, this growth has not managed to shift these almost one billion people in countries such as China, India, Indonesia, Pakistan, Nigeria, or South Africa out of poverty (WBGU

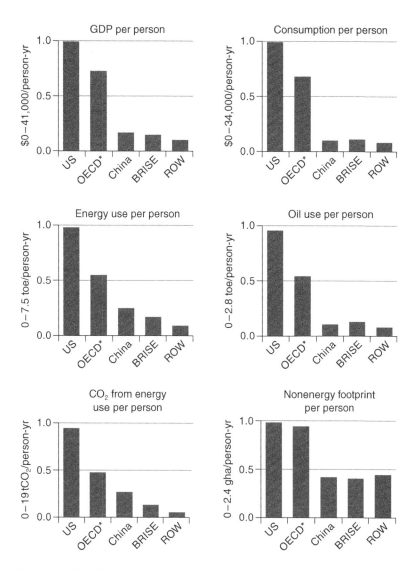

Figure 2.4 World inequity, 2010.

Source: Randers 2012, 29; reprinted from *2052*, copyright 2012 by Jørgen Randers, used with permission from Chelsea Green Publishing (www.chelseagreen.com).

Notes
Definitions: OECD* = OECD-less-US; BRISE = big emerging economies; ROW = rest of the world. Populations in billions: US = 0.3, OECD-less-US = 0.7; China = 1.3, BRISE = 2.4, ROW = 2.1. Abbreviations: toe = tonnes of oil equivalents, tCO_2 = tonnes of CO_2, gha = hectares of average global productivity.

2011, 48, 50). For the case of India, the physicist, political activist, and Altern-ative Nobel Peace Prize (the Right Livelihood Award) laureate of 1993 Vandana Shiva showed how the globalised neoliberal corporate economy has indeed increased the gross domestic product, yet has, at the same time, under-mined and aggravated the living conditions of the majority of Indians with every fourth going hungry (Shiva 2013, 21, 135–6; cf. 7.4.3.1), whereas a quarter of the Indian economy is controlled by a minority of very rich people (ibid., 101–2, 234). This is because the increasingly liberalised market which has determined the global economy since the 1980s[48] is aligned with the inter-ests of society's rich minority (Meadows *et al.* 2005, 234). *It is not true that a magic hand automatically distributes profits obtained in this globalised neoliberal corpo-rate economic system to the poorest part of the population.*[49] *For this to happen, the state has to create a functioning redistribution scheme,* which bluntly speaking means taking from the rich and giving to the poor. Without such a fair redis-tribution scheme within a country, but also between countries worldwide, eco-nomic growth is incapable of lifting the 20 per cent of poorest people in the world out of poverty and of avoiding an ever-widening socio-economic gap in industrialised countries.

So let us assume that governments are wise enough, freed from the lobbying of the rich, to redistribute the benefits of economic growth wisely to all members of society as well as setting incentives for moving from brown to green economic growth.[50] In that case, there might be the option that growth can lift people out of poverty without destroying the Earth's carrying capacity. Therefore, demonis-ing economic growth altogether is not constructive. Meadows *et al.* propose an economic growth check before deciding for more economic growth. It must be asked 'what the growth is for, and who would benefit, and what it would cost, and how long it would last, and whether the growth could be accommodated by the sources and sinks of the earth' (2005, 255). So the important questions are what shall be obtained with the help of this growth, where in the world it takes place, what its social and environmental consequences are (for example con-cerning working conditions and handling of produced pollution), whether enterprises contributing to it are structured democratically and are non-corrupt, and in which sectors the obtained profit is invested. If such a growth check was implemented consistently on a global scale, only the kind of growth would take place 'that would serve important social goals while enhancing sustainability. Once any physical growth had accomplished its purposes, society would stop its pursuit' (ibid., 255–6). The post-growth discourse (cf. 2.4) does not aim at for-bidding poor countries their right to development which can be achieved with the help of economic growth under certain, well-defined, conditions:

> Insofar as development requires physical expansion, it should be equitable, affordable, and sustainable, with all real costs counted. … We need to encourage technologies that will reduce the ecological footprint, increase efficiency, enhance resources, improve signals, and end material deprivation.
>
> (Ibid., 278)[51]

A comprehensive understanding of development is expressed in the concept of 'buen vivir', which became a core constitutional principle in Ecuador in 2008 (Constitution of Ecuador 2008) and in Bolivia in 2009 (Constitution of Bolivia 2009). It is about striving for a good life for all while respecting nature as the main foundation for human well-being. This can be achieved in a diversified economy re-embedded into its societal foundation, as expressed in the Bolivian Constitution (art. 306, subsection III):

> A diverse economy interlinks the different forms of economic organisation according to the principles of complementarity, reciprocity, solidarity, redistribution, equality, juridical security, sustainability, equilibrium, justice and transparency. The social and communal economy will complement the individual interest with the collective 'vivir bien'.

If this concept was set as an overarching framework and thoroughly abided to, if the majority of economic growth took place in the green economy, and if the poor countries and the majority of their population profited from it, as well as the increasing number of poor people in the industrialised countries, which can only be achieved by installing a fair redistribution scheme, only then would there be no denying the fact that economic growth can reduce poverty. Yet, economic growth in the current economic and social system is very unlikely to provoke these effects because incentives to achieve its active redistribution are too few and it is very difficult to work against the vested short-term interests of the minority of the rich within a state and of the 20 per cent of rich people worldwide.

2.3.3 Reasons for clinging to the economic growth lie

Relying on continued economic growth as the only means to solve society's problems is a short-sighted strategy and is already creating major problems for industrialised societies with more severe ones to be expected. So why does the belief in growth still persist so obstinately? This is for two interrelated reasons. First, economic growth is considered to be the precondition for achieving prosperity and well-being. Achievements such as public education, healthcare, and increased life expectancy depend on rising incomes and are thus growth-dependent (Jackson 2009, 49, 55). The second reason is the fact that any proposal on the reduction of economic growth immediately raises the question of redistribution (Meadows *et al.* 2005, 178; Paech 2015, 26–7). Economic growth is needed to keep the economy and the whole society and its political system as they currently function in a stable state. Economic growth allows a country to 'share the pie' without reducing the share of others, which is why policy-makers are swift to convert already existing or awaited distributional conflicts into growth targets. This redistribution scheme had functioned more or less until the 1990s in the now highly industrialised countries. Economic growth had permitted, via job creation and subsequent supplement tax income, the redistribution of wealth to all parts of society *without* touching the wealth and privileges of the rich (Randers 2012, 23, 204). Yet, this has irreversibly stopped working. The growth rates the industrialised countries used to have were already stagnated or even declined.[52] This trend will continue. Sinking economic growth rates are and will be a matter of fact for already highly industrialised societies (cf. 2.4.3.3). Political leaders denying this and continuing to tell their voters that a further creation of growth is possible is to be considered as, either out of sheer ignorance or out of fear of telling the truth, clinging to the economic growth lie and standing in the way of long-term sustainable solutions to restructuring economy and society. What is already happening now is that 'all stare at and hope for economic growth, and from behind the ecological societal conflict becomes ever more firmly established' (Beck 1993, 31, own translation). Therefore societies need to find other redistribution schemes than growth (Randers 2012, 263), if they want to avoid the impoverishment of an increasing proportion of the population and subsequent social unrest (cf. 2.4.3.4).

2.4 Approaches for redefining economy and society

Making the sustainability revolution come true requires a profound shift in organising economy and society. This means abandoning the still predominant one-dimensional economic growth paradigm as a unique steering instrument and striving for the well-being of society's members through other means. The latter includes social development and might include a green version of economic growth, yet only as a means to a broader end.[53] Yet, the transition is severely impeded by 'political, institutional and economic path dependencies, interest structures and veto players' (WBGU 2011, 4) of the first modernity with its economy built on the use of fossil fuels (ibid.). However, remaining within this paradigm inhibits learning effects and leads to mere 'incremental policies of short-term crisis management and the ever-procrastinating negotiation of compromises' (ibid., 270) with instruments that were developed for the problems of the first modernity only (ibid., 78, 79). Nevertheless, the shift from first to second modernity has already been going on for a while. What will be the consequences of such a fundamental reorientation within a country but also across countries? How will the role of the state, the economy, and civil society change as well as the role of and the interaction between government levels from local to global?

The following subsections present approaches for redefining the relationship between economy and society. These approaches contribute to substituting the 200-year-old, still mainstream narrative of the 'model of prosperity based on the unlimited availability of fossil fuels and other resources' (ibid., 84) with the model of prosperity within planetary boundaries. This can only be achieved in a process of re-embedding economy into its social and environmental foundations following Polanyi's (2001) original idea, in contrast to the dis-embedding paradigm of the industrial society (WBGU 2011, 91). These approaches exceed the narrow views of neoclassical and even more neoliberal economics of conceiving economy as mere market relations (Bourdieu 1983, 184) by presenting correctives, extensions, and alternatives to self-regulating profit-driven market economies, following the conception that economy is embedded into a social and environmental context (Elsen 2007, 6, 29). Their ideas are not completely new but build on thinking that has always existed, yet has been marginalised by mainstream economic thinking (ibid., 46–7). Altering the interrelationship between economy and society is a complex task and can be facilitated by following the figure of thought of an overarching social contract for sustainability. Since the post-growth society and economy resulting from closing this contract would look very different from the industrial one, this chapter will highlight what changes are required and how society and economy can be organised in a system that does not depend on economic growth. A central operating level in a post-growth society and economy is the local and regional one where social and solidarity economies become effective.

Scientific analysis (cf. 2.2, 2.3, and 2.3.1) points to the narrow time frame of action which creates the risk of people resigning or blanking the issue out, believing that the future of the Earth and their (grand)children is lost anyway: 'Where there is no escape, people ultimately no longer want to think about it' (Beck 2009, 37). In face of the challenges to arrive at a sustainable society and economy there is the danger that irreversible climate change with concomitant huge social inequalities and incalculable environmental consequences is accepted as inescapable, thus, instead of caring for the common good, people might tend to primarily care for their family and personal security against the ever-increasing risks (Jackson 2009, 171). And even if people are willing not to resign and to become active, society might remain in the hamster-wheel-like paradigm of economic growth, because alternatives are not tried out due to multiple path dependencies. This makes it ever more important to tackle these dependencies and to spread already existing alternatives to the current way society and economy operates.

The transition to a sustainable society and economy must take place at all societal levels. For example, regarding the problem of climate change, interrelationships must be made transparent and incentives must be set:

> Policy makers are called upon to make the impact that energy generation has on environment and climate visible for the market, for instance through carbon pricing, or a cap on emissions accompanied by the introduction of tradable emissions certificates. The transformation can succeed only if the use of climate-damaging technologies becomes economically unattractive.
>
> (WBGU 2011, 172)

This top-down action must be complemented from the bottom up. Fortunately, organising a post-growth society and economy, at least at the local and regional level, is not something that has to be learned from scratch, since alternatives, for example from social and solidarity economy, even if having been marginalised by mainstream economy, have never stopped existing around the world.

As the world has been increasingly struck by social and environmental crises, they have been regaining strength[54] and constitute a starting point for pointing society and economy into the right direction (Shiva 2013, 12). However, the upscaling of these alternatives needs a joint vision, a joint goal which must be to not undermine the living conditions of people in the Global South or those of future generations.[55] The starting point is first to perceive and second to acknowledge the current state of the Earth, to have understood its causes, to then develop a vision, and to make it come true with people operating on every horizontal level and vertical sector of society.[56] For this to come true the role of social innovation is essential and the knowledge and ideas of as many actors as possible must be drawn on. This is a strong argument working against an eco-dictatorship (cf. 2.1 and 6.2.1).

It is not an axiomatic natural law that economic growth thinking determines the functioning of society, but economic history since the industrial revolution has shaped industrialised society's thinking this way. This 'law' is indeed revocable, since economy, even if especially financial economy seems to be a self-contained uncontrollable system, is still run by human beings, thus members of society who have the power to modify social norms (Jackson 2009, 188) and values. Consequently, they can also alter the logic of the economic system, either because they are themselves convinced of a change in this direction, or since pressure from political, economic, or civil society actors becomes so immense that they have to redirect economic thinking and acting this way:

> If social forms of living and values change, then economic principles must also be transformed. If, for instance, the majority of the population rejects the values of economic growth (for whatever reason), then our thinking about the structuring of labor, the criteria of productivity and the direction of development will become dubious and a new type of pressure for political action will arise.
>
> (Beck 2009, 201)

2.4.1 Re-embedding economy

Polanyi (1979; 2001) reflected on the interrelationship of economy and society and on the significance the first should have in the latter. He described how in the course of industrialisation, most strongly in the nineteenth century, economy was disembedded from social structures, thus also from social control, gaining predominance in society and creating in fact a new form of society which has been determined by the market mechanism (Polanyi 1979, 131–3): 'Instead of economy being embedded in social relations, social relations are embedded in the economic system' (Polanyi 2001, 57). This type of economy is independent from society and institutionally disconnected from the political sphere. It follows a distinct logic and motivations and is determined by the rules of the price-setting self-regulating liberal market aiming at making profit by selling goods (Polanyi 1979, 152). Yet, this specific understanding of economic activity only emerged with the rise of industrialisation and within the scope of national economics, suppressing and marginalising other pre-existing diverse forms of economy. Polanyi (1979, 47) shows that in all societies except modern market society, economy is still embedded in society serving societal aims. He labels modern market society's restricted understanding of the term 'economy' as 'economic error in reasoning' (ibid., 438, own translation).[57] It is not that he condemns market activities per se, but believes that the market economy has taken a harming all-dominant position in society. 'Not "the market" ... is the problem but its depiction as "the economy" and, as described by Polanyi, the absolutisation of the market mechanism as coordination principle of economic activity and increasingly of the whole society'[58] (Elsen 2007, 16, own translation). Reducing economy to market activities implicates the commodification of resources, meaning to price them and to put them for sale on the market. Commodities are market goods, thus they are things deliberately fabricated to be sold on a market (Polanyi 2001, 72). However, in the system of the liberal economy also objects that are not produced for a market are considered to be and treated like commodities. This is what Polanyi (2001, 73) calls 'the commodity fiction'. He especially refers to the resources of labour, land, and money whose commodification constitutes the foundation of market economy (ibid., 70–2). For each of them a separate market is created (ibid., 69) with prices being set that are accordingly called 'wages, rent and interest' (ibid.). This means that everything that is going on outside these created markets is not to be considered as economic activity, since it does not have a market price and thus cannot be sold. He identifies the commodification of these three resources as a major reason for the disembedding of economy:

> Labor and land are no other than the human beings themselves of which every society consists and land the natural surroundings in which it exists. To include them in the market mechanism means to subordinate the substance of society itself to the laws of the market.
>
> (Ibid., 71)

In the current global economic system environment and society are subordinated to market laws, which has led to the current unsustainable societal and environmental conditions (cf. 2.1, 2.2., 2.3, 2.3.1, and 2.3.2). A re-embedding of economy into its social and environmental basis (Polanyi 1979, 143) is overdue.

Based on Polanyi's and also on Habermas' reasoning (cf. 6.2.2), Biesecker (2000) and colleagues developed the approach 'Vorsorgendes Wirtschaften' ('caring economy', author's translation), convinced that a new enlarged conception of economy is needed to solve urgent pending socioeconomic and environmental problems:

> Today the term economy no longer only refers to eliminating relative scarcity. Economics is specifically asked to think about mastering abundance and its costs. This means on the one hand dealing with absolute scarcities

(for example on the part of the environment) and on the other hand to take into account the question of just distribution of costs and benefits of global economic activity. And this is not possible without integrating societal models, norms and values.

(Biesecker and Kesting 2003, 173, own translation)

The approach criticises that mainstream economic thinking only puts into focus the market economy and that it takes for granted that the environment delivers resources and is used as a sink (ibid., 2–3) and that the care economy, referring to all unpaid care and subsistence work which is still mostly performed by women, despite being excluded from the market, self-evidently serves as its social basis.

Unlike mainstream economy, emanating from the market, the approach starts from a 'lifeworld' (cf. 6.2.2) perspective. Acting economically rationally is defined as 'what permanently creates good living conditions for people and nature' (Biesecker and von Winterfeld 2014a, 217, own translation). It is thus guided by the necessity of a good life with the care economy as well as the regenerative performances of nature taking centre stage (ibid., 215). The approach undoes the narrowed understanding of economy as mere market economy, defining economy as consisting of market economy and care economy, with the latter being the basis for the former (Biesecker and Kesting 2003, 168). Caring is understood as caring for oneself, for others – including future generations – and for the environment (ibid., 169). Mainstream economic thinking is enlarged by re-embedding the market economy 'into the social lifeworld and both into the environment' (ibid., 4, own translation), consequently acknowledging economic limits (ibid.). Thus, it clearly opposes the economic growth paradigm with concomitant distorting measuring in gross domestic product terms.

2.4.2 A new social contract for the socio-ecological transition

The 'fossil-nuclear metabolism' of the industrialised society has no future. The longer we cling to it, the higher the price will be for future generations. However, there are alternatives which would at least give all people access to the chance of a good life within the boundaries of the natural environment. Without a global agreement to actually dare to experiment with these alternatives, we will not manage to find our way out of the crisis of late modernity.

(WBGU 2011, 25)

This is the backdrop against which '*a new global social contract for a low-carbon and sustainable global economic system*' (ibid., 1) is deemed to be necessary.

Social contract theory which emerged in early modern philosophy of the seventeenth century asks 'how an agreement based on an (imagined) contract between rulers and ruled can guarantee orderly cohabitation in a national and social confederation' (ibid., 276). Its basic concept is that 'free and equal individuals surrender their rights to a government, and precisely this act of surrender obliges the state to protect its citizens, which in turn leads to obligations on the part of the citizens' (ibid.). Translated into a sustainability contract this means that

> individuals and civil societies, states and the global community of states, as well as the economy and science, carry the joint responsibility for the avoidance of dangerous climate change, and the aversion of other threats to humankind as part of the Earth system.
>
> (Ibid., 2)

Thus, individuals and collective actors such as corporations surrender their 'rights'[59] to harm the environment to the state, expecting in turn public innovations in the direction of sustainability which can be justified normatively with the pressing need for a sustainability transition. The state assumes a strong role and makes use of its legislation competence to devise a legislative framework conducive to the transition with the aim of protecting its citizens from dangerous climate change and the undermining of their livelihood. This in turn binds the citizens to change established routines and their individual behaviour in the direction of a more sustainable lifestyle, which can for example include doing voluntary work or paying carbon taxes (ibid., 276).

The figure of thought of the social contract that is used to frame the socio-ecological transition differs from traditional contract theory in four main points (ibid., 8). First, due to globalisation processes, the nation state is no longer the point of reference but the contract must have a global dimension.

Second, traditional contract theory assumed – wrongly, as shown by Nussbaum (2006) – equality between all members of society, which would imply the same opportunity to participate in and shape societal processes. Yet, the different types of capital (Bourdieu 1983)[60] are unequally distributed not only between different world regions but also within one state according to different social positions. Furthermore, as demonstrated by Pateman (1988), the functioning of the traditional social contract is based on a sexual contract, taking women's bodies and labour as granted for the functioning of society without granting them equal rights as members of society. For these two sub-reasons a social contract remains incomplete without also conceiving a redistribution mechanism of opportunities for participation across social positions and gender.

Third, the traditional social contract uses the environment as an infinite source and sink for human activity, granting human beings an unlimited right to exploit natural resources.[61] This idea must be turned completely upside down in a social contract for sustainability, acknowledging human activity as being dependent on the environment and therefore respecting the Earth's planetary boundaries in order not to undermine humankind's livelihood.

Fourth, the image of a self-organised civil society as major societal actor and driver is not an element in traditional social contract theory in which the individual by granting his[62] rights to the sovereign assumes the passive role of a state-protected subject.

In this new contract the state must assume a 'proactive' and 'enabling' role. This state is conceived as serving its citizens (Biesecker and Kesting 2003, 461). 'Proactive' means that sustainability is determined as overarching priority, options for participation are augmented and diversified, and incentives for sustainable economic behaviour are given (WBGU 2011, 2). For example, the state could bind unleashed market forces by changing legislation for putting a price on social and environmental externalities of products,[63] for introducing higher taxes, for increasing investments of the gross domestic product into green sectors (Randers 2012, 166–7), for reducing consumption,[64] and for introducing a yearly individual yet transferable CO_2 emission allotment (Paech 2015, 41). The enabling state fosters self-organisation (WBGU 2011, 204) and should promote the sustainability commitment of economic and civil society actors (ibid., 205).[65] Whereas the concept of the proactive state ascribes the need for action primarily to political and administrative actors, the enabling state supports citizens' initiatives that emerge in economy or civil society (Biesecker and Kesting 2003, 461). This double concept of the state ascribes it a more active role than the 'liberal model of the minimal state' (WBGU 2011, 204) and also than the 'purely moderating and remedial role that is typical for pluralistic negotiation democracies' (ibid., 203), yet without reaching the 'command and control function' (ibid., 204) of socialist systems.

To balance and to legitimise the state's strong role and to control its increased power, citizens must actively participate in and co-shape the transition (ibid., 205). The contract brings together three types of cultures: 'a culture of attentiveness (born of a sense of ecological responsibility), a culture of participation (as a democratic responsibility), and a culture of obligation towards future generations (future responsibility)' (ibid., 2). The relatively strong role of the state must be balanced by a 'democratic mandate' (Jackson 2009, 168), thus by the opening up and fostering of participation options (Biesecker and Kesting 2003, 453; WBGU 2011, 8; Biesecker and von Winterfeld 2014a, 220; Biesecker and von Winterfeld 2014b). Biesecker and von Winterfeld (2014a, 220, own translation) point to the fact that this means realising the overarching contract in many small local social contracts, meaning 'in social experiments and social struggles', thus acting at the local level with the global social contract in mind. A sustainable economy and society can only be achieved in a broad cooperative negotiation process (Biesecker and Kesting 2003, 169, 191), also because as the state on its own has nothing up its sleeves to achieve a sustainable society and economy (WBGU 2011, 203).

Randers (2012, 212, 248) also argues for a stronger state, not believing that the big increases in investment needed to obtain a green economy would occur in a free market. Yet, in opposition to the ideas expressed in the last paragraph, he does not believe in the power of a countervailing democratic force, being convinced that a strong state needs to act even against the will of the majority to achieve the sustainability aims for the eventual benefit of all (ibid., 248–9; cf.

2.3.1). Almost 30 years of economic globalisation, expressing itself in liberalisation, deregulation, and privatisation tendencies, have not found solutions to the problems that neoliberal economists say a free market could solve (Elsen 2007, 17; Randers 2012, 248). On the contrary, social and environmental externalities are bigger than ever before due to the deregulation in the global neoliberal corporate economy, for example in the financial and agriculture/food economy, having led to multiple crises (Shiva 2013, 5–6; cf. 2.4.3.7). This is also because in this profit-driven system marked by 'mergers and speculative financial transactions there is no growth in the real economy but a rising pressure for cost reduction to obtain high capital yields'[66] (Elsen 2007, 18, own translation). Randers (2012, 210) believes a form of 'modified capitalism'[67] will have emerged before 2052 whose overarching aim will be marked by sustainability values and collective well-being. Governments will make legislation that diverts investment flows from the most profitable projects to the perhaps more expensive in the short and middle run but more sustainable ones. Economic actors will be obliged to follow a transparent reporting of the social and environmental impacts of their actions which will have been co-developed and monitored by the public, especially civil society, and although private enterprises will still be operating, economy will comprise a large public share. However, countering Randers' pessimistic view of the power of democratic systems, precisely the implementation of such a modified form of capitalism can be accelerated if the reasoning behind and the functioning of a post-growth society and economy is understood by an increasing proportion of the population (cf. 6.2.6).

2.4.3 Out of the growth trap: conceiving a post-growth society and economy

This subsection argues why a radical and timely system shift to a post-growth society and economy is necessary if catastrophic irreversible climate change seriously wants to be avoided, remaining within the safe operating space. It first explains why both relative and absolute decoupling of economic growth from growth in material throughputs and environmental impacts are a dead-end road, if they continue to be paired with the goal of economic growth, before arguing for a new kind of macro-economics not dependent on economic growth rates. Section 2.4.3.3 explains why the path to a post-growth society and economy has already been taken, and Section 2.4.3.4 shows why a post-growth society and economy is also indispensable to achieve equity within a country and between world regions. Section 2.4.3.5 carves out the 'philosophy' standing behind a post-growth society and economy by highlighting people's underlying values and motives in it. Section 2.4.3.6 shows how a post-growth society and economy practically functions, paying specific attention to the role of work in it. The last subsection gives examples of how economic crises can be the starting point to shift direction towards a post-growth society and economy.

2.4.3.1 Why decoupling is insufficient

While a non-growing economy is beyond the imagination of most economists, the above considerations, especially Section 2.2, as well as mere logical thinking leads to ever continuing economic growth to be questioned. 'Green economy' or 'green growth' advocates believe in the compatibility of economic growth and decarbonisation. According to this concept a low-carbon economy can be achieved by decoupling economic growth from growth in material throughputs and environmental impacts, principally greenhouse gas emissions, mainly by technological innovations that increase efficiency and consistency (Jackson 2009, 14; WBGU 2011, 177; Paech 2015, 33). The decoupling strategy is twofold. Relative decoupling refers to reducing energy intensity through increasing resource efficiency (Jackson 2009, 68–71; Seidl and Zahrnt 2010b, 30). Thus, in a process of dematerialisation an equal output is reached with less energy and material input (Meadows *et al.* 2005, 178). Absolute decoupling is more ambitious, since it demands economic growth to be virtually totally independent from resource consumption and environmental pollution by very increased efficiency, dematerialisation, and technological innovation (Lieb 2003; Binswanger *et al.* 2005; Jackson 2009, 67; Krausmann *et al.* 2009; Seidl and Zahrnt 2010b, 30).

The question is whether absolute decoupling can be introduced as an overarching principle in all sectors, beyond its realisation in single branches of economic activity, and whether it would then be sufficient to keep a world population of nine billion people within ecological boundaries, including avoiding catastrophic climate change (Jackson 2009, 67–8). With humankind being faced with the looming consequences of its self-endangering behaviour for the first time, there is no historical or scientific experience to draw on in this question. If major technological innovations were implemented to immensely reduce resource intensity and if consumer demand was shifted to more sustainable products (Jackson 2009, 75), the compatibility of economic growth with a low-carbon economy cannot be completely excluded, yet several factors make achieving this goal highly improbable on a global scale.[68]

The problem with the decoupling strategy is that it does not give up the Keynesian aim of shifting the economy back on the path of growing consumption (Jackson 2009, 103–4). Remaining in this thinking makes the system-inherent growth drivers urge for 'ever more unsustainable resource throughput' (Jackson 2009, 118–19). This increases the possibility of 'rebound' effects, which occur if more energy-efficient products are bought and used more often. In that case relative decoupling can decrease the possibility of absolute decoupling (Jackson 2009, 30; Seidl and Zahrnt 2010a, 21; Seidl and Zahrnt 2010b, 30). Several studies have shown that absolute decoupling is no feasible strategy for the necessary decarbonisation of economy (Lieb 2003; Binswanger *et al.* 2005; Krausmann *et al.* 2009).

In fact, post-growth economists are convinced that only in a non-growing economy is there the possibility that more sustainable technologies do not

negatively impact on the ecosystem (e.g. Paech 2015, 36). Post-growth economists do not believe in the possibility of achieving a low-carbon economy via
decoupling, being convinced that relying on economic growth to solve world
society's complex problems is a short-sighted strategy. If the economy grew, as
wished by mainstream economists, at around 2 per cent a year from 2050
onwards, it would be 40 times bigger in 2100 than today (Jackson 2009, 82).
Jackson (ibid.) asks how the world would look with such an economy. Fortunately, this is a mere hypothetical question, as such growth rates will not be
achieved (cf. 2.4.3.3). In fact, in Western industrialised countries, due to the
saturation of the market, which expresses itself in a rising saving rate and a
falling consumption rate due to rising income (Reuter 2010, 94), growth rates
have continuously fallen since the 1960s (Seidl and Zahrnt 2010b, 33; cf.
2.4.3.3). Post-growth economists believe that absolute decoupling can only be
achieved in a non-growing economy and that this new type of economy will
require far-reaching changes in the economic but also underlying social system
to become growth-independent yet remain stable (Daly 1991; Latouche 2006;
Victor 2008; Jackson 2009, 118–19; Kallis 2011; Costanza *et al.* 2015).

> The truth is that there is as yet no credible, socially just, ecologically sus-
> tainable scenario of continually growing incomes for a world of 9 billion
> people. In this context, simplistic assumptions that capitalism's propensity
> for efficiency will allow us to stabilize the climate or protect against resource
> scarcity are nothing short of delusional.... [I]t is entirely fanciful to suppose
> that 'deep' emission and resource cuts can be achieved without confronting
> the structure of market economies.
>
> (Jackson 2009, 86)

Post-growth economists acknowledge the basic incompatibility of an infinitely
growing economy 'within a finite ecological system' (ibid., 14). They warn that
the current 'green' growth strategy is very likely to lead to irreversible climate
change in the second half of this century. Therefore, the logic of economic
growth needs to be questioned *now* and the 'green cloak' policy of most economic and political actors needs to be dismantled. *Real* sustainability and green
economy means abandoning the economic growth paradigm as the overarching
aim of politics and economy,[69] to set as the overarching goal the prosperity and
the well-being of society, and to orient the whole of the economy towards it.
Post-growth economists believe neither that prosperity can be equalised with
economic growth nor that 'continued economic growth is a *necessary condition*
for a lasting prosperity' (ibid., 49).

2.4.3.2 Why a different kind of macro-economics is needed

Despite economic growth being unsustainable, it is continuously clung to
(cf. 2.3.3), knowing that putting into practice 'de-growth'[70] demands such as
reducing consumption would create instability, since they can lead to 'rising

unemployment, falling competitiveness and a spiral of recession' (Jackson 2009, 65). As explained above (2.4.3.1), post-growth economists do not believe in the possibility of making growth sustainable, so they must answer the question how 'to make de-growth stable' (Jackson 2009, 128). This will be explained in this subsection as well as under 2.4.3.5 and 2.4.3.6. To propose growth-independent alternatives that still guarantee economic stability and employment,[71] it first has to be understood why human beings rely on economic growth despite knowing that it endangers our livelihoods.

Economic growth can be defined as 'the increase in monetarily measured economic performance of a national economy. Measured variable is the change rate of the inflation-adjusted gross domestic product' (Seidl and Zahrnt 2010b, 24, own translation). The gross domestic product is 'the sum of all economic output (gross value added), the sum of all incomes (wages and dividends/profits) and the sum of all expenditures (consumption and investment)' (Jackson 2009, 221, endnote 4) within a country. Despite the fact that the gross domestic product is an inappropriate measuring tool for human well-being and prosperity as expressed in national welfare and social progress (Nordhaus and Tobin 1973) and despite alternative tools being available (Stiglitz *et al.* 2009), it is still widely used as the main instrument to diagnose the state of economies.

The main problem with this measurement is that it merely measures the market economy's activities (Jackson 2009, 179). Thus, 'by counting only the monetary value of things exchanged in the economy' (ibid., 125), it 'excludes the existing stocks' (WBGU 2011, 75) and does not depict economic activities happening outside the market. This is highly problematic since it distorts the picture of economic activities going on and depreciates 'goods and services that do not have a market price, or are not actually traded, such as ecosystem services, housework, voluntary work or subsistence economic activities' (ibid.; similarly Jackson 2009, 125). This 'asymmetric accounting' (Daly 2012, 75) means on the one hand that the cited positive economic activities going on outside the market are not counted in the gross domestic product, and that on the other hand the social and environmental costs of economic activities, such as the consumption of natural capital up to environmental destruction and pollution, are not subtracted from the gross domestic product but contrarily added as income despite being contrary to achieving human well-being (Daly 2012, 75; Jackson 2009, 125). 'The cost of, for example, remedying environmental damages leads to a higher GDP per capita, even though it only serves the restoration of the status quo' (WBGU 2011, 75). Moreover, taking into consideration the finiteness of resources is completely absent from this measuring tool (Jackson 2009, 125), and aspects that are highly important to assess the well-being of a society are not reflected either, such as the quality of the education and health systems (WBGU 2011, 75) as well as the distribution of income (Stiglitz *et al.* 2009).

The aforementioned points show that more realistic approaches to measure welfare are needed (Seidl and Zahrnt 2010b, 29). Such approaches already exist. For example, the Stiglitz-Sen-Fitoussi-Commission on the Measurement of Economic Performance and Social Progress proposes including the value of leisure time, non-remunerated services like household and voluntary work as well as subsistence agriculture into the measuring of welfare (Stiglitz *et al.* 2009). Most advanced as far as policy implementation is concerned is the state of Bhutan with its 'Gross National Happiness Index'. This measuring tool was commissioned by the Bhutan government and sets the citizens' happiness as the overarching policy goal, aligning all policies to it (Givel and Figueroa 2013).

Conceiving alternative growth-independent welfare measuring tools is a good starting point to achieve a 'new ecological macro-economics' (Jackson 2009, 137), yet it must be supplemented by the elaboration of a comprehensive post-growth theory of macroeconomics able to explain how economic stability can be achieved without relying on ever-increasing economic growth (ibid., 122–3). Major groundwork in this direction was performed by Herman E. Daly with the concept of a steady-state economy, which he defines as

> an economy with constant stocks of people and artefacts, maintained at some desired, sufficient levels by low rates of maintenance 'throughputs', that is, by the lowest feasible flows of matter and energy from the first stage of production (depletion of low-entropy materials from the environment) to the last stage of consumption (pollution of the environment with high-entropy wastes and exotic materials).
>
> (1991, 17)

According to Jackson (2009, 141) such an economy must emanate from

> relax[ing] the presumption of perpetual consumption growth as the only possible basis for stability and to identify clearly the conditions that define a sustainable economy. These conditions will still include a strong requirement for economic stability … but … need to be augmented by conditions that provide security for people's livelihoods, ensure distributional equity, impose sustainable levels of resource throughput and protect critical natural capital…. [N]ew macro-economic variables will need to be brought explicitly into play. These will almost certainly include variables to reflect the energy and resource dependence of the economy and the limits of carbon. They may also include variables to reflect the value of ecosystem services or stocks of natural capital.

A key task of such a new economic theory is to change existing conceptions about labour and capital productivities, since 'the continued pursuit of labour productivity drives economies towards growth simply to maintain full employment' (ibid., 176). In the face of ending growth and the environmental state of the planet it makes sense, not to aim for high productivities but rather to 'engage in structural transition towards low-carbon, labour-intensive activities and sectors' (ibid.).

2.4.3.3 Why the post-growth society and economy is already under way

The path to a post-growth society and economy,[72] consciously or unconsciously, has already been taken (Reuter 2010, 85, 89–92). The economy, at least in Western industrial countries, cannot rely any more on rising economic growth rates (Reuter 2010; Paech 2015, 39). Most of these countries reported 'in the first years of the new millennium an on average growth of less than one per cent' (Reuter 2010, 89–90, own translation),[73] and this trend is expected to continue in the future. According to Randers' (2012, 232–3; cf. 2.3) forecast, the worldwide gross domestic product growth rates will diminish until at a point in the second half of this century there will be no economic growth at all, and in the already industrialised countries it will even stagnate decades before (Randers 2012, 284–5; cf. 2.3). And even if high economic growth rates were still achievable, they would not suffice to allow for full employment under the current conditions.[74] Also, if the looming climate catastrophe makes human-kind wise enough to take mitigation options (cf. 2.2), economic growth will decline since consumption will be reduced or shifted to more sustainable sectors (IPCC 2015, 24). The economic growth that is still expected under this scen-ario will be needed for climate change mitigation and adaptation (Jackson 2009, 84–5).[75] Post-growth economists expose mainstream economists' central lie of economic growth automatically leading to a higher level of prosperity and well-being, to welfare and employment for all. While this is only in part still true for developing and newly industrialising countries, it does not depict the situation in the already highly industrialised world regions where productivity is already high. 'The hopes for economic growth as a diverse societal problem solver have not been fulfilled since the 1970s in the industrial countries.' (Seidl and Zahrnt 2010b, 31, own translation). Rather an almost jobless growth has been recorded for almost 40 years due to an already high labour productivity mainly because of technological progress (Gorz 1997, 129, 145–6; Seidl and Zahrnt 2010b, 32). 'All labor policy, whether governmental or in-plant, has been subject since at least the eighties to the law of *redistributing the systematically produced lack of work*' (Beck 2009, 145). Consequently, economic growth does not have the power any more to reduce social disparities of wealth and income (Gorz 1997, 129, 145–6; Seidl and Zahrnt 2010b, 32). The rise of mass unemployment and the resulting reinforced disparities in income and wealth since the beginning of the 1970s can be explained 'as a consequence of the interaction of a lacking expansion of the service sector, an insufficient creation of public or publicly financed workplaces and an insufficient reduction in working time' (Reuter 2010, 92, own translation). Nevertheless, politics is continuously oriented on the outdated model of a society based on gainful employment which no longer represents societal realities (Elsen 2007, 24). Therefore, the economy needs to be redirected as quickly as possible towards different goals. The way to a post-growth economy and society is already predetermined. The earlier the current economy and society is accordingly started to be rebuilt, the higher the level of prosperity and well-being within ecological boundaries will be for society's members. The later the conversion takes place, the shorter the remaining time span to avoid catastrophic climate change (cf. 2.2) and the higher the economic, social, and environmental costs will be. This choice is what Paech (2015, 36) pointedly names 'by design or by disaster'. The main challenge of a post-growth economy is 'to organise the negative growth in a socially compatible and economically resilient way' (ibid., own translation). The only growth that is to be found in a post-growth economy and society in the long term is qualitative growth in well-being and prosperity.

2.4.3.4 Achieving equity within a country and around the world

Apart from the need to remain within ecological boundaries, the shift to a post-growth economy and society is necessary to achieve equity on a global scale and within a country. The ecological footprint (cf. 2.3) varies greatly between countries (Shiva 2013, 19). As a matter of fact, if the countries in the Global South had the same consumption rates as the industrialised countries, the world's resources would have already been exhausted.[76] Allowing the current level of material consumption enjoyed by the industrialised countries to the whole world population would by far exceed the Earth's carrying capacity (Meadows *et al.* 2005, 278; Shiva 2013, 39). This logically puts the responsibility on the industrialised countries to reduce their consumption to set an example for the rest of the world, which naturally believes it has the same 'right' of pollution and consumption as the industrialised countries which have already used it up endangering several planetary boundaries. 'A high-carbon lifestyle in western industrial societies' (WBGU 2011, 197) has led to climate change, whose detrimental impacts also undermine the livelihood of people in the Global South who already do and will even more suffer most from a development they have, if at all, least and only marginally contributed to.

The concept of a post-growth economy is not to be understood as a universal key and application principle for every world region. The countries in the Global South cannot be denied their right to economic growth to shift their populations out of poverty. However, for economic growth to reach this goal, it must be embedded into its social and environmental foundations (cf. 2.3.2) and be relatively and possibly absolutely decoupled from resource consumption (cf. 2.4.3.1). It is the duty of industrialised countries to de-grow to increase the scope for economic growth and resource consumption within ecological boundaries for the developing and newly industrialising countries so that they can manage to meet the basic needs of their populations (Elsen 2007, 99; Jackson 2009, 41). A well-functioning society, be it on the global scale or within a country, only supports inequality up to a certain extent (Elsen 2007, 72). However, both the current national and the global trend completely ignore this fact. Prosperity and well-being in its current form of the richest fifth of the global population is only possible because it 'is founded on ecological destruction and persistent social injustice' (Jackson 2009, 15). Yet, as especially international migration flows in 2015 have shown, people can hardly be prevented from migrating to where they hope to be able to live a good life. And also within a country, problems arise, if a minority of rich becomes ever richer, while the majority of the population is threatened by downward social mobility. The post-growth economy tries to reorganise economy and society in a way that global and national inequalities are reduced and a good life for all becomes possible without undermining the carrying capacity of the Earth. Thus, a post-growth economy

> operates within clear ecological limits, and focuses on social equity and environmental compatibility. Primarily recommended is a government information and communication policy that triggers a value change towards frugality, towards solidarity, a pronounced environmental consciousness, and greater social participation.... [A]ny steering by means of state policies must be legitimised through participation and social debate. Management by governance should encompass social redistribution, the democratisation of decision-making processes, renunciation of the present consumer behaviour, and the introduction of new welfare indicators and new narratives for a 'good life.'
>
> (WBGU 2011, 177)

2.4.3.5 What the 'good life' is about

A post-growth society and economy is about finding ways for people 'to flourish, to achieve greater social cohesion, to find higher levels of well-being and yet still to reduce their material impact on the environment' (Jackson 2009, 35). Such a society and economy can only be achieved under two conditions. First, there must be a worldwide understanding for the need of a transition and consequently an agreement to align all actions with sustainability generally and climate change mitigation specifically (WBGU 2011, 64). Second, reaching this consensus is only possible in a broad societal discussion and participation process in which action situations[77] for communication and compromise-finding are created that allow experiments and (re)negotiation of what living a 'good life' implies (Seidl and Zahrnt 2010c, 227; Biesecker and von Winterfeld 2014a, 215–16). The 'good life' cannot be dictated from above but 'must match perceptions of what a good and successful life is, and these again must be widely shared and attractive' (WBGU 2011, 67). This necessitates an individual learning process of every member of society in which knowledge is gained, understanding of the necessity of a change is increased, and personal values, habits, and behaviour are subsequently modified.

Since in a post-growth society and economy there is no bigger pie to distribute from, the piece of the pie becomes smaller for those that were used to having the bigger pieces, provided a fair redistribution scheme is applied. This causes fears of loss aversion and about the future amongst the rich.[78] A post-growth society is often associated with minimisation, frugality, and relinquishment. These terms are so contradictory to the current striving of economy and society, that it is hard to believe that a movement has evolved whose members voluntarily reduce their consumption and change their lifestyles, interestingly not perceiving this as a loss but as a deliberate gain in life quality and personal freedom through a 'Liberation from Excess' (Paech 2012, 3). So a value change is already under way. There is the chance that in highly industrialised societies the idea of how a good successful life looks will be more and more decoupled from materialistic values and coupled to post-materialistic ones.

However, achieving a change in this direction is still at odds with the principles of the consumption society surrounding us in which sustainable behaviour is continuously regarded as a sacrifice and a reduction in personal freedom. The process of industrialisation with its concomitant economic-growth-based system has distorted the original sense of freedom (Polanyi 2001, 257). In this process, 'the "good life" has increasingly become synonymous with material wealth' (WBGU 2011, 67). Social status has become closely linked to material goods. Here, it should be added that in all European societies the gap between the rich and the poor has widened, which is even more problematic in a consumption society. This is so because in such a society there is the pressure to show one's social status by acquiring material goods which is made difficult for an ever-growing majority of people.

Yet, since it is distributional equity that is highly correlated with the quality of life (Jackson 2009, 154–5) and not the absolute quantity of material goods acquired, a high quality of life does not depend on a high consumption rate but can, even more sustainably and more likely, be achieved in a post-growth society with a shift from materialistic individualism to post-materialistic values and participation (ibid., 169). That the equation referred to in the previous paragraph is false can easily be shown when psychologically digging deeper into the real motives behind the striving for material goods. Then it becomes obvious that they are actually of a social nature: striving for acceptance and recognition by others. Material goods have for long become the wrong substitutes for needs that could and should be satisfied in a non-materialistic way: for example spending more time with family and friends and becoming engaged in and participating in the local community (Gorz 1988, 65–6; WBGU 2011, 69).[79]

Achieving a post-growth economy and society requires a profound restructuring of growth-dependent and growth-promoting political and economic institutions. Yet realisable concrete concepts are still in the fledging stage, and there is little experience of how to transform them in a way that they can still exercise their functions independent of growth (Seidl and Zahrnt 2010a, 17). Therefore, it is ever more important to initiate joint learning processes. Experiments must be allowed, and existing diverse grassroots initiatives that are often highly networked and operate at the local level must be made visible and given a voice, because 'as laboratories for social change' (Jackson 2009, 152) they show the route to a sustainable lifestyle. Citizens will only back the path to a sustainable economy and society if they have participated in its elaboration, thus having become familiarised with the issues, having interacted actively, having formed an opinion, and undergone a value change. Information, education, and participation are ever more crucial, 'since the hitherto existing model of unlimited freedom needs to be withdrawn and the ecological and social costs of this freedom need to be widely thematised' (Seidl and Zahrnt 2010c, 226, own translation) to perceive the change as a gain instead of a loss. In this process there is no master plan but numerous transition paths according to differing local conditions. However, all share the same overarching goal and are marked by a high degree of citizen participation and options for self-organisation (cf. 6.3.2).

2.4.3.6 How a post-growth society and economy looks

In a post-growth economy, economic growth is slowed down because of three major macro-economic measures that aim at achieving economic and ecological stability:

- respect of ecological limits (Daly 1991; Daly 1996; Jackson 2009, 198);
- structural conversion to more service activities with a high proportion of public ones (Jackson 2009, 199–200; Reuter 2010, 85, 97); and
- allocation of the majority of financial investment to ecological projects (Jackson 2009, 177, 199; Randers 2012, 84), for example in the field of urban green spaces or ecosystem protection and maintenance.

The macroeconomy is liberated from the dilemma of economic growth (cf. 2.3.3; Jackson 2009, 169), and politics can abandon its alignment with economic growth and aim instead at reducing non-renewable energy and resource consumption and at restructuring growth-promoting and -depending institutions to make them growth-independent (Seidl and Zahrnt 2010b, 33–4). The primacy of environmental investment leads to a rise in public investment (Jackson 2009, 200) to 'ensure that long-term public goods are not undermined by short-term private interests' (ibid., 166). Yet, also, ownership schemes that go beyond the classical distinction between public and private can be a way to organise and provide public services beyond the market and have become more and more widespread (Elsen 2007, 256–7; Jackson 2009, 201; Reuter 2010, 95). Especially basic services for the local community can be organised in and delivered by social and solidarity economies (Elsen 2007, 280; cf. 2.4.4). In this sense, Seidl and Zahrnt (2010c, 224, own translation) expect

> that increasingly hybrid forms of private, public and semi-public co-producers of public goods will emerge. Considerations on efficiency, an increasing demand for societal participation, shortened times of gainful employment and consequently increased informal work, voluntary work as well as new forms of social entrepreneurship are indicative of this.

Following Elsen (2007, 150), a post-growth economy follows four main core guiding ideas. First, 'efficiency', 'sufficiency', and 'consistency' are the central principles on how to handle resources in the restructuring of economy and society. The first refers to the 'reduction of material and energy input in production for the same output' (Biesecker and Kesting 2003, 240, own translation). The second designates the 'reduction of material and energy flows' (ibid., own translation), and the third means

> to manage in a way that the material and energy flows are both from the resource and from the 'waste' side compatible with the environment, that is that they can be integrated by the environment both in the composition and in the time structure into its reproduction cycle.
>
> (Ibid., own translation)

Second, 'the creation of socio-economic cycles'[80] (Elsen 2007, 111, own translation), as part of regional markets, 'via embedding, networking and controlling economic transactions' (ibid.) results in shorter value chains to keep the added value in the region and to become more independent from the volatility of the global (financial) economy and from the practical constraints of export-orientated economies (Elsen 2007, 153–7; Shiva 2013, 265). Subsistence economy, for example in the field of urban food production, is a main pillar of this regionalised economy (cf. 7.4.2). It is supplemented by regional enterprises, for example in the field of 'community supported agriculture',[81] which provide goods supplementing those created by prosumers[82] and those that cannot be created by them.

Third, in a post-growth economy the understanding of work and the role it plays in people's lives differs from its understanding and role in the growth economy. In a post-growth understanding, 'work' is a holistic, overarching term comprising a diversity of human activities. Such a pluralised concept of work, arguing for a new equilibrium between gainful employment and other types of work, has been discussed for decades in literature and has gained highest argumentative power in times of the growth-turn. As expressed in the approach of the caring economy (Biesecker 2000), it considers productive and reproductive activities, thus gainful employment as well as non-gainful work such as care work and voluntary work, as equal and interrelated. This conceptualisation enlarges the conventional restricted understanding of work as a mere production factor, thus being limited to gainful employment in the industrial economic growth society by encompassing the environmental, social, and economic sustainability dimension (Biesecker and Kesting 2003, 32, 377, 384–7; Elsen 2007, 150). It points back to Polanyi's re-embedding conception, who early on pointed to the detrimental social consequences of the commodification of work:

> To **SEPARATE LABOR** from other activities of life and to subject it to the laws of the market was to annihilate all organic forms of existence and to replace them by a different type of organization, an atomistic and individualistic one.
>
> (2001, 163)

In a post-growth economy the process described by Polanyi is partly reversed by equally redistributing the remaining available gainful employment amongst the workforce by a reduction in working hours, job sharing, and the creation of tax-funded public green jobs (Gorz 1988, 199; 1997, 114, 136; Meadows *et al.* 2005, 261; Jackson 2009, 114, 134, 200; Reuter 2010, 92–3; Randers 2012, 263). Reducing the hours of an individual's employment not only opens up possibilities to bring more people into employment but also increases the free time of those having worked full-time before (Jackson 2009, 134) with the possibility of unfolding, self-actualising, and becoming engaged in meaningful creative activities (Gorz 1988, 235). The additional time gained can for example turn consumers into modern more self-sufficient persons who refresh manual and social competences by engaging in community activities such as urban gardening or agriculture[83] (Gorz 1988, 198; Paech 2015, 29).

Since, as outlined in the preceding paragraph, in a post-growth economy the term 'full employment' does not refer any more exclusively to the sphere of gainful employment but to all fields of work, all members of society can be integrated into a form of work which puts an end to unemployment (Biesecker and Kesting 2003, 391–2). A necessary precondition for this is sufficient social security (ibid., 392). The most radical proposal to decouple income and social security from employment in order to achieve a more equal society, to promote and enable participation in the form of political activism, meaningful work, and activities is the introduction of an (unconditional) basic income (Habermas 1985, 253; Beck 1986, 236; Jackson 2009, 196). According to Gorz (1997, 113–16, 134–8), for this concept to deliver the desired effects, it is fundamental that it is truly unconditional[84] and that the income is set above the poverty level. The first condition prevents rendering its recipient a suppliant of the welfare state, since it gives the individual the freedom to reject unworthy work or working conditions. The second condition prevents neoliberal trials (Friedman 1962) to misuse it as a means to subsidise unqualified labour. Without this second condition in place recipients would have to accept jobs in the low-pay sector to bulk their income up which is the true reason for neoliberals supporting the version of an unconditional insufficient basic income (Gorz 1997, 134–6). Contrary to the neoliberal view, an unconditional basic income should be seen as an option for everyone to engage in a variety of occupations that are freed from the need to yield profit in monetary terms (Gorz 1997, 161). In this sense, an unconditional basic income catalyses the emergence of a 'multiple activity society' (ibid., 130, own translation; cf. 7.4.2), as an alternative to the dysfunctional labour society, in which the citizens lead a multiactive self-determined life which can but does not have to include gainful employment. Gainful employment does not take centre stage any more but is downgraded to one amongst many other meaningful work activities that increase life satisfaction and social capital (Gorz 1997, 124). Meaningful work caters for participation-enabling processes of communication and the building of relationships for example in the local community (Elsen 2007, 113). The concept acknowledges the diversity of societally meaningful and necessary work, and can be linked to Hannah Arendt's conception of action referring to the plurality of meaningful human activities that can never be done alone but depend on the communication with others, thus 'always establishes relationships' (1958, 190).

While the implementation of 'a low basic income' (van Parijs 1992, 230) could be achieved for its major part without increased state expenditures by a restructuring of current welfare spending,[85] it should not be concealed that the aforementioned shift to public investment requires higher state expenditures (Reuter 2010, 99), which entails higher taxation if public sector debts want to be avoided (Jackson 2009, 25). In a non-growing economy this inevitably means touching upon the private assets of the rich.[86]

Fourth, in a 'multiple activity society' local initiatives, either initiated bottom-up by the citizens themselves or by the local authority, take centre stage, since they 'provide meaningful work, offer people capabilities for flourishing, contribute positively to community and have a decent chance of being materially light' (Jackson 2009, 132). On the condition that they are not misused by the local authority to cut back state services (cf. 1.1, and Chapter 3), these initiatives can become capable of delivering local services, for example in the field of green spaces maintenance or food production and might develop into institutions with a higher organisational degree, for example food cooperatives (cf. 2.4.4). They enable participation, strengthen social capital, and make the community more resilient to economic crises (Jackson 2009, 182, 193; cf. 2.4.4).

Yet, the problem of these economic initiatives is that they remain quasi invisible in economic terms, since they only marginally contribute to the gross domestic product (Jackson 2009, 130–1). Being labour-intensive, often involving a large share of voluntary work and not being primarily profit-orientated, these social and solidarity economies run counter to mainstream economic thinking (ibid., 196). They are often not competitive in conventional economic terms. At the same time they deliver important social, environmental, and economic functions for the local community and thus require support from the local authority on the one hand, and a special legal status and protection on the other (cf. 2.4.4). Only then will they be able to deliver their meaningful services through meaningful work in the long run. Thus, the local authority is in the duty to play an active role in creating scope for the development of such self-organised initiatives (Gorz 1997, 133; Elsen 2007, 157–60; Jackson 2009, 182).

2.4.3.7 Creating a post-growth economy out of crises

Around the world there are examples of post-growth economies evolving out of economic crises. In Argentina, after the economic crisis in 2001, it was only thanks to the set-up of decentralised barter economy schemes that the provision of the population with essential goods could be upheld (Elsen 2007, 200–2). In Cuba, the end of the Soviet Union and the subsequent need to become quasi self-sufficient due to international sanctions and the breaking away of remaining imports has led to a flourishing of social and solidarity economies primarily in the field of urban food production which have in many places evolved into institutions with a higher organisational structure – cooperatives – providing work and feeding the population at the same time (cf. 2.4.4 and 7.4.2).

Economic crises are times in which the questioning of the current functioning of economy becomes louder. The multiple crises from 2008 onwards which started on the food market, continued on the financial market, and finally reached the whole economy is the most evident signal that the current functioning of the globalised economy is incompatible with the ecological and social limits of reality (Shiva 2013, 5–6) and that 'for the advanced economies of the western world, prosperity without growth is no longer a utopian dream. It is a financial and ecological necessity' (Jackson 2009, 185). The crises would be an opportunity to invest in a profound reorientation towards a post-growth economy and society. However, instead of touching on private assets by introducing a Europe-wide progressive tax on assets[87] and by fighting tax evasion, allowing a partial debt cancellation,[88] and strengthening options for social and solidarity economies to evolve (cf. 2.4.4), debts were not reduced, the assets of the rich remain untouched and austerity policy measures (privatisation, cutting public spending in fields like health and education down to the local level) were introduced that are most strongly felt at the local level and brought more and more people close to the poverty line.[89]

2.4.4 Implementing the growth-turn at the regional and the local level: social and solidarity economy as one approach

According to Randers (2012, 191), in times of growing global economic upheaval and decreasing access to fossil fuels, stability and orientation can be built up and regional resilience strengthened if regions increasingly draw on their own resources, becoming more independent from the global economy. In this sense, coping with unavoidable de-growth is a key task for sustainable regional development and is generally more easily realisable in a decentralised state granting a high degree of local autonomy. Regions most advanced in this process have fostered local and regional economies, especially in the agriculture and energy sector, that have often evolved from bottom-up activities (Elsen 2007, 149; Paech 2015, 41). Elsen (2007, 46) analyses the emergence of local independent socioeconomic complementary structures across the globe. Instead of waiting for a change in macroeconomic and political guiding principles, they have, for about 30 years, mostly starting from highly informal civil society initiatives or bottom-up movements, gained in importance. They often tie in with and reactivate suppressed social and solidarity economies which are 'variations of a plural economy which have survived the complete penetration by the market economy in peripheral world regions or in the economies of poverty' (ibid., own translation). Their initiators share the belief in socioeconomic self-organisation instead of waiting for external market or state solutions. When these initiatives and movements gain in organisational capability, developing a higher organisational structure, they can evolve into forms of social and solidarity economy as part of organised civil society (Elsen 2007, 165) and can also enter and effect innovative change in the (local) political and economic system, for example by transferring principles of participatory democracy into them (Elsen 2007, 6, 13, 46, 232–3).

The term 'social and solidarity economy'[90] 'is not about a uniform economic position, … [but] instead is a normative real phenomenon which at the same time is to be found worldwide historically and currently in diverse manifestations' (ibid., own translation). It can be considered as the practical re-embedding of economy at the local and regional level via the strengthening and recreating of economies following the needs of the local community (ibid., 42; cf. 2.4.1), functioning according to a redefined concretised concept of economic rationality as 'what does not endanger the social and ecological livelihoods of the community and what grants access of all members of society to these bases'[92] (Elsen 2007, 85, own translation). Its underlying economic logic is directed towards social and environmental aims, promotes a diversity of economic activity, and expresses itself in economic actors bringing in comprehensive perspectives (ibid., 99, 112, 147–8, 150). It relies on self-organisation, communication, cooperation, mutuality, and solidarity as guiding principles (ibid., 52, 108–9, 112, 265, 267) and preserves and promotes social and human capital (ibid., 150). This kind of economy is thus rooted in the 'lifeworld' of local actors, aiming at 'social integration, fulfilment of demand, and securing the livelihood of the local population and the sustainability of the community'[93] (ibid., 26, own translation).

Social and solidarity economies can be understood as alternative drafts to irrational growth-driven processes of neoliberal corporate globalisation producing disembedded markets and weakened democratic systems, since they show that an alternative, more democratic way of conceiving economy and its relationship with society and the environment and of being economically active is possible (ibid., 99, 267). Social and solidarity economies at the local and regional level are examples of socially and environmentally embedded institutions responding to global disembedding processes by relocalisation and the local embedding of economies. This implies a high density of networked, self-organised institutions providing local basic goods and services while being embedded in regional economic structures (Gorz 1997, 118–19; 138; Elsen 2007, 150–1, 317). This does not mean making the local economy totally autonomous or even walling it off from the market. Instead politically controlled and democratically legitimised 'diversified regional economic cultures with inter- and intraregional cooperation relationships'[94] (Elsen 2007, 153, own translation) are created. On the one hand economies and policies aiming at sustainability are always embedded at the local or regional level, while on the other hand the local level never acts independently of superior levels but is placed within a multilevel and multisectoral approach. Opening up options for sustainable local development, social and solidarity economies are never bound to one place, but instead are often highly networked with similar initiatives around the world, creating and spreading 'best practices' and joint learning options from the local to the global level.

In this kind of economy the conception of meaningful work takes centre stage (ibid., 113). Emanating from a comprehensive conception of work (cf. 2.4.3.6), meaningful work is made accessible locally and regionally with the help of social and solidarity economies. Arendt's (2007, 13) statement that modern societies will run out of work, which has been taken up and modified by Rifkin (2004), only refers to gainful employment performed in the official labour market. While there is an increasing lack of work as activity of employed persons in the official labour market, the amount of available work in the local community has been increasing (Habermas 1985, 71–2; EC 1995; Elsen 2007, 113). This is due *inter alia* to an ageing trend in European society resulting in an increasing demand for care work, to the need to make European cities, towns, and villages climate-resilient, and not least to the necessity to host and integrate a rising number of migrants which is a task primarily accomplished at the local level. The mentioned societal and environmental changes require a large amount of work to be dealt with successfully and to be possibly turned into opportunities and benefits for the local community. Yet, these changes happen in times in which the state draws back from essential public services for a lack of financial resources, which partly results in privatisation. However, the market only enters where it sees an opportunity for making profit, which by implication connotes a neglect of public services, for example the care of urban green spaces, that are often considered secondary in the face of pressing social tasks. Following Habermas, commercial privatisation is no solution to the problem, since

> it is difficult to see how relocating problems that, since the end of the nineteenth century, and for good reasons, have been shifted from the market to the state – that is, how shoving problems back and forth between the media of money and power – is going to give us new impetus
>
> (Habermas 1984, xliii)

Commercial privatisation can only be reversed with difficulty and lowers the chances of equal access for all citizens in large measure.[95]

One central question to which social and solidarity economy can deliver an answer, if political framework conditions are supportive, is how the available work at the local level can be tapped via the creation of economic activities that primarily serve the common good instead of profit interests. Political support and concomitant funding structures for local and regional social and solidarity economy solutions that bring people into meaningful work while at the same time delivering highly needed services for the local community and driving local sustainable development are necessary (Elsen 2007, 116).[96] This requires giving up the predominant alignment of (social) policies on gainful employment in the official labour market with concomitant solely individual solution strategies (ibid., 14, 115–16). Alternatives of economic activities based on collective self-organisation are a central element to respond to crises via solutions that are tailored to local needs (ibid., 150). This would be a kind of social policy that focuses on providing equal opportunities instead of primarily being based on the more expensive and less efficient measures that concentrate on *ex-post* redistribution schemes. However, this line of reasoning is not to be misunderstood as a plea for abolishing the welfare state (cf. also 1.1 and Chapter 3). The state is not to be let off the hook in social policy. Instead it should recognise and foster social and solidarity economy options as complementary structures and adjust its funding structures accordingly, following the model of the proactive enabling state (cf. 2.4.2). The availability of funding structures for social and solidarity economy options is especially important in times of economic crises in which it is even more difficult to gain access to seed money in the form of credits (Elsen 2007, 259). Arguing with a lack of public financial resources falls short, if considering 'that precisely major corporations, which cause the biggest societal damage, do not only pay no, barely or no taxes but are moreover to a high degree directly or indirectly subsidised'[97] (ibid., 116, own translation). They receive public money from the EU and national authorities. If parts of this money shall be branched off to support social and solidarity economies, this implies a stringent application of the principle of connexity according to which 'legally described functions (duties) should correlate with the resources allocated' (World Bank, United Cities, and Local Governments 2009, 145). Due to an ageing and immigration trend in Europe there is a huge amount of human capital available that has either already dropped out of the official labour market or due to language, legal, and administrative barriers does not enter it. Thus, besides removing legal and administrative barriers to bring people into gainful employment in the official labour market, local options for work in social and solidarity economy must be tapped.[98] This would enable meaningful activities for citizens and ensure equal access to commons as well as the provision with basic goods and services for the local community (Elsen 2007, 55–6, 112–13) and is therefore to be preferred to commercial privatisation options.

One way of organising economic activities according to the principles of social and solidarity economy is offered by cooperatives as a form of enterprise. Their function varies according to their location. 'In developing and transition countries they can pave the way for entering the market from the informal sector. In industrial countries they facilitate opening up especially labour-intensive sectors for local markets'[99] (ibid., 47, own translation). Apart from their work-providing function, they are also effective at ensuring the access to commons for all members of society and are one form of participation (ibid., 256). This is due to their five central criteria of organisation (ibid., 145–6): they are organised democratically (the vote of every member counts equally), manage common property which is used by all members, their action is geared to local needs and not mainly to making profit, the profit they make is earmarked, and they are socially embedded in the local community. Cooperatives can be considered to be a collective form of privatisation, yet as distinguished from commercial privatisation they offer 'protection from crowding out due to collective ownership which is not liable to a speculative price increase'[100] (ibid., 294, own translation).

With regard to urban and regional sustainable development, cooperatives are an especially interesting form of enterprise. For example, in the field of food production producer–consumer cooperatives strengthen rural–urban linkages by installing a direct link between producers and consumers. This form of community-supported agriculture (cf. 2.4.3.5) provides the first group with a stable guaranteed income and the latter with fresh regional food from a known source at a fair price that directly benefits the producer (Elsen 2007, 288). Compared to this specific form of cooperative, multi-stakeholder cooperatives are more complexly structured, consisting of at least two groups pursuing distinct promotion interests (ibid., 307). They have the capability to provide public services concerning urban and environmental development while at the same time organising the locally necessary work and making it available for local citizens (ibid., 46, 309). Under a conducive policy with a supporting legal framework and funding structures, cooperatives, as a new type of 'private–public partnership', could fulfil important functions in local social politics by including civil society actors as major players to fulfil tasks that are currently neglected due to tight local public budgets (ibid., 308). They could provide citizens, also socially disadvantaged ones, with the option to self-organise their matters in cooperation with private and public actors and thus to actively participate in the local community (ibid.). Since cooperatives, as a form of socioeconomic self-organisation, transgress the boundaries of civil society and private household, economy and state (ibid., 42), they can 'act like incubators, transforming informal into formal solutions or formal into community-based ones' (Elsen and Schicklinski 2016, 225). They cannot be exclusively assigned to belonging to the 'system' or to the 'lifeworld' (cf. 6.2.2), yet they are the form of enterprise most embedded in the 'lifeworld' of local actors (Elsen 2007, 313). Under a conducive legal framework and with solid support from public authorities, they could, more than at present, contribute to comprehensive solutions to local challenges overcoming the sectoral division into state, market, and civil society (ibid., 20; cf. 6.2.2).

Notes

1 This is not to deny the fact that the richer part of the world's population, be it within industrialised countries or in countries of the Global South in comparison to the majority of the population, has been and will always be in a better position to protect itself from risks, which is exemplified for example in the case of climate change mitigation. This is recognised also by Beck when stating that '*new international inequalities*' (Beck 1986, 30; Beck 2007, 78, own translation) are created by the risks of the second modernity. Some groups of people are more concerned by the produced risks than others. Although risks have almost exclusively been produced by industrialised societies, their adverse impacts hit poor people in the industrialised countries and in the Global South even harder – although risks have become universal, they are unevenly distributed.

2 Modernisation risks produce an 'ecological expropriation' (Beck 2007, 79, own translation), yet not coming along with a change in ownership (ibid.). This can for

example be studied in already falling real estate prices in regions threatened by rising sea levels because of climate change.

3 Beck (1996); ©Springer, with permission of Springer.

4 This counts for already industrialised societies. It would be cynical to prescribe zero economic growth to countries of the Global South now given that they contributed nothing or very little to the Earth being in overshoot. However, the relation between economic growth and development needs to be carefully scrutinised in this discourse (cf. 2.4.3.4).

5 The term was first used in German ('Nachhaltigkeit'), with reference to the forestry sector, by Carlowitz (1713), designating a situation in which no more wood was cut than could grow again in a certain time span.

6 The idea of 'planetary boundaries' was first brought forward by the German Advisory Council on Global Change in 1994 under the name of 'the concept of the Earth system's planetary guard rails' (WBGU 2011, 32).

7 From Steffen *et al.* (2015). Reprinted with permission from AAAS.

8 Cf. Note 7.

9 This boundary is split up into phosphorus and nitrogen flows. The use of fertilisers is the main reason for the biochemical flows boundary being transgressed (Steffen *et al.* 2015, 1259855-7).

10 Cf. Note 7.

11 Cf. Note 7.

12 Cf. Note 7.

13 Cf. Note 7.

14 For example, the knowledge of the interconnection between biosphere integrity and climate change is still low, however it is known that on the one hand many species are highly important for climate regulation due to their carbon sequesting function (Hicks *et al.* 2014) and that on the other hand climate change may cause the extinction of species.

15 'It is *extremely likely* that more than half of the observed increase in global average surface temperature from 1951 to 2010 was caused by the anthropogenic increase in GHG [greenhouse gas] concentrations and other anthropogenic forcings together' (IPCC 2015, 5).

16 The United Nations Framework Convention on Climate Change (UNFCCC), established in Rio de Janeiro in 1992, 'is the main multilateral forum focused on addressing climate change' (IPCC 2015, 29). The Kyoto Protocol of 1997, entering into force in 2005 and expiring in 2020, is the first binding agreement under international law to keep global warming below 2°C compared to pre-industrial levels. However, it was not signed by the largest emitter, the USA, and signatories lag behind the pledges made. At the Twenty-first Conference and Meeting of the Parties to the UNFCCC in Paris from 28 November to 12 December 2015, a binding follow-up agreement under international law, the Paris Agreement, was adopted in which 195 countries agreed to aim to 'holding the increase in the global average temperature to well below 2°C above pre-industrial levels and to pursue efforts to limit the temperature increase to 1.5°C above pre-industrial levels' (UNFCCC 2015, art. 2, no. 1, section (a)). The reached agreement is in so far a dangerous one, as it gives the impression that now that the international community of states has reached a binding agreement under international law for the time after 2020, climate change can be dealt with effectively. However, this agreement is too weak to entail indispensable fast-track action to be able to reach a decarbonisation of the atmosphere fast enough to prevent irreversible climate change and to achieve global climate justice, since it does not contain concrete binding obligations to heavily reduce carbon emissions *before* 2030. In the *non-legally binding* preamble the signatories themselves

[note] with concern that the estimated aggregate greenhouse gas emission levels in 2025 and 2030 resulting from the intended nationally determined contributions do not fall within least-cost 2°C scenarios …, and also [note] that much greater emission reduction efforts will be required than those associated with the intended nationally determined contributions in order to hold the increase in the global average temperature to below 2°C above pre-industrial levels.

(Ibid., preamble, no. 17)

The made pledges will result in at least 2.7°C and probably in over 3°C of warming. Regarding global climate justice, to only 'pursue efforts' to keep global warming under 1.5°C is insufficient to stop already happening extreme devastating effects, especially for the Global South. Also, a fair cost-sharing between countries of the Global South and industrialised countries has not made it into the binding text, which only obliges developed countries to report on the finance they provide to countries of the Global South. It is only mentioned in the preamble to '*strongly [urge]* developed country Parties to scale up their level of financial support, with a concrete roadmap to achieve the goal of jointly providing USD 100 billion annually by 2020 for mitigation and adaptation' (ibid., preamble, no. 115).

Furthermore, the issue of climate refugees is absent from the agreement. It is not mentioned in the main text and barely in the preamble in the 'loss and damage' section (ibid., preamble, no. 50), only requesting the Executive Committee of the Warsaw International Mechanism to propose recommendations on how to deal with the increasing number of climate refugees. *Global climate justice will not be achieved with this agreement*, also because the establishment of an international tribunal for climate justice, as requested by civil society, is mentioned nowhere in the text.

The clause on the necessity of innovation to successfully combat climate change names 'economic growth' and 'sustainable development' in the same breath (ibid., art. 10, no. 5), disregarding the incompatibility of global economic growth with sustainable development and functioning climate change mitigation and adaptation, thus disregarding the need for a post-growth society and economy in developed countries.

With regard to food production, article 2 (ibid., art. 2, no. 1, subsection (b)) stresses that the agreement aims at 'increasing the ability to adapt to the adverse impacts of climate change and foster climate resilience and low greenhouse gas emissions development, in a manner that does not threaten food production'. This is too vague an expression and can easily be misused by the industrial conventional food and agriculture lobby not to switch to organic sustainable food production but to continue their highly climate-harming way of operating.

Since every party is free to leave the agreement, neither concrete years nor numbers are named about each country's reduction commitments, and no sanctions are foreseen for violation of the agreement, it is highly improbable that the stated goal 'to achieve a balance between anthropogenic emissions by sources and removals by sinks of greenhouse gases in the second half of this century' (ibid., art. 4, no. 1) will be achieved. The language used in the agreement corresponds less to language used in binding treaties under international law and resembles more a non-binding agreement (for example in several places 'should' instead of 'shall').

17 Anthropogenic greenhouse gases comprise CO_2, methane (CH_4), nitrous oxide (N_2O) as well as fluorinated gases, and CO_2 takes a predominant role therein, being responsible for approximately 73 per cent of total anthropogenic greenhouse gas emissions in 2010 (IPCC 2015, 84).

18 For example, according to Robine *et al.* (2008, 171), in the summer of 2003 'more than 70,000 additional deaths occurred', mainly affecting elderly and sick people.

19 Parts per million.

20 The 2°C threshold was proposed first by the German Advisory Council on Global Change as part of its 'concept of the Earth system's planetary guard rails [which it] has ... developed since 1994' (WBGU 2011, 32). However, to stop already happening extreme devastating effects, especially for countries in the Global South, the temperature rise would have to be limited to 1.5°C (World Bank 2014).

21 'The creation of a low-carbon global economy is conceivable only if the new powers [China, India, Brazil and further newly industrialising countries] share this development path' (WBGU 2011, 90).

22 Brown growth still heavily relies on fossil fuels as the main energy source and thus produces high rates of CO_2 emissions.

23 Even if the Organisation for Economic Co-operation and Development (OECD) countries completely stopped their emissions, the most stringent mitigation scenario would not be followed if the rest of the world followed a brown growth path as the OECD countries have done until now (IEA 2008, 48).

24 'The global mean surface temperature change for the period 2016–2035 relative to 1986–2005 ... will *likely* be in the range 0.3°C to 0.7°C (*medium confidence*)' (IPCC 2015, 10).

25 Even if greenhouse gas emissions were completely stopped now, sea level rise will continue for thousands of years (WBGU 2011, 90).

26 A resource-efficient low-carbon economy can be achieved, if 2 per cent of the global gross domestic product is shifted away from climate-damaging projects to be invested in 11 pivotal sectors: agriculture, fisheries, water, forests, renewable energy, manufacturing, waste, buildings, transport, tourism, and cities (UNEP 2011, 22, 23). Setting up a global carbon pricing system to accelerate decarbonisation, either in the form of a cap and trade system or tax system (WBGU 2011, 10, 162) would greatly facilitate this redirection of investment (Randers 2012, 254). In fact, 'it would take no more than a tax increase of a few percentage points to bring in enough money to solve the climate problem within a generation' (ibid., 336).

27 Reprinted from *2052*, copyright 2012 by Jørgen Randers, used with permission from Chelsea Green Publishing (www.chelseagreen.com).

28 Overshoot in system theory designates a situation in which 'the ecological footprint is above the sustainable level, but not yet large enough to trigger changes that produce a decline in its ecological footprint' (Meadows *et al.* 2005, 174).

29 Cf. Note 27.

30 This is lower than Randers had expected and will be reached not because society will abandon the growth paradigm, but because, first, due to an ageing and shrinking population there will be a smaller workforce, and, second, (as the main reason) productivity growth will be slower due to already more industrialised economies, greater inequity, and social unrest (Randers 2012, 162) (my Note).

31 This designates 'a process wherein current warming leads to more future warming, which in turn leads to even more warming in an unstoppable causal feedback loop' (Randers 2012, 235) (my Note).

32 Cf. Note 27 (my Note).

33 Cf. Note 27.

34 This would correspond to the IPCC's most stringent mitigation scenario (2015, 22), yet still rising emission levels in all other regions except OECD-less-US beyond 2010 make passing the 2°C threshold very likely. The remaining global carbon budget will be used up by 2030, which means that in 2052 the global temperature will have passed the 2°C threshold (Randers 2012, 118).

35 Cf. Note 27.

36 Cf. Note 27.

37 Like Beck (cf. 2.1), Meadows *et al.* (2004, 269) compare this shift to the industrial revolution, and additionally to the first big shift in human society, the agricultural revolution, and equally stress that like the preceding revolutions it is not plannable.

However, as the WBGU (2011, 1, 27) notes, in contrast to the past two big transitions, the pending sustainability transition must be actively and consciously brought about in a limited time frame to remain within the 2°C threshold; see Note 27.

38 Cf. Note 27.

39 Cf. Note 27.

40 Cf. Note 27.

41 Cf. Note 27.

42 Randers assumes that crises will accumulate from 2030 onwards, requiring more investment to mitigate the damage, for example investments in climate change mitigation and adaptation measures (2012, 93, 163, 306).

43 For example the German economic miracle after the Second World War shifted the majority of Germans out of poverty and into employment, thus ensuring upward mobility (Hogwood 2015, 136).

44 The WBGU (2011, 109) brings to mind that around half of the world's population has *not* benefited from industrialisation-related economic, technical, and scientific achievements.

45 The least developed countries are not completely decoupled from the world market, yet they do not participate as sovereign partners in it, since profit from economic activity in them mostly remains with the big corporations having their headquarters in the rich part of the world. The least developed countries serve the rich countries as sinks for environmental waste (for example electronic scrap), as extraction sites for raw products (for example metals, raw earths) and as production sites with no or low social and environmental standards, thus providing cheap labour supply and using local ecosystem services for the production process and the environment as a sink, leaving the countries to cope with the resulting social and environmental damage. It is true that the corporations need to pay the least developed countries' national governments for obtaining operating licences, yet this money seldom reaches the majority of the population due to non-democratic structures or corruption. In most cases profit is only shared with the rich minority of the country; the majority of the population remains poor. Nigeria is an exemplary case for this situation. It is the country with the highest oil extraction rate in Africa, yet the majority of its population lives on less than $1 per day (BBC News 2012). Such dislocation of contaminating industries in the scope of globalisation does not only affect least developed countries but also newly industrialising countries of the Global South.

46 Income inequality has risen in OECD countries since the middle of the 1980s (OECD 2008). For example, in Germany between 2000 and 2006 the proportion of the overall population receiving a medium income decreased from 62 to 54 per cent, while the proportion of richer and poorer people both increased, with a larger increase in the number of poorer people though (Grabka and Frick 2008), and wealth inequality rose ever more from 2002 to 2007 (Frick and Grabka 2009).

47 The Human Development Report (UNDP 2015, 228–9) distinguishes between a greatly varying national poverty line which is determined by each country's authorities and the international poverty line of $1.25 a day (in purchasing power parity terms) which was set by the World Bank.

48 Whereas the goal of classical national economy following Adam Smith (1966) was to use free markets to increase the welfare of nations, this idea was modified in neo-liberalism which can be considered as a reduction of economic thinking to the idea of egoistic individuals striving for profit maximisation to increase their self-interest (Elsen 2007, 68).

49 Daly goes even further in not only saying that economic growth primarily serves the rich but that they deliberately keep alive the growth lie despite knowing that the limits of growth have already been reached 'because they have found ways to privatize the benefits of growth while socializing the even greater costs' (2012, 76).

50 This refers to the shift from an economy based on non-renewable climate-harming resources such as fossil fuels to renewable ones.

51 In this regard the case of the yearly recurrent deliberate large-scale slash-and-burn of rainforest in Indonesia to make space for oil palm plantations, whose palm oil is then exported to the EU as one major importer in order to produce biodiesel, illustrates what kind of economic growth is not needed in the countries of the Global South. The practice has destructive social and environmental consequences locally and regionally. Apart from aggravating global climate change, it maximises profit for a tiny part of the Indonesian population and foreign corporations based in the industrialised countries, while the majority of the population, not only in Indonesia but in the whole region, is heavily threatened by health problems, does not receive any economic benefit, and is left with ruined livelihoods.

52 Considered from an ecological economist point of view 'economic growth has already ended in the sense that the growth that continues is now *uneconomic*; it costs more than it is worth at the margin and makes us poorer rather than richer' (Daly 2012, 73). This is because

> growth takes an economy up a nonlinear cost curve to the point where further abatement becomes unaffordable. At that point a rational society would stop the expansion of its activity level, since further growth will no longer increase the welfare of its citizens.
>
> (Meadows *et al.* 2005, 224)

53 However, proponents of a post-growth society and economy (e.g. Paech and Jackson, cf. 2.3.3) reject the need for any type of economic growth for reaching a state of well-being.

54 Also in Europe, especially with the multiple crises from 2008 onwards and subsequent austerity policies, these kinds of economies have resurged (Monzón Campos and Ávila 2012, 85–92).

55 The German term 'Enkeltauglichkeit' ('grandchild suitability') pointedly expresses against what demand all policies and actions must be measured.

56 The 17 Sustainable Development Goals (UNGA 2015), divided into 169 targets and accepted by all 193 UN member states as part of the 2030 Agenda for Sustainable Development, which replaced the eight Millennium Development Goals (MDGs) (ibid.) on 1 January 2016 to guide action until 2030, could provide the basis for such a joint vision. Whereas the MDGs were targeted exclusively at countries of the Global South, the Sustainable Development Goals are valid for and targeted at all countries (ibid., 3).

57 He points to the fact that the etymological meaning of 'economy' goes back to the Greek word 'oeconomia', designating the 'principle of householding', thus 'production for one's own use' (Polanyi 2001, 53), which is diametrical to the idea of capital accumulation and profit-making for their own sake.

58 From: Elsen (2007); ©Juventa.

59 Quotation marks are used here since morally speaking human beings do not have the right to cause irreversible damage to the environment; they have just done it and so far have not been stopped by a higher power, only single state restrictions have curtailed their 'right' so far.

60 Bourdieu (1983) distinguishes three forms of capital: economic capital, which is directly convertible into money; cultural capital, which is acquired via a longer learning process to obtain an academic title (besides two further subforms of cultural capital); and social capital, which designates resources that are based on the belonging to a social group.

61 John Locke's version is an exception here (von Winterfeld and Biesecker 2013, 388–93). In the chapter on property of the 'Two Treatises of Government', even if

he interprets God's commandment to subject earth as authorisation to take possession of it, which in his interpretation inevitably leads to private property:

> The law man was under was rather for appropriating. God commanded, and his
> wants forced him to labour. That was his property which could not be taken
> from him wherever he had fixed it. And hence subduing or cultivating the earth,
> and having dominion, we see are joined together. The one gave title to the
> other. So that God, by commanding to subdue, gave authority so far to appropri-
> ate: and the condition for human life, which requires labour and materials to
> work on, necessarily introduces private possessions
>
> (Locke 2003, 114, §35)

this is in no way a carte blanche to infinitely exploit its resources disregardless of
detrimental consequences for the environment and other human beings: 'God and
his reason commanded him to subdue the earth, *i.e.* improve it for the benefit of
life' (ibid., 113, §32). It may only be used to satisfy one's own needs – 'especially
keeping within the bounds, set by reason, of what might serve for his use' (ibid.,
113, §31) – and only to the extent that there is still enough left for other human
beings – 'for he that leaves as much as another can make use of' (ibid., 114, §33),

> as much as any one can make use of to any advantage of life before it spoils, …
> whatever is beyond this, is more than his share, and belongs to others. Nothing
> was made by God for man to spoil or destroy.
>
> (Ibid., 113, §31)

62 Here, solely the male form is used since in classical contract theory, with the exception of Hobbes, the relationship between the state and the individual was exclusively
conceived as one between the state and a male individual (Pateman 1988, 5–6).

63 Under Sustainable Development Goal 12 'Ensure sustainable consumption and production patterns', target 12.c demands to 'rationalize inefficient fossil-fuel subsidies
that encourage wasteful consumption by removing market distortions, … including
by restructuring taxation and phasing out those harmful subsidies, where they exist,
to reflect their environmental impacts' (UNGA 2015, 23, Sustainable Development
Goal 12, target 12.c). By such an internalisation of social and environmental
externalities, the price distortions fossil-fuelled industries have benefited from would
finally be abolished (WBGU 2011, 274). This way, the product price would eventually mirror all real costs in the product cycle from production to recycling/waste
removal (Meadows *et al.* 2005, 257–8), thus telling 'the complete economic and
ecological truth' (von Weizsäcker 1994, 143, own translation). This means for many
products a rise in price that consumers must be willing to pay unless the state invests
in subsidies into these sustainable products to decrease end-consumer prices.

64 Currently the consumption level 'in the OECD countries … is four times the global
average' (Randers 2012, 169).

65 The shift from a 'patronizing welfare state without user participation' (Rosol 2014,
253, endnote 14) to a proactive enabling one implies an altered relationship
between citizens and the state, yet must not be misunderstood as carte blanche for
drawing back welfare state functions (cf. also 1.1 and Chapter 3).

66 Cf. Note 58.

67 Cf. Note 27.

68 This does not exclude that it can be achieved in specific economic sectors and on a
regional scale.

69 This holds true for industrialised countries. The developing and newly industrialised
countries have the right to further grow to increase productivity to develop:

> the remaining growth possible – whatever space there is for more resource use
> and pollution emissions, plus whatever space is freed up by higher efficiencies

and lifestyle moderations on the part of the rich – would logically and, one would hope, joyfully be allocated to those who need it most.

(Meadows *et al.* 2005, 256)

However, these countries should pursue a strategy of real green growth, meaning to shift investments in green sectors of economy such as renewable energy resources and sustainable agriculture to avoid the social and environmental externalities that the now industrialised countries produced. However, the current global corporate economy works in the opposite way, forcing countries of the South to function according to the mere dictate of profit and growth, as Shiva (2013) has shown for India.

70 'De-growth' is the translation of the French term 'décroissance' and was coined by the French economist Serge Latouche (2006). It designates the reduction of economic activity, including sinking consumption rates and a smaller economic output, having meanwhile evolved into a social movement (Jackson 2009, 226, endnote 24).

71 This statement should not wrongly make the reader believe that the economic system in its current functioning would ensure this stability and employment. It has been shaken by severe economic crises from the beginning of its implementation and since the 1970s it has no longer been able to guarantee full employment (cf. 2.4.3.3).

72 'Post-growth economy' is the translation of the German term 'Postwachstumsökonomie' introduced by Paech (2008; 2009).

73 This is problematic when aiming for full employment in the conventional economic growth-based system, since 'an economic growth of estimated 1.1 to 2.4 per cent [is] needed to keep the existing workplaces' (Seidl and Zahrnt 2010a, 20, own translation).

74 Taking Germany as an example, according to Reuter (2010, 93, own translation), the gross domestic product would have to, 'rise from today 2.4 billion to 2.7 billion euros, corresponding to a growth of just under 13 per cent, to allow for full employment'.

75 Different studies estimate these costs between 1 and 3 per cent of the annual global gross domestic product (e.g. Stern 2007).

76 For example, 'for most metals, the average use rate of a person in the industrialized world is 8 to 10 times the use rate of people in the nonindustrialized world' (Meadows *et al.* 2005, 100).

77 The term 'action situation' is used consistently in this thesis for what is more commonly known as 'action arena'. In her later works, Ostrom stuck to the term 'action situation', abandoning the one of 'action arena' to designate 'the 'black' box where policy choices are made' (McGinnis 2011, 172).

78 The term 'rich' is vague and relative to the society one lives in. Fears of loss aversion are not expected to be highest amongst the very rich who can easily give away a part of their wealth without having to profoundly change their way of life. They might be stronger amongst people with a 'middle' social position that have had to work for their social advancement, now fearing social decline.

79 This statement does not refer to the satisfaction of basic material needs. They remain the foundation for leading a 'good life'. There is a correlation between economic growth and prosperity/well-being 'up to a certain threshold which lies approximately at 50 per cent of rich industrial countries' per capita income' (Seidl and Zahrnt 2010b, 31, own translation). Yet,

beyond that, immaterial factors play a role in the 'pursuit of happiness' in all cultures, such as the recognition received from others, being embedded in different kinds of communities and networks, yet also the fulfilment of aesthetic and hedonistic pleasures.

(WBGU 2011, 80)

80 Cf. Note 58.
81 Community supported agriculture is a form of solidarity agriculture in which consumers co-finance an agricultural holding by buying harvest shares which increases transparency and trust between consumers and producers (Paech 2015, 39).
82 A prosumer is a person that equally produces and consumes a good, thus practising subsistence economy.
83 In this thesis, when using the term 'urban gardening', 'urban agriculture', or 'urban food production', it is referred to urban *and* peri-urban activities, thus taking place either in the urban or suburban area. Urban gardening and urban agriculture (also called urban farming) are the two forms of urban food production referred to in this thesis. While urban gardening can also include growing non-edible plants, urban agriculture refers to growing edible plants on a larger scale than urban gardening activities and might also include animal husbandry for obtaining fish, meat, and dairy products.
84 Here his thinking has evolved from earlier publications (e.g. Gorz 1988, 253) (e.g. when he was already a proponent of a basic income, yet still believed that this should not be granted without a return service by the recipient).

85   As long as we are speaking of a low basic income, much of it can be financed simply by a relabeling of the corresponding part of existing transfers (pensions, unemployment benefits, etc.) and by the abolition of a number of tax exemptions … or tax rebates … that no longer serve a purpose. Moreover, the increase in the tax yield required for the transfers themselves will be partly offset by a decrease in the administrative cost of the transfer system. In an era of computerized payments, the bulk of this cost is the cost of checking entitlements. Obviously, the less conditional the system, the lower the latter cost…. There is no doubt, however, that the introduction of a significant basic income would involve some increase in marginal tax rates.

(van Parijs 1992, 230)

86 One policy measure to do so would be the EU-wide introduction of a progressive tax on assets. So far it only exists in some member states of the EU (for example France), which incentivises the rich to shift their residence abroad.
87 In Europe the rich, also in crisis-struck countries, have been largely spared from the crisis (European ATTAC Network 2013, 2–3), having partly even profited from it, for example via acquiring property that the state is forced to privatise.
88 Germany was abated about half of its external debts in the London Agreement on German External Debts of 1953 (Osmańczyk and Mango 2003), which was a major reason for its post-war economic miracle (Habermas 2015), besides relying on an immigrant workforce.
89 This primarily but not exclusively refers to Greece, the European country most affected by the crises (ATTAC 2013, 2–3).
90 Equivalents in other languages are 'Gemeinwesenökonomie', 'Economía popular y solidaria', 'Community Economy', 'Économie sociale', 'Économie solidaire' (Elsen 2007, 145).
91 Cf. Note 58.
92 Cf. Note 58.
93 Cf. Note 58.
94 Cf. Note 58.
95 This can be seen for example in the massive privatisation of council flats and houses under Thatcher in the United Kingdom in the 1980s, greatly reducing the number of available council flats and houses (Hodkinson and Lawrence 2011).
96 This does not mean permanent financial subsidies from the state (Habisch 2002, 355). Initial financial subsidies and financial possibilities in times of crisis as well as tax shelters are an option. Most important however are conducive legal framework

conditions that do not discriminate against organisational forms of the social and solidarity economy compared to other more mainstream forms of economic organisation.

97 Cf. Note 58.
98 The programmes that have been installed since the beginning of the 1990s in structurally weak regions in Europe have tried to involve civil society actors in urban and regional development. However, often they have aimed at organising 'labour-intensive non-profitable fields of action without public subsidies especially via the employment of disadvantaged persons' (Elsen 2007, 160, footnote 210, own translation), which shows the risk of a state drawing on the workforce of citizens while at the same time cutting back public spending.
99 Cf. Note 58.
100 Cf. Note 58.

References

Arendt, Hannah. 1958. *Charles R. Walgreen Foundation lectures, The human condition.* Chicago IL, London: University of Chicago.

Arendt, Hannah. 2007. *Vita activa oder Vom tätigen Leben*, 5th edn. München, Zürich: Piper.

BBC News. 2012. 'Nigerians living in poverty rise to nearly 61%'. *BBC News*, 13 February. www.bbc.com/news/world-africa-17015873 [27 August 2016].

Beck, Ulrich. 1986. *Risikogesellschaft: Auf dem Weg in eine andere Moderne.* Frankfurt am Main: Suhrkamp.

Beck, Ulrich. 1993. *Die Erfindung des Politischen: Zu einer Theorie reflexiver Modernisierung.* Frankfurt am Main: Suhrkamp.

Beck, Ulrich. 1996. 'Weltrisikogesellschaft, Weltöffentlichkeit und globale Subpolitik: Ökologische Fragen im Bezugsrahmen fabrizierter Unsicherheiten'. In *Kölner Zeitschrift für Soziologie und Sozialpsychologie Sonderhefte, Umweltsoziologie*, eds Andreas Diekmann and Carlo J. Jaeger, 119–47. Opladen: Westdeutscher Verlag.

Beck, Ulrich. 2007. *Weltrisikogesellschaft: Auf der Suche nach der verlorenen Sicherheit.* Frankfurt am Main: Suhrkamp.

Beck, Ulrich. 2009. *Risk society: Towards a new modernity.* Theory, culture and society series. London: Sage.

Biesecker, Adelheid. 2000. *Vorsorgendes Wirtschaften: Auf dem Weg zu einer Ökonomie des Guten Lebens.* Bielefeld: Kleine.

Biesecker, Adelheid and Stefan Kesting. 2003. *Mikroökonomik: Eine Einführung aus sozial-ökologischer Perspektive.* München: Oldenbourg Wissenschaftsverlag.

Biesecker, Adelheid and Uta von Winterfeld. 2014a. 'All inclusive? Vorsorgendes Witschaften und neue Gesellschaftsverträge'. I, *Social Innovation, Participation and the Development of Society: Soziale Innovation, Partizipation und die Entwicklung der Gesellschaft*, eds Walter Lorenz and Susanne Elsen, 211–31. Bozen: Bozen University, Brixener Studien zu Sozialpolitik und Sozialwissenschaft, Creative Commons Attribution-ShareAlike 4.0 (CC BY SA 4.0). www.unibz.it/it/library/Documents/bupress/publications/fulltext/9788860460707.pdf [17 September 2016].

Biesecker, Adelheid and Uta von Winterfeld. 2014b. Weshalb und inwiefern moderne Gesellschaften Externalisierung brauchen und erzeugen. www.kolleg-postwachstum.de/sozwgmedia/dokumente/WorkingPaper/wp2_2014.pdf [27 August 2016].

Binswanger, Mathias, Guido Beltrani, Annette Jochem, and Oliver Schelske. 2005. 'Wachstum und Umweltbelastung: Findet eine Entkopplung statt?' Umwelt-Materialien 198.

www.mathias-binswanger.ch/inhalt/Artikel_in_Fachzeitschriften/Wachstum_und_
Umweltbelastung.pdf [28 August 2016].

Bourdieu, Pierre. 1983. 'Ökonomisches Kapital, kulturelles Kapital, soziales Kapital'. In
Sonderband 2, Soziale Ungleichheiten: Soziale Welt, ed. Reinhard Kreckel, 183–98. Göttingen.

Carlowitz, Hans C. 1713. *Sylvicultura oeconomica: Oder haußwirthliche Nachricht und
Naturgemäßige Anweisung zur wilden Baum-Zucht*. Leipzig: Johann Friedrich Braun.

Constitution of Ecuador. 2008. *Constitución de la Republica del Ecuador 2008*.

Constitution of Bolivia. 2009. *Constitución política del estado plurinacional de Bolivia*.

Costanza, Robert, John H. Cumberland, Herman E. Daly, Robert Goodland, Richard B.
Norgaard, Ida Kubiszewski, and Carol Franco. 2015. *An introduction to ecological economics*. Boca Raton FL, London, New York: CRC.

Daly, Herman E. 1991. *Steady-state economics*, 2nd edn. Washington DC, Covelo: Island
(orig. pub. 1977).

Daly, Herman E. 1996. *Beyond growth: The economics of sustainable development*. Boston
MA: Beacon.

Daly, Herman E. 2012. 'The end of uneconomic growth: Glimpse 4–1'. In *2052: A global
forecast for the next forty years*, ed. Jørgen Randers, 73–6. White River Junction VT:
Chelsea Green.

Elsen, Susanne. 2007. *Die Ökonomie des Gemeinwesens: Sozialpolitik und Soziale Arbeit im
Kontext von gesellschaftlicher Wertschöpfung und -verteilung*. Weinheim, München:
Juventa.

Elsen, Susanne and Judith Schicklinski. 2016. 'Mobilising the citizens for the socio-
ecological transition'. In *Cities in transition: Social innovation for Europe's urban sustainability*, eds Thomas Sauer, Cristina Garzillo, and Susanne Elsen, 221–38. Abingdon/
New York: Routledge.

European ATTAC Network (ATTAC). 2013. 'For a Europe-wide coordinated levy on
wealth'. Association pour la Taxation des Transactions financière et l'Aide aux Citoy-
ens. www.attac.org/sites/default/files/EAN-Wealth-Levy-Concept.pdf [27 August 2016].

European Commission (EC). 1995. 'Local development and employment initiatives: An
investigation in the European Union'. Internal document SEC 564/95. http://book-
shop.europa.eu/en/local-development-and-employment-initiatives-pbCM8995082/ [27
August 2016].

Frick, Joachim R. and Markus M. Grabka. 2009. 'Gestiegene Vermögensungleichheit in
Deutschland'. Deutsches Institut für Wirtschaftsforschung. Wochenbericht 4. www.
diw.de/documents/publikationen/73/93785/09-4-1.pdf [27 August 2016].

Friedman, Milton. 1962. *Capitalism and freedom: With the assistance of Rose D. Friedmann*.
Chicago IL: University of Chicago Press.

German Advisory Council on Global Change (WBGU). 2011. Flagship report. World in
transition: A social contract for sustainability. Berlin: WBGU. www.wbgu.de/file
admin/templates/dateien/veroeffentlichungen/hauptgutachten/jg2011/wbgu_jg2011_
en.pdf [27 August 2016].

Givel, Michael and Laura Figueroa. 2013. 'Early happiness policy as a government
mission of Bhutan: A survey of the Bhutanese unwritten constitution from 1619 to
1729'. *Journal of Bhutan Studies*, 31: 1–21. www.bhutanstudies.org.bt/publicationFiles/
JBS/JBS_Vol.31/vol.31–1.pdf [27 August 2016].

Gorz, André. 1988. *Métamorphoses du travail: Quête du sens. Critique de la raison
économique*. Paris: Galilée.

Gorz, André. 1997. *Misères du présent, richesse du possible*. Paris: Galilée.

Grabka, Markus M. and Joachim R. Frick. 2008. 'Schrumpfende Mittelschicht: Anzeichen einer dauerhaften Polarisierung der verfügbaren Einkommen?' Deutsches Institut für Wirtschaftsforschung. Wochenbericht 10. www.diw.de/documents/publik ationen/73/79586/08-10-1.pdf [27 August 2016].

Habermas, Jürgen. 1984. *The theory of communicative action. Volume one: Reason and the rationalisation of society.* Translated by Thomas McCarthy. Boston MA: Beacon (orig. pub. 1981).

Habermas, Jürgen. 1985. *Die Neue Unübersichtlichkeit: Kleine Politische Schriften V.* Frankfurt am Main: Suhrkamp.

Habermas, Jürgen. 2015. 'Habermas: Warum Merkels Griechenland-Politik ein Fehler ist'. *Süddeutsche Zeitung.* 22 June. www.sueddeutsche.de/wirtschaft/europa-sand-im-getriebe-1.2532119 [8 December 2016].

Habisch, André. 2002. 'Sondervotum des sachverständigen Mitglieds Prof. Dr. André Habisch: Soziales Kapital, Bürgerschaftliches Engagement und Initiativen regionaler Arbeitsmarkt- und Sozialpolitik'. In *Bericht. Bürgerschaftliches Engagement: Auf dem Weg in eine zukunftsfähige Bürgergesellschaft,* ed. Enquete-Kommission 'Zukunft des Bürgerschaftlichen Engagements' des Deutschen Bundestages, 350–6. Opladen: Leske + Budrich.

Hicks, Charlotte, Stephen Woroniecki, Max Fancourt, Mari Bieri, Helena Garcia Robles, Kate Trumper, and Rebecca Mant. 2014. 'The relationship between biodiversity, carbon storage and the provision of other ecosystem services: Critical review for the forestry component of the international climate fund'. UNEP. www.gov.uk/ government/uploads/system/uploads/attachment_data/file/331581/biodiversity-forests-ecosystem-services.pdf [27 August 2016].

Hodkinson, Stuart and Beth Lawrence. 2011. 'The neoliberal project, privatisation and the housing crisis'. *Corporate Watch,* 50/51(Autumn/Winter). https://corporatewatch. org/magazine/50/autumnwinter-2011/neoliberal-project-privatisation-and-housing-crisis [27 August 2016].

Hogwood, Patricia. 2015. 'Social wellbeing and democracy'. In *The Routledge handbook of German politics and culture,* ed. Sarah Colvin, 133–46. London, New York: Routledge.

International Energy Agency (IEA). 2008. *World energy outlook 2008.* Paris: IEA. www. worldenergyoutlook.org/media/weowebsite/2008-1994/weo2008.pdf [27 August 2016].

Intergovernmental Panel on Climate Change (IPCC) ed. 2015. *Climate change 2014: Synthesis report. Contribution of working groups I, II and III to the fifth assessment report of the Intergovernmental Panel on Climate Change.* Geneva. www.ipcc.ch/report/ar5/syr/ [27 August 2016].

Jackson, Tim. 2009. *Prosperity without growth: Economics for a finite planet.* London: Earthscan.

Kallis, Giorgos. 2011. 'In defence of degrowth'. *Ecological Economics,* 70(5): 873–80.

Krausmann, Fridolin, Simone Gingrich, Nina Eisenmenger, Karl-Heinz Erb, Helmut Haberl, and Marina Fischer-Kowalski. 2009. 'Growth in global materials use, GDP and population during the 20th century'. *Ecological Economics,* 68(10): 2696–705.

Latouche, Serge. 2006. *Petit traité de la décroissance sereine.* Paris: Mille et une nuits.

Lieb, Christoph M. 2003. 'The environmental Kuznets curve: A survey of the empirical evidence and possible causes'. University of Heidelberg Department of Economics. Discussion Paper Series 391. www.uni-heidelberg.de/md/awi/forschung/dp391.pdf [27 August 2016].

Locke, John. 2003. 'Two treatises of government'. In *Rethinking the Western tradition: Two treatises of government and a letter concerning toleration,* ed. Ian Shapiro, 1–209. New Haven CT, London: Yale University.

McGinnis, Michael D. 2011. 'An introduction to IAD and the language of the Ostrom workshop: A simple guide to a complex framework'. *Policy Studies Journal*, 39(1): 169–83.

Meadows, Donella H., Dennis L. Meadows, and Jørgen Randers. 1992. *Beyond the limits: Confronting global collapse, envisioning a sustainable future*. White River Junction VT: Chelsea Green.

Meadows, Donella H., Jørgen Randers, and Dennis L. Meadows. 2005. *Limits to growth: The 30-year update*, 3rd edn. London: Earthscan.

Meadows, Donella H., Dennis L. Meadows, Jørgen Randers, and William W. Behrens. 1972. *The limits to growth*. New York: Universe.

Monzón Campos, José Luis, and Rafael Chaves Ávila. 2012. 'The social economy in the European Union'. European Economic and Social Committee. www.eesc.europa.eu/resources/docs/qe-30-12-790-en-c.pdf [27 August 2016].

Nordhaus, William D. and James Tobin. 1973. 'Is growth obsolete?' In *The measurement of economics and social performance*, ed. Milton Moss, 509–64. www.nber.org/chapters/c3621.pdf [27 August 2016].

Nowotny, Helga, Peter Scott, and Michael Gibbons. 2013. *Re-thinking science: Knowledge and the public in an age of uncertainty*. Cambridge: Polity (orig. pub. 2001).

Nussbaum, Martha C. 2006. *The Tanner lectures on human values. Frontiers of justice: Disability, nationality, species membership*. Cambridge MA: Belknap Press; Harvard University Press.

Organisation for Economic Co-operation and Development (OECD). 2008. *Growing unequal? Income inequality and poverty in OECD countries*. Paris: OECD.

Organisation for Economic Co-operation and Development (OECD). 2010. *Perspectives on global development 2010: Shifting wealth*. Paris: OECD.

Osmańczyk, Edmund J. and Anthony Mango, eds. 2003. *Encyclopedia of the United Nations and international agreements: G to M*. New York: Taylor & Francis.

Paech, Niko. 2008. 'Regionalwährungen als Baustaine einer Postwachstumsökonomie'. *Zeitschrift für Sozialökonomie*, 45(158/159): 10–19. www.postwachstumsoekonomie.de/material/grundzuege/ [27 August 2016].

Paech, Niko. 2009. 'Postwachstumsökonomie: ein Vademecum'. *Zeitschrift für Sozialökonomie*, 46(160/161): 28–31. www.postwachstumsoekonomie.de/material/grundzuege/ [8 December 2016].

Paech, Niko. 2012. *Liberation from excess: The road to a post-growth economy*. Translated by Benjamin Liebelt. München: Oekom.

Paech, Niko. 2015. 'Wachstumsdogma zur Postwachstumsökonomie'. In *Die Kunst des Wandels: Ansätze für die ökosoziale Transformation*, eds Susanne Elsen, Günther Reifer, Andreas Wild, and Evelyn Oberleiter, 25–44. München: Oekom.

Pateman, Carole. 1988. *The sexual contract*. Stanford CA: Stanford University Press.

Polanyi, Karl. 1979. *Ökonomie und Gesellschaft*. Frankfurt am Main: Suhrkamp.

Polanyi, Karl. 2001. *The great transformation: The political and economic origins of our time*, 2nd edn. Boston MA: Beacon (orig. pub. 1944).

Randers, Jørgen. 2012. *2052. A global forecast for the next forty years*. White River Junction VT: Chelsea Green.

Reuter, Norbert. 2010. 'Der Arbeitsmarkt im Spannungsfeld von Wachstum, Ökologie und Verteilung'. In *Ökologie und Wirtschaftsforschung, Postwachstumsgesellschaft: Konzepte für die Zukunft*, eds Irmi Seidl and Angelika Zahrnt, 85–102. Marburg: Metropolis.

Rifkin, Jeremy. 2004. *The end of work: The decline of the global labor force and the dawn of the post-market era*. New York: Jeremy P. Tarcher/Penguin (orig. pub. 1995).

Robine, Jean-Marie, Siu L. K. Cheung, Sophie Le Roy, Herman van Oyen, Clare Griffiths, Jean-Pierre Michel, and François R. Herrmann. 2008. 'Death toll exceeded 70,000 in Europe during the summer of 203'. *Comptes Rendus Biologies*, 331(2): 171–8.

Rosol, Marit. 2014. 'Community volunteering as neoliberal strategy? Green space production in Berlin'. *Antipode: A Radical Journal of Geography*, 44(1): 239–57.

Seidl, Irmi and Angelika Zahrnt. 2010a. 'Anliegen des Buches und Übersicht'. In *Ökologie und Wirtschaftsforschung, Postwachstumsgesellschaft: Konzepte für die Zukunft*, eds Irmi Seidl and Angelika Zahrnt, 17–22. Marburg: Metropolis.

Seidl, Irmi and Angelika Zahrnt. 2010b. 'Argumente für einen Abschied vom Paradigma des Wirtschaftswachstums'. In *Ökologie und Wirtschaftsforschung, Postwachstumsgesellschaft: Konzepte für die Zukunft*, eds Irmi Seidl and Angelika Zahrnt, 23–36. Marburg: Metropolis.

Seidl, Irmi and Angelika Zahrnt. 2010c. 'Verbindungslinien: Inhaltliche Zusammenhänge zwischen den Themen'. In *Ökologie und Wirtschaftsforschung, Postwachstumsgesellschaft: Konzepte für die Zukunft*, eds Irmi Seidl and Angelika Zahrnt, 221–8. Marburg: Metropolis.

Shiva, Vandana. 2013. *Making peace with the earth*. London: Pluto.

Smith, Adam. 1966. *The wealth of nations*, vol. II. London: Dent (orig. pub. 1776).

Steffen, Will, Katherine Richardson, Johan Rockström, Sarah. E. Cornell, Ingo Fetzer, Elena M. Bennett, Reinette Biggs, Stephen R. Carpenter, Wim de Vries, Cynthia A. de Wit, Carl Folke, Dieter Gerten, Jens Heinke, Georgina M. Mace, Linn M. Persson, Veerabhadran Ramanathan, Belinda Reyers, and Sverker Sörlin. 2015. 'Planetary boundaries: Guiding human development on a changing planet'. *Science*, 347(6223): 736–1259855-10.

Stern, Nicholas. 2007. *The economics of climate change: The Stern review*. Cambridge: Cambridge University Press.

Stiglitz, Joseph E., Amartya Sen, and Jean-Paul Fitoussi. 2009. 'Report by the commission on the measurement of economic performance and social progress'. www.stiglitz-sen-fitoussi.fr/documents/rapport_anglais.pdf [27 August 2016].

United Nations Development Programme (UNDP). 2015. 'Human development report 2015. Work for human development: Statistical annex'. UNDP. http://hdr.undp.org/sites/default/files/hdr_2015_statistical_annex.pdf [27 August 2016].

United Nations Environment Programme (UNEP). 2011. 'Towards a green economy: Pathways to sustainable development and poverty eradication'. UNEP. https://sustainabledevelopment.un.org/content/documents/126GER_synthesis_en.pdf [27 August 2016].

United Nations Framework Convention on Climate Change (UNFCCC). 2015. 'Adoption of the Paris Agreement. Conference of the Parties, twenty-first session, Paris, 30 November to 11 December 2015. Agenda item 4(b), Durban Platform for Enhanced Action (decision 1/CP.17), Adoption of a protocol, another legal instrument, or an agreed outcome with legal force under the Convention applicable to all Parties'. FCCC/CP/2015/L.9. https://unfccc.int/resource/docs/2015/cop21/eng/l09r01.pdf [27 August 2016].

United Nations General Assembly (UNGA). 2015. 'Draft resolution referred to the United Nations summit for the adoption of the post-2015 development agenda by the General Assembly at its sixty-ninth session. Transforming our world: The 2030 Agenda for Sustainable Development'. Seventieth session Agenda items 15 and 116. www.un.org/ga/search/view_doc.asp?symbol=A/70/L.1&Lang=E [27 August 2016].

van Parijs, Philippe. 1992. 'The second marriage of justice and efficiency'. In *Arguing for basic income: Ethical foundations for a radical reform*, ed. Philippe van Parijs, 215–40. London, New York: Verso.

Victor, Peter A. 2008. *Advances in ecological economics. Managing without growth: Slower by design, not disaster*. Cheltenham: Edward Elgar.

von Weizsäcker, Ernst Ulrich. 1994. *Erdpolitik: Ökologische Realpolitik an der Schwelle zum Jahrhundert der Umwelt*. Darmstadt: Wissenschaftliche Buchgesellschaft.

von Winterfeld, Uta, and Adelheid Biesecker. 2013. 'Es geht nicht allein: Vorsorgendes Wirtschaften braucht neue Gesellschaftsverträge'. In *Wege vorsorgenden Wirtschaftens*, ed. Netzwerk Vorsorgenden Wirtschaftens, 385–403. Marburg: Metropolis.

Wackernagel, Mathis. 1994. 'Ecological footprint and appropriated carrying capacity: A tool for planning towards sustainability'. PhD thesis. Vancouver: University of British Columbia. https://open.library.ubc.ca/cIRcle/collections/ubctheses/831/items/1.0088048 [27 August 2016].

Watkins, Kevin, Haishan Fu, Ricardo Fuentes, Arunabha Ghosh, Chiara Giamberardini, Claes Johansson, Christopher Kuonqui, Andrés Montes, David Stewart, Cecilia Ugaz, and Shahin Yaqub. 2005. 'Human development report 2005: International cooperation at a crossroads'. Aid, trade and security in an unequal world. UNDP. http://hdr.undp.org/sites/default/files/reports/266/hdr05_complete.pdf [27 August 2016].

World Commission on Environment and Development. 1987. 'Our common future'. Transmitted to the General Assembly as an Annex to document A/42/427 – Development and International Co-operation: Environment. United Nations (UN) General Assembly Resolution 42/187. www.un-documents.net/our-common-future.pdf [26 September 2016].

World Bank. 2014. 'Turn down the heat: Confronting the new climate normal'. International Bank for Reconstruction and Development, World Bank. www-wds.worldbank.org/external/default/WDSContentServer/WDSP/IB/2014/11/20/000406484_20141120090713/Rendered/PDF/927040v20WP00O0ull0Report000English.pdf [27 August 2016].

World Bank, United Cities, and Local Governments. 2009. 'Decentralization and local democracy in the world: First global report by United Cities and Local Governments, 2008'. Washington DC: World Bank, United Cities and Local Governments. www.cities-localgovernments.org/gold/Upload/gold_report/01_introduction_en.pdf [27 August 2016].

3 Governing commons

In today's globalised neoliberal corporate economy with its commodification and privatisation tendencies it becomes ever more difficult to ensure access to natural and social resources for the majority of a still growing population. Whereas in the Global South people virtually lose their livelihoods through a global economy oriented on profit and reckless economic growth with its disastrous consequences of climate change, land grabbing and corporations' seed control (Shiva 2013, 5–6, 30), in many European cities the effects of privatisation and commodification on people's access to commons such as green spaces is not life-threatening, yet still alarming, as shown by the empirical data (cf. 5.3). The question is in what kind of city citizens want to live. This can be one with a majority of privatised green spaces with no access or only fee-based access for citizens, a city marked by the disappearance of inner-city green spaces and a high rate of urban sprawl due to construction and infrastructure development, which results in the loss of one of the most important resources, the soil. Or it can be a city that endeavours to reduce the inner-city vacancy rate and to build reasonably upward instead of increasing urban sprawl (cf. 9.4.2.2 – concept of the 'green compact city') and that encourages citizens to take care of urban green spaces, which are accessible free of charge and do not risk being privatised, and supports them, *without* functionalising them for neoliberal city development. Due to the important diverse functions of urban green spaces for a liveable city (cf. 5.2.1), the question must be raised as to how they can be governed sustainably. Since they can be regarded as commons (cf. 6.3.1.2), this chapter sheds light on this term and on the theory of the governance of commons developed by Ostrom, who gained, in 2009, as the first and only woman so far, the Nobel Laureate in Economic Sciences for her groundbreaking work in institutional economics. Whereas Section 3.1 explains the difference of commons in relation to other types of goods, Section 3.2 contrasts Ostrom's theory with the conventional economic one. Section 3.3 explains the main principles of the governance of commons, while Section 3.4 responds to critiques that have been raised against her theory. Finally, in Section 3.5, policy implications emerging from her theory are summarised.

3.1 Commons – a special type of goods

'Conventional [economic] theory relied on a tripartite categorization of property rights (private, state, or communal)' (Poteete *et al.* 2010, 46). The latter is supposed to result in the 'tragedy of the commons', which led to the long-standing doctrine that either nationalisation or privatisation is the solution to collective action problems occurring in the governance of commons (cf. 3.2). Ostrom challenged this binary logic by showing that a sustainable collective self-organised governance of commons beyond institutional arrangements relying either on the market or the state is possible. She developed a quadripartite scheme of goods and services determined by the degree of two attributes: exclusion and subtractability of use (cf. Table 3.1).

In this scheme, a common

> such as a lake, an ocean, an irrigation system, a fishing ground, a forest, the Internet, or the stratosphere, is a natural or man-made resource from which it is difficult to exclude or limit users once the resource is provided by nature or produced by humans (Elinor Ostrom, Roy Gardner, and James Walker 1994). One person's consumption of resource units, such as water, fish, or trees, removes those units from what is available to others.
>
> (Ostrom 2005, 79–80)

In contrast to toll and private goods, it is very difficult to exclude potential beneficiaries from using commons, and in contrast to public and toll goods an increased use of commons lowers the possibility for further actors to use it. This high degree of subtractability can even lead to a total depletion of the resource (cf. 3.2).

The scheme puts an end to mixing up commons with public goods. Conventional economic theory did not pay attention to the attribute of subtractability and solely distinguished goods according to the attribute of exclusion. However,

Table 3.1 Four types of goods

| | | Subtractability of use | |
		High	Low
Difficulty of excluding potential beneficiaries	High	*Common-pool resources:* groundwater basins, lakes, irrigation systems, fisheries, forests, etc.	*Public goods:* peace and security of a community, national defence, knowledge, fire protection, weather forecasts, etc.
	Low	*Private goods:* food, clothing, automobiles, etc.	*Toll goods:* theatres, private clubs, daycare centres

Source: Ostrom 2005, 24.

since '"overuse" problems are chronic in CPR [common-pool resource] situations, but absent in regard to pure public goods' (Ostrom 1990, 32) it is important to additionally distinguish goods according to their degree of subtractability.

3.2 Countering the 'tragedy of the commons'

Ostrom disproved the long-standing economic theorem that the self-governance of commons inescapably leads to the depletion of the resource due to overuse. The expression 'tragedy of the commons' is commonly ascribed to Garett Hardin, according to whom 'Freedom in a commons brings ruin to all' (1968, 1244).[1] In other words, 'in an open access CPR with no governance arrangements in operation, appropriators will tend to over-exploit the resource and may destroy it entirely' (McGinnis 2011, 175). 'Hardin envisioned a pasture open to all in which each herder received a direct benefit from adding animals to graze on the pasture and suffered only delayed costs from overgrazing' (Ostrom 2007, 15183). According to Hardin, this situation inevitably leads to the depletion of the resource, due to 'the paradox that individually rational strategies lead to collectively irrational outcomes' (Ostrom 1990, 5), here the overgrazing of the pastures. Following from this reasoning, it seems logical to demand, as Hardin did, either privatisation or nationalisation with a subsequent allocation of the right of use of the resource to solve the problem. Hardin's thoughts were developed further in game theory. However, the problem with models of conventional theory is that they depict human behaviour in a very narrow way. They are thus not useful for predicting human behaviour for the majority of collective action situations (Ostrom 2005, 7–8; Poteete *et al.* 2010, 220–8; Sauer 2012a, 143–4), but only to make predictions for social dilemma situations[2] which are characterised by the actors' access to mutual and exhaustive information, their synchronous and autonomous decision-making, their impossibility to communicate and the lack of a central authority to ensure the implementation of agreed decisions (Ostrom 2009a, 7). In this specific situation, 'regardless of the microsituational structure or broader context [cf. Figure 3.2], all individuals in a dilemma situation would maximize short-term returns to self…. No one would cooperate' (Poteete *et al.* 2010, 218).

Overcoming the limited view of conventional economic theory, Ostrom's decade-long empirical and theoretical interdisciplinary work with multiple methods (Poteete *et al.* 2010, 215–16) has brought three important findings. First, case studies from all over the world have shown that local actors are indeed able to devise institutions to sustainably self-govern commons, thus remaining in communal property without being either privatised or nationalised (Ostrom 1990, 1; 2005, 221; Poteete *et al.* 2010, 45–6, 94, 218). Second, neither market nor state solutions can guarantee the sustainable governance of commons (Ostrom 1990, 1; McGinnis and Walker 2010, 46; Poteete *et al.* 2010, 46). Third, there is no institutional magic bullet for solving collective action problems (Poteete *et al.* 2010, 220), since 'collective action related to common-pool resources (CPRs) is far more complicated than the conventional theory had assumed' (ibid., 215). Therefore, mere state and market solutions must be supplemented by a broad range of institutionally diverse approaches (Ostrom 2007, 15181; Sauer 2012b, 138). There are drawbacks in every property rights regime, whether common, private, or public property. Yet, an overuse of a resource is quasi guaranteed if it is open access without any regulations (Ostrom 2009b, 218–19). Therefore a system of rules needs to be developed and abided by to sustainably self-govern commons.

It is Ostrom's merit to have developed an empirically valid broad economic 'theory of self-organized collective action to complement the existing theories of externally organized collective action: the theory of the firm and the theory of the state' (Ostrom 1990, 57). In comparison to these theories, this 'more general behavioral theory of human action' (Poteete *et al.* 2010, 220) explains how institutional arrangements that effectively govern commons function and can be modified by actors (Ostrom 1990, xiv). The theory accounts for the complex real context in which the action situation is embedded (cf. Figure 3.1) while still depicting scientific results as concisely as possible (Sauer 2012a, 138; 2012b). It explains why and under which conditions actors behave cooperatively in social dilemma situations in preference to 'always maximiz[ing] expected, short-term, material returns to self in isolation from other actors' (Poteete *et al.* 2010, 215). The theory 'has the potential to initiate a paradigm shift in economics' (Sauer 2012a, 151, own translation) in the direction of true sustainability economics (cf. 2.4.3.2). Such economics would acknowledge the need for institutional diversity, admitting and supporting solutions that go beyond the binary logic of market or state (Sauer 2012a, 138, 152; 2012b). This shift is necessary because economic reality is marked by institutional diversity, as shown by Ostrom (1990, 14): 'Institutions are rarely either private or public – "the market" or "the state". Many successful CPR institutions are rich mixtures of "private-like" and "public-like" institutions defying classification in a sterile dichotomy.'

3.3 Principles of the governance of commons following Ostrom

Ostrom's research stresses the important role of commons for the sustainable governance of resources (Ostrom 2009b, 218). This section aims at showing under which conditions a sustainable collective self-organised governance of commons is possible. This is necessary to assess the potential of new civil-society-driven self-organised institutional arrangements at the local level for the socio-ecological transition. To analyse the complex setting of commons, Ostrom developed a comprehensive theoretical framework which will be presented and linked to the already earlier conceived design rules before turning to two specific variables in the framework that are amongst those having turned out to be of major importance for successfully governing commons: social capital and learning.

3.3.1 IAD and SES framework and design rules

Capturing and modelling the collective self-organisation of commons turned out to be a very demanding task due to the complex institutional diversity encountered in the empirical field research: 'The many relevant variables, the immense number of combinations of these variables that exist, and their organization into multiple levels of analysis make understanding organized social life a complex endeavor' (Ostrom 2005, 11). To bring down this real-world diversity into a theoretical framework, the Institutional Analysis and Development (IAD) framework was developed, which is a conceptual 'diagnostic tool that can be used to investigate any broad subject where humans repeatedly interact within rules and norms that guide their choice of strategies and behaviors' (Ostrom and Hess 2007, 41). The IAD framework has been developed further into the broader SES framework (Poteete *et al.* 2010, 216–17, 234–6), which also incorporates 'the biophysical and ecological foundations of institutional systems' (McGinnis 2011, 181).

The broad eight first-tier variables depicted in Figure 3.1 can be differentiated in 56 second-tier variables (Poteete *et al.* 2010, 237). Together they form 'a nested, multitier framework' (Ostrom 2007, 15181). Due to the diversity of locally self-organised commons, not the whole range of variables are relevant for each case and those that count often take effect in an interrelated way (Poteete *et al.* 2010, 238). Furthermore, their influence also depends on past action in the

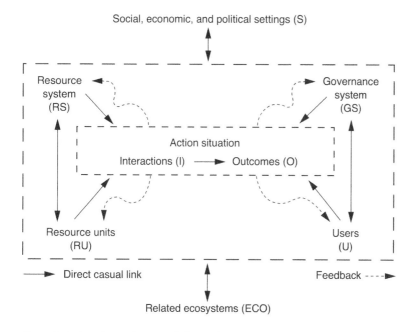

Figure 3.1 A multitier framework for analysing an SES.

Source: Ostrom 2007, 15182, copyright (2007) National Academy of Sciences, USA.

Table 3.2 Second-tier variables affecting the probability of self-organisation

Resource System (RS)	Governance System (GS)
RS3: *size of resource system* RS5: *productivity of system* RS5a: *indicators of the productivity of system* RS7: *predictability of system dynamics*	GS6a: *local collective choice autonomy*
Resource Units (RU)	Users (U)
RU1: *resource unit mobility*	U1: *number of users* U2: *socioeconomic attributes of users* U5: *leadership/entrepreneurship* U6: *norms/social capital* U7: *knowledge of SES/mental models* U8: *importance of resource*

Source: adapted from Sauer 2016, 49.

SES (Ostrom 1990, 202; 2007, 15182). The framework (cf. Figure 3.1) models SES as being composed of a *Resource System* (the commons) and *Resource Units* variables on the one hand and of *Governance System* and *Users* variables on the other hand which all influence *Interactions* and *Outcomes* of an action situation. The action situation is embedded in *Related Ecosystems* on the one hand and in the wider *Social, Economic and Political settings* on the other (Ostrom 2007, 15181). The framework reflects Ostrom's interdisciplinary approach by taking into consideration both social and ecological variables, revealing their interrelatedness. From this system, 12 variables could be identified as being of particular relevance to the capabilities of the actors to self-organise the governance of a commons (Poteete *et al.* 2010, 238–9).

Poteete *et al.* (2010, 243) found that

> even in a group that differs on many variables, if at least a minimally winning subset of users harvesting from an overused but valuable resource are dependent on it (U8), share a common understanding of their situation (U7), trust one another (U6), and have autonomy to make their own rules (GS6a), it is more likely that they will estimate that the expected benefits of governing their resource are greater than the expected costs.

The framework confirmed and refined the eight design rules that need to be followed for a successful self-governance of commons (ibid., 100–1), first defined 26 years ago (Ostrom 1990):

- *Boundaries of the resource system as well as social boundaries must be unambiguously defined.* The latter refers to designating which are the individuals or households holding a right to the resource (ibid., 90; Poteete *et al.* 2010, 100).

- *Actors' benefits and costs must be proportionate*, meaning that 'rules-in-use should allocate benefits associated with a common-pool resource in proportion to contributions of required inputs. Rules that respect proportionality are more widely accepted as equitable' (Poteete *et al.* 2010, 100).
- The majority of actors affected by the resource system have the *right to participate in determining common rules* (Ostrom 1990, 90; Poteete *et al.* 2010, 100).
- '*The individuals charged with monitoring rule adherence and resource conditions should be accountable to users*.... Robust, self-organized resource regimes tend to select their own monitors'[3] (Poteete *et al.* 2010, 100).
- 'Sanctions for violated rules should be graduated. *Graduated sanctions* signal that infractions are noticed while allowing for misunderstandings, mistakes, and exceptional circumstances that lead to rule breaking. They encourage individuals who have broken a rule to resume compliance in order to enjoy ongoing trust' (ibid., 100–1).
- 'There should be *rapid, low-cost, local arenas to resolve conflicts among users or between users and officials*. Some conflicts arise because participants interpret in different ways a rule that they have jointly made. Simple, local mechanisms that get conflicts aired immediately and produce resolutions that are generally known in the community can limit the number of conflicts that reduce trust' (ibid., 101).
- 'The *rights of local users to make their own rules* should be recognized by the national or local government' (ibid.).
- '*When common-pool resources are part of a larger system, governance activities should be organized in multiple nested layers*. Small-scale units can match rules to local conditions, but larger-scale institutions are also needed to govern interdependencies among smaller units' (ibid.).

3.4 Critique of Ostrom's theory

Critique of Ostrom's theory can be broadly divided into six interrelated points. Ostrom's theory has been criticised for being too behavioural (e.g. Clement 2010; 2012; Johnson 2004) and is situated by a number of scholars from political ecology and economy (e.g. Obeng-Odoom 2016a, 14; 2016b, 374) in conventional neoclassical economics. They reproach it with taking a too rationalist-individualistic approach (Obeng-Odoom 2016b, 373, 384–5) and with remaining in the mental framework of the *homo oeconomicus* (Obeng-Odoom 2016a, 14) with its cost–benefit analysis and utility maximization features (Exner 2015, 123, 125–6). They acknowledge Ostrom's merit in 'expanding economic thinking beyond questions of individualistic rational behaviour' (Forsyth and Johnson 2014, 1093), yet criticise that her methodological basis to explain collective action processes remains focused on 'rational choice theory and methodological individualism' (ibid.).

The second critique states that in its endeavour to 'contribute to an empirically-grounded theory of social action' (Johnson 2004, 409–10), Ostrom's theory neglects a historical dimension and specificness (Obeng-Odoom 2016b, 386; Johnson 2004, 407). Political ecologists and economists 'emphasize the historical struggles that determine resource access and entitlement, and the ways in which formal and informal rules create and reinforce unequal access to the commons' (Johnson 2004, 409). Thus, they accuse it of not being normative enough and of being too pragmatic, neglecting political economists' and ecologists' focus on critically examining issues of 'inequality, poverty and exclusion' (ibid., 420) and of paying sufficient attention to 'aspects of context, culture and meaning' (Forsyth and Johnson 2014, 1100).

The third critique claims that Ostrom's theory insufficiently analyses the role of inner-and outer group power relations and discourses (e.g. Exner 2015, 122; Clement 2012; Epstein *et al.* 2014; Agrawal 2014). Commons are not spared from underlying internal local power structures that can be extremely hierarchical or patriarchal (Lipietz 2009; Euler 2016; DeCaro 2011, 5). Von Winterfeld *et al.* (2012, 8) point to the fact that participation processes are not void of power structures and that every member of a community must have the same possibility to participate. Since commons are governed by a group of people, the question must be raised of how to define who is included and who is excluded. Johnson (2004, 417) draws attention to studies that have shown that even in cases when a local common property regime was successful in maintaining the resource for sustainable use, this does not automatically mean that the local economy is also 'based on equity, welfare and social security'. Referring to outer-group power relations, several scholars see the major threats to a successful governed common not as in the first place stemming from a lacking organisational structure within the commons, leading to overexploitation, but from external capitalistic and imperialistic forces and power constellations (Obeng-Odoom 2016b, 399, 407–8; Habermann 2011, 156). Lipietz (2009) warns that commons should not be seen separately from the state and the market. The successful organisation in a commons structure does not protect the commons from being under threat from external powers (cf. also von Winterfeld *et al.* 2012).

Fourth, Ostrom's theory is also criticised for paying insufficient attention to inequality issues (Epstein *et al.* 2014; Agrawal 2014). According to Johnson (2004, 409), Ostrom did not consider how to '[deal] with the problem of creating and sustaining resource access for poor and vulnerable groups in society', thus achieving 'a more inclusive and meaningful form of governance' (Forsyth and Johnson 2014, 1103–4). If all members of the community are supposed to be able to equally participate in a democratic way, it is not sufficient to treat them equally, just granting equal rights, since preconditions to participate differ along the heterogeneity of people (Euler 2016, 104). Therefore, disadvantaged social groups must first be enabled to participate (cf. 6.3.2.2) and attention must be paid to gender relations (Gottschlich 2013), for example since commoning per se is no guarantee that an unquestioned gender-based division of work ceases to exist (ibid., 9).

A fifth critique blames Ostrom of being too market-friendly and too state-hostile (Obeng-Odoom 2016b, 383).

She presented a way to deal with environmental problems that did not require government involvement. Ostrom offered a vision of local self-governance that lay between big government and private property. This represented what seemed to be an alternative to capitalism and socialism.

(Cobb 2016, 267)

For those who aim at criticising statal or capital structures, using Ostrom's theory is the wrong approach (Exner 2015, 130).

A sixth strand faults an unclear demarcation line between commons and partnership agreements, falling under private property rights (Block and Jankovic 2016; Block 2011, 9, 4; Agrawal 2014, 86–7). Araral (2014) points to the fact that the successful commons as described by Ostrom in 1990 are 'not strictly CPRs in which exclusion is difficult but are in fact some form of limited access, private property rights in which exclusion to the resource system is highly feasible' (ibid., 19): 'when … [a] common resource is divided into individual units or when a small group takes possession of it … [, f]rom a social perspective, it is privatized either way' (Cobb 2016, 267).

Ostrom belonged to the 'second-generation theories of rational choice and collective action' (Araral 2014, 13) which

suggest the possibility of self-governance as a viable solution to collective action problems in the commons … [and] point to the centrality of trust and reciprocity as the core determinant of collective action not only in the commons but of the evolution of social order more generally.

(Ibid., 14)

Despite the critiques, one has to admit that Ostrom's theory 'introduced frameworks, theories and models that have helped foster a conversation amongst social science scholars and ecologists' (ibid., 13). 'The SES framework holds great potential for social science integration, and may serve as a bridge between political ecology and commons theory' (Epstein *et al.* 2014). Clement's (2010, 129) proposal of 'a "politicised" institutional analysis and development framework' by 'integrat[ing] explicit second-tier variables on power and discourses into the SES framework' (ibid., 3) could contribute to this endeavour and make institutionalists' research more critical. She argues that it is necessary and possible to combine the approach of institutionalists and power-centred analysts since they complement each other (ibid., 136) to more easily arriving at consistent policy recommendations (ibid., 149).

3.5 Policy implications

The mentioned critique does not belittle Ostrom's merit in having delivered a comprehensive theory for explaining the successful governance of commons. Policy-making from the local to the international level does not only have to take notice of its existence but also orientate policy according to it. Yet, there is the high risk that policy is continuously devised 'with a presumption that individuals cannot organize themselves and always need to be organized by external authorities'[4] (Ostrom 1990, 25). This is, first, because this thinking corresponds to conventional long-term scientific consensus and, second, because orientating policy on Ostrom's theory would let new actors enter the action situation, which contains the 'risk' of a shift in power structures and would demand higher organisational skills of coordination from the local authority.

External authorities can greatly influence the emergence of self-organisation (Ostrom 1990, 212; Poteete *et al.* 2010, 242–3), since they 'can do a lot to enhance or impede the likelihood and performance of self-governing institutions' (Poteete *et al.*, 242). The local authority, for example, has the power 'to extend autonomy to local groups' (ibid., 241), which can take various forms 'from informal mechanisms that will ensure consultation to formal mechanisms including signed petitions, special elections, legislation, and court proceedings' (Ostrom 1990, 220). Self-organisation generally more easily emerges in democratic regimes (cf. 6.2.1). One reason for this is that in a democracy it is more probable that citizens are allowed and supported to self-organise. This support can take various forms. A major one is to provide institutions that facilitate the creation of social capital (Bray *et al.* 203; Merino and Robson 2005; Ostrom 2009b, 224), most importantly institutions for conflict resolution to prevent 'conflict over rule interpretation and adjustment ..., which ... may destroy the process of building capital before it gets very far' (Ostrom and Ahn 2003, xxiv). Another, more technical form of support are 'formal laws, government agents, and courts' (ibid., xxii), as they provide actors with the will to self-organise 'technical advice, information, and complementary monitoring and sanctioning systems' (ibid.).

Considering a *'polycentric governance system'* (Ostrom 2005, 283) as most suitable to cope with collective action problems, Ostrom developed its seven major characteristics on the basis of her theory:

- It has 'multiple governing authorities at differing scales rather than a monocentric unit' (Ostrom 2010b, 552).
- Every system unit 'exercises considerable independence to make norms and rules within a specific domain (such as a family, a firm, a local government, a network of local governments, a state or province, a region, a national government, or an international regime)' (ibid.).
- 'Some units are general-purpose governments while others may be highly specialized' (Ostrom 2005, 283).
- 'The users of each common-pool resource would have some authority to make at least some of the rules related to how that particular resource will be utilized' (ibid.).
- Since 'major universities and research stations are located in larger units but have a responsibility to relate recent scientific findings to multiple smaller units within their region' (ibid.), 'a more effective blend of scientific information with local knowledge' (ibid.) becomes feasible.

• Since they

> have overlapping units, information about what has worked well in one setting can be transmitted to others who may try it out in their settings. Associations of local resource governance units can be encouraged to speed up the exchange of information about relevant local conditions and about policy experiments that have proved particularly successful.
>
> (Ibid.)

• 'When small systems fail, there are larger systems to call upon – and vice versa' (ibid.).

The existence of a conflict-regulation mechanism is of paramount importance in a polycentric system, since because of its units' autonomy and concurrent interrelatedness, the conflict potential is high (Ostrom 2005, 286). Considering the list of characteristics, this system provides options for monitoring, for reciprocal learning and experimenting, for developing trust, and consequently enhancing cooperation levels, as well as for transferring gained knowledge to other contexts and for the subsequent adaptation of policies (Ostrom 2010b, 552, 555–6). There can therefore be considered the governance system that best lets society's innovative potential unfold and thus the most apt to drive the socio-ecological transition at all levels and in all sectors.

Notes

1 However, as Sauer (2016, 40) points out, Hardin was not the first to use the expression 'tragedy of the commons'; it first appeared as early as in 1832 in a lecture by William F. Lloyd (1980, 473).
2 A social dilemma designates

> settings where uncoordinated decisions motivated by the pursuit of individual benefits generate suboptimal payoffs for others and for self in the long run. Individual maximization of short-term benefits to self leads individuals to take actions that generate lower joint outcomes than could have been achieved.
>
> (Ostrom 2009a, 6)

3 Italics added in this and the remaining direct citations of this chapter.
4 With this term Ostrom refers to governance bodies of all levels outside self-governing institutions.

References

Agrawal, Arun. 2014. 'Studying the commons, governing common-pool resource outcomes: Some concluding thoughts'. *Environmental Science and Policy*, 36: 86–91.

Araral, Eduardo. 2014. 'Ostrom, Hardin and the commons: A critical appreciation and a revisionist view'. *Environmental Science and Policy*, 36: 11–23.

Block, Walter E. 2011. 'Review of Ostrom's governing the commons'. *Libertarian Papers*, 3(21). http://libertarianpapers.org/wp-content/uploads/article/2011/lp-3-21.pdf [27 August 2016].

Block, Walter E. and Ivan Jankovic. 2016. 'Tragedy of the partnership: A critique of Elinor Ostrom'. *American Journal of Economics and Sociology*, 75(2): 289–318.

Bray, David B., Leticia Merino-Pérez, Patricia Negreros-Castillo, Gerardo Segura-Warnholtz, Juan M. Torres-Rojo, and Henricus F. M. Vester. 2003. 'Mexico's community-managed forests as a global model for sustainable landscapes'. *Conservation Biology*, 17(3): 672–7.

Clement, Floriane. 2010. 'Analysing decentralised natural resource governance: Proposition for a "politicised" institutional analysis and development framework'. *Policy Sciences*, 43: 129–56.

Clement, Floriane. 2012. 'Comment. For critical social-ecological system studies: Integrating power and discourses to move beyond the right institutional fit'. *Environmental Conservation*, 40(1): 1–4.

Cobb, Clifford W. 2016. 'Editor's introduction. Questioning the commons: Power, equity, and the meaning of ownership'. *American Journal of Economics and Sociology*, 75(2): 265–88.

DeCaro, Daniel A. 2011. 'Considering a broader view of power, participation, and social justice in the Ostrom institutional analysis framework'. *Grassroots Economic Organizing (GEO) Newsletter*, 2(9). http://geo.coop/node/651 [27 August 2016].

Epstein, Graham, Abigail Bennett, Rebecca Gruby, Leslie Acton, and Mateja Nenadovic. 2014. 'Studying power with the social-ecological system framework'. In *Understanding Society and Natural Resources: Forging New Strands of Integration Across the Social Sciences*, eds Michael J. Manfredo, Jerry J. Vaske, Andreas Rechkemmer, and Esther A. Duke, 111–35. Dordrecht, Heidelberg, New York, London: Springer.

Euler, Johannes. 2016. 'Commons-creating society: On the radical German commons discourse'. *Review of Radical Political Economics*, 48(1): 93–110.

Exner, Andreas. 2015. 'Commons. Ein nomadisierender Begriff im Wandel von Bedeutungsfeldern: Anmerkungen zur theoretischen Analyse des Werks von Elinor Ostrom und linksalternative Bezüge darauf'. *Emanzipation. Zeitschrift für Sozialistische Theorie und Praxis*, 5(9): 119–33.

Forsyth, Tim and Craig Johnson. 2014. 'Elinor Ostrom's legacy: Governing the commons and the rational choice controversy'. *Development and Change*, 45(5): 1093–110.

Gottschlich, Daniela. 2013: 'Doing away with "labour": Working and caring in a world of commons. Expeditions into (re)thinking the role of human (re)productive activity and its inherent nature in a generative commons network'. Presentation Keynote Working and Caring. www.boell.de/de/node/277315 [8 December 2016].

Habermann, Friederike. 2011. 'Eccomony. Peerökonomie, Gemeingüter, Solidarisches Wirtschaften'. In *Ausgewachsen! Ökologische Gerechtigkeit. Soziale Rechte. Gutes Leben.*, eds Werner Rätz, Tanja V. Egan-Krieger, Barbara Muraca, Alexis Passadakis, Matthias Schmelzer, and Andrea Vetter, 152–60. Hamburg: VSA.

Hardin, Garrett. 1968. 'The tragedy of the commons'. *Science*, 162(3859): 1243–8. www.sciencemag.org/cgi/reprint/162/3859/1243.pdf [27 August 2016].

Johnson, Craig. 2004. 'Uncommon ground: The "poverty of history" in common property discourse'. *Development and Change*, 35(3): 407–33.

Lipietz, Alain. 2009. 'Questions sur les "biens communs"'. Intervention au débat de la Fondation Heinrich Böll, FSM de Belém, Janvier 2009. http://lipietz.net/spip.php?article2344 [27 August 2016].

Lloyd, William F. 1980. 'On the checks to population'. *Population and Development Review*, 6(3): 473–96.

McGinnis, Michael D. 2011. 'An introduction to IAD and the language of the Ostrom workshop: A simple guide to a complex framework'. *Policy Studies Journal*, 39(1): 169–83.

McGinnis, Michael D. and James M. Walker. 2010. 'Foundations of the Ostrom workshop: Institutional analysis, polycentricity, and self-governance of the commons'. *Public Choice*, 143(3–4): 293–301.

Merino, Leticia and Jim Robson, eds. 2005. *Managing the commons: Indigenous rights, economic development and identity*. Mexico.

Obeng-Odoom, Franklin. 2016a. 'Property in the commons: Origins and paradigms'. *Review of Radical Political Economics*, 48(1): 9–19.

Obeng-Odoom, Franklin. 2016b. 'The meaning, prospects, and future of the commons: Revisiting the legacies of Elinor Ostrom and Henry George'. *American Journal of Economics and Sociology*, 75(2): 372–414.

Ostrom, Elinor. 1990. *Governing the commons: The evolution of institutions for collective action*. New York: Cambridge University.

Ostrom, Elinor. 2005. *Understanding institutional diversity*. Princeton NJ: Princeton University Press.

Ostrom, Elinor. 2007. 'A diagnostic approach for going beyond panaceas'. *Proceedings of the National Academy of Sciences*, 104(39): 15181–7. www.pnas.org/content/104/39/15181.full.pdf [27 August 2016].

Ostrom, Elinor. 2009a. 'A polycentric approach for coping with climate change'. Policy Research Working Paper 5095. http://papers.ssrn.com/sol3/papers.cfm?abstract_id=1494833 [27 August 2016].

Ostrom, Elinor. 2009b. 'Gemeingütermanagement: Perspektiven für bürgerschaftliches Engagement'. In *Wem gehört die Welt? Zur Wiederentdeckung der Gemeingüter*, eds Silke Helfrich and Heinrich-Böll-Stiftung, 218–28. Munich: Oekom. www.boell.de/sites/default/files/assets/boell.de/images/download_de/economysocial/Netzausgabe_Wem_gehoert_die_Welt.pdf [27 August 2016].

Ostrom, Elinor. 2010b. 'Polycentric systems for coping with collective action and global environmental change'. *Global Environmental Change*, 20(4): 550–7.

Ostrom, Elinor and T. K. Ahn. 2003. 'Introduction'. In *Foundations of Social Capital*, eds Elinor Ostrom and T. K. Ahn. Cheltenham, Northampton MA: Edward Elgar.

Ostrom, Elinor and Charlotte Hess. 2007. 'A framework for analyzing the knowledge commons'. In *Understanding knowledge as a commons: From theory to practice*, eds Charlotte Hess and Elinor Ostrom, 41–81. Cambridge MA: MIT.

Ostrom, Elinor, Roy Gardner, and James Walker, with Arun Agrawal, William Blomquist, Edella Schlager, and Shui Yan Tang. 1994. *Rules, games, and common-pool resources*. Ann Arbor MI: University of Michigan.

Poteete, Amy R., Marco A. Janssen, and Elinor Ostrom. 2010. *Working together: Collective action, the commons, and multiple methods in practice*. Princeton NJ: Princeton University Press.

Sauer, Thomas. 2012a. 'Elemente einer kontextuellen Ökonomie der Nachhaltigkeit: Der Beitrag Elinor Ostroms'. In *Ökonomie der Nachhaltigkeit: Grundlagen, Indikatoren, Strategien*, ed. Thomas Sauer, 135–60. Marburg: Metropolis.

Sauer, Thomas. 2012b. 'Die Rolle der Gemeingüter in den Städten: Die kontextuelle Ökonomie der Postwachstumsgesellschaft'. *Gegenblende. Das gewerkschaftliche Debattenmagazin*, 6 August. www.gegenblende.de/++co++21cdfd5c-dfcb-11e1-94df-52540066f352 [27 August 2016].

Sauer, Thomas. 2016. 'Patterns of change: A general model of socio-ecological transition'. In *Cities in transition: Social innovation for Europe's urban sustainability*, eds Thomas Sauer, Cristina Garzillo, and Susanne Elsen, 39–58. Abingdon/New York: Routledge.

von Winterfeld, Uta, Adelheid Biesecker, Christine Katz, and Benjamin Best. 2012. 'Welche Rolle können Commons in Transformationsprozessen zu Nachhaltigkeit spielen?' Impulse zur WachstumsWende. Wuppertal: Wuppertal Institute for Climate, Environment and Energy. https://epub.wupperinst.org/frontdoor/index/index/docId/4480 [27 August 2016].

4 Methodological approach

This research is embedded into the ROCSET[1] project which is part of the WWWforEurope project whose general aims as well as the more specific ones of ROCSET are outlined in Section 4.1. Then, briefly, the theoretical approach of ROCSET is presented before turning, in Section 4.3, to the strategy for this research.

4.1 Embedding the research into an interdisciplinary multi-stakeholder project

This research is strongly linked to the FP7[2] Collaborative Research Project WWWforEurope running from April 2012 to April 2016, which sought to develop a research-based proposal for a development strategy for a more dynamic, inclusive, and sustainable Europe. Its leading question reads 'What kind of strategy is necessary and feasible for a European development beyond economic growth, under the terms of scarcity of resources, providing wealth, work and social inclusion for citizens, reducing ecological destruction and sustaining local and global commons?' The complex project with in total 34 partners from 14 European countries has provided researchers from different disciplines with the opportunity to work interdisciplinarily in the project's areas and respective workpackages. The collaboration of researchers from diverse backgrounds entails also contrasting views, for example on which role economic growth shall play in realising the socio-ecological transition (cf. 2.3 and 2.4).

One project area particularly explored the role of regions and cities in the transition. Within this area, the ROCSET workpackage examined the institutional preconditions of the socio-ecological transition at the city level. This was done by evaluating the potential of new institutional arrangements, looking specifically at the influence of civil society bottom-up initiatives, assuming that they are important in preserving urban commons. Here, the focus lay on the three urban resource systems of energy, water, and green spaces deemed particularly relevant to the transition (Sauer *et al.* 2016).

4.2 Applying Ostrom's theory to urban resource systems –
the WWWforEurope project ROCSET

Ostrom's theory on the sustainable governance of commons (cf. 3.2 and 3.3) had so far mainly been applied to small local rural resource systems. A main idea in the research design for the work in ROCSET was to understand whether her theory on collective action is transferrable to more complex bigger urban resource systems with less clearly defined boundaries (Sauer 2012a, 153). There-fore, ROCSET explored the potential of new innovative self-organised institutional arrangements in the three urban resource systems water, energy, and green spaces 'to understand better their role in safeguarding the resilience of the ecological resource system under scrutiny' (Sauer 2016, 41) and to answer the overarching research question: 'What is the transformative role of institutional diversification and innovation in the governance of core urban common pool resources?' (ibid., 39).

Ostrom's IAD and SES frameworks (cf. 3.3.1) were taken as a basis 'for comparisons of the governance of different resource systems in different institutional settings in Europe' (ibid., 47), because with their help it becomes possible 'to assess institutional diversity beyond market or governmental organisations' (Kalff and Sauer 2016, 14). Emanating from these frameworks, seven specific research questions were developed, related to Figure 4.1 (Sauer 2016, 46–58). Starting at the top of the cycle, each variable refers to a specific research question:

1   Is the urban governance of ecological resource systems observed in the European cities framed by a common understanding of sustainability transition?

2   Which kinds of citizen participation and users' self-organisation can be observed in local urban resource systems like energy, water, and green spaces?

3   Who are the actors and what are the factors motivating them to pursue a socio-ecological transition in these urban resource systems?

4   What are the lessons learned and the reputations gained from leadership in local resource management?

5   Could we observe transitional socio-ecological norm adoption towards trust and cooperation in the urban context?

6   Does local decision-making autonomy matter in socio-ecological transitions in relation to superior governance levels?

7   To what extent do citizens have an equal voice in the governance of urban resource systems in terms of delegated power and citizen control?

(Ibid., 57–8)

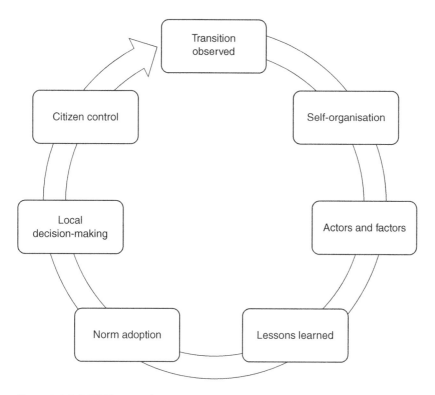

Figure 4.1 ROCSET research questions.
Source: Sauer 2016, 58.

4.3 Research strategy

To arrive at a holistic presentation of the strategy for this research, Section 4.3.1 links the research questions to the research design, justifying the use of the latter. Section 4.3.2 explains the methods of data collection and displays the collected data, and Section 4.3.3 explains the process of data analysis and interpretation.

4.3.1 Research design

In the data analysis phase of the ROCSET project, diverse types of civil society action in the green spaces resource system became evident in the data that are examined in detail in the scope of this research (cf. 7.3, 7.4). The research draws on a mixed methods approach, with a focus on qualitative data (cf. 4.3.3.3), since to answer this research's underlying questions, the qualitative data delivers more profound insights. Fifty-five expert interviews from civil society, economic, and governmental[3] actors from 29 cities in 11 countries of the EU and in three non-EU countries (cf. 4.3.2.2) together with solicited documents (cf. 4.3.2.4) form a case study, the main corpus of analysis, and are triangulated with quantitative questionnaires (cf. 4.3.2.3, cf. Figure 4.2). The analysed data was obtained within the scope of the ROCSET project, which had also defined the selection choice strategy for cities and respondents.[4] Both the research design of ROCSET and of this research follow a linear, not a circular, model. Thus, the sample structure is not developed out of the first collected data, but is finished before data collection starts. Also, data collection and analysis are two distinct consecutive steps (Flick 2009, 142; cf. 4.3.1.2 and 4.3.2.1).

4.3.1.1 Case study design

The green spaces resource system across the 29 European cities from which the qualitative data comes is considered as a one-case qualitative observational[5] case study analysing within-case synchronic spatial variation (Figure 4.2; Gerring 2007, 21, 27–8, 65–6, 197, 216). A

> *case* connotes a spatially delimited phenomenon (a unit) observed at a single point in time or over some period of time.… A case may be created out of any phenomenon so long as it has identifiable boundaries and comprises the primary object of an inference.
>
> (Gerring 2007, 19)

Here, the main unit of analysis, the case, is the socio-ecological transition in the green spaces resource system across 29 European cities. The research design is embedded, since the single case consists of multiple units of analysis – the cities – which are subunits of the case – the main unit of analysis – and in which data is collected (Yin 2014, 50, 238; cf. Figure 4.2). This embedded design makes the research more complex, yet it also 'adds significant opportunities for extensive analysis, enhancing the insights into the single case' (Yin 2014, 56). Each city can be considered as a policy unit from which data on the use of natural resources and socio-ecological interaction within this unit is collected (Poteete *et al.* 2010, 67).

The research design of a case study was chosen because the type of research questions posed suggested this approach. The delivered case study is both descriptive and explanatory (Yin 2014, 8). Whereas the first aspect 'describe[s] a phenomenon (the "case") in its real-world context' (ibid., 238), the explanatory part helps to understand, by looking at the 55 within-case observations across 29 subunits of analysis (cf. Figure 4.2), 'how or why some condition came to be' (ibid., 238).

The research design of a *single* case study was chosen for a theoretical and for a practical reason. First, according to Gerring (2007, 7) 'the product of a good case study is *insight*'. This case study delivers insight into the socio-ecological transition of the green spaces resource system in European cities. Its interest lies

Type of data

Qualitative data:
one-case qualitative observational case study analysing within-case synchronic spatial variation in the resource system green spaces

a) Expert interviews:
13% politics/administration,
38% economy,
49% civil society,
1–4 interviews per city

b) Documents:
1 'case study' report and
1 personal report per city

Quantitative data:
167 questionnaires from 40 cities
(24% administration,
38% economy, 38% civil society)

Population: local experts from politics/administration, economy and civil society from all European cities

Sample: main unit of analysis: the case (the socio-ecological transition in the resource system of green spaces across 29 European cities)

Subunits of analysis:
29 cities

Within-case observations:
55 interviews

Three-part qualitative strategic sampling strategy

1) Contrasting sampling:
selection of 40 cities
(in the scope of ROCSET)

2) Selection of 29 cities:
12 EU and two non-EU
(in the scope of the PhD)

3) Purposive sampling:
selection of 55 local experts
(in the scope of ROCSET)

Figure 4.2 Nested mixed methods research design.

Source: own.

in depicting in depth the specific features of the socio-ecological transition in the green spaces resource system by drawing on a total of 29 subunits that altogether deliver 55 within-case observations (interviews) to arrive at a 'kaleidoscopic picture' (Kalff 2016, 88) of the state of the transition in this resource system across European cities and of civil society's role in it. It thus aims at 'provid[ing] an in-depth elucidation of [the case]' (Bryman and Bell 2011, 60) without profoundly analysing one specific city. The decision to merely concentrate on the green spaces resource system and to examine civil society action in depth in this resource system across 29 cities emerged after having conducted cross-case analyses in the scope of ROCSET between the three resource systems under scrutiny. In the data analysis and interpretation phase of the ROCSET project it turned out that, compared to the other two resource systems of water and energy, more civil society action was palpable in the green spaces resource system. Keeping in mind that civil society action was modelled as an independent variable (cf. 1.2), the green spaces resource system can be considered as an influential and crucial case (Gerring 2007, 89–90). The first applies because it shows 'influential configurations of the independent variable' (ibid., 89), and the second because it is, compared to the other two resource systems, 'most … likely to exhibit a given outcome' (ibid.). Thus, this resource system best lends itself to better understanding civil society's role in the socio-ecological transition of European cities and to answering the question under what local conditions and to which extent civil society can be a transition driver at the local level. It is thus chosen for a deeper analysis in the scope of this research.

Second, due to the research design of the ROCSET project, only one to four interviews on green spaces were obtained per city. This limited amount of qualitative data per city does not lend itself to considering each city as a separate case in a multiple-case design and to being able to deliver the knowledge to create 29 in-depth holistic case city case study reports. A second round of data collection in a reduced selection of cities from the 29-city sample would have been necessary to collect sufficient data per city to conduct a case study with each city representing a case. Then, however, valuable data from the excluded cities would have remained unconsidered since in the scope of a one-person PhD project it would not have been possible to conduct a multiple case study with more than three cities. The author's concurrent role as research assistant in ROCSET and PhD candidate, however, would not have allowed in the available time span a second round of data collection to be conducted in a reduced number of cities. It was thus decided to conduct a single case study which allowed, in the given time frame, reanalysis and further analysis of the data in depth in a second round – after the first round in the scope of ROCSET – according to this study's research questions. This way the questions that emerged in the data analysis and interpretation phase of ROCSET could be answered.

4.3.1.2 Sampling strategy

The three-part sampling strategy to arrive at the case with its subunits of analysis and within-case observations is qualitative (cf. Figure 4.2; Mason 2002, 123; Yin 2014, 21, 45–49). It thus does not claim, as random sampling in inductive statistics does, to generate generalisable results in the statistical sense (Mason 2002, 120; Bryman and Bell 2011, 62). It follows a strategic strategy (Mason 2002, 123–5) with 'the aim to produce, through sampling, a relevant range of contexts or phenomena, which will enable you to make strategic and possibly cross-contextual comparisons, and hence build a well-founded argument' (ibid., 123–4), which needs to be transparently presented. Thus, it must be explained how the created sample can be justified and how it relates to the wider population from which it is drawn. In this case the wider population is all civil society, economic, and governmental actors dealing with the issue of sustainability in general and the governance of urban green spaces in particular either in their free time or for work in potentially all European cities (cf. Figure 4.2).

First, in the scope of the ROCSET project 40 cities were selected. This city sample is not random, since ROCSET's aim was to arrive at 'an equal representation of the European population' (Kalff and Sauer 2016, 16), which would not have been possible in the study since 'random selections of a number as small as 40 cities can over- or underrepresent certain areas, regions, or countries' (ibid.). Therefore, cities were selected contrastingly through theoretical reasoning before collecting the data (Kruse 2014, 246, 251) according to population and economic growth indicators (Kalff and Sauer 2016, 23–7). With this strategy, following 'the principle of maximal structural variation' (Kruse 2014, 246, own translation), it was tried to represent the heterogeneity of European cities (Kruse 2014, 58, 254, 636).

Second, the sample for this thesis contains those 29 cities out of the ROCSET sample that deliver interview data referring to the green spaces resource system.[6]

Third, the field researchers selected, based on desktop research and information given by 'keyholders',[7] the interview partners (cf. 4.3.2.1). This strategy can be described as purposive, since interviewees are selected 'on the basis of their likely ability to contribute to theoretical understanding of a subject' (Bryman and Bell 2011, 492). To give insight into the case of the socio-ecological

Table 4.1 Countries in European regions

Country	Region
Denmark, Sweden, United Kingdom	Northern Europe
Czech Republic, Poland, Romania	Eastern Europe
Greece, Italy, Spain, Turkey (Istanbul)	Southern Europe
Austria, France, Germany, Switzerland	Western Europe

Source: United Nations, Department of Economic and Social Affairs, Population Division (2015, 3).

Table 4.2 Twenty-nine cities for data collection

Country	City	Performance average population growth	Performance average GDP growth	Regarded time span
Austria	Innsbruck	A	A	1996–2007
	Linz	U	A	1996–2007
Czech Republic	Jilhava	U	A	1996–2007
Denmark	Aalborg	A	A	2005–7
	Copenhagen	O	U	2005–7
France	Paris	U	A	1996–2007
	Strasbourg	U	U	1996–2007
Germany	Dortmund	S	A	1996–2007
	Potsdam	O	A	1996–2007
	Saarbrücken	S	O	1996–2007
Greece	Larisa	O	U	1996–2007
	Thessaloniki	S	U	1996–2007
Italy	Milano	S	U	1996–2007
	Napoli	S	A	1996–2007
	Roma	S	A	1996–2007
Poland	Krakow	S	A	2001–7
	Lodz	S	A	2001–7
	Lublin	S	U	2001–7
Romania	Sibiu	S	O	2001–7
	Timisoara	S	O	2001–7
Spain	Bilbao	U	O	1996–2007
	Madrid	U	A	1996–2007
Sweden	Goteborg	O	A	1996–2007
	Umea	O	A	1996–2007
Switzerland	Lugano	O	–	1990–2008
	St. Gallen	S	–	1990–2008
Turkey	Istanbul	O	–	
United Kingdom	Glasgow	S	O	1996–2007
	Leeds	U	A	1996–2007

Source: adapted from Kalff and Sauer 2016, 28.

Notes
O: overperformer; U: underperformer; A: close to average; S: shrinking city; –: no data available.

transition in the green spaces resource system across 29 European cities, the number of 55 interviews should be considered to be sufficient since it is 'large enough to make meaningful comparisons in relation to [the] … research questions, but not so large as to become so diffuse that a detailed and nuanced focus on something in particular becomes impossible' (Mason 2002, 136). As in the

Figure 4.3 Map of 29 selected cities.
Source: own.

two previous sampling parts to arrive at the final number of cities, in this part a random sampling was neither feasible nor desirable, since the aim of the actors' selection process was to gain insight into local experts' views on the process and the current state of the socio-ecological transition of the green spaces resource system in the respective city, assuming that these actors would also be able to best report on the city's situation (Littig 2011, 1343). Random sampling is excluded since experts are already drawn from a reduced population, which refers to persons in local governmental, economic, and civil society institutions (Kalff and Sauer 2016, 30–2). The selected interviewees can be considered as true experts in the field of local transition in the green spaces resource system (Bogner and Menz 2009, 67–74; Meuser and Nagel 2009, 37–51). Experts are understood in this thesis as people serving as a '*source of special knowledge about the social facts of the case to be researched*'[8] (Gläser and Laudel 2010, 12, own translation). This definition necessitates that experts are immediately involved in local sustainability issues. Chosen experts hold key positions within the local authority, the economic sector, and civil society. Sustainability questions are either part of their daily job (for politicians, administrative staff, economic actors, and some civil society actors), or they engage with the topic in their free time (most civil society actors).[9] The question in the interview guide 'To what extent are you involved in sustainability issues in [name of the city]?' served as a control question to check whether the chosen actor truly was considered to be an expert in local sustainability issues. No interviewees had problems in explaining their connection to the local sustainability topic in general or to the local green spaces resource system specifically (Kalff and Sauer 2016, 36).

Before going to the cities, the field researchers conducted desktop research and contacted the keyholders to compile a preliminary list of actors according to the field research design following specific rules for the type of actors to be contacted (cf. Table 4.3).[10] Only in a small number of cases where it proved unfeasible to define an actor before going to the city and also in cases when the originally defined actor was not available any more when the field research had already started was the actor determined only when already in the city, sometimes with the support of other actors (snowball system). The final actors list was then approved by the project team before conducting the interviews. This combined way of selection ensured that chosen local interviewees, especially civil society actors, were very often known local personalities of the local 'sustainability scene' with a rich knowledge of (historical) local transition processes, and almost all of them deal, either in their job or in voluntary work, with sustainability issues on a regular, often day-to-day basis. The sampling strategy (4.3.1.2) tried to arrive at a non-biased sample, on both the city and the actor level, thus ensuring that the cities and actors selected represent the whole range of European cities and possible actors from the three sectors (Lewis and Ritchie 2003, 272, 284). As pointed out by Kalff and Sauer (2016, 14–15), interviewing actors from different sectors implies getting diverse, sometimes contradicting answers for the same city. All these narrations are to be taken seriously as examples/illustrations of processes, practices, and dynamics in the local arena. At a later stage in the data analysis phase, they need to be presented with the quantitative data and the secondary material to deliver a coherent narrative/description of the socio-ecological transition in the green spaces resource system across 29 European cities.

4.3.2 Sample

This subsection details the used methods of data collection and the kind of data collected.

4.3.2.1 Methods of data collection

In the scope of the ROCSET project, 15 field researchers were recruited to collect data in 40 cities in 14 countries. In order to increase the research's quality criteria of objectivity, reliability, and validity, before collecting the data from June to October 2013, information on the project's research aims and field research design, especially on the selection procedure for the local actors (cf. Table 4.3) and the specific type of data to be collected was presented in a manual and deepened in a two-day workshop (Arthur and Nazroo 2003, 133). Here, the field researchers were also trained on using the interview guide in role plays (Flick 2009, 172, 386).

This briefing was considered to be necessary due to the complexity of the data collection process (Arthur and Nazroo 2003, 133–4) with a large amount of quantitative and qualitative data in different languages to be collected by different field researchers and a predefined selection procedure of single actors to be applied consistently across all cities. It was necessary to ensure that all field researchers contributing to the case study entered the field with the same state of knowledge (Yin 2014, 79–82) on the aims of the study, the field research design, and the specific steps to be taken in the field. Despite these precautions interviewer effects cannot be totally eliminated. Every interviewer has a unique way of asking questions, of explaining the research's aim, and of using mime and gesture. This effect is potentially even stronger in a multilingual research field (cf. 4.3.2.1). Furthermore, knowledge on the respective city and the specific resource system as well as knowledge about and experience in conducting qualitative interviews and collecting quantitative data varies across the 15 researchers. Apart from training the field researchers, interviewer effects were also tried to be minimised by choosing field researchers with experience in collecting qualitative and quantitative data.

Reliability during the data collection process was increased in the following ways. To provide for the highest possible degree of systematic, comprehensive, and consistent data collection and subsequent analysis, in the phase of data collection, the manual was guiding the field researchers on what kind of data was to be collected in what way. Moreover, information on actors to be interviewed had to be registered in the actors list and any arising issue with importance to steps of the research process was to be included in the personal reports. Not only before entering the cities but also while working there, the field researchers regularly reported to the project team to ensure a smooth process and quick support in case of locally emerging problems. From the beginning of the data analysis phase a case study database was set up (Yin 2014, 45) including all data collected. Despite the diversity and large amount of data to be collected, in the vast majority of cities data could be collected smoothly without delay.

Before starting the audio recorder and the interview and/or the questionnaire, interviewees were informed about the project and questions could be asked. After this clarification phase, '*informed consent*' (Christians 2005, 65) was obtained by the participants about the exclusive and anonymous use of the data for research purposes and in the case of the interview for obtaining the permission for registration. Due to the length and complexity of the questionnaire, which took around one hour to be filled in, not only were the interviews conducted in direct meetings with the actors but also the questionnaire was filled in with the field researcher present to guarantee the right understanding of the questions.[11] This way a very high return rate for both quantitative and qualitative data was achieved (Kalff and Sauer 2016, 30).

Since interviews were conducted in the local language,[12] the field researchers translated the interview guide and the questionnaire from English into the respective language and after having collected the data, delivered both the interview transcript in the original language and the translated English version. Collecting interviews in the local language was deemed necessary to ensure that respondents entirely understood the questions and were able to express themselves fully without meeting language barriers (Enzenhofer and Resch 2011), and thus to reach a high level of reliability and validity of the data. However, due to translation challenges, working in a multilingual research field with different researchers involved also bears the risk of decreasing the quality criteria of objectivity, reliability, and validity. Fifteen field researchers were involved in first translating the interview guide and the questionnaire from English into the local language, then transcribing interviews in the local language[13] and finally translating the transcripts into English. Despite the initial briefing, every researcher pursues an individual way of conducting the interview and this individuality increases further if several different local languages are used instead of English everywhere. Furthermore, transcription and translation work cannot be completely standardised, since working with language in general is a complex task and transferring content from one language to the other an even more complex one. So the fact that several researchers were involved in the translation process (Inhetveen 2012, 30), that a dozen different languages were the starting point for translation, and that, even when translating only from one language to the other, 'translating opens up a range of possibilities, and … the translator has to make decisions between divergent, but equally eligible options' (ibid., 34) makes working with multilingual data a challenging task. This bears the risk of not getting every meaning across as it was originally meant, of producing translation mistakes, and, thus, of a change or loss in meaning. Translating implies linguistic and sociocultural challenges. The translator can be faced with terms to translate for which no equivalent exists in the other language or with grammatical structures that equally pose translation difficulty. The translation of proverbs and idioms is especially challenging since socio-historical context knowledge on both languages must be accessed to arrive at a valid translation (Bryman and Bell 2011, 488). Translation 'is therefore a sense-making process that involves the translator's knowledge, social background, and personal experience' (ibid.). To increase reliability and validity of the translated qualitative data, the manual provided field researchers with some basic transcription rules. A word-by-word transcription was required. However, repetitions and word fillers like 'erm', as well as pause indications, gestures, mimes, or other utterances such as laughter or other non-verbal expressions of feelings were generally not transcribed. Only if the field researchers considered for example a pause or a non-verbal expression as important for better understanding the content of the interview, they were free to transcribe accordingly. Also, questions related to transcription and translation were discussed in the briefing. Furthermore, the field researchers were asked to complete the first transcription and corresponding translation as soon as possible after having conducted the interview to send it to the research team which checked whether the interview had been transcribed and translated according to the rules and gave feedback to the field researchers, this way facilitating data analysis later. Last, the research team carried out spot checks of comparing the original transcript to the translated English version. The 'local language' strategy was chosen because the risk of decreased reliability and validity was deemed to be higher if all the research had been conducted in English. Also, remembering the socio-scientific nature of the study and the research's aim of giving insight into the state of the socio-ecological transition in the green spaces resource system from the actors' perspective, it was not necessary to capture underlying moods or atmospheres but the mere semantics of the interviews (Kalff and Sauer 2016, 37). For the topic under question and the concomitant research questions a relatively simple transcription system is sufficient (Flick 2009, 299–300; Kuckartz 2014, 136). Since the content is to the fore (Flick 2009, 299–300; Mayring 2010b, 55) with the language merely seen as the device to transmit it, neither a narrow transcription nor a subsequent in-depth analysis and interpretation are required, as would have been necessary for a linguistic or conversation analysis or a psychological inquiry or biographical study.[14]

Concerning the quantitative data, a high degree of reliability and validity throughout the translation process was tried to be upheld by sending the English questionnaire to the field researchers before the briefing so that they could familiarise themselves with its content and ask questions in the briefing. Furthermore, the research team was available via email in the event of any questions in the translation phase, and it also checked translated questionnaires before the field research started.[15] To arrive at a close and valid translation of the English questionnaire, this strategy was deemed necessary due to the complexity and length of the questionnaire.

4.3.2.2 *Qualitative data: expert interviews*

For carving out the knowledge of local experts, it is common to draw on individual interviews which are mostly based on an interview guide (Gläser and Laudel 2010, 43, 111). In fact, interviews were guideline based, following a semi-structured interview guide which was pre-tested before the briefing (Gläser and Laudel 2010, 107, 150; Flick 2014, 482) and adapted accordingly. The sample of 55 interviews consists of one to four interviews per city and stems from 29 cities from all four European regions – 14 countries in total (cf. Figure 4.2, Tables 4.1 and 4.2). All but two cities belong to the EU. Regarding the three sectors (politics/administration, economy, civil society), four interviews with politicians and three with civil servants, thus 13 per cent, were conducted. Twenty-one interviews stem from the economic sector (38 per cent), and the majority (27, thus 49 per cent) were obtained from civil society respondents (cf. Table 4.4). In all three sectors fewer women than men were interviewed (69 per cent male and 31 per cent female respondents).

The interview length stretched from 18 to 114 minutes with an average duration of 56 minutes. The interviews aimed at capturing the actor's individual

Table 4.3 List of actors relevant to the green spaces resource system

Actor	Profession	Conducted inquiry
1	Politician with a particular interest in sustainability (mayor for smaller cities).	Interview
2	Head of environmental/sustainability department (or other department dealing with environmental issues or sustainability).	Interview
3	A representative of the private sector with particular relevance to the issue of sustainability. This could be from the local chamber of commerce of a major business in the city.	Interview, questionnaire
4	A civil society representative (or leader of bottom-up initiatives, NGO, etc.).	Interview, questionnaire
5	Director/manager of urban planning department (or department in charge of green spaces).	Questionnaire
6	A civil society representative (or leader of bottom-up initiatives, NGO, etc.).	Questionnaire
7	A representative of the private sector with particular relevance to the issue of green spaces (forest owners, park manager, local chamber of commerce, etc.).	Questionnaire

Source: adapted from Kalff and Sauer 2016, 31.

view and estimation of the transition in the green spaces resource system in the respective city.[16] To this end, in the semi-structured interview guide questions were clustered according to the ROCSET research questions (cf. 4.2). Although the wording and the order of the questions in the guide were not mandatory and additional questions could be asked apart from the compulsory ones (Gläser and Laudel 2010, 42), all questions should be asked where possible in the given order to not let the interviewer forget to pose a question and to simplify comparability and thus facilitate later data analysis. Questions in brackets were additional deepening questions that had to be asked if the respondent had not automatically already answered them in the previous more general question.

It is potentially problematic to use the interview guide designed according to the ROCSET research questions also for this research. In the data analysis phase of the ROCSET project, three major types of civil society action became evident that deserved a deeper analysis. Also, as explained above (cf. 4.3.1.1), due to time constraints it was not possible to obtain further data, which would have allowed the construction of a new interview guide closely adapted to this project's research questions. However, this is not considered to be a major caveat of this study, since the data obtained in the scope of ROCSET with the present interview guide was rich enough and had not yet been fully exploited in the scope of ROCSET, justifying a second round of analysis in the scope of this study. As detailed below (cf. 4.3.3.1), the data was reanalysed including those interview questions (on personal involvement and motivation) that were, since

Table 4.4 Interview distribution across cities and sectors

Country	City	Politics (P) or Administration (A)	Economy (E)	Civil society (C)
Austria	Innsbruck	–	E	–
	Linz	–	E	C
Czech Republic	Jilhava	–	E	C
Denmark	Aalborg	–	–	C
	Copenhagen	A	E	C
France	Paris	–	E	C
	Strasbourg	–	–	C
Germany	Dortmund	–	–	C
	Potsdam	–	E	C
	Saarbrücken	–	E	C
Greece	Larisa	–	E	C
	Thessaloniki	–	E	C
Italy	Milano	–	E	C
	Napoli	–	E	C
	Roma	P	–	–
Poland	Krakow	P/A	E	C
	Lodz	–	E	C
	Lublin	P	–	C
Romania	Sibiu	A	E	C
	Timisoara	–	E	C
Spain	Bilbao	–	E	C
	Madrid	–	E	C
Sweden	Goteborg	–	E	C
	Umea	–	E	–
Switzerland	Lugano	–	E	C
	St. Gallen	–	–	C
Turkey	Istanbul	P	–	C
United Kingdom	Glasgow	–	E	C
	Leeds	–	E	C

Source: own.

not relevant to answering the ROCSET research questions, not considered in the first analysis round.

4.3.2.3 *Quantitative data: questionnaires*

Although the focus of data analysis lies on the qualitative interview case study data (cf. 4.3.2.2), the quantitative data is additionally used in a mixed methods approach to cross-check findings (cf. 4.3.3.3). The quantitative data is not part of the case study but draws from the sample of all 40 cities of the ROCSET project (cf. Figure 4.2). It would be problematic to compare qualitative findings of a smaller sample of 29 cities to a bigger quantitative one of 40 cities if the focus on analysis was equally strong for both data types. Yet, since the quantitative data is only used additionally, this potential caveat is negligible. However, when cross-checking the qualitative with the quantitative data it needs to be kept in mind that the answers obtained for the overall quantitative sample might vary in comparison to a smaller sample of just 29 cities.

Altogether 167 questionnaires from 40 cities were collected. Forty-one questionnaires (24 per cent) were filled in by administrative actors and 63 (38 per cent) each by economic and civil society actors. Most actors who were interviewed also filled in a questionnaire.[17] The rest of the quantitative data was obtained from further actors identified by the field researcher (cf. Table 4.5).

4.3.2.4 Secondary data: documents

To supplement the qualitative and quantitative primary data, documents as secondary data were used. According to Flick (2014, 360) documents 'can be a very instructive addition to interviews' and 'should be seen as a way of contextualizing information' (ibid., 357). Here, 'solicited documents' (Flick 2009, 256) were drawn on; thus material was deliberately produced for the research. This refers to two types of data. First, there are 29 'case study' reports – one per city, written by the field researchers, that portray the state of the socio-ecological transition for the city with a section on characteristics of the green spaces resource system through the eyes of the respective field researcher.[18] The reports are thus based on the field researcher's on-the-spot experience and their incorporation of a wide array of sources from desktop research before and after the field phase, such as official reports, newspaper articles, and websites on the respective city.

Second, for each city a personal report was produced by the field researchers in which they were supposed to reflect on the field research and to cite met challenges and problems in the different steps of the field research in order to facilitate later data analysis and interpretation and to increase its validity and reliability.

4.3.3 Data analysis and interpretation

This subsection explains how the qualitative and quantitative data was analysed and how it was triangulated for interpretation.

4.3.3.1 Qualitative content analysis

The interviews were analysed drawing on qualitative content analysis. Grounded theory was not an option for the following reasons. The ROCSET research design does not aim at generating theory from the data but rather tested whether Ostrom's theory on collective action was applicable to urban resource systems (Kalff and Sauer 2016, 14). To answer the ROCSET research questions, the research design relies on a one-time round of field research and a predefined semi-structured interview guide. Data generated this way can hardly be analysed with grounded theory, which requires a less narrow and more open approach with multiple rounds of data collection in the cities as well as a more open interview guide. However, such an approach would not have been feasible within the given time and financial frame of ROCSET. Several visits would have required an extension of the field work time and field researchers would have had to be trained more intensively to cope with a more open interview guide. Meeting the qualitative research criteria of reliability, validity, and objectivity would have become even more difficult due to the fact that the overall ROCSET study involved 167 interviews from 40 cities being held by 15 different field researchers. To be more easily able to compare data collected by a team of researchers in 40 different places, the research design needed to be comparatively highly structured 'to ensure some consistency in approaches and issues covered' (Arthur and Nazroo 2003, 111). Working with the data obtained as described, a content analysis approach thus makes more sense and also matches better with regard to this study's research questions. The aim of this study was to get a 'surface' knowledge from the local experts' perspective on transition processes going on in the green spaces resource system in several European cities. The research is not interested in carving out information on the actors' personality or the deep structures of the interviews, for which a grounded theory approach would have been more apt.

Qualitative content analysis is drawn on, since it is a way of generalisingly and systematically extracting information from large amounts of texts and processing this information independently from the source text (Gläser and Laudel 2010, 46; Mayring 2010a, 607). This way it is possible to reduce the amount of text (Flick 2014, 435) while maintaining the information relevant for answering the research questions. The method aims at the content that is to be found on the 'surface of … [the] text' (ibid.). Contrary to grounded theory, it does not aim at bringing to light 'the deep structures of the text'[19] (Mayring 2010a, 607, own translation). The major instrument to conduct qualitative content analysis is the category system, which is developed before the data is analysed (Gläser and Laudel 2010, 47; Kuckartz 2010, 93; Mayring 2010b, 49, 59). Depending on the methodological approach used, the terms 'code' and 'category' are used as key concepts (Kuckartz 2010, 61). This thesis sticks to the term 'category', which designates an analytical identifier for a central concept (Kruse 2014, 387–8; Kuckartz 2010, 57, 59, 198). The building of categories and the assigning of text passages to them (coding) (Kuckartz 2010, 23; Flick 2014, 373) makes comparing the information stemming from a large number of interviews easier (Flick 2014, 435). Coding refers to the complex process of matching text segments representing 'semantic units of meaning'[20] (Kuckartz 2010, 63, own translation) that are relevant to answering the research questions with a 'category'.

The data set consisting of 55 qualitative semi-structured interviews is a 'cross-sectional … analysis [approach which] implies … making comparisons across the whole … data set, on certain specific themes' (Mason 2002, 199). Analysis was facilitated and also made more transparent to increase internal validity by the use of the qualitative data analysis software MaxQDA (version 11) with which a project database was created containing all interviews from the three resource systems.[21] MaxQDA allows the creation of 'a hierarchical code system with up to ten levels' (Flick 2014, 469) and to extract all text segments that have been coded with one category (Kuckartz 2010, 12, 25; Mayring 2010b, 113). Data analysis showed a great variety and even contradicting statements of different actors coming from different sectors in the same city, which will be shown in the empirical findings section.

4.3.3.2 *Quantitative analysis and analysis of secondary data*

The data from the questionnaire was exclusively analysed in the scope of the ROCSET project.[22] The raw data was inserted by each field researcher into an online tool. Spot checks were conducted to see whether the inserted data into this tool matched the original paper version of the questionnaire. The first two sections of the questionnaire, referring to the respondents' socioeconomic background and their assessment of what a future strategy on sustainability for the respective city should look like, were analysed jointly with the questionnaires for the resource systems of energy and water. The remaining sections specifically refer to the green spaces resource system. For this part, with the help of the data analysis and statistical software STATA (version 13),[23] an analysis for each question was produced, also paying attention to regional (cf. Table 4.1) and sector differences, which was compiled in a single Word document. This document was taken as a basis by the author for data triangulation (cf. 4.3.3.3).

Additional to the primary qualitative and quantitative data, secondary data, more specifically solicited documents, was drawn on. The field researchers, based on a template, had to provide the research team with a general report for each city incorporating their desktop research work in the run-up and aftermath of the field research and the experiences and collected documents from the cities during the field research. The report consists of a general section as well as a specific one for each resource system, depicting the state of the socio-ecological transition of the city through the eyes of the respective field researcher (cf. Garzillo and Ulrich 2015). An evaluation grid was elaborated to assess the degree of civil society action for each city and to get a general feeling of the dynamics going on in each city (Table 4.5). Yet, since the focus of analysis does not lie on the individual city (cf. 4.3.1.1), this data is only used additionally to cross-check results from the interviews.

4.3.3.3 *Triangulation – 'mixed methods'*

Figure 4.2 visualises the study's nested mixed methods research design, also in relation to the ROCSET project, from which the data was taken. A mixed methods study can be defined as 'a single study embracing both qualitative and

Table 4.5 Evaluation grid on civil society action per city

[Name of city] – features	Scale
Civil society action Citizens involved in the governance of urban green spaces?	Less active civil society–active civil society–very active civil society Citizens hardly involved–citizens could be more involved–citizens involved
Overview of eco-social strategies/activities/actions[1] that aim at improving sustainability locally	No strategies/actions–no strategies/very few actions–few strategies/action–some strategies/actions–numerous strategies/actions
Cooperation level between civil society, local authority, and local economy in governing green spaces (any conflicts/obstacles/need for clarification?)	High–middle–low–very low
(Local) policy framework facilitates–fosters/hinders civil society action or is neutral?	Fosters–neutral–hinders
Local decision-making autonomy from higher governance units or external decision makers?[2]	High–middle–low–very low
Private[3]/public/private–public partnerships?	
Official/statistical unemployment rate[4]	

Source: own.

Notes
1 Initiated by the local authority (not necessarily with civil society involvement) or new institutional arrangements/mixed forms of state, market, and civil society.
2 For example private investors.
3 Including, besides commercially private forms, democratically citizen-controlled private forms of the 'third sector' (for example cooperatives, local employment initiatives).
4 The data contained in the case study reports is hardly comparable since no uniform data from one international organisation is available for the city level. Data stems from local, regional, or national sources, applying different methods in measuring official unemployment. This results in huge discrepancies, for example the unemployment rate in 2012 in Dortmund was 12.9 per cent (Stadt Dortmund, Dortmunder Systemhaus – Bereich Statistik 2013, 11), in Timișoara 1.03 per cent (Timișoara City Hall 2013, 16). Apart from providing data on the national level (e.g. monthly updates: http://europa.eu/rapid/press-release_STAT-14-4_en.htm [30 July 2016], Eurostat provides data on the regional level (http://appsso.eurostat.ec.europa.eu/nui/show.do?dataset=lfst_r_lfu3rt &lang=en [30 July 2016] and on the city level in the urban audit database (http://appsso.eurostat. ec.europa.eu/nui/submitViewTableAction.do [30 July 2016], yet not all 29 cities are covered.

quantitative components, with a case study potentially being one of the components' (Yin 2014, 239). The primary focus of this study lies on the in-depth single case study on the green spaces resource system which draws on two types of qualitative data (interviews and documents) while being embedded in and encompassed by 'a larger, mixed methods study' (ibid., 193; cf. also Yin 2006, 44–5) providing 'a more superficial analysis conducted on a larger sample'

(Gerring 2007, 22). The latter refers to the quantitative data stemming from respondents from 40 cities. Mixed methods analysis allows different types of data analysis to be combined. Here two qualitative analysis types are combined with one quantitative one. As far as the time sequence is concerned, qualitative and quantitative data are collected simultaneously and are then also analysed simultaneously. This is valid for the first round of data analysis within the ROCSET project. The second round of qualitative data analysis for this study comes later and is thus conducted sequentially with regard to the quantitative analysis from the first round. Referring to the degree of interaction between the two different data types, they were analysed separately according to the respective research paradigm so as to produce three different sets of data analysis outcome. Results from all analysis strands could then be triangulated (Yin 2014, 193).

Notes

1 'The Role of Regions in the Envisaged Socio-Ecological Transition', www.foreurope. eu/index.php?id=794 [28 July 2016].
2 Seventh Framework Programme of the Directorate-General for Research and Innovation of the European Commission.
3 This includes answers from local politicians and civil servants from the local authority.
4 For a detailed description of the ROCSET research strategy and design, including the choice of the city sample and the selection of the interviewees, cf. Kalff and Sauer (2016, 13–32).
5 Gerring (2007, 215) delineates the observational from the experimental one by stating that in the first 'the causal factor of interest is not manipulated by the researcher'. However, even in an observational design absolute objectivity is impossible.
6 The field researchers were asked to choose between putting the research focus on either the resource system of water or green spaces for each city according to which resource system they consider to be more relevant for the socio-ecological transition in the respective city. The interview with actors 3 and 4 would then focus on either green spaces or water, while interviews with actors 1 and 2 should focus on energy (cf. Table 4.3). However, respondents were free to choose another focus, if they felt more at ease speaking about that focus. This way interview data on green spaces from 29 cities was obtained which however is not equally divided between the three sectors politics/administration, economy, and civil society (cf. 4.3.2.2).
7 A 'keyholder' per city, an employee of the city administration, served as the field researcher's contact person in the respective city to help with identifying and contacting appropriate interview and questionnaire partners in case a first list of actors could not be easily compiled by the field researcher (Kalff and Sauer 2016, 16).
8 Gläser and Laudel (2010); ©Springer, with permission of Springer.
9 This is a schematic description referring to the required actors' selection process (cf. Table 4.3). In fact, in the course of the interview it turned out that many actors who were chosen for their professional dealing with sustainability issues were also active for it in their free time and vice versa.
10 Actually, the field research design and consequently the list of actors are more complex than depicted in Table 4.3 due to the fact that not only data on the green spaces resource system but also data on energy and water was collected. Since this study concentrates on the green spaces resource system and exclusively uses the data from this system, only the parts of the field research design relevant to this are

presented. For a complete overview of the field research design, cf. Kalff and Sauer (2016, 13–38).

11 In a very limited number of cases, due to time constraints of the respondent, the questionnaire was not filled in in a face-to-face situation but beforehand. Open questions could still be clarified when collecting the questionnaires in the majority of these cases. For the rest, ambiguities could be clarified via email or phone.

12 'Local' here implies that data from the same country was collected in different languages, if the local language differs from city to city (Switzerland). Thus, interviews were conducted in 12 different languages (German, Czech, Danish, French, Greek, Italian, Polish, Romanian, Spanish, Swedish, Turkish, and English) (cf. 4.4).

13 For transcription the open source software 'Express Scribe Free' (http://download. cnet.com/Express-Scribe-Free/3000–7239_4–10060252.html [28 July 2016] was used by the author and by almost all other field researchers.

14 Also, the latter two would probably have drawn on narrative interviews instead of semi-structured ones.

15 This refers to those transcripts that were translated into languages at least one member of the research team masters.

16 The interviewees were asked about their personal involvement in local sustainability matters and their motivation for becoming involved, about challenges to urban sustainable development, and about defining factors, actions, and actors for urban sustainability. The interview guide then continues with a section specific to the green spaces resource system. They were questioned about the state of local resources, access and participation in local resource governance, lessons learned from local resource governance, room for local autonomy, room for self-governance, strategic sustainability goals, policy instruments, and rules missing or to be changed.

17 Political actors (cf. Table 4.3) were exempted from filling in the questionnaire, which turned out to be a wise decision due to the questionnaire's complexity and length and the actors' restricted time frame.

18 The reports (Garzillo and Ulrich 2015; cf. 4.3.2.4) cannot be considered to be case study reports resulting from an in-depth case study as for example described in Yin (2014, 177–206). Yet, they are very useful to cross-check hypotheses in the phase of data interpretation. They contain a general city profile, providing background information, giving factual data on size, population, climate, special characteristics, etc., and providing information on basic government/administrative structure as well as on economic conditions (growth trend, key businesses and industries, employment, etc.). Furthermore, local lifestyle and key challenges and trends (economic, social, and environmental) are addressed. Apart from that, a resource-system-specific synthesis for water, energy, and green spaces refers to availability, affordability, and consumption levels, key issues, key actors/partnerships, and key actions/measures/initiatives. Governance, specifically multi-level governance (province, national, EU), and citizen participation and bottom-up action is also looked into. Finally, trends and challenges for the future are outlined.

19 Mayring (2010a); ©Springer, with permission of Springer.

20 Kuckartz (2010); ©Springer, with permission of Springer.

21 This project database was created by Yannick Kalff.

22 In the ROCSET project, the author was responsible for the analysis of the qualitative data for the green spaces resource system. Stephanie Barnebeck simultaneously analysed the corresponding quantitative data.

23 For a detailed description of the quantitative data methods, cf. Kalff and Sauer (2016, 33–4).

References

Arthur, Sue and James Nazroo. 2003. 'Designing fieldwork strategies and materials'. In *Qualitative research practice: A guide for social science students and researchers*, eds Jane Ritchie and Jane Lewis, 109–37. London, Thousand Oaks CA: Sage.

Bogner, Alexander and Wolfgang Menz. 2009. 'Das theoriegenerierende Experteninterview: Erkenntnisinteresse, Wissensformen, Interaktion'. In *Experteninterviews: Theorien, Methoden, Anwendungsfelder*, 3rd edn, eds Alexander Bogner, Beate Littig, and Wolfgang Menz, 61–98. Wiesbaden: VS Verlag für Sozialwissenschaften.

Bryman, Alan and Emma Bell. 2011. *Business research methods*, 3rd edn. Oxford: Oxford University Press.

Christians, Clifford G. 2005. 'Ethics and politics in qualitative research'. In *The SAGE handbook of qualitative research*, eds Norman K. Denzin and Yvonna S. Lincoln, 139–64. Thousand Oaks CA, London, New Delhi: Sage.

Enzenhofer, Edith and Katharina Resch. 'Übersetzungsprozesse und deren Qualitätssicherung in der qualitativen Sozialforschung'. *Forum: Qualitative Social Research*, 12(2): Art. 10. www.qualitative-research.net/index.php/fqs/article/view/1652/3177 [27 August 2016].

Flick, Uwe. 2009. *An introduction to qualitative research*, 4th edn. Los Angeles CA: Sage.

Flick, Uwe. 2014. *An introduction to qualitative research*. Los Angeles CA, London, New Delhi, Singapore, Washington DC: Sage.

Garzillo, Cristina and Peter Ulrich, eds. 2015. 'WWWforEurope, Annex to MS94: Compilation of case study reports. A compendium of case study reports from 40 cities in 14 European countries'. Work Package 501 MS94: 'Final draft report', 94th edn. www.foreurope.eu/fileadmin/documents/pdf/Workingpapers/WWWforEurope_WPS_no094_MS94_Annex.pdf [27 August 2016].

Gerring, John. 2007. *Case study research: Principles and practices*. New York: Cambridge University Press.

Gläser, Jochen and Grit Laudel. 2010. *Experteninterviews und qualitative Inhaltsanalyse: Als Instrumente rekonstruierender Untersuchungen*, 4th edn. Wiesbaden: VS Verlag für Sozialwissenschaften.

Inhetveen, Katharina. 2012. 'Translation challenges: Qualitative interviewing in a multilingual field'. *Qualitative Sociology Review*, 8(2): 28–45. www.qualitativesociology review.org/ENG/Volume22/QSR_8_2_Inhetveen.pdf [27 August 2016].

Kalff, Yannick. 2016. 'Socio-ecological transitions in the energy system: The local government view'. In *Cities in transition: Social innovation for Europe's urban sustainability*, eds Thomas Sauer, Cristina Garzillo, and Susanne Elsen, 59–92. Abingdon/New York: Routledge.

Kalff, Yannick and Thomas Sauer. 2016. 'Selecting forty cities'. In *Cities in transition: Social innovation for Europe's urban sustainability*, eds Thomas Sauer, Cristina Garzillo, and Susanne Elsen, 13–38. Abingdon/New York: Routledge.

Kruse, Jan. 2014. *Grundlagentexte Methoden, Qualitative Interviewforschung: Ein integrativer Ansatz*. Weinheim: Beltz Juventa.

Kuckartz, Udo. 2010. *Einführung in die computergestützte Analyse qualitativer Daten*, 3rd edn. Wiesbaden: VS Verlag für Sozialwissenschaften.

Kuckartz, Udo. 2014. *Qualitative Inhaltsanalyse: Methoden, Praxis, Computerunterstützung*, 2nd edn. Weinheim: Beltz Juventa.

Lewis, Jane and Jane Ritchie. 2003. 'Generalising from qualitative research'. In *Qualitative research practice: A guide for social science students and researchers*, eds Jane Ritchie and Jane Lewis, 263–85. London, Thousand Oaks CA: Sage.

Littig, Beate. 2011. 'Interviews, expert'. In *International encyclopedia of political science*, eds Bertrand Badie, Dirk Berg-Schlosser, and Leonardo Morlino, 1343–6. London, Thousand Oaks CA, New Delhi: Sage.

Mason, Jennifer. 2002. *Qualitative researching*. London, Thousand Oaks CA, New Delhi: Sage.

Mayring, Philipp. 2010a. 'Qualitative Inhaltsanalyse'. In *Handbuch Qualitative Forschung in der Psychologie*, 1st edn, eds Günter Mey and Katja Mruck, 601–13. Wiesbaden: VS Verlag für Sozialwissenschaften.

Mayring, Philipp. 2010b. *Beltz Pädagogik, Qualitative Inhaltsanalyse: Grundlagen und Techniken*, 11th edn. Weinheim: Beltz.

Meuser, Michael and Ulrike Nagel. 2009. 'Experteninterview und der Wandel der Wissensproduktion'. In *Experteninterviews: Theorien, Methoden, Anwendungsfelder*, 3rd edn, eds Alexander Bogner, Beate Littig, and Wolfgang Menz, 35–60. Wiesbaden: VS Verlag für Sozialwissenschaften.

Poteete, Amy R., Marco A. Janssen, and Elinor Ostrom. 2010. *Working together: Collective action, the commons, and multiple methods in practice*. Princeton, NJ: Princeton University Press.

Sauer, Thomas. 2012a. 'Elemente einer kontextuellen Ökonomie der Nachhaltigkeit: Der Beitrag Elinor Ostroms'. In *Ökonomie der Nachhaltigkeit: Grundlagen, Indikatoren, Strategien*, ed. Thomas Sauer, 135–60. Marburg: Metropolis.

Sauer, Thomas. 2016. 'Patterns of change: A general model of socio-ecological transition'. In *Cities in transition: Social innovation for Europe's urban sustainability*, eds Thomas Sauer, Cristina Garzillo, and Susanne Elsen, 39–58. Abingdon/New York: Routledge.

Stadt Dortmund, Dortmunder Systemhaus – Bereich Statistik, ed. 2013. *Jahresbericht Dortmunder Statistik 2013 Bevölkerung*. Dortmund.

Timişoara City Hall. 2013. 'STAREA ECONOMICĂ, SOCIALĂ ŞI DE MEDIU A MUNICIPIULUI TIMIŞOARA (Economic, Social and Environmental Situation of Timişoara Municipality)'. www.primariatm.ro/uploads/files/PID/starea_economica_2013.pdf [8 December 2016].

United Nations, Department of Economic and Social Affairs, Population Division. 2015. World urbanization prospects: The 2015 Revision. Classification of countries by major area and region of the world. https://esa.un.org/unpd/wpp/General/Files/Definition_of_Regions.pdf [8 December 2016].

Yin, Robert K. 2006. 'Mixed methods research: Are the methods genuinely integrated or merely parallel?' *Research in the Schools*, 13(1): 41–7.

Yin, Robert K. 2014. *Case study research: Design and methods*, 5th edn. Los Angeles CA, London, New Delhi, Singapore, Washington DC: Sage.

5 Urban spaces–green spaces, and observed socio-ecological transition

Urban green spaces are

> public green spaces located in urban areas, mainly covered by vegetation (as opposed to other open spaces) which are directly used for active or passive recreation, or indirectly used by virtue of their positive influence on the urban environment, accessible to citizens, serving the diverse needs of citizens and thus enhancing the quality of life in cities or urban regions.
>
> (URGE-Team 2004, 13)

They are relevant for cities due to their interconnected ecological, social, and economic benefits. By their mitigation and adaptation capacities, urban green spaces play an important role in building climate-resilient cities, and they also contribute to biodiversity conservation. They are spaces for recreation and can even be used productively, creating new employment options. Despite these important functions, continuing urbanisation is one of the most severe risk factors threatening their existence. This means that the pressure on urban green spaces will further increase, making the urban environment a field of action for civil society actors trying to obtain changes in the governance of green spaces.

While Section 5.1 explains the relevance of cities for the socio-ecological transition, Section 5.2 examines why green spaces are essential for cities and in what way they are threatened, and Section 5.3 explores how they can become spaces of civil society action.[1]

5.1 The relevance of cities for the socio-ecological transition

Cities can be described as places 'where the opportunities and threats to sustainable development come together' (EC 2015, 1). Cities have largely contributed to climate change, and it is in cities that major actions for climate change mitigation and adaptation must take effect. Worldwide, this century will be marked by urbanisation. Europe already has an urbanisation rate of 73 per cent with a rising trend (UNESA 2014, 1), reaching around 80 per cent by 2020 (Vancutsem 2008, 4). Around 75 per cent of greenhouse gas production emanates from cities, while they occupy only about 2 per cent of the global land area. Thus, cities are crucial for the success of the socio-ecological transition due to ongoing worldwide urbanisation and connected rising energy demand. These urbanisation processes must be steered into the direction of low-carbon cities, which is even more difficult, since no learning model for the perfect low-carbon country or city exists so far (WBGU 2011, 3, 83).

Historically, the city has been considered the manifest of modernity. Having arrived at the crisis of modernity with a necessary concomitant critical analysis of the limits of growth, the city is a major playing field. Due to increasing urbanisation, cities will be even more important and gain more political power with concomitant possibilities to determine the path to sustainability. 'Cities are characterised by the huge complexity and heterogeneity of actors and interest groups' (ibid., 335). Due to their high level of cultural and social diversity, they will also increasingly be the spot of societal innovation. This makes cities the pivotal point to achieve equitable and sustainable post-fossil-carbon societies. Cities can be living laboratories trying out alternative social, cultural, political, and technological innovations. Their cultural diversity is an advantage in this respect.[2]

5.2 The relevance of green spaces for cities

The year 2015 was declared International Year of Soils by the General Assembly of the United Nations (FAO 2015), since soil is an essential natural, only very slowly renewable, resource on which food sovereignty and security[3] depend and which highly impacts on climate change mitigation (cf. 5.2.1). Target 12.2 of Sustainable Development Goal 12 is 'Ensure sustainable consumption and production patterns' and foresees 'achiev[ing] the sustainable management and efficient use of natural resources' (UNGA 2015, 22) by 2030. As part of this goal, achieving sustainable land use governance is crucial for the socio-ecological transition in Europe. The governance of the green spaces resource system in European cities plays a growing role in this process due to increasing urbanisation. Preserving bio-diverse urban green spaces is necessary due to the multiple functions they provide, which are not distinct but mutually influence each other.

5.2.1 Ecological, social, and economic benefits

Target 11.7 under Sustainable Development Goal 11 'Make cities and human settlements inclusive, safe, resilient and sustainable' aims at 'provid[ing] universal access to safe, inclusive and accessible, green and public spaces, in particular for women and children, older persons and persons with disabilities' (ibid., 22). Having access to green spaces is a major component of city dwellers' well-being. Urban green spaces can be productive also in economic terms. By producing urban timber, fruits, compost but also increasingly vegetables originating from urban gardening and urban agriculture, they can create new employment options (ibid.) increasingly in the social and solidarity economy (cf. 2.4.4 and 7.4.2). The creation of seed banks (IPCC 2015, 27) helps to preserve traditional endemic species and thus also provides a basis for the reintroduction, continuation, and expansion of sustainable gardening and agriculture in the city.

5.2.2 *Risk factors for urban green spaces*

Despite the important benefits of green spaces, continuing urbanisation is one of the most severe risk factors threatening their existence, especially in growing cities. This means that the pressure on urban green spaces will further increase, which has made the local city level a field of action for civil society actors trying to obtain changes in the governance of urban green spaces. These actors counter land consumption taking place in various forms by extensive inner-city densification, urban sprawl, infrastructure development, often linked to speculation and privatisation tendencies. The question arises of how urban green spaces can be held available and accessible for all and possibly be expanded whilst ensuring their biodiversity and allowing for a diversity of uses for local needs at the same time.

5.3 The state of the local socio-ecological transition and of the green spaces resource system – decreasing availability of urban green spaces

Chapters 5–9 try to respond to the overarching research question with its two subquestions (cf. 1.2) by presenting theory and empirical findings in relation to each other, following the logic of the research's variables. Whereas the dependent variable (Y) and the independent variable (X) were already presented above (cf. 1.2), the importance of the latent variable[4] (L) and the intervening variables (I) (cf. Figure 5.1) emerged out of the empirical data during the data analysis process. This section gives an insight into the state of the socio-ecological transition in general and into the state of the transition in the green spaces resource system specifically across the cities as assessed by the interviewees. The collected quantitative and qualitative data yields insights into the actors' understanding of the sustainability concept and into their estimation of the state of the socio-ecological transition in general and of the state of the green spaces resource system in particular. Actors draw a differentiated picture of the state of the transition and of the green spaces resource system across the cities, and their answers also reveal reasons for the decreasing availability of urban green spaces. Additionally, it is shown how urgent actors think the transition is.

Urban green spaces are constantly reduced for building and infrastructure development. Ongoing *urban sprawl* consumes land, thus making urban green spaces and agricultural land disappear (Linz, a3, 59–61;[5] Lublin, a4, 52; Lugano, a3, 29 and a4, 22–30; Rome, a1, 43). *High development pressure* (Leeds, a3, 61–3;

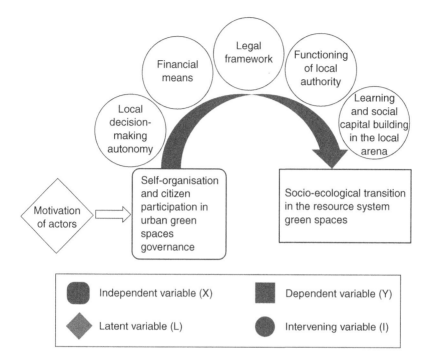

Figure 5.1 Relation between the research variables.
Source: own.

Potsdam, a3, 58) sometimes leads to construction even in environmentally sensitive areas (Lublin, a4, 26–9; Lugano, a4, 22–30). Large traffic infrastructure projects frequently entail urban sprawl. For example, along the third bridge in Istanbul irregular building activity has been emerging. This starts with shanty houses, later being replaced by proper houses for which eventually a permit is obtained (Istanbul, a1, 39). Increased soil sealing *endangers biodiversity* (Strasbourg, a4, 36) and even poses a risk to inhabitants (Bilbao, a4, 36). This is because, when river flooding areas are (re)developed into urban green spaces rather than built on, they can also serve as compensation areas in the case of flooding, thus reducing flooding risk to inhabitants. Many times, no ecological compensation areas are created or they are insufficiently created, and thus do not compensate for the biodiversity loss that occurs. For example, trees planted will need a minimum of 20 years to replace those which have been lost (Timisoara, a4, 63).

Exodus from the city occurs if living conditions in the city are not attractive enough, for example due to high traffic density, related pollution problems, lack of urban green spaces, but also high rents. In these cases, citizens opt for living outside the city and commuting to work, thus aggravating the traffic problem, as well as increasing the vacant building rate in the city (Dortmund, a4, 23;

Lublin, a4, 52; Lugano, a3, 29). This situation is made even worse if motorways are then built through the city in order to facilitate increased commuting by car, further decreasing living quality for those remaining in the city (Linz, a4, 35). Many cities are already highly densified, with little urban green space left (Lugano, a3, 108–9 and a4, 49–56; Paris, a3, 29). For example, Thessaloniki has less than three square metres of urban green space per inhabitant, which is far below the EU average (Thessaloniki, a3, 80 and a4, 21). The city is character-ised as 'an uninterrupted mass of concrete that stops at the waterfront just because it cannot go further' (Thessaloniki, a3, 31). 'In some … districts … there is a complete lack of green spaces' (ibid.). The latter is also reported from Sibiu (a4, 149–50). In Lugano, bringing people back to live in the city is seen as the biggest challenge. If people came back to live in the city, this would also break the vicious cycle of people moving out of the inner city and thus not being interested any more in putting bottom-up pressure on the state to regain access to inner-city urban green spaces (Lugano, a3, 60–6, 115).

Some cities pursue the strategy of further inner-city *densification* to prevent urban sprawl (Cracow, a4, 13, 53), which however needs to be combined with the aim of increasing inner-city quality of life. This has worked out, for example, in Zurich, which has managed to attract people back to the city after a general exodus in the 1980s. An example of how it has done this is by transforming streets into recreation areas (Lugano, a3, 68). Yet, if the principle of 'inner city development before outer city development' (Saarbrücken, a4, 24) is exagger-ated, without paying attention to a sufficient amount of inner-city urban green spaces and to the creation of affordable living space, people cannot be con-vinced to live there (Bilbao, a4, 36; Larissa, a3, 28; Lugano, a4, 34; Saarbrücken, a4, 23–4, 51; Strasbourg, a4, 23–4, 58). An example is Lugano, where, besides being highly densified already, the high rents in the inner city deter people on an average income from living there. Tenants are almost exclusively banks and service enterprises or foreign investors, increasing inner-city vacancy rates, since the latter might not rent but just keep the real estate for speculation purposes (Lugano, a3, 60–6, 114–15).

Densification due to inner-city building or traffic infrastructure development very often *reduces* still existing urban *green spaces* (Aalborg, a4, 74–5; Cracow, a4, 13, 47; Linz, a3, 59–61; Lodz, a4, 23, 38; Lugano, a4, 52; Timisoara, a4, 30, 68, 100–2; Umea, a3, 66–70), also because the more densely built an area is the more profit can be made (Leeds, a3, 60–3). For example, in Innsbruck it was dis-cussed whether to turn allotment gardens situated near a shopping mall into an industrial area (Innsbruck, a3, 85). Another example of densification is Lublin, which is developing into a car-friendly city to the detriment of pedestrians and non-motorised traffic by 'gigantomania in road investments' (Lublin, a4, 29). Despite a bypass road being planned, there is enormous investment in building roads throughout the city, thus reducing urban green spaces and other public space: 'This eliminates a piece of the square here, a piece of playground there, a bit of something else' (ibid.). In one case, the pedestrians' shortcut route to the central train station through a park was blocked by building a highway through the park, which increases traffic density even more since pedestrians now opt to go by car in order to reach the station. However, the risk of urban green spaces disappearing is even higher for smaller, less well-known spaces, which are threatened by the construction of car parks and roads, partly demanded by private persons and enterprises. This form of urban green space destruction is not being sufficiently countered by the local authority (Linz, a3, 59–61; Lublin, a4, 38–40).[6]

City development can also be mismanaged by *building speculation*, sometimes linked to corruption and clientelism. It leads to high consumption of territory and *reduces affordable housing space*. Real estate serving speculation purposes or holiday houses provoke a *high inner-city vacancy rate* (Lugano, a4, 30). In Naples, building speculation contributed to a doubling in the number of buildings being built in the past 20 years (Naples, a4, 26). Unrequired, often supersized, buildings are erected in places that, when taking into consideration the common good of the city, should not be built on (Lugano, a4, 34; Milan, a3, 27, 35 and a4, 66–9). This is often due to deals between politicians, the finance sector, and the building industry and serves the financial interest of a few. This mechanism has led to major architectural blunders in several European cities, contradicting the principles of sustainable city development.

The multiple crises from 2008 onwards have slowed down building activity. However, in some cities the crises have also led to *public poverty*, i.e. scarce public resources regarding the city budget. This can result in cities selling public land to private investors to replenish their budget in the short term, or of sacrificing urban green spaces in order to cut costs. Even if the quantitative data does not show a privatisation trend (cf. Schicklinski 2016, 114), the qualitative data delivers examples of privatisation from a number of cities. The mechanism is drastically expressed by an Italian interviewee who states that 'the city is kidnapped by the building speculative trends because the local authority sells its territory for its budget' (Milan, a3, 31). Good ideas to minimise the reduction of urban green spaces for building development exist, such as the *redevelopment of brownfields*, and are also anchored in the City Development Plan. However, they are not put into practice due to a lack of resources (Milan, a3, 31). Instead, the city administration has tried to make money by giving permission to build car parks, even on urban green spaces (Milan, a4, 75). Examples of cost cutting affecting urban green spaces are when cities close parks down, officially for regeneration reasons, yet citizens suspect that it is done to save maintenance costs (Lublin, a4, 38–40). Some actors propose connecting income tax not to residence but to place of work in order to make commuters pay for the costs of city development, and to shift rich exurbs' resources to less affluent city budgets (Dortmund, a4, 109).

Istanbul is one of the cities with the highest pressure on still existing urban green spaces, due to an ever-rising population and political and economic actors following the *growth paradigm* at all costs for profit interests. Urban green spaces are being consistently and rapidly reduced by building and infrastructure development for roads, mosques, shopping malls, or the third bridge:

Roads pass through the green spaces; they build highways and bridges on them; the green land is redeveloped to bring in more money and is turned into shopping malls.... The green is disappearing.... Now they are building sideways to the third bridge. Millions of trees will be cut down. And the prime minister says they will plant more trees. And where will they plant them, on concrete?

(Istanbul, a1, 19)

This situation is also mentioned by a civil society actor who equally points to the speed with which urban green spaces disappear, which leads to the situation that 'in Istanbul people picnic on the sides of the highways' (Istanbul, a4, 42). This is not a form of an organised protest gathering but simply occurs because the remaining urban green spaces are highly insufficient to satisfy the city population's need to be outside in nature (Istanbul, a4, 42). The result is an *overuse* of the remaining urban green spaces (Istanbul, a4, 44). It is highly difficult to exit this growth logic due to existing *property rights* and the *distribution of power*, and respondents even predict an aggravation for the future (Istanbul, a4, 42–6). The land development plan was stipulated long ago, all land is titled land. New urban green spaces could only be created if the metropolitan municipality decided to buy land, transformed it into urban green spaces, and opened them up for the citizens. Thus, the fate of urban green spaces depends on the goodwill of the metropolitan municipality, since it is responsible for creating new urban green spaces, and the existing urban green spaces are only available as long as the national and local government decide to protect them (Istanbul, a1, 37–41).

A *shared vision of sustainability and city development* is too often *still missing* or not visible enough (Milan, a3, 27–33; St. Gallen, a4, 9), but would be the starting point to achieve a more *sustainable land use* in and around cities (cf. 8.4.5). The need to build a less dense city and to also leave room for public space, especially public green spaces is not a top priority for the majority of stakeholders (Lublin, a4, 27–9). Especially cities with a long industrial tradition or which were used as military bases, often still have large areas of *fallow land*. Sustainable land use means that instead of sealing urban green spaces, industrial brownfields and former military sites would be reused for building or infrastructure development and for expanding these spaces (Dortmund, a4, 77; Potsdam, a3, 20; Saarbrücken, a4, 23), even if this can be complicated by shifted land tenure, often meaning that land has been privatised. For example, the Cracow municipality sold a piece of land for a cheap price to a private company, which uses only parts of it, making redevelopment for housing, commercial use, or green spaces impossible since the new owner does not want to cooperate (Cracow, a4, 53). Some cities' shape is particularly suited for redeveloping urban green spaces. As a respondent from Leeds explains, the medium-sized city's shape of a 'wagon wheel' (Leeds, a4, 59) lends itself to the creation of green 'spokes' (ibid.), rather like 'green corridors' (ibid.). This feature also opens up possibilities to 'revillagiz[e] the city' (ibid.) and even to 'relocaliz[e] [the] economy' (ibid.). *Inner-city urban green space* could also be *regained* by retransforming inner-city car parks. However, this presupposes a united vision of a traffic-calm inner city, often counteracted by the interests of local enterprises, or public bodies in favour of creating parking spaces in order to generate public funds. Creating a traffic-calm, green inner city instead requires financial resources and thus necessitates strong and united political will (Lugano, a4, 56; Saarbrücken, a4, 62).

Notes

1 More detailed theoretical insights and empirical results of this chapter's topic are presented in Schicklinski (2016).
2 Within the WWWforEurope project and based on ROCSET data (cf. 4.1), Dohse and Gold (2014) examined the cultural diversity–innovation nexus in 40 European cities. They report a 'positive relationship between cultural diversity and economic development' (ibid., 46), state that 'local actors identify ... the increase in city dynamics as major benefits of cultural diversity' (ibid., 45), and conclude that 'increasing cultural diversity increases the cities' creative and innovative potential' (ibid., 47).
3 Food sovereignty is to be distinguished from food security. The latter refers to the quantity of food available yet does not inform about production conditions, distributional processes, and consumption patterns, thus dissimulating power structures (Salzer 2013, 281). By contrast, food sovereignty refers to everyone's right to good sustainably produced quality food and also to the right of a group of people to determine its agricultural and food policy itself (ibid.).
4 'In psychology, there are many constructs ... like ... self-efficacy' (Borsboom *et al.* 2002, 203) that represent 'an unobserved attribute' (ibid.) assuming 'a causal role in bringing about' (ibid.) an 'observational behaviour' (ibid.). Such 'hypothetical constructs that cannot be directly measured' (MacCallum and Austin 2000, 202) are called 'latent variables'. They are needed to explain situations in which 'observable phenomena are influenced by underlying and unobserved causes' (Bollen 2002, 606). In this research the different kinds of actors' motivations influencing on the observable phenomenon of 'self-organisation and citizen participation in green spaces governance in European cities' cannot be directly observed and measured and are thus modelled as a latent variable.
5 Referring to the city of Linz, actor 3 (cf. Table 4.3), transcript lines 59–61.
6 The case of Lublin resembles the situation of German cities in the 1960s and 1970s, when urban planning was oriented towards transforming cities into car-friendly ones (Reichow 1959), disregarding the needs of pedestrians and cyclists. This is a trend that Germany then tried to reverse from the 1990s onwards. It seems that particularly cities in Eastern Europe as well as Istanbul still cling to a growth paradigm when it comes to urban development, which has partly been overcome in other regions of Europe.

References

Bollen, Kenneth A. 2002. 'Latent variables in psychology and the social sciences'. *Annual Review of Psychology*, 53(1): 605–34.
Borsboom, Denny, Gideon J. Mellenbergh, and Jaap van Heerden. 2002. 'The theoretical status of latent variables'. *Psychological Review*, 110(2): 203–19.
Dohse, Dirk and Robert Gold. 2014. 'Cultural diversity and economic policy'. WWW forEurope Working Paper 64. www.foreurope.eu/fileadmin/documents/pdf/Working papers/WWWforEurope_WPS_no064_MS102.pdf [27 August 2016].
European Commission (EC). 2015. Issues paper for discussion in the forum 'CITIES –

cities of tomorrow: Investing in Europe'. Brussels, 17–18 February 2014. http://ec.
europa.eu/regional_policy/sources/conferences/urban2014/doc/issues_paper_final.pdf
[27 August 2016].

Food and Agriculture Organization of the United Nations (FAO). 2015. 2015 international year of soils: Healthy soils for a healthy life. www.fao.org/soils-2015/about/en/
[27 August 2016].

German Advisory Council on Global Change (WBGU). 2011. Flagship report. World in
transition: A social contract for sustainability. Berlin: WBGU. www.wbgu.de/file
admin/templates/dateien/veroeffentlichungen/hauptgutachten/jg2011/wbgu_jg2011_
en.pdf [27 August 2016].

Intergovernmental Panel on Climate Change (IPCC), ed. 2015. *Climate change 2014:
Synthesis report. Contribution of working groups I, II and III to the fifth assessment report of
the Intergovernmental Panel on Climate Change.* Geneva. www.ipcc.ch/report/ar5/syr/ [27
August 2016].

MacCallum, Robert and James T. Austin. 2000. 'Application of structural equation
modeling in psychological research'. *Annual Review of Psychology*, 51(1): 201–26.

Reichow, Hans B. 1959. *Die autogerechte Stadt: Ein Weg aus dem Verkehrs-Chaos.* Ravens-
burg: Otto Maier.

Salzer, Irmi. 2013. 'Gutes Essen für alle! Keine Ernährungssouveränität ohne Commons'.
In *Was allen gehört: Commons – neue Perspektiven in der Armutsbekämpfung*, ed. Die
Armutskonferenz, 279–87. Wien: Verlag des Österreichischen Gewerkschaftsbundes.

Schicklinski, Judith. 2016. 'Socio-ecological transitions in the green spaces resource
system'. In *Cities in transition: Social innovation for Europe's urban sustainability*, eds
Thomas Sauer, Cristina Garzillo, and Susanne Elsen, 93–124. Abingdon/New York:
Routledge.

United Nations, Department of Economic and Social Affairs, Population Division
(UNESA). 2014. 'World urbanization prospects: The 2014 revision, highlights'. (ST/
ESA/SER.A/352). https://esa.un.org/unpd/wup/Publications/Files/WUP2014-Highlights.
pdf [25 September 2016].

United Nations General Assembly (UNGA). 2015. 'Draft resolution referred to the
United Nations summit for the adoption of the post-2015 development agenda by the
General Assembly at its sixty-ninth session: Transforming our world: the 2030 Agenda
for Sustainable Development'. Seventieth session Agenda items 15 and 116. www.
un.org/ga/search/view_doc.asp?symbol=A/70/L.1&Lang=E [27 August 2016].

URGE-Team. 2004. 'Making greener cities – A practical guide: Development of urban
green spaces to improve the quality of life in cities and urban regions'. UFZ-Bericht
Nr. 8/2004 (Stadtökologische Forschungen Nr. 37). Leipzig: UFZ Centre for Environmental Research Leipzig-Halle. www.urge-project.ufz.de/CD/pdf/Part_1_Booklet/high_
resolution/Booklet_2_Section_A_300dpi.pdf [27 August 2016].

Vancutsem, Didier. 2008. 'Land use management for sustainable European cities: Base-
line study – Development phase'. http://urbact.eu/sites/default/files/import/Projects/
LUMASEC/outputs_media/LUMASEC_Baseline_Study.pdf [27 August 2016].

6 Social innovation and urban spaces of civil society action

This research assumes that social innovation most often emerges in civil society, then possibly spreading to the state and market sector and that this innovative potential is one reason for civil society's power to correct state and market failures. This hypothesis requires a first step to circumscribe the term 'social innovation' and a second step to explain what is meant by civil society's corrective power. Here, keeping the research question in mind, it is also examined how social movements emerge and what the chances are that a broad social movement for the socio-ecological transition gains force.

Section 6.3 explores how urban green spaces can become spaces of civil society action. Referring to the independent variable, an overview of existing civil society activities in the cities is provided to examine civil society's position vis-à-vis state and market players and to explore their impact at the local level. The macro-level is left to circumscribe at a meso-level the two main forms of civic activities, namely citizen participation and self-organisation. An attempt has been made to explain from the data where civil society's transformative role springs from by providing a deepened analysis of actors, processes, and contributions of citizen-driven activities within the governance of urban green spaces and urban food production across European cities. 'Best practice' examples are given, and activities are classified, first, according to involved actors and types of actions as well as conflicts and then according to a developed participation model (cf. Figure 6.1). To understand a possible impact of self-organisation and citizen participation on the transition in the green spaces resource system, it has to be examined to what extent citizens are involved in local decision-making regarding green spaces and if opportunities for citizens to self-organise exist. Therefore, civil society actions in the cities are empirically presented in detail, carving out their occurrence and different forms.

6.1 Social innovation

A sustainability transition requires totally new thinking and thus cannot cope without social innovation (Meadows *et al.* 2005, 274; WBGU 2011, 321). The term has become omnipresent in current policy discourses. In a publication by the European Commission, social innovations are generally defined as innovations that are social in both their ends and their means.... We define social innovations as new ideas (products, services and models) that simultaneously meet social needs (more effectively than alternatives) and create new social relationships or collaborations. In other words they are innovations that are not only good for society but also enhance society's capacity to act.

(Bureau of European Policy Advisers European Commission 2011, 33)

A more detailed definition of different types of social innovation is given by Zapf (1989, 177, own translation), who also describes their relation to their technical counterparts:

Social innovations are new ways to reach goals, especially new forms of organisation, new regulations, new lifestyles, *that change the direction of social change*, that solve problems better than former practices and that are therefore worth being imitated and institutionalised.

Social innovations can be preconditions, concomitants or consequences of technical innovations.

Looking back in time, the term 'innovation', then referring to 'entrepreneurial innovation', was first mentioned by Joseph A. Schumpeter in 1934 (1983, xxiv), defining the latter as the 'central autonomous cause of economic development' (ibid.). For him, innovation is 'the commercial or industrial application of something new – a new product, process, or method of production, a new market or source of supply; a form of commercial, business, or financial organization' (ibid., xix) which evolves in a 'process of Creative Destruction' (ibid., xx). This creative aspect also becomes obvious in his theory of innovation, which states that 'innovation combines factors in a new way, or ... it consists in carrying out New Combinations' (Schumpeter 2005, 88). Here, he is close to Bandura's (1997, 473) assessment of creativity's role for innovative processes, who writes that 'few innovations are entirely new. The second type of creativity largely involves synthesizing existing knowledge into new ways of thinking and doing things'.

From Schumpeter's point of view the personality of an entrepreneur is no mere 'profit maximiser'.... Besides the joy in creating, improving, and prevailing against others, he considers as central drive and cause for entrepreneurial action the fact that in the case of success it is connected with upward mobility and recognition.

(Biesecker and Kesting 2003, 249, own translation)

Innovative entrepreneurs can handle an evolving situation of insecurity which evolves since they leave tried-out behavioural paths and also operate against resistance. This capacity makes social innovators the right persons to cope with the challenges of the second modernity in which uncertainty has become the norm.

Problems can no longer be 'solved' one and for all or even appear to be capable of solution in this simplistic sense. Instead, they form a non-linear sequence which leads to new potentialities, and so to uncertainties, into which they are embedded. Any 'solution', therefore, merely offers a temporary reprieve – which leads on inexorably to the next 'challenge'.

(Nowotny *et al.* 2013, 48)

Schumpeter's concept of entrepreneurial innovation is clearly tied to the economic realm, whilst the first two definitions given in this chapter leave open whether social innovation is most likely to emerge in economy, politics, or civil society. Other scholars, for example Geoff Mulgan (2006, 145), do not identify one primary locus of social innovation either, but rather attribute it to all societal realms, with sometimes a predominant role for one of them, depending on different historical contexts:

During some periods in recent history, civil society provided most of the impetus for social innovation…. The great wave of industrialization and urbanization in the nineteenth century was accompanied by an extraordinary upsurge of social enterprise and innovation: mutual self-help, microcredit, building societies, cooperatives, trade unions, reading clubs, and philanthropic business leaders creating model towns and model schools…. At other times governments have taken the lead in social innovation.[1]

Consequently, 'leaders of social innovation have included politicians, bureaucrats, intellectuals, business people, as well as NGO activists'[2] (ibid., 148). However, he points to politics' crucial role 'in scaling up social innovations … [by its] unique capacities to do this by passing laws; allocating public expenditure; and conferring authority on public agencies'[3] (ibid., 153). This hints at conducive conditions for social innovation to emerge and to be scaled-up, which he quite specifically carves out for different types of social innovation belonging to the three realms of society:

For social movements, basic legal protections and status, plus open media are key. In business, social innovation can be driven by competition, open cultures, and accessible capital, and it will be impeded where capital is monopolized by urban elites or government. In politics and government, the conditions are likely to include competing parties, think tanks, innovation funds, contestable markets, and plentiful pilots, as well as creative leaders…. In social organizations, the acceleration of social innovation is aided by practitioner networks, allies in politics, strong civic organizations … and the support of progressive foundations and philanthropists.[4]

(Ibid., 155)

He equally cites existing barriers in politics and civil society: whereas in politics and administration 'there are few incentives for either politicians or officials to take up new ideas ... [and] anyone who does promote innovations risks upsetting powerful vested interests'[5] (ibid., 156), he deplores that public and private support is missing for social innovation emerging in civil society. While innovations in the economic sector receive 'public subsidy ... and private investment in incubators, venture capital, and startups. The equivalent potential supports for social innovation – foundations and public agencies – are much weaker' (ibid.).

The concept of change agents expands Schumpeter's concept of innovative entrepreneurs horizontally and vertically to further actors within the economic sector, to civil society and politics as well as to all governance levels from local to international. In economy, within the production cycle, these 'pioneers of social change ... [are not only] the inventors, investors, entrepreneurs, developers or distributors of new concepts, products and services, but also ... [the] "enlightened consumers" through demanding new products, and letting them circulate' (WBGU 2011, 243). This stresses the power of smart consumers for the socio-ecological transition. Change agents bring topics on the political agenda, take a facilitator or mediator role, network between different groups, and thus they have the capacity to bridge across sectors and levels (Elsen 2007, 210; WBGU 2011, 243). They can be individual people, groups of people, and also bigger organisations to be found from the micro- to macro-societal level and in all sectors of society (WBGU 2011, 243, 345–6). They develop experimental and unconventional solutions (Elsen 2007, 209) and have sufficient bridging social capital (cf. 6.3.2.2) to spread their ideas.

Lastly, the concept of social innovation can also be looked at from the angle of local development and is then, first, and quite generally, meant 'in the sense defined by Max Weber: innovation in the relations between individuals and between groups' (Moulaert 2000, 71), playing a key role in the economic and social development of European cities (ibid., 13). This more restricted concept defines social innovation as happening at the local level from below, though it can be actively fostered by 'the establishment of communication channels between privileged and underprivileged citizens in urban society, and the creation of grass-roots democracy' (ibid., 71). It is thus solely attributed to civil society, even if it can be supported by politics.

6.2 The corrective power of civil society

Conditions for civil society to unfold on and to influence the state and the market are best in democratic systems. Why there is no alternative to a democratic transition path is explained in Section 6.2.1. Perceiving civil society as a corrective power to state and market forces necessitates locating it in relation to the state and the market, which is done in Section 6.2.2. Subsequently, in Section 6.2.3, the ambivalence of the term 'civil society' is addressed, and light is shed on the emergence of social movements in Section 6.2.4. Section 6.2.5 leaves the macro-level to see how modes of participation have changed requiring a new way of making politics. Section 6.2.6 explains why a socio-ecological transition is not feasible without transdisciplinary learning processes.

6.2.1 *The transformative power of democratic systems*

Randers' (2012, 6, 255; cf. 2.3) analysis places low hopes in the capacity of current democratic systems of solving the world's problems and avoiding catastrophic climate change in the second half of this century, lamenting their system inertia. Indeed, with irreversible climate change looming around the corner, there is the risk that politics opts for less democratic choices (Beck 2007, 86). However, according to the German Advisory Council on Global Change (cf. 2.4.2), a strong participatory democracy is not contradictory to a strong state. Sustainable behaviour can, on the one hand, be 'inflicted' from above by laws, regulations, and economic incentives, which is in certain fields even necessary to represent the interests of the unborn (Beck 1993, 27). Yet, on the other hand, if citizens do not see the point in behaving sustainably beyond their short-term interests, they will not back politicians' decisions in that direction. While in non-democratic systems they can be forced to some extent to behave in a certain way, this is more difficult in democracies in which citizens tend to opt for those political representatives proposing short-term options, naturally contradicting sustainability. Therefore, even more importantly as long as immediate environmental threats are not too overwhelmingly obvious, information about and education for sustainability is crucial to make citizens understand what is at stake and how social environmental, and economic issues are globally intertwined. This stresses, besides the responsibility of the public educational system, the importance of civil society actors in the transition (WBGU 2011, 273). If the environmental question has become omnipresent in society because civil society actors have understood its importance, politics, economy, and science cannot deny this and have to adjust their ways of operating (Beck 1993, 84).[6] Some argue that time for action is too short to allow for this learning process in a participatory democratic system. Yet, swift political action and reform decisions with the economic crisis in 2008 were possible also in democratic systems (WBGU 2011, 193), because there was a joint consensus of the need to act. Reaching such a consensus that is supported by the majority of the population is only possible in democratic systems. Refusing democratic options would also be a kick in the teeth of those that were at the origin of the environmental movements, triggering worldwide change and modifying political and also economic institutions from the bottom by putting the environmental issue on the international agenda against the vested interests of policies and industry (Beck 2007, 90).[7] It is the merit of these bottom-up movements that the state of the Earth has become a worldwide concern, even if necessary reactions are far lacking behind. The battle is by far not won, which is why Beck (2007, 90, own translation) pleads for an 'ecological extension of democracy' with the extension of a public sphere to all realms and levels of society in order to increase transparency and to exert a control function on risk-producing institutions (ibid., 91, 174).

The main difference in Randers' and Beck's analysis of societal conditions lies in their different assessment of the role of democracies in the socio-ecological transition. Randers (2012, 27) believes that 'democratic society will pursue short-term satisfaction and choose their leaders accordingly … [which will] require an element of benevolent authoritarianism'[8] to make the sustainability revolution come true. Beck's analysis centres around the merging of subpolitics next to traditional institutions of representative democracy. Subpolitics for the environmental cause have already infiltrated all spheres and levels of society. That the 'sustainability revolution has started'[9] (Randers 2012, 13) is primarily thanks to civil society actors having entered the action situation and having become active for the cause of the socio-ecological transition. And this has predominantly happened in democratic societies in which citizens are not punished or even risk their life for uttering their opinion, for participating and self-organising in community matters. This has happened where they are not totally engaged in a daily fight for survival, be it due to conflicts or economic hardship, and in which they are generally more educated and thus also more informed about their rights as human beings. These considerations also show the special responsibility on civil society actors in the industrialised countries for whom it is easier to engage in voluntary work than people in the Global South.

There is no alternative to a democratic transition path, since only democracies '[allow] broad and liberal discourse, thereby promoting the establishment of a social consensus for the necessary transformation' (WBGU 2011, 46), and since only via the involvement of all societal actors can all available creative innovative ideas be considered and the best solution be found (ibid., 194). Even if 'in welfare states the idea of socioeconomic self-help is not anchored any more in the collective memory like in transition and developing countries in which it is present in daily life'[10] (Elsen 2007, 191, own translation), in democratic systems it is generally easier to build social capital and to create and run socioeconomic alternative structures in the form of self-organised institutions to collectively improve local living conditions, since actors can interact without being oppressed and have more probably learned to create a 'public sphere' (cf. 6.2.2) in which to negotiate between different interests and to peacefully solve conflicts. Even in cases where it is obvious which measures have to be implemented, such as introducing a CO_2 tax, the implementation of the measure has to take place in a participatory negotiation process of all involved to find the best and most equitable way of implementing it. There is not one predefined best transition path, but several options (WBGU 2011, 318). The best solution can only be reached in a broad democratic process within and across countries. This includes not knowing whether the chosen path is the best one; doubts are part of the process in reflexive modernity, in contrast to the first modernity where doubts, for example the questioning of expert knowledge, were suppressed (Beck 1993, 268).

6.2.2 Civil society in relation to the state and the market

For answering the research question, the interrelationship of civil society actors with state and market actors needs to be examined. To do so, it is useful to draw on Habermas' (1995a, 180, 183, 452; 1995b, 8) twofold societal model of 'life-world' and 'system' developed in the scope of his theory of communicative action. Civil society's inherent force is based on its embeddedness in and its functioning according to the logics of the 'lifeworld' – in opposition to the con-ception of 'system' that the state and the market follow (Habermas 1985, 155–6, 189, 255). Civil society's functional 'lifeworld' logics are different from the 'system' logic of the state and the market. While the coordination principles of the 'lifeworld' are communication, cooperation, and solidarity, the economic system is steered by capital and competition and the political system by (organ-isational) power and law (ibid., 158; Habermas 1995a, 247, 541, 455). Civil society's functioning according to 'lifeworld' logics means that it is centred around communicative action. The 'lifeworld' can be described as the ever, yet unconsciously, present backdrop or horizon in which communicative action is embedded (Habermas 1995a, 188, 191–2, 199, 272). It is the 'context-forming background of processes of reaching understanding' (Habermas 1987b, 204) which includes subconscious and unquestioned assumptions such as culture and language (Habermas 1995a, 191–92): 'Communicative action takes place within a lifeworld that remains at the backs of participants in communication' (Haber-mas 1984, 335). Whereas action in the systems of state or market has a well-defined goal, namely increasing power or making profit, the result of communicative action cannot be defined beforehand. It remains open and is only formulated and negotiated within the process of communicative action by the participants themselves (Biesecker and Kesting 2003, 177). Reaching, main-taining, and renewing a consensus can become the inherent goal of communica-tive action:

> In communicative action participants pursue their plans cooperatively on the basis of a shared definition of the situation. If a shared definition of the situation has first to be negotiated, or if efforts to come to some agreement within the framework of the shared situation definitions fail, the attainment of consensus which is normally a condition for pursuing goals, can itself become an end.
>
> (Habermas 1987b, 126)

The underlying drivers of communicative action which are (1) to negotiate a joint definition of the situation and (2) to reach a consensus grants communica-tive action the power to substantially change the involved actors. Even basic validity claims can be questioned (Habermas 1995a, 199) and thus altered. Thus, responsibility is shifted to every participant to co-define the basis of joint action which might also include a modification of values and norms (Biesecker and Kesting 2003, 160). However, in order to analyse societal processes, a mere 'lifeworld' focus is insufficient. The 'system' must also be kept in mind, trying to understand 'how the lifeworld – as the horizon within which communicative actions are "always already" moving – is in turn limited and changed by the structural transformation of society as a whole' (Habermas 1987b, 119). This is important, because the 'lifeworld' does not operate in a social vacuum but is surrounded and impacted by the 'system':

> In fact, however, their [the members of a socio-cultural lifeworld] goal-directed actions are coordinated not only through processes of reaching understanding, but also through functional interconnections that are not intended by them and are usually not even perceived within the horizon of everyday practice.
>
> (Ibid., 150)

Polanyi's disembedding and commodification theses (cf. 2.4.1) can be compared to Habermas' description of two major processes that modern societies that are geared towards ever-increasing economic growth have been undergoing: (1) the uncoupling of 'system' and 'lifeworld' logics and (2) the colonisation of the 'lifeworld' by the imperatives of ever more complex state and market systems (Habermas 1985, 182; 1995a, 8; 1995b). The first process explains how the two-dimensional society with its concomitant diverging functional logics has emerged. In a process that could also be understood as a continuation of the disembedding of economy described by Polanyi, the state and the market have developed into highly specialised and autonomous subsystems functioning according to logics very different from those of the 'lifeworld':

> Modern societies attain a level of system differentiation at which increasingly autonomous organizations are connected with one another via dilinguistified media of communication: these system mechanisms – for example, money – steer a social intercourse that has been largely disconnected from norms and values, above all in those subsystems of purposive rational economic and administrative action.
>
> (Habermas 1987b, 154)

The second process connects to the first one. The state and market system do not only become highly specialised and autonomous but also call on the 'lifeworld' for their purposes (Habermas 1995a, 526). The colonisation of the 'lifeworld' by the 'system' damages the first (ibid.). These damages are 'deformations that inevitably turn up when forms of economic and administrative rationality encroach upon areas of life whose internal communicative structures cannot be rationalized according to those criteria' (Habermas 1987b, 285). For example, 'the destruction of urban environments as a result of uncontrolled capitalist growth … can be explained as a "misuse" of the media of money and power' (ibid., 293–4). Like Polanyi, Habermas warns of commodification tendencies. The colonisation of the 'lifeworld' implies a commodification of more and more spheres of life (Habermas 1985, 69–70) and decreases the possibility of social capital to evolve and flourish therein (Elsen 2007, 74). Habermas' model of a two-dimensional society (Biesecker and Kesting 2003, 159) transgresses and expands a dual state–market logic and enables civil society's role as a counterweight to state and market forces. This role is necessary because of the ever-expanding colonising 'system' into the 'lifeworld':

> The point is to protect areas of life that are functionally dependent on social integration through values, norms, and consensus formation, to preserve them from falling prey to the systemic imperatives of economic and administrative subsystems growing with dynamics of their own, and to defend them from becoming converted over, through the steering medium of law, to a principle of sociation that is, for them, dysfunctional.
>
> (Habermas 1987b, 372–3)

The three coordination principles of communication, capital, and power need to be brought into a new balance with the 'lifeworld' principle gaining in power (Habermas 1985, 158, 255). Such a new power balance can only be achieved by the action of counter-institutions emerging in civil society and functioning according to 'lifeworld' principles. Such institutions introduce alternative economic and direct democratic political options: there is the need for 'counter institutions that develop from within the lifeworld in order to set limits on the inner dynamics of the economic and political-administrative action systems' (Habermas 1987b, 396). They follow the principle of communicative action with its inherent logic of 'communicative rationality' (ibid., 333). The latter is the underlying logic of the consensus-orientated process of communicative action:

> Processes of reaching understanding aim at an agreement that meets the conditions of rationally motivated assent [*Zustimmung*] to the content of an utterance. A communicatively achieved agreement has a rational basis; it cannot be imposed by either party, whether instrumentally through intervention in the situation directly or strategically through influencing the decisions of opponents. Agreement can indeed be objectively obtained by force; but what comes to pass manifestly through outside influence or the use of violence cannot count subjectively as agreement. Agreement rests on common *convictions*.
>
> (Habermas 1984, 287)

Thus, communicative action is geared towards reaching a consensus via 'discursive processes of will-formation and consensus-oriented procedures of negotiation and decision making' (Habermas 1987b, 371) and is therefore always directed towards peaceful conflict regulation. Habermas' plea for communicative rationality can be considered to be the basic argument for civil society's innovative power and driving role in the socio-ecological transition.

> The communicative rationality and the reciprocal interaction between different reasons, processes of differentiation, or new combinations, for example in the development of socio-ecological economies, are drivers of

social innovation. This is due to their function as 'centers of concentrated communication' (Jürgen Habermas 1987a, 364) rooted in direct lifeworld concerns. The logic of these 'centers of concentrated communication' can 'develop into autonomous public spheres' (ibid.) with the potential to draw attention to and to counter two important phenomena of modern times: the 'uncoupling' of system and lifeworld logics and the colonisation of life-world by the imperatives of systems (Stephen Kemmis 2001, 96).

(Elsen and Schicklinski 2016, 223–4)

Via citizen participation and self-organisation new actors evolve in the local action situation that claim their right to participate politically and economic-ally. Habermas stresses the importance of promoting the lower action situation to make this possible. This is where an autonomous public sphere can emerge, where communication and creating a debate grow stronger, forming public dis-courses with the power of influencing policy from below by bringing in innov-ative new issues and thus with the power of weakening the functional logics of market and state (Habermas 1985, 159–60):

The problem seems more to be how in autonomous publics the ability to self-organisation can be unfolded to the extent that the purposeful decision-making processes of a utility-value-oriented lifeworld can contain the sys-temic imperatives of economic system and apparatus of state and can make *both* media-steered subsystems dependent on lifeworld imperatives.

(Ibid., 255, own translation)

This process is of key importance for the socio-ecological transition. Yet, strengthening civil society does not mean letting the state off the hook (cf. 2.4.4). It means reaching a new interplay between community, political, and economic actors, with the state keeping the responsibility for core tasks. It means the containment of state and market power, a redirection of the steering potential in society. There is no denying the fact that civil society actors have already gained in power in the last decades:

Twenty years ago, Jeremy Rifkin described the reasons for the rapid global growth of the 'third' sector. The withdrawal of the state-run as well as the economic sector from local communities and their concerns leaves a crucial vacuum (Rifkin 2004, 275–93). This vacuum is filled by civil society actors taking over responsibility for social, cultural, and ecological matters and for the rebuilding of community.

(Elsen and Schicklinski 2016, 225–6)

Civil society can indeed be considered as a corrective power with the capacity of correcting state and market failure (Biesecker and Kesting 2003, 460). 'Shift-ing balances become visible within processes of social innovation and democrat-isation and approaches to socio-ecological development especially on the local level' (Elsen and Schicklinski 2016, 238). Civil society actors at the local level were the ones who pointed to the detrimental effects of industrial activities in their neighbourhood. They were the first to develop environmental awareness, which then spread to other sectors and higher governmental levels. Some of these civil society actors also joined forces and developed into powerful internationally operating non-governmental organisations (NGOs). Therefore, small social movements at the local level are no drop in the ocean but 'prepare the fertile soil for institutional reforms'[11] (Diekmann and Jaeger 1996, 23, own translation), thus indirectly influencing discourses, even if they are not yet granted participation options.

This suggests a transformative role of civil society actors. Yet, it must be mentioned that the socio-ecological transition, or sustainability revolution, is not to be understood as a violent opposing, rejecting, overthrowing, or dismantling of existing political and economic structures and institutions. 'Lifeworld's' functioning principle of communicative action strongly opposes this approach. It would not be target-aiming either, since civil society actors would not be able to organise economy and society on their own (Jackson 2009, 172). Furthermore, change agents are to be found in all three societal realms. Revolution in this book is understood as a profound, massive, overarching, and comprehensive transformation of society and economy which then function according to a changed vision, goal, and inherent logics. It entails profound changes in existing economic and political institutions without aiming at completely abolishing institutions in power. However, it includes changes in the distribution of power and financial allocation, which inescapably creates distributional conflicts between societal groups that makes the enabling of direct democratic processes and the opening up of broad participatory discourse action situations for consensus oriented conflict resolution even more important.

6.2.3 Civil society – an ambivalent term

Civil society is a term frequently called upon, yet provoking an international discussion of what is meant by civic activities and how these activities relate to the state and the market. It is an ambivalent term for at least four reasons.

First, practising subpolitics (cf. 6.2.5) is open to everyone (Beck 1993, 159). Also organisations like the mafia or, looking back into history, the parks movement in nineteenth-century England and the United States (US) (Pincetl 2007, 1870)[12] are part of civil society. 'Local self-organization can also be dominated by local elites to use rules as tools to advantage themselves' (Ostrom 2005, 220). Civil society organisations may accumulate social capital (cf. 3.3.2), which results in advantages for their members yet leads to disadvantages for those excluded from the organisations (Ostrom and Ahn 2003, xiv). Thus, when speaking about civic activities it must be clear that it refers to activities that are done not for profit interest or solely personal gain or that of a closed social group but for the common good of the community. It does not refer to actors of a 'counter-modernity' (Beck 1993, 15, own translation) which equally evolve in the process of reflexive modernisation, yet whose reaction to the more complex and insecure world of the second modernity consists of erecting (new) borders or assembling neonationalistic and neofascist tendencies (Beck 1993, 15–16, 97–8, 100).

Second, the term 'civil society' needs to be delineated against that of 'third sector'. Elsen (2007, 43, own translation) points out that the latter is used to designate 'all which is neither assigned to the state or the market nor to the lifeworld'.[13] This includes for example also (big) NGOs and quasi-autonomous NGOs (QUANGOS). It is a misleading term since it keeps up the belief that a clear assignment to one sector is always possible. It furthermore gives the impression of a residual category, gathering heterogeneous forms, everything that does not fit into the state–market dichotomy (Elsen 2007, 43–4). Moreover, one basic logic of action which is ascribed to the 'third sector', namely doing economy not primarily for profit, is also valid for some forms of organisation that are not subsumed in this sector (Biesecker and Kesting 2003, 196; Elsen 2007, 43–4, 265). Therefore, the term 'intermediary sector' is more appropriate (Seibel 1994, 33; Elsen 2007, 44, 147–8, 317). It designates the locus where "intermediary" institutions' (Seibel 1994, 53, own translation) emerge 'as interactive nexuses of households, enterprises, and state levels' (Biesecker and Kesting 2003, 195, own translation). This sector is the locus of 'hybrid forms of organisation which transversely to societal sectors pursue both social and ecological and economic aims, act in the economic system, yet are part of organised civil society'[14] (Elsen 2007, 45, own translation). This intermediary civil society sector does not only compensate failures of market and state (Seibel 1994, 45–53) but, by allowing and combining new institutional arrangements such as still more informal citizens' initiatives or networks or already more organised forms of social and solidarity economies, for example cooperatives, has the potential to build a 'bridge between the heterogeneous and separate spheres of political-administrative and economic system and the concerns and potentials of lifeworlds'[15] (Elsen 2007, 267, own translation). This way, forms of socioeconomic self-organisation as part of social and solidarity economy cross the border from the 'lifeworld' to the state and the market (ibid., 45) to a large extent overcoming the 'lifeworld'–'system' dichotomy (ibid., 86) and countering their decoupling as well as the colonisation of the former by the latter.

Third, striving for equity between different world regions, generations and gender must be an internalised value of civil society. The social and environmental side effects of the risk society and a globalised neoliberal corporate economy do not stop at borders. Consequently, bottom-up solutions must always be devised in a locally embedded yet globally connected network of civil society actors (Roth 2002, 350). A civil society of the twenty-first century deserving this term has to think of the terms 'local' and 'global' in the same breath, enable a growing social group of socially, environmentally, and economically disadvantaged persons[16] to participate and self-organise as well as to fight for their interests, if it does not want to be confronted with the reproach of being a 'gated community' (ibid.) closing itself in 'cosy' conflict-distant issues that do not touch the issue of distributional justice between different world regions, generations, and gender.

Fourth, the term 'civil society' is closely linked, via the concept of 'social capital', to self-organisation. It is indisputable in the scientific discussion that civic activities build social capital. Yet, what is specifically meant with this term must be clearly defined. 'The notion of social capital ... is not to be mixed up with a nonbinding call for "more cooperation"'[17] (Habisch 2002, 355–6, own translation). Social capital is not evolving automatically by becoming engaged in voluntary work. In international scientific discussion, social capital is defined as 'an attribute of individuals and of their relationship that enhances their ability to solve collective action problems' (Ostrom and Ahn 2003, xiv). They name three types of social capital with particular relevance to collective action: '(1) trustworthiness, (2) networks, and (3) formal and informal rules or institutions' (ibid.). Social capital is created by interaction and negotiation processes between local actors. In decade-long empirically meticulous detailed work Ostrom studied the functioning of social capital and figured out eight basic rules that have to be in place to achieve cooperation despite existing incentives for free riding to achieve a successful governance of commons (Roth 2002, 352–3; cf. 3.3.1). Two of these rules refer to the participation right of the actors[18] to commonly set working rules as well as to create well-functioning institutionalised local action situations for conflict regulation (Ostrom 1990, 88–102).

> To be able to do so 'individuals need to invest in those working rules in the form of devising, revising, monitoring, and sanctioning' (Ostrom and Ahn 2003, xxiii). This continuous process is only conceivable in an 'autonomous public sphere' as conceptualised by Habermas.
>
> (Elsen and Schicklinski 2016, 224)

In fact, Ostrom's concept on social capital and her theory on the collective governance of commons and Habermas' theory of communicative action (cf. 6.2.2) 'overlap in at least two main points' (ibid.). Besides being both persuaded that 'forms of self-organization strengthen the collective capacity for action' (Habermas 1987a, 364), they both acknowledge the significance of socially embedded and interconnected institutions and emphasise the great importance of communication for negotiation and conflict management. Communication is essential for 'achieving a common understanding of the problems jointly faced. Discourse frequently generates ideas concerning various ways of coping more effectively with these problems' (Ostrom 2005, 65). The overuse of commons due to actors' selfish behaviour can only be prevented if the evolvement of communication between actors is allowed for and fostered. Communication can be regarded as the basic foundation of sustainable governance of commons in particular (Poteete *et al.* 2010, 215) and of civic engagement in general, since it is the precondition for social capital to be built up, leading to cooperation between actors. Civil society institutions create social capital and thus are able to overcome cooperation dilemma and to achieve cooperation for collective problem solutions to the benefit of all parties (Habisch 2002, 352). In this sense, we can only speak of the building of social capital if citizens have created cooperative structures in which the set rules are followed, which is ensured by a jointly developed self-control and sanctions system (ibid., 356). Discussing the concept of civil society and orienting policy accordingly needs to be guided by this 'ambitious concept of social capital'[19] (ibid., 355, own translation). Understanding social capital this way, implies an altered relationship between civil society and the state (ibid., 351). It implies the possibility of conflictual processes to evolve and of existing power structures to shift (Elsen 2007, 38–9). Ostrom's concept of social capital suggests a necessary rethinking with the local authority. Civic activities are already drawn on to compensate state and market failure, yet up to now autonomous self-organised socioeconomic solutions are either not permitted or not recognised and fostered sufficiently (ibid., 75). Socioeconomic self-organisation needs to be acknowledged as the right of citizens to defend themselves 'against the encroachments of the market on essential life interests'[20] (ibid., 38, own translation). The local authority needs to acknowledge citizens' self-organisation as an essential part of civic activities. If it seriously wants to increase framework conditions for civic engagement and promote it, it first of all has to support and foster citizens' self-organisation capabilities by providing them with adequate instruments (Habisch 2002, 354, 356).[21]

6.2.4 The emergence of social movements

Since social movements can take the role of innovative pioneers (Habermas 1985, 234), they are important social phenomena with the potential of driving social change. In order to examine the conditions under which a broad social sustainability movement can emerge and gain in power, the emergence of past social movements needs to be understood. Social movements usually emerge in opposition to statal structures as one form of self-organisation. Although environmental movements have existed since the beginning of industrialisation, they reached a new dimension in the 1970s. Whereas, in the nineteenth century, 'the selective critique expressed by conservation organizations (which in addition involved neither large costs for nor fundamental critique of industrialization) was never able to shake off the nimbus of hostility to progress and backwardness that surrounded it' (Beck 2009, 162), the environmental conservation movement that emerged in the 1970s gained such influence that it achieved major political and economic changes in the direction of environmental protection (cf. 6.2.1). The movement was composed of 'decentralised citizens' initiatives and demonstrations' (WBGU 2011, 242), and was fighting against tangible visible environmental destruction (such as the *waldsterben*, the pollution of rivers). Over time, it also opposed more complex issues, fighting against environmental degradation and risks whose social and environmental externalities can be charged to future generations (for example nuclear waste, climate change).

'The current potentials for protest are very difficult to classify, because scenes, groupings, and topics change very rapidly' (Habermas 1987b, 393). Social movements mostly emerge in protest to existing societal conditions, which implies that they might also disappear, if their goals have been reached or if their action opens up further action situations and their actors assume roles in more institutionalised processes. However, they do not necessarily have to vanish. They can also collaborate closely with the local authority and still comply with their initial mission of critically observing and triggering policy innovation in local governance (Moulaert 2000, 77).

This research is specifically interested in the emergence of a continuously growing type of social movement whose joint and unifying topic is its critique of growth (Habermas 1985, 155; 1995a, 577, 579). On the backdrop of the 'life-world' being threatened by commodification and bureaucratisation of the systems market and state, they claim bottom-up forms of self-organisation to contain the power the market and state exercise over the 'lifeworld' (Habermas 1985, 155–6) and can thus be understood as one form of resistance against 'life-world'-colonising trends (Habermas 1995a, 579, 582).

Beck's (2007, 80) question 'Which shape an ecological labour movement could take?' is justified, since starting from the beginning of industrialisation up to now labour movements have primarily fought for the social rights of the workers, disregarding environmental damage as long as economic activity assured their employment and increasing income.[22] Workers are an integral part of the processes of industrialisation that have led to the current state of the planet. They benefit from economic growth on the one hand, but on the other hand they suffer from its consequences, either in direct exposure to health risks at their place of work or indirectly through the short- and long-term consequences of environmental damage provoked by industrial activity. The environmental movements of the 1970s and onwards have not managed to connect the environmental issue to that of workers' social rights. Here lies a big untapped potential for different civil society actors to join forces and to create social change, in industrialised countries and in the Global South. In the latter the probability of unacceptable working conditions is even higher. Serving as supplier countries for products and raw materials to the industrialised countries, both social rights of the workers and environmental standards are often disregarded, thus exposing the workers to extreme health risks. Yet, despite mostly higher socio-environmental risks for workers in the Global South, it is less probable that an environmental workers' movement arises in that part of the world, since there the majority of workers have few possibilities for choosing a less harming job to earn an income. Chances for the evolution of such a movement and for its success are higher in industrialised countries with a 'parliamentary democracy, a (relative) independence of the press and an advanced wealth production in which for the majority of the population the risk of cancer [for example] … does not fade into the background in face of a famine' (Beck 2007, 90, own translation).[23]

Social movements mostly emerge and grow in the urban space. The innovative and corrective power of urban social movements is expressed by Castells (1983, 278), describing them as a 'conscious collective practice originating in urban issues, able to produce qualitative changes in the urban system, local culture, and political institutions in contradiction to the dominant social interests institutionalized as such at the societal level'. He carves out the features of urban social movements as striving for 'local government, self-reliance, and citizen participation' (ibid., 285). In concrete terms, and coming close to the conceptions of social and solidarity economy (cf. 2.4.4), urban demands brought forward by urban social movements

> tend to create an alternative economic basis of community-orientated social relations, and, at the same time, their satisfaction could provide a new source of legitimacy for decentralized political power. Community-orientated neighbourhoods could become the social fabric required for a more effective functioning of urban services through self-management, while they could establish the political institutions in the grassroots by bringing the state down to the community level. Participatory democracy appears to be the political prerequisite for achieving … economic redistribution by means of urban services.
>
> (Ibid.)

One strong international urban social movement has been the 'Right to the city'. This term was first used by Lefebvre (2009, 107, own translation), who considers it to be an umbrella term for a group of inherent rights of city dwellers, of which citizen participation and self-organisation, including the common production of space by (re)appropriating space and thereby turning it into commons, are part (ibid., 77, 94, 104, 107, 125, 133). Purcell and Tyman (2015, 2), having applied Lefebvre's concept of a right to the city to urban food production (cf. 7.4.1), define it as 'a declaration by people that they intend to struggle for a radically democratised city beyond both capitalism and the state, a city where inhabitants produce and directly manage urban space for themselves, through free activity'. Purcell and Tyman (2015, 4) argue that for Lefebvre political activism is always linked to controversies about space: 'Any revolutionary "project" today, whether utopian or realist, must, if it is to avoid hopeless banality, make … the reappropriation of space … into a non-negotiable part of its agenda' (Lefebvre 1991, 166–7). The goal of the struggle, which 'is already underway, in the everyday practices of urban inhabitants' (Purcell and Tyman 2015, 2) is 'a city that esteems use value over exchange value … where inhabitants are active participants rather than passive consumers' (ibid., 5). Concurring with Lefebvre, Harvey (2012, 87–8) believes that urban social movements unavoidably have to deal with the issue of urban commons. He sees a crucial role for urban social movements as an all-embracing collective undertaking towards more democratisation, environmental sustainability, social equality, and the re-thinking of values which together lead to profound social change (ibid., xvi, 4). In this process of change, urban social movements are conceived as a counter force from below to the uncontrolled growth-determined capitalist forces that disregard political, social, and environmental effects (ibid., xv).

There is only a small corpus of research on urban movements focusing specifically on green spaces. Barthel and colleagues researched urban environmental movements' part in the protection of urban green space. They specify four major functions which these movements can fulfil in protecting urban green spaces. First, 'they can counter shorter-term and profit-driven interests on urban land through their engagement in place-based struggles'[24] (2015, 1331). Second, 'through their intervention in the planning and use of urban space, environmental movements participate in shaping ecosystem processes and services' (ibid.). Third, they 'can push existing administrative systems to recognise the value of urban green areas' (ibid.). Fourth, they

> challeng[e] longstanding ideas of how we should understand 'the city', its identity and for what and whom it exists. [They] ... have the ability to bring new and lay narratives into public debates that can help to express the connectedness and dependency of urban dwellers on ecosystem services such as local food.
>
> (Ibid.)

Particularly, over about the last 20 years, numerous diverse heterogeneous social movements around the world have emerged to drive the socio-ecological transition. They mostly start locally as 'one-issue initiatives'[25] (Elsen 2007, 321), being embedded in the local context, and often become increasingly interconnected and networked, achieving impact also at the regional, national, and international level (ibid., 13, 49, 321). They fight for global social, environmental, and economic rights and develop sustainable alternatives to the globalised neoliberal corporate economic system (ibid., 13, 166; Fischer-Lescano and Möller 2011, 24). These movements have realised and taken action against the fact that 'in the neoliberal economic constitution primarily liberal property-, patent- and free-trade rights are protected and the social rights are often downgraded to *soft-law* principles in unbinding codes of conduct' (Fischer-Lescano and Möller 2011, 46, own translation).[26] 'They are fed up with the power of corporations, they are fed up with the destruction of democracy and people's rights' (Shiva 2013, 260). They respond to an unjust globalised neoliberal corporate economic system which plunders the Earth's natural resources for profit interests of a rich minority, destroying the livelihood of people in the Global South (cf. also ibid., 20; 7.4.3).

A main challenge of the socio-ecological transition is to let these various social movements 'become the "critical mass" required' (WBGU 2011, 261), to let them 'achieve a shared feeling of collective self-efficacy' (ibid.) and to unite them 'in a widespread social movement' (ibid.). The socio-ecological transition can only be successful if supported by a broad societal coalition of actors from the market, state, and civil society. Therefore, social movements emerging in civil society need to have the capacity to also reach state and market actors. This can then produce what Randers (2012, 255) calls the 'sustainability crowd'.[27] These are people from all societal sectors[28] that oppose the infinite economic growth paradigm, having understood that to protect the planet and humankind's livelihoods a thinking beyond making short-term profit and achieving short-term benefits is required.

6.2.5 Bottom-up politics and changing modes of participation

Whereas in the first modernity, civil society action, for example in the form of social movements, centred around obtaining social rights and abolishing privileges of the advantaged social classes, in the second modernity the ecological question turns into a central reason for civil society actors to become active (Beck 1996, 123–4). It offers a unique chance for all concerned people to join in a global project of socio-ecological transition to ensure the survival of the Earth and its inhabitants (Beck 1993, 247). The fact that climate collapse is in sight, as bad as it is, might also be a great chance for democracy (WBGU 2011, 29), since it forces people 'to sit down at a table to find and enforce solutions to the self-inflicted endangering that crosses all borders' (Beck 1986, 63, own translation). This process can be labelled '*reflexive politicization*' (Beck 2009, 77) and points to a broadened understanding of politics. Politics is considered a matter for all citizens, not only for elected representatives. It becomes the 'politics of *society*' (Beck 1993, 17, own translation). Thus, it is no longer exclusively practised by political actors of the representative democratic system but involves a broader realm of society, of individual and collective actors (ibid., 155, 162–3), for example social movements and citizens' initiatives. This 'unbinding of politics' (Beck 1986, 311, own translation) and the rise of 'subpolitics' (Beck 2007, 154, own translation) point to the emergence of a 'new political culture' (Beck 2009, 185). Its core is the locally situated but globally connected self-organisation of politics (Beck 1993, 156, 215) with the power to shape society from the bottom up (ibid., 164). This way the rules of the political game can be modified (ibid., 207). This is also made easier since '*reflexive politicization*' (Beck 2009, 77) happens at a time of a double weakening of the nation state in the course of globalisation from above and from below (Nowotny *et al.* 2013, 22–3). On the one hand European integration has entailed the cession of national sovereignty in numerous policy domains to the European level. On the other hand 'decentralization in political authority and administration came to be regarded as a requirement of good governance' (ibid., 7) and has been initiated and set as a principle in numerous European countries.

With the help of subpolitics, national politics and the interests of global corporations that counteract the goals of the socio-ecological transition can be undermined by multilevel coalitions from local to global unified in the fight for a common idea. These new actors call into question the 'old' institutions of the first modernity. Citizens all over the world have noticed that they are not at the mercy of global corporations and national governments but that for example their purchasing power is a powerful weapon. Boycotting socially and environmentally unsustainable products is a form of direct democracy, exercised by an active and conscious consumer society comprising smart consumers, in coalition with public media, who have become aware of every individual's global responsibility and have started to act. In the process of reflexive modernisation, consensus is increasingly reached by discussing topics transparently and publicly (Habermas 1995a, 218), which also modifies the framework conditions of economic action (Beck 1993, 200). Economic actors increasingly have to explain and justify their actions in front of an awakened public.

The above-mentioned example of conscious consumers refutes wide-spread complaints about decreasing participation levels in democracy. These complaints go up to the point of diagnosing a 'post-democracy' (Crouch 2004, 1)

> which designate[s] a society in which, despite democratic mechanisms like elections still in place, a more egalitarian society remains out of reach. This is because political processes are mainly determined by economic lobbyists, whereas the majority of citizens only assume a passive recipient position (Crouch 2004, viii, 4).
>
> (Elsen and Schicklinski 2016, 222)

Indeed, in times of globalisation, the influence of the economic sector on political decision processes has increased, whereas the power of national parliaments and political parties has decreased (von Braunmühl 2010, 191). Yet, if to speak of a democracy crisis, one has to specify which type of democracy is meant. 'Agree[ing] with Crouch's analysis up to this point' (Elsen and Schicklinski 2016, 222), it must however be stressed that the widely lamented disenchantment with politics does 'not really reflect a general legitimisation crisis, but ... [indicates] a growing disappointment with the effectiveness and accountability of democratic systems' (WBGU 2011, 207). Thus, it can also be considered to be a major 'paradigm shift. The existing crisis of representative democracy expressing itself in decreasing participation levels in elections goes along with increasing and diverse forms of participation and self-organisation' (Elsen and Schicklinski 2016, 222). There is a 'growing self-confidence and participatory interest of the citizens' (Beck 2009, 195). Yet, people increasingly 'become active predominantly outside of the parliamentary system' (WBGU 2011, 192). Individualisation processes of the second modernity (cf. 2.1) mean 'the loss of traditional normative securities [which is] also the cause of the search for new forms of social embedding'[29] (Elsen 2007, 45, own translation). People are unified by one common issue, often a specific tangible one, to be solved and punctually, often spontaneously, become politically active for the joint aim. '*Temporary* coalitions between *different groups* and *different camps* are formed and dissolved, depending on the *particular issue* at stake and on the *particular situation*' (Beck 2009, 100). Patterns of participation and civic activities are changing, yet are not decreasing or becoming less reliable (Beck 1996, 143; Enquete-Kommission 'Zukunft des Bürgerschaftlichen Engagements' des Deutschen Bundestages 2002, 49–51). Also the new social media catalyse new forms of spontaneous participation and self-organisation – 'new, in particular informal forms of organisation with distinctive flexibility and big individual room for manoeuvre'[30] (ibid., 50, own translation).

> This is a form of democracy that goes beyond the voting right. Citizens ask for more co-determination and for a different culture of political participation. Civic engagement is much more than volunteer work within predefined boundaries. It is a bottom-up reaction to the aforementioned tendencies and can thus be considered as political action.
>
> (Elsen and Schicklinski 2016, 222)

These activities might then, in a second step, develop into institutions with a higher organisational level. New institutional arrangements are forming that offer a new way of social embedding more adapted to the needs and demands of the modern individualised person (Elsen 2007, 45). To achieve broad support from bottom-up actors for the transition, it is essential that participation options respond to this changed demand from the citizens' side. New options for citizen participation and self-organisation need to 'respect the autonomy demands of individuals, and encourage change agents' own initiative whilst also providing them with stability and continuity' (WBGU 2011, 209).

6.2.6 Transformative transdisciplinary learning processes

The 'overspecialization' (Beck 2009, 158) of sectors in industrial society in general and of science in particular is the cause of side effects (cf. 2.1) due to the fact that these overspecialised subsystems function according to their inherent specific rationalities (Beck 1993, 74), disregarding the knowledge of other such systems. Subpolitics can help to reduce this trend by returning to and developing further the 'specialization in the context' (Beck 2009, 158) by starting to think in transdisciplinary networks (Beck 1993, 189) and to foster a joint learning process. In such a process risks are no longer minimised and hidden, but 'methodically and objectively interpreted and scientifically displayed' (Beck 2009, 158). Learning takes places by taking small steps, conducting actions as experiments and learning from one's own mistakes and those of others. This requires building up a public sphere with industry, politics, science, and the population participating. In this regard Nowotny *et al.* (2013, 23) describe how

> new kinds of more open regulation are emerging. These regulations are preceded by elaborate negotiations, mediations, consultations and contestations which take place within the public arena.... This is no longer the domain of a relatively closed bureaucratic-professional-legal world of regulation, but of broader cultural-political movements embodying antagonistic forms of interaction.

For such a new interplay of actors to unfold and persist, several changes are necessary. One has to abandon the belief that expert knowledge is exclusively found in public administrations and with official experts and instead also acknowledge local lay experts' knowledge (Nowotny *et al.* 2013, 10, 35). Also, citizens have to stop believing that political leaders know all the solutions and instead have to allow them to make mistakes and to learn from them. 'They [political leaders] do not know any better than anyone else how to bring about a sustainable society; most of them don't even know it's necessary to do so' (Meadows *et al.* 2005, 280). Acknowledging the potential of change agents also shifts the focus away from political leaders as sole problem solvers in the socio-ecological transition. Despite their important role due to their ability to influence law-making and allocate public resources,

> a sustainability revolution requires each person to act as a learning leader at some level, from family to community to nation to world. And it requires each of us to support leaders by allowing them to admit uncertainty, conduct honest experiments, and acknowledge mistakes.
>
> (Ibid.)

Furthermore, all societal groups need to have the right to participate in decision-making which has to start with an open-ended discussion and not with an already defined outcome, and socially disadvantaged groups need to be enabled to participate equally (cf. 6.3.2.2). This requires a transparent dialogue between all actors in a public sphere, which is easier to achieve with the help of negotiation and mediation institutions (Beck 1986, 190–1).

6.3 Spaces of civil society action

Urban green spaces can be turned into spaces of civil society action if actors become aware of their power to turn these spaces into urban green commons. To better understand the process of space creation, the approach of sociology of space is presented before explaining how urban green commons are made.

6.3.1 Space, actors, commons: creating space

Even though in urban and regional sociology city and space are considered to be highly interconnected notions (Löw *et al.* 2008, 9), existing theories mainly describe space as being related to places and territories (Löw 2001, 9). This approach is insufficient to explain civil society action around urban green spaces, especially their (re)appropriation. Löw has advanced the notion of space by proposing an action-related theory of space, which seems to be suitable to understand civil society action in the field of urban green spaces. The approach is outlined in the following subsection, before linking the creation of space to 'commoning' and the urban green commons concept, which can be considered to be an application of Ostrom's theory to urban green spaces.

6.3.1.1 The approach of sociology of space

Before the emergence of action-related theories of space, theories could be divided into absolutistic and relativistic ones, with the majority of sociologists adhering to the first group. The absolutistic view conceives space as a container that embraces objects and human beings and in which action takes place. 'Space is used as a synonym for soil, territory or place'[31] (Löw 2001, 264, own translation). The relativistic view states 'that space arises from the structure of the bodies' relative positions. Considered from a relativistic point of view, space is the sole result of the relationships' (Löw *et al.* 2008, 9, own translation). Both approaches consider space and action as two phenomena detached from each other, and in neither approach can space be conceived as resulting from human action (Löw 2001, 264). Therefore, Löw develops – out of the relativistic concept – a procedural notion of space, which postulates that '*spatial structures* are, like temporal structures also, forms of *social structures*'[32] (Löw 2001, 167, own translation). The approach tries to understand 'how space is made relevant in communications … or how space is produced in processes of perception, remembrance or imagination and how it becomes manifest in social structures' (Löw *et al.* 2008, 9, own translation). Two interacting processes constitute spaces. First, spaces 'emerge … through the active combination of elements by people. This means that via processes of perception, imagination and remembrance, social goods and people/ living beings are combined to spaces' (ibid., 64, own translation).[33] 'Commoning', for example in the form of urban gardening on an abandoned brownfield site (cf. 6.3.1.2 and 7.3), can be considered as such a process. Here, a group of actors actively takes care of urban green spaces and in this way (re)combines existing elements or adds new ones to alter existing space and thereby creating a new one.[34] Second, the process of 'spacing' (ibid.) means that 'space is … constituted by the placing of social goods and people, or the placing of primarily symbolic markings to mark ensembles of goods and people as such' (ibid., own translation). 'Spacing' manifests for example in citizens' movements that appropriate abandoned urban space, for example former military fields, to put pressure on local authorities to turn them into green spaces instead of starting building development (cf. 7.3). By physically 'taking possession' of the space, activists symbolically mark it as possible valuable urban meeting space for social interaction. Their action carries a political demand as it points to a lack of sufficient urban green spaces and to ongoing densification, urban sprawl, and concomitant soil-sealing.

If spaces are created repeatedly, they become institutionalised. The aforementioned process thus creates spatial structures that then shape – 'alongside political, economic, legal … and temporal structures [–] … the social structure'[35] (Löw 2001, 171–2, own translation). In relation to green spaces, we could for example speak of institutionalised urban green commons (cf. 6.3.1.2) as spatial structures, if local policy-makers had recognised civil society's legitimate role in participating in the governance of urban green spaces and had allowed for, fostered, and perpetuated diverse forms of collectively caring for green spaces. This reasoning advances the duality of action and structure, as described by Anthony

Giddens (1984), stressing that space itself needs to be thought of as social structure, meaning that 'spaces do not merely exist, but that they are created in (usually repetitive) action and as spatial structures, embedded in institutions, guide action'[36] (Löw 2001, 172, own translation).

A historic example of how the creation of space by human action influences social structures and ultimately leads to social change can be found in the Madrid Citizen Movement in the second half of the 1980s.[37] Currently, in cities where citizens create space, 'reclaiming' the city by protest actions in urban space in order to direct attention to the lack of green spaces and related building speculation and privatisation trends can open up public discussion about the use of space for different interests. This, to a certain extent, changes the social structure, since citizens become aware that they can take part in designing their city. The implication of this could be that city populations then demand more citizen participation and options for self-organisation in other policy fields and not only the governance of urban green spaces.

6.3.1.2 Creating urban green commons

The concept of self-organisation (cf. 6.3.2) is tightly linked to the one of commons. Commons are

> both natural and depletable resources such as water, land and forest, and renewable, social or cultural resources such as seeds, algorithms, software, public space or the electromagnetic spectrum, [all of which are] considered to be jointly owned by a group of people; ... because they are elementary to our lives.[38]
>
> (Helfrich 2014, 90, own translation)

They are thus a special type of goods (cf. also 3.1) and can be governed successfully through self-organisation if certain rules are followed (cf. 3.3.1).

Commons are collectively governed by commoners, which works out if they have undergone learning processes and are able to cooperate and self-organise (Helfrich and Bollier 2014, 19). Harvey (2012, 79) stresses the interplay between civil society and the local authority in commoning, describing it as a 'mix of individual and private initiative ... [with] the local state [being] ... involved through regulations, codes, standards, and public investments, along with informal and formal neighborhood organization'. This shows that in most cases, self-organisation, even if emerging alongside traditional governance structures, has to adhere to local regulations and can even be advanced by them.

With regard to urban green spaces, the urban green commons concept serves to circumscribe the creation of commons in the governance of urban green spaces. Colding and Barthel (2013, 159) define 'urban green commons'

> as physical green spaces in urban settings of diverse ownership that depend on collective organization and management and to which individuals and

interest groups participating in management hold a rich set of bundles of rights, including rights to craft their own institutions and to decide whom they want to include in management schemes.

While ownership of the land can vary (for example public or private)[39] and different organisational structures exist (for example allotment gardens, community gardens), urban green commons are marked by the fact that their governance right lies in the hands of the group of actors (Colding *et al.* 2013, 1). Urban green commons allow city dwellers to actively become engaged with urban nature by jointly taking care of urban green spaces, thus facilitating ecological processes (ibid.). They emerge since urban green spaces are lacking and people, instead of acquiescing, become active locally in order to bring about a change (Colding and Barthel 2013, 162). They counter 'three dominant trends in cities – those of privatization of land, lowering contact between people and nature, and the impoverishment of ecological habitats and functions' (Colding *et al.* 2013, 1), therefore being a major contributing factor to making cities more ecologically and socially sustainable (ibid., 11).

6.3.2 Civic activities: citizen participation and self-organisation

> The complexity and uncertainty of socio-ecological problems can only be dealt with in a broad societal participatory learning process. In this process, civil society has increasingly been recognised as a creative, steering, and corrective power in society and in the economic, political, and scientific systems. It is also a discrete societal actor, following the needs of the lifeworld.
>
> (Elsen and Schicklinski 2016, 238)

With the stronger role of a proactive and enabling state (cf. 2.4.2), citizen participation and self-organisation become ever more important as a countervailing power. Meanwhile, citizens have been less regarded by public authorities 'as passive recipients of public good to be distributed or re-distributed according to expert systems' (Nowotny *et al.* 2013, 7). Yet, despite numerous statements, increased options for true citizen participation and self-organisation have only sluggishly been given, because increasing citizens' power implies 'the restriction of the powerful's power'[40] (Elsen 2007, 316, own translation). In his theory on reflexive modernisation, Beck (1993, 164, own translation) describes a civil society 'takes in hand by itself its matters in all areas and spheres of activity of society'. In this sense, citizen participation and self-organisation can be considered as a 'subpolitisation of society' (ibid., own translation) through which social change is created. Civic activities are an important source of social innovation (Enquete 2002, 128). They need to find conducive framework conditions to unfold more easily:

> A fundamental shift is needed to overcome the obvious knowledge–behaviour gap to open up arenas where unconventional bottom-up initiatives

and top-down approaches can meet to approve and enable societal innovations. In particular, the political and administrative systems are challenged to come to a new culture of interplay with civil society actors to demonstrate that they consider civic engagement to be 'more than a political residual'[41] (Roth 2002, 350, own translation). Roth criticises that instead of drawing on the diverse forms of civic engagement that are evolving because citizens are increasingly aware of their competence, 'political democracy is still enclosed representatively and colonised by the political parties' (ibid., own translation).

(Elsen and Schicklinski 2016, 235–6)

Opening up opportunities to citizen participation as well as strengthening 'the capability of individuals and groups to self-organise and to represent their own and common concerns depends on personal, social, economic, and political preconditions' (ibid., 238). Local authorities, taking the discourse on citizen participation and self-organisation seriously, should find ways to implement direct democracy tools such as community parliaments or citizen assemblies (WBGU 2011, 336). 'In particular, the local level enables widespread, synergetic, and participatory solutions and can be a laboratory for politics of possibilities from below' (Elsen and Schicklinski 2016, 238). 'New forms of direct democracy and public participation[42] as well as opportunities for social learning' (ibid.) and self-organisation need to be provided.

6.3.2.1 Communalities and differences

Allowing more options for direct democracy is expressed in the slogan 'Democracy beyond voting', which has become a buzzword in current policy discourses. For example, for the Working Group on Public Participation in relation to the EU Water Framework Directive public participation generally signifies 'allowing people to influence the outcome of plans and working processes' (European Commission (EC) 2003, iv). The group distinguishes between three stages of participation mentioned in the directive: *information supply*, consultation, and active involvement according to the respective level of involving citizens (ibid.). The model assumes that the lower stages are a prerequisite for the higher ones. In order to be able to participate, citizens need to be informed, for example through a website, which constitutes one form of communication from public authorities to citizens.

Consultation takes place, if citizens' input and ideas are asked for in written or oral form, building a two-way information channel, for example via surveys or public meetings without voting (EC 2003, 13). Thus, public authorities ask for citizens' points of view, yet citizens are not requested to elaborate a common group opinion, nor are public authorities obliged to take citizens' opinions into consideration (European Environment Agency (EEA) 2014, 12).

Active involvement generally signifies that 'interested parties participate actively in the planning process by discussing issues and contributing to their solution' (EC 2003, 13). Measures include 'citizen's juries, consensus confer-ences, task-forces and public meetings with voting' (Reed 2008, 2424).

This three-stage model can be zoomed in on by classifying in a more detailed way its highest stage of active involvement, as done for example by Wright *et al.* (2010, 42–5). For them, information and consultation are only pre-stages of citizen participation. Real citizen participation starts when citizens can take part in decision-making. An example would be elaborating a group proposal in which the decision-makers assure citizens that their views will be taken into consideration, which is commonly also known as *stakeholder engagement*.

The next higher level is usually known as *delegated decision-making*. Here decision-making authority is partly granted to citizens, for example in the form of participatory budgeting.

The highest level of citizen participation is reached when citizens are given decisive power (*co-decision-making*). They are on an equal footing with public authorities and are also co-accountable for the results (EC 2003, 13; Figure 6.1).

Defining self-organisation requires a description of its relationship with, and delimitation to, the closely linked concept of citizen participation. There is a growing corpus of literature on the citizen participation–environmental decision-making nexus, and yet self-organisation's influence on environmental decision-making has, to date, hardly been researched. One reason might be that citizen participation is easier to define and classify into different forms than self-organisation, as undertaken in the preceding paragraph. Another reason might be that the environmental legal framework from the international to the local level increasingly requires participatory procedures, for example the United Nations Convention on Access to Information, Public Participation in Decision-Making and Access to Justice in Environmental Matters (United Nations Economic Commission for Europe (UNECE) 1998),[43] or the European Union Water Framework Directive (European Parliament and Council of the

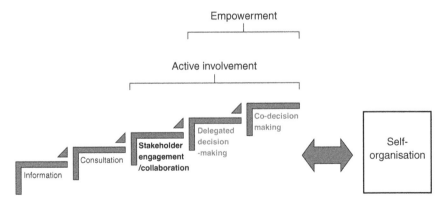

Figure 6.1 Citizen participation and self-organisation.

Source: own representation, based on Arnstein 1969, 217; EC 2003, iv; Wright *et al.* 2010, 42; Davies and Simon 2013, 5.

European Union 2000). The United Nations convention even sets citizen participation in environmental matters as a democratic and human right (EEA 2014, 13) by giving citizens the 'rights of access to information, public participation in decision-making, and access to justice in environmental matters' (UNECE 1998, 518). In contrast, the concept of self-organisation is not yet a subject matter in the environmental legal framework. Self-organisation is more dynamic and can occur in manifold ways, and thus its concept is more difficult to grasp and lay down in legislative texts. However, an additional reason could be that both in theory and in practice the two concepts are often used interchangeably (Boonstra and Boelens 2011, 109) without doing justice to their inherent meaning. The following paragraphs try to define commonalities and differences between the two concepts and propose a model to illustrate the ideas (cf. Figure 6.1).

An important distinction between citizen participation and self-organisation is the possible locus of initiative-taking. In the case of citizen participation, it lies exclusively with public authorities, whereas with self-organisation 'the initiative is taken by members of civil society or business, indifferent to public policy objectives' (ibid., 109). Citizen participation can precede self-organisation, yet it is not a prerequisite for it as the participation ladder model by Wright *et al.* (2010, 42) might misleadingly suggest. They developed their model on the basis of Arnstein's (1969, 217) eight-step model, adding self-organisation as the highest level of the participation ladder. However, self-organisation goes beyond the scope of citizen participation as far as the degree of decisive power of those involved is concerned. Thus it includes all types of self-organised activities that do not compulsorily have to stem from participatory measures. They can also be started by citizens themselves (Wright *et al.* 2010, 45). Therefore, self-organisation can also emerge independently of existing citizen participation options (cf. Figure 6.1).

Whereas citizen participation

> refers to goals set by government bodies on which citizens can exert influence through procedures set by these government regimes themselves …, self-organization stands for the actual motives, networks, communities, processes and objectives of citizens themselves, at least initially independent of government policies and detached from participatory planning procedures.
>
> (Boonstra and Boelens 2011, 109)

Both citizen participation and self-organisation are essential components of civil society activities. Depending on the institutional setting, the one or the other makes more sense. Furthermore, self-organisation can develop out of citizen participation and vice versa. Moreover, self-organisation can also emerge as a result of non-involvement by local politics and administration, for example out of missing citizen participation, or it can deliberately be started by citizens as a protest movement against political or administrative action. Especially, 'socio-economic self-help is always political' (Elsen 2007, 51, own translation), since it questions established responsibilities and power structures (ibid., 146, 190). It can be a way 'to sustainably ensure access via cooperation to personal and common livelihoods' (ibid., 51, own translation) and is thus 'real social self-help, since it takes place collectively and has a social background of origin.... In addition, it pursues primarily social goals with economic means' (ibid., 51, own translation; cf. 2.4.4). Yet, in industrialised market societies with concomitant welfare states the capability for socioeconomic self-organisation as a form of autonomous self-help has been unlearned, in contrast to developing and newly industrialising countries (ibid., 191) where market and state are less present and self-organisation is often a means of survival. With people relying to a great extent on state and market solutions, the capacity for socioeconomic self-organisation to organise local matters according to the needs of the local community must thus be re-learned and pursued, also against the resistance of state and market actors who fear losing their power (ibid., 321).

6.3.2.2 Enabling participation and self-organisation of socially disadvantaged groups

For the socio-ecological transition to be successful, all societal groups must be included. This challenge should not be underestimated, since people with less spending power are virtually forced to spend as little money as possible for all products. With the internalisation of social and environmental externalities (cf. 2.4.2) product prices would rise, which can easily turn less wealthy people into opponents of the transition (WBGU 2011, 191). The provision of an unconditional basic income would provide the material security for less wealthy citizens to become more conscious consumers on the one hand and to actively participate and self-organise in the local community on the other (Elsen 2007, 56; cf. 2.4.3.6). Yet, increased material security does not automatically lead to intensified civic activities among this group, since 'the capability of individuals and groups to self-organise and to represent their own and common concerns depends on personal, social, economic, and political preconditions' (Elsen and Schicklinski 2016, 226). At present, major studies still show a 'close connection between socioeconomic factors such as income, educational level and professional position on one hand and the extent of realised commitment on the other'[44] (Enquete 2002, 48, own translation). The capability to self-organise 'is the core competence of active citizenship. However, it follows the social mechanism of silent selectivity, varying along the demarcation line of social inequality' (Elsen and Schicklinski 2016, 226). To explain these interrelationships, Bourdieu's (1983) theory of social capital can be drawn on (cf. 2.4.2). It helps

> to understand the intrinsic and sociocultural depth effects of a lack of cultural and social capital. Having such capital is a precondition for individuals' active and self-confident participation in all societal sectors. Therefore, having it makes the emergence of [citizen] participation and

self-organisation more probable. However, all civil society actors, also those who are not adept at articulating their needs and opinions in public, must have adequate options to participate.

(Elsen and Schicklinski 2016, 226)

Keeping Bourdieu's theory in mind, it becomes evident that

> the same treatment of 'relevant actors' promotes existing inequality in participatory developments. If all societal groupings shall truly be involved, those people that are less apt to express themselves need to be met in the community, since they have learned that their competences, wishes and opinions are not in demand.
>
> (Elsen 2007, 42, own translation)

Therefore, access to civic activities must be opened up and facilitated specifically to this group, so that they get in touch actively with sustainability topics and joint learning and awareness-raising become possible. The local authority must not only provide options for citizen participation and give room for self-organisation to evolve, but they must also ensure that all groups of society have access to these options and that they are enabled to use them. 'Socioeconomic self-organisation of disadvantaged persons ... necessitates for its enabling ... the opening of established societal systems, a material and immaterial framing and innovative institutional arrangements' (ibid., 326, own translation). In practical terms, and with regard to the present and expected composition of the European population, this means for example for the local authority to provide written and oral information in more than just the local language and to provide translation services to cater for the needs of migrants as well as to provide assistance to the elderly and disabled to enable them to become active in citizen participation and self-organisation locally. Providing participation options for migrants is especially important to counter their double discrimination of, first, often being excluded from the labour market[45] and, second, from civil rights, if not allowed to vote, not even in local elections.[46] 'The activation and facilitation of civic engagement [in general and in particular amongst socially disadvantaged groups] can be supported by intermediaries, operating as facilitators and change agents' (Elsen and Schicklinski 2016, 227). With regard to migrants, the role of second- or third-generation migrants[47] as facilitators is precious and greatly needed.

Drawing on the distinction between bonding and bridging social capital made by Putnam and Goss (2001, 28–30), Elsen (2007, 146) explains that socially disadvantaged persons have the former, which however is mostly not sufficient to enable participation and socioeconomic self-organised solutions in the local community. Since socioeconomic self-organisation questions existing power structures, it is only realisable, if also having bridging social capital to be able to create a 'connection to social influential forces apt to organise' (ibid., 146, own translation). Intermediaries are a necessary bridging force here. In this sense, for example the urban gardening movement (cf. 7.4) could be very important. For the first time, a social movement has emerged that could bring together 'the reflexive, alternatively economic and environmental movements and the alternative social and sociopolitical movements and their addressees which are less apt to express themselves' (ibid., 110, own translation). The first group is 'part of the alliance of "dissidents of the growth's society", described by Habermas (1985, 157, own translation), that aims to strengthen the vital foundations of lifeworlds against administrative powers and money through forms of self-organisation at the grassroots level' (Elsen and Schicklinski 2016, 137). It is already aware of a necessary socio-ecological transition at all societal levels and in all fields and has the 'bridging social capital' that the second group is lacking. Joining forces between the two groups would have an amplifying effect for the transition from below. Urban gardening and agriculture brings together people from all social backgrounds. This also increases the likelihood that the first group becomes sensitised to the problems of the second and that the socio-ecological transition is brought forward at the local level taking along all societal groups, sensitising the citizens for the interconnectedness of social, environmental, and economic problems. From this movement social and solidarity economies could emerge on the one hand 'for lack of other possibilities of securing one's livelihood and socioeconomic participation' (Elsen 2007, 145, own translation) and on the other hand 'as explicit and reflexive alternative draft to the encroachments of the globalised market economy' (ibid., own translation).

With the rapidly increasing number of refugees in Germany and other countries of the EU, enabling the participation of socially disadvantaged groups has become an immense task. Coping with this task would not be possible without numerous civil society actors who, in 2015, were the first to find swift unbureaucratic solutions to provide refugees with the provision of basic goods, while politics and administration from the EU to the local level were still occupied with clarifying responsibilities. For the long-term integration of the newly arriving refugees, community gardens, especially in Germany, can draw on past experiences. The foundation 'anstiftung & ertomis'[48] scientifically accompanies the development of the urban gardening movement in the German-speaking area. It recently conducted a survey in German community gardens to understand how they reach out to refugees in order to spread this knowledge to other gardens. Some of these gardens were deliberately set up on the premises of accommodation for refugees, others were started intentionally in the context of flight and asylum on premises outside the refugees' accommodation, and the third type are gardens that have integrated specific parts for refugees after their foundation (anstiftung & ertomis 2015). To successfully integrate the refugees in the garden project,[49] it is important not to set up more than a manageable number of rules in the garden, since too many complicated rules can inhibit refugees from participating (ibid.). Participation on an equal footing in direct democratic discussion and decision processes needs to be learned, which by itself already needs time and patience. This is all the more true if the participants, as is the case for many refugees, are not used to democratic ways of interacting and deciding, be it between different social positions, genders, or generations.

In order to allow for the participation of disadvantaged groups, Elsen demands an enabling social policy fostering their democratic socioeconomic self-organisation (cf. 2.4.4). Such a policy would aim at sustainable local development (Elsen 2007, 19, 34) and would '[combine] support of disadvantaged social groups with demands for their greater self-reliance and self-help' (WBGU 2011, 204).[50] Community gardens are self-organised civil society projects that enable participation, not only across social positions, generations, and gender but, with increasing immigration to the EU, also across different cultures, religions, and languages. By doing so they carry out social work tasks, delivering a precious service to the whole local community, which should be acknowledged as such by the local authority.[51] Yet, so far, social, economic, and labour market policy have largely ignored such projects of self-organisation with the potential to develop into social and solidarity economies (Elsen 2007). Even worse, where these projects emerge, they are far too often still treated as supplicants by the local authority, having to ask and being grateful for services that the local authority should provide them for free, in the case of community gardens to be able to make the garden run smoothly.[52] If the socio-ecological transition is supposed to succeed, enabling and supporting bottom-up self-organised initiatives such as urban gardening is of key importance, since these projects are rooted in local issues and have the potential to actively involve all citizens irrespective of their socioeconomic background.

6.3.2.3 Existing civil society action

The research in the ROCSET project revealed that citizens more easily and more often participate and self-organise in the green spaces resource system than in water or energy up to the point that citizens' 'self organisation has even become a transition driver in some cities' (Barnebeck *et al.* 2016, 194). The qualitative data analysis delivers examples for all stages of citizen participation and self-organisation (cf. Figure 6.1). Yet, only *consultation* and *self-organisation* are mentioned in all regions. Altogether, *citizen involvement in the governance of urban green spaces* is rated as non-existent or low by actors from several cities (Bilbao, a4, 41–7, 53–4, 92; Gothenburg, a3, 76–80; Sibiu, a3, 86–91 and a4, 109, 114–15, 121–5; Strasbourg, a4, 118–22). This is either because no participatory options are offered, or when enshrined in the legal framework and also offered, they are not adopted well by citizens. Expert knowledge of civil society can deliberately be ignored (cf. 9.4), as in the case of Timisoara, where an NGO provided knowledge on the city's richest urban green space and biodiversity site next to the river and advised the local authority not to seal and build on this ecological corridor, but without success (Timisoara, a4, 99–100). Nevertheless, other actors see citizens involved in the governance of urban green spaces via participatory measures and report that they contribute to the governance of urban green spaces by self-organising (Bilbao, a3, 58, 83–4, 104–8; Copenhagen, a2, 80–1, 94 and a3, 37; St. Gallen, a4, 9; Timisoara, a3, 156–61). For example, in Lublin a consultative committee at the mayor's office made up of civil society and economic representatives was created (Lublin, a4, 22).

In the last ten years the availability and quality of green spaces has been improved mainly by reclaiming land or by opening new spaces by either the local authority or by residents or community groups, by investments or new regulations by the local government, and by community actions with or without changing the function of existing open green spaces. The impact of new spaces by residents or community groups is stronger in the South and North than in the East and West. Community actions which do not change the functions of urban green spaces are relevant especially in the North and South, and community actions that change the functions of urban green spaces are not common in the East. These regional differences, as well as the ones displayed in Figures 6.2 and 6.3 suggest a higher degree of civil society action and of interaction between civil society and the local authority in Northern Europe in comparison with the remaining regions. The figures also back the hypothesis that civil society's impact on the governance of urban green spaces is lowest in the East. Only in the North are civil society groups involved with urban green spaces common, with local authorities and civil society closely collaborating.

These quantitative tendencies connect to the qualitative finding that all factors for successful self-organisation and citizen participation were mentioned either in Northern, Western, or Southern Europe and are also backed by the 'case study' reports: 15 cities, that is about half of all observed, could be classified

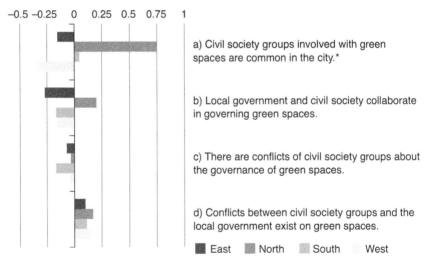

Figure 6.2 Regional differences in civil society involvement in the governance of urban green spaces.

Source: Schicklinski 2016, 101.

Notes
Scaled from –2: strong disagreement, to 2: strong agreement.
* $p < 0.001$.

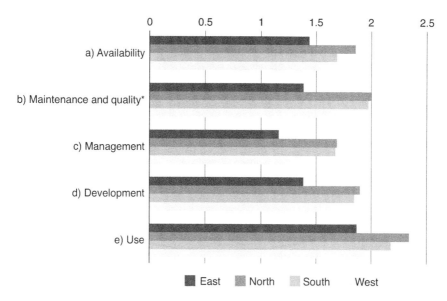

Figure 6.3 Regional differences in the contribution of the non-profit sector to urban green spaces.

Source: Schicklinski 2016, 101.

Notes
Scaled from 0: none, to 4: very high.
* $p < 0.05$;

as having a very active civil society in the field of urban green spaces. Seven – about one-quarter – were observed to have an active civil society and another seven a less active one (cf. Figure 6.4). With six Eastern and six Northern cities in the sample, as well as eight Southern and nine Western ones, it is interesting to see that the majority of cities from all regions except the East can be classified as having a very active civil society. In these cities the degree of civil society action as well as cooperation between civil society and the local authority in the governance of green spaces is highest. Yet, these indications should be interpreted cautiously as a sample of 29 cities covering the four European regions cannot be considered to be representative in the quantitative sense and because the qualitative data indicates forms of citizen participation and self-organisation for every region. Also, as shown in the first paragraph of this section, citizen involvement is rated differently by actors in the interviews, even from the same city. Keeping in mind the low number of actors consulted in each city, no conclusions for the individual cities can be drawn. Yet, when also taking into consideration the quantitative data and the 'case study' reports, one can say that the degree of citizen participation and self-organisation varies greatly across cities due to historically grown national

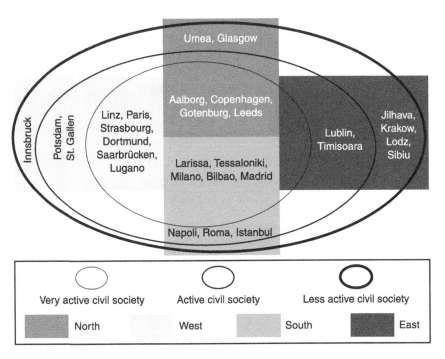

Figure 6.4 Classification of cities according to the degree of civil society action as emerging from the document analysis.

Source: own.

and regional differences in legal frameworks, in political and economic conditions, and due to different urban contexts.

Existing civil society activity can be better understood when presenting the results of data analysis along *forms and outcomes of self-organisation and citizen participation*; *actors, actions and conflicts* and *emerging issues*. These elements will be presented in the following subsections.

6.3.2.4 Forms and outcomes of citizen participation and self-organisation

Citizen participation procedures are enshrined in the legal framework of most countries in the EU. Yet, the level of citizen participation actually applied at the local level greatly differs across the cities. An attempt has been made to cluster observed forms of citizen participation referring to the participation model (Figure 6.1) explained under 6.3.2:

- The lowest stage of *information* exists for example when providing a citizens' phone hotline and a website (Madrid, a3, 53) or when letting citizens attend municipality council sessions (Istanbul, a1, 54–7).

- The second stage of *consultation* can be seen across all regions, either at the district or municipality level. The local authority listens to citizens, citizens associations, and neighbourhood commissions in information sessions or gets their opinion via questionnaires (Gothenburg, a4, 64–6; Istanbul, a1, 71; Lugano, a3, 78; Sibiu, a2, 167–75). Citizens give input to the elaboration of the zoning plan in a workshop and afterwards via internet (Jihlava, a3, 41), or the mayor broadly invites to a public reflection for green areas (Copenhagen, a4, 53). District councils with a right to be heard by the municipal council exist for local decisions, constituting the intermediary link between the municipal council and the citizens (Copenhagen, a2, 55; Larissa, a4, 63; Lublin, a1, 25 and 39–41; Milan, a4, 77). They organise for example citizens' meetings whose results are communicated to the municipality. NGOs participate in round tables, or in the 'department for social affairs … [there is] a unit … for dealing with non-government organizations' (Cracow, a1, 54).

- The third stage of *stakeholder engagement* is only mentioned in one city (Naples, a4, 19, 81–5). Here, city consultative committees on the municipality level exist, for example the Environmental Committee, for which each citizen can enrol to participate. Citizens take part in decision-making by elaborating a joint group proposal on a round table which is then presented to the Chancellor. He/she has to take it into consideration, yet is not obliged to present it to the council.

- The fourth stage of *delegated decision-making* can be found in the form of the participatory budget through which citizens have a say in allocating the city's resources, as mentioned in several cities (Lodz, a3, 59; Lublin, a4, 35; Potsdam, a3, 114).

- The fifth stage of *co-decision-making* exists where there is collaboration in different councils – for example in a green council in which associations are involved (Aalborg, a4, 83–7). With Switzerland generally known for its system of direct democracy, another example is a referendum on a regeneration project of a park (Lugano, a3, 47). Citizens' committees approving of local decisions on green spaces also fall into this category yet can only wield influence if decisions on green spaces are taken by the local authority and not being postponed for years (Naples, a3, 30, 52–6).

Amongst the different *reasons for allowing citizen participation*, as traced for example by Häikiö (2012, 421–9) and earlier by Habermas (1973, 95–6, 187), following Naschold (1972, 42–6), the one of *increasing legitimacy* is mentioned by several actors, stating that citizen participation is necessary, since 'when there was an involvement of … citizens of the district, things have been going on, much less when things came from above' (Rome, a1, 35). To avoid legal problems at a later stage of the planning process, citizens should be involved early (Lugano, a3, 117–18).[53] Even social peace can be endangered if no options for citizen participation exist (Bilbao, a3, 104). Citizen participation is further considered to be necessary for *improving the quality of decision-making*, stressing that citizen participation is necessary to find the best policy solution due to the inclusion of local knowledge of citizens (Sibiu, a2, 174–5). This means that all stakeholders are taken seriously and are considered experts. Citizen participation is also a means of *creating social support amongst stakeholders.* An active civil society can support the work of politicians working for the transition. This is for example the case if individuals or associations' representatives become involved in various councils (Aalborg, a4, 83–7). Monitoring and evaluating local politics and policies is a form of citizen participation that can contribute to *rising levels of transparency and trust.* The right to do so needs to be in citizens' hands, for example by monitoring the local budget (Thessaloniki, a4, 86, 90; Naples, a3, 46). Here, self-organisation and citizen participation is seen as a basic control element of the local authority in a democracy, especially in the case of a weak opposition.

Self-organisation capabilities regarding the green spaces resource system are reported from all regions. They range from small citizens' initiatives on the neighbourhood level, often emerging in opposition to planned construction on urban green spaces, to the formation of bottom-up social movements, for example in the field of urban food production. They arise as well in bigger associations and NGOs with a higher organisational degree and financial structure (Larissa, a4, 81–3; Leeds, a3, 88 and a4, 15–19, 114–16; Naples, a3, 72–4 and a4, 57). Forms of self-organisation can be clustered according to often intertwined goals. The main ones are to *protest against building or infrastructure development on urban green spaces* (cf. 7.3) and to *use common green spaces for urban food production* (cf. 7.4), sometimes after citizens have appropriated – often contested – commons.

From all regions *citizens' protests* due to conflicts between preserving urban green spaces and building and infrastructure development are reported. Urbanisation increases building density and sealing and is exacerbated by real estate and infrastructure speculation. This creates conflicts, out of which self-organisation can emerge, often starting with protests of informal citizens' movements (Cracow, a2, 37–9 and a3, 74–6, 128–34). Measures to achieve the *(re)appropriation of urban green spaces* take various forms, ranging from protest movements (Lodz, a4, 36) and collective legal actions, mostly with organised NGOs filing a suit against the government (Istanbul, a1, 39 and a4, 48), to fruitful collaboration amongst various civil society actors (Saarbrücken, a4, 68–73). Initiatives sometimes succeed, sometimes not or only partially, due to existing power structures or due to the fact that they come late in the planning phase.

In an increasing number of cities, self-organisation helps to *mitigate public poverty.* Especially in cities in which local governments have severe difficulties in affording the provision of urban green space, new self-organised initiatives have emerged on the grassroots level for maintaining and even developing those, thus tackling local challenges and becoming active players in local governance processes (cf. 7.4.2.2). Tasks previously accomplished by public authorities are taken over by civil society, citizens, or associations, and in some cases by economic actors, alleviating the public budget. This tendency has been intensified as a result of the multiple crises in 2008/9 and subsequent austerity policies hitting hard on local public budgets (Rome, a1, 35). The crises also led to self-organisation *mitigating rising private poverty levels* in some places: urban green spaces are used for growing food for self-consumption (cf. 7.4.1).

Actors also raise positive and negative *outcomes of citizen participation and self-organisation*. Positive outcomes are cited in all regions except the East. Citizen participation and self-organisation lead to *shared experiences* of a community in jointly being active for the common good, thus creating a consciousness for common matters and building a more attentive community, which is the *basis for sustainability* (Rome, a1, 33). It is seen that the results of participatory processes are better than those achieved in top-down procedures without citizen participation (Linz, a4, 82–4). *The more people are involved, the more satisfied they are* with the result and the more they use the city, identifying with it and its public space (Copenhagen, a2, 80–1). Even if citizens have not got through with their opinion, participatory processes increase the acceptance of political decisions, since citizens have the feeling of having been listened to, thus of having been taken seriously (Copenhagen, a4, 53). Citizen participation creates a feeling of *ownership* and *responsibility* with the citizens, raising their interest in the common good (Copenhagen, a3, 37; Potsdam, a4, 195; Rome, a1, 35). Local participatory processes can be seen as joint experiments that are evaluated after implementation. If they work, they can be scaled up ('think big – start small – scale fast' Copenhagen, a3, 18, 37). In Spain, citizens' movements mushroomed after the end of the dictatorship. They have achieved an increase in green spaces in the neighbourhoods and have gained influence in the governance of parks (Madrid, a4, 57–60; cf. 6.3.1.1). The adoption of urban green spaces by civil society and economic actors (cf. 7.4.2.2) can be a counterweight to private actors' building and dumping activities on empty spaces (Naples, a4, 49). This can even weaken organised crime as in the case of associations managing land withdrawn from the mafia (Naples, a4, 69–73). This exemplifies civil society's correcting role towards state and market from below.

Negative outcomes and shortcomings of participatory procedures are also cited. The 'participation paradox' (Seley 1983, 20), meaning that groups with higher capacities to express their opinions are primarily listened to by policy-makers, disadvantaging less powerful civil society groups, is existent. This implies that there is the risk of only the strongest and best lobbyists influencing political decisions with the rest remaining unheard (Gothenburg, a4, 68). The *misuse of citizen participation*, either for political reasons or for particular interests of citizens, is mentioned in every region (Cracow, a3, 28). Individuals and associations try to get through particular interests, sometimes related to a NIMBY[54] attitude, hindering the socio-ecological transition (Cracow, a1, 51–2; Gothenburg, a4, 68). In several places participatory tools are only applied because they are required by law without having an influence on further policy outcomes ('Citizen involvement is such a bit – "must have it", "a tick a box", and when they got the job, then they make [!] just what they would do anyway' (Copenhagen, a3, 37); similarly Istanbul, a4, 34, 62; Lodz, a4, 13; Paris, a4, 66).

They are often only applied if they fit the political planning process and are only suggested at a late stage (Cracow, a4, 77; Saarbrücken, a4, 55).

6.3.2.5 Actors, actions, and conflicts

This subsection presents the transition actors, the actions they pursue, and the conflicts that emerge, as described by the respondents. Insight is gained by studying examples of (un-/less) successful actions and actors' (non-)involvement in them. In all cities of the green spaces sample there are governmental, economic, and civil society actors involved, yet the degree and quality of their collaboration differs greatly from city to city.

Across cities, actors from politics, administration, and civil society have shown *leadership* in the governance of urban green spaces (the local government administration, the mayor, politicians of the ruling parties, local environmental NGOs, other local community groups). In contrast to the other two resource systems (Barnebeck 2016, 133, 138–9, 155–6; Kalff 2016, 66–72, 89, 91), local community groups play a major role in the green spaces system. The regional distribution shows that *civil society is less influential in the East*, since local environmental NGOs and other community groups assume the leadership role less often than in the other regions (cf. Figure 6.5).

Such *facilitating intermediary actors* are crucial to trigger and sustain learning processes of all actors involved which are processes of change and development. They can be active in all sectors and also across them. Processes are very often driven by committed key persons that have first adopted changing and newly evolving norms and significantly pushed for their manifestation in rules. Here, successful norm adoption has led to higher levels of trust and cooperation between stakeholders and to vivid institutionalised interaction processes with the joint goal of the socio-ecological transition. In all regions individual persons coming from all sectors are highly influential and can become such *key change agents*. They often have a known reputation, like for example a dedicated mayor driving forward sustainability issues (Sibiu, a2, 69). Highly driven individuals working as civil servants in the Environment Department can be decisive (Gothenburg, a4, 46). The same applies to well-informed leading figures from civil society that are good networkers implementing innovative ideas, for example in the field of urban food production (Leeds, a4, 70–2). In addition, the position of the city's semi-public enterprises[55] on sustainability issues influences the city's orientation towards sustainability (Copenhagen, a2, 57–8; Saarbrücken, a4, 33–4).

Many actors explicitly cite *civil society* as influential (Copenhagen, a4, 39; Lodz, a4, 32–6; Lugano, a4, 44–6; Thessaloniki, a3, 42–4 and a4, 13): in some cities the sustainability topic was brought up by citizens' movements, then taken up by politicians. High pressure from NGOs on the local authority can lead to the official involvement of civil society actors in local politics, for example in committees. This can have a spillover effect to also involving individual citizens, for example via local councils (Copenhagen, a2, 54–5).

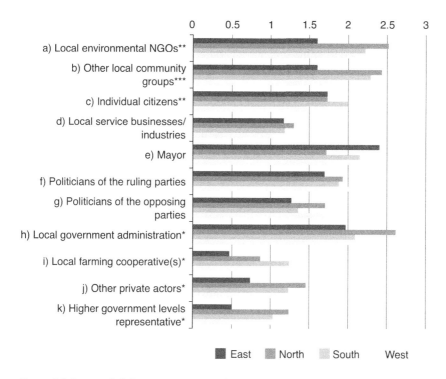

Figure 6.5 Regional differences in actors showing concrete leadership (reputation and capability) in the governance of urban green spaces.

Source: Schicklinski 2016, 110.

Notes
Scaled from 0: none, to 4: very high.
* $p < 0.05$;
** $p < 0.01$;
*** $p < 0.001$.

The role of *science* is seen as bringing in a neutral perspective, highlighting problems and pointing to the future (Linz, a3, 47). Universities should be rooted locally, work project-orientated in an innovative way, and collaborate with the local authority and the economic sector (Aalborg, a4, 47–51; Lodz, a3, 102–5; Lublin, a1, 43–51; Rome, a1, 78; St. Gallen, a4, 10). Innovation means strengthening these university–community linkages (Leeds, a4, 31–6). Science plays an important role in underlining the urgency of sustainability issues in public opinion (Aalborg, a4, 47).

There is a wide range of *successful actions* referred to in all regions. Numerous *information* and *awareness-raising* events have been held all over Europe. These include lectures (Jihlava, a4, 25), research studies conducted by NGOs (Larissa, a4, 17, 48), tree-planting actions (Jihlava, a4, 25), park-cleaning events (Larissa, a4, 67), or picnics (Thessaloniki, a3, 43). They are organised, depending on the city, mainly by civil society or by the local authority, often in collaboration with each other, sometimes also involving the economic or science sector. Tendering *sustainability prizes* within the city or taking part in (inter)national tenders as a whole city is becoming more common and seems to be a functioning incentive (Copenhagen, a4, 15; Innsbruck, a3, 147–9). In several cities citizen movements get together to protect endangered green areas (cf. 7.3). The local authority can encourage and facilitate participation and self-organisation, for example by coordinating volunteers' involvement and by supporting emerging initiatives financially or by providing space, material, and soil. Actions across sectors help to mitigate *public poverty* (cf. 7.4.2.2). Civil society and sometimes economic actors contribute voluntarily to the governance of urban green spaces (Milan, a3, 37 and a4, 101–2; Naples, a3, 71–6 and a4, 32, 47, 57; Thessaloniki, a3, 20–1, 42–4, 85 and a4, 13). Cooperation takes different forms, for example *spontaneous self-organised initiatives* from the bottom or actions proposed by the city, such as the *adoption of urban green spaces* by associations and private enterprises to take care of them (cf. 7.4.2.2). Across European cities, urban commons are increasingly used for *food production*, which in most cases is a self-organised activity. In some cases these movements start as small spontaneous bottom-up initiatives, evolving into growing social movements in which sometimes associations join or out of which in some cases new associations or cooperatives are formed. For example, an *urban garden network* was created by individuals and neighbourhood associations without any support from the city council, operating on public abandoned space (Madrid, a3, 58–59). Urban food production can also be a means of *combatting private poverty* by providing fresh local food to contribute to food sovereignty (cf. 7.4.2.1 and 7.4.1).

The reduction of green spaces due to infrastructure and building development, often linked to privatisation, has generated *conflicts* between urban stakeholders with highly diverging interests and a different understanding of the value of green spaces (Cracow, a1, 71–5; Istanbul, a4, 48; Lublin, a1, 23; Milan, a3, 55). This often leads to diametrical visions for city development. Conflicts are a challenge on the one hand and part of the problem-solving process on the other hand if stakeholders have access to institutionalised conflict management tools. Such tools seem to be widely missing, since only a minority of actors consider conflicts as a constructive component of the sustainability discourse driving forward the socio-ecological transition.

Cited conflicts can be clustered into four different types:

- First, they emerge due to different ideas on the *use of existing green spaces*. These can be intergenerational conflicts (Strasbourg, a4, 91), conflicts about different forms of usage (Aalborg, a4, 74–5), for example between dog owners and non-dog owners (Milan, a3, 55; Saarbrücken, a4, 53), or between cyclists and pedestrians (Glasgow, a4, 26; Madrid, a3, 49). Conflict can also emerge on the conversion of use, for example when urban gardening activities are started on urban green spaces (Innsbruck, a3, 77; Strasbourg, a4, 89–90) or around the usage for recreational activities and nature protection (Copenhagen, a3, 82; Innsbruck, a3, 81–5; Rome, a1, 43; Saarbrücken, a3, 38).

- Second, conflicts emerge around the *accessibility of green spaces*. Parks can be closed in the evening (Strasbourg, a4, 90), or access can be restricted by entrance fees (Potsdam, a3, 142–5). The city can partly assign the care of urban green spaces to associations, which can also lead to restricted access (cf. 7.4.2.2).
- Third, in all regions there are conflicts *between preserving green spaces and building and infrastructure development* which in some cities heavily reduce green spaces (Cracow, a4, 49; Leeds, a3, 61–3; Milan, a4, 75; Saarbrücken, a3, 26), often entailing persisting citizen protests (cf. 7.3).
- Fourth, conflicts can emerge *between sectors* – mostly civil society and the local authority (Cracow, a4, 50–1; Milan, a3, 54–5) – but also within a sector. For example, conflicts between civil society actors (Cracow, a1, 51; Gothenburg, a4, 35) or within the city administration between departments (Copenhagen, a2, 104–6) have been reported. Here, the quantitative sector analysis reveals that administration clearly rejects the existence of conflicts between itself and civil society, whereas civil society and economic actors confirm the existence of such conflicts.

The various conflicts around urban land use raise the question of what kind of local control system is adequate to deal with this *new complexity and multiplication of actors* entering the governance of urban green spaces. This increases the conflict potential since rule definition, for example around fallow land, permanent permits etc., is further complicated by an increasing number of involved actors. In some cities, 'boundary rules' (Ostrom 2005, 194)[56] have partly been shifted: new actors from civil society and economy are now eligible to enter positions that before were reserved for governmental actors only. The process determining who can or has to enter positions and, at a later stage, can or must leave them (ibid., 194) has only just started. This leads to conflict and sometimes disappointment and to the retreat of new actors that invested time and commitment. Due to not yet clearly defined boundary rules, they become tired of participating or self-organising.

Notes

1 Mulgan (2006); © 2006 by Tagore LLC.
2 See Note 1.
3 See Note 1.
4 See Note 1.
5 See Note 1.
6 This is easier to achieve in democratic societies, yet also in non-democratic ones: widely helped by the internet and social media, political and economic actors counteracting long-term sustainability and for example threatening the social and environmental consequences of industrial production are made increasingly accountable by citizens, for example Chinese citizens' demands in the Tianjin catastrophe (heavy explosion in a warehouse) in August 2015 (BBC News 2015).

7 This awareness-raising was also made possible by the interplay between civil society actors and the rise of a mass-medial public sphere (Beck 1993, 226–7).

8 Reprinted from *2052*, copyright 2012 by Jørgen Randers, used with permission from Chelsea Green Publishing (www.chelseagreen.com).

9 See Note 8.

10 From: Elsen (2007); ©Juventa.

11 Diekmann and Jaeger (1996); ©Springer, with permission of Springer.

12 This social movement was composed of wealthy Britons and Americans who campaigned for workers to be able to use urban parks for recreational activities and gardening. An underlying reason however was to prevent social upheavals, since it was also a form of self-help of the poor to save them from hunger (Bailey 1978; Gaskell 1980).

13 See Note 10.

14 See Note 10.

15 See Note 10.

16 These different forms of discrimination are interlinked. For example, it is highly probable that the average female worker in a textile factory in Bangladesh is triple-discriminated against: economically because she neither receives a fair salary nor works in a safe place (as several fires with lethal consequences due to missing or not observed safety measures in textile factories in the Global South have shown), environmentally, first because she is threatened by climate-change-related sea level rise caused almost exclusively by the industrialised countries, and second because she is exposed to health-harming substances at the workplace, and socially because due to cultural constraints she, not her husband, is, beyond her gainful employment, mostly responsible for household, care, and family work.

17 Habisch (2002); ©Springer, with permission of Springer.

18 This book uses the more general term of 'actors' to also refer to the more specific one of 'users' used by Ostrom with regard to the governance of commons. The latter can be defined as 'the individuals who routinely extract resource units from … [a] resource system; these users may or may not be organized into a single user group' (McGinnis 2011, 181).

19 See Note 17.

20 See Note 10.

21 Concretely, 'Ostrom recommends to offer citizens that want to engage in civic activities as "social capital investors" with sets of self-organisation rules' (Habisch 2002, 354, own translation, see Note 17).

22 In contrast to the labour movement, in the agrarian movement of the nineteenth century, which evolved as a reaction to the transition from a feudal to an industrial society, the environment indeed played a role. This anti-industrialisation movement was not just directed against capital but was pointing out the destructive side effects of rapidly growing industrialisation on the environment. However, as Polanyi points out, the underlying reason for this movement, which was primarily carried forward by aristocrats who had been losing influence, power and workforce, was that it actually tried to 'recover its past by presenting itself as the guardian of man's natural habitat, the soil' (2001, 186).

23 In this context, it is interesting to follow the rise of an environmental labour movement in the South Italian city of Taranto, which is known for being Italy's biggest steel production site. Workers there have always been exposed to severe health risks, yet never complained even after the death of colleagues, because they preferred to work under health-damaging conditions instead of losing their job. Only when children in their families also began to die because of the steel plant's pollution, did they join in an environmental labour movement to obtain improved production conditions (Barca and Leonardi 2016).

24 Barthel *et al.* (2015); copyright ©2013 by Urban Studies Journal Limited. Reprinted by permission of SAGE Publications, Inc.

25 See Note 10.
26 The interrelationship of social, environmental, political, and economic rights becomes most evident in the increasing practice of expropriation and eviction in the form of land-grabbing. For example, in Cambodia, where approximately 80 per cent of the population is dependent on smallholder subsistence agriculture (Saracini 2011, 6), within a couple of years more than half of the arable land was sold or leased to foreign private agro-industrial investors (ibid., 4). This human-rights-violating practice destroys local rural communities' livelihoods (cf. 7.4.3.1), increasing migration to the cities.
27 See Note 8.
28 Randers (2012, 255) enumerates environmentalists and political and economic leaders, such as heads of global corporations, global intergovernmental institutions, and NGOs like the IPCC, UNEP, or the World Wide Fund for Nature (WWF). This list has to be enlarged to also include numerous diverse actors at the local level such as local political and administrative actors, heads of local small and medium-sized enterprises and local yet internationally connected small NGOs and local sections of big international NGOs.
29 See Note 10.
30 Enquete-Kommission 'Zukunft des Bürgerschaftlichen Engagements' des Deutschen Bundestages (2002); ©Springer, with permission of Springer.
31 Löw (2001); reproduced with permission of Palgrave Macmillan.
32 See Note 31.
33 This process is called 'Syntheseleistung' (Löw *et al.* 2008, 8, 64) – 'attainment of composition'.
34 The example of the NGO 'Donne Nissà' in Bolzano (Italy) illustrates this process of 'Syntheseleistung'. When a member of the association passed an abandoned brown-field site belonging to the city, the idea was born to turn it into an urban garden. With this idea in mind, the association approached the local authority and received their permission for the project. The group of gardeners started to transform the space into an urban garden by recombining existing elements (soil, division of the whole space into beds for subgroups of gardeners and into common space) or adding new ones (fertile soil from outside, seeds, plants, gardening tools, rules for smoother inter-action and communication between the ever growing number of gardeners), thus altering the existing space and creating a new one. So, after perceiving the potential of this space and after having created a vision for its transformation, this was put into practice.
35 See Note 31.
36 See Note 31.
37 The movement was part of the Spain-wide neighbourhood movement which evolved in the 1970s around different urban issues despite political oppression. Castells (1983, 215) characterises it as 'the largest and most significant urban movement in Europe since 1945 ... dealing with all matters of everyday life, from housing to open spaces'. He describes its contribution to social change:

> Under the influence of social processes to which it contributed substantially, Spanish cities changed, political institutions were turned upside down, social relationships in the neighbourhoods dramatically improved, and perhaps most significantly, the urban culture, namely, society's conception of what a city should be, was fundamentally altered.... Open space was provided, ... some environ-mental protection was legislated for; ... community life was enhanced.
>
> (Ibid., 216)

The Madrid Citizen Movement 'decisively changed the city ... and actively particip-ated in the transformation of the political system' (ibid., 258). This does not only mean that it was one factor for the decline of the dictatorship, but its claims were implemented at a very practical policy level:

> Beyond the measures put into effect in Madrid between 1975 and 1980, there was a *total rectification of the model of urban development as well as of official urban policy*.... The building of urban motorways were [!] stopped; sudden and dramatic changes of land-use were avoided (for instance, the railway stations remained in the centre of the city); ... private parks were opened to public use ...; pedestrian zones were extended.
>
> (Ibid., 259)

Moreover, its 'demands for participatory democracy actually reshaped the institutions of city government while opening a serious debate on the meaning of democracy within the political parties themselves' (ibid., 261).

38 Translated and reproduced from Helfrich (2014).
39 The urban green commons concept thus also includes private urban green spaces which are not the centre of interest of this research (cf. Chapter 5). Yet, they should not be excluded from the analysis if civil society action is going on in them.
40 See Note 10.
41 Roth (2002); ©Springer, permission of Springer.
42 The term 'public participation' is a synonym of 'citizen participation' preferred in this book.
43 The convention is commonly known as the Aarhus Convention.
44 See Note 30.
45 Migrants (except the highly qualified) generally have more difficulty in finding work than locals, for example because of language barriers but also because their professional qualification obtained abroad is not or is only partly recognised.
46 Non-EU residents do not have the right to vote or to candidate in local elections. In Germany some cities have at least formed advising migrants' councils (for example Freiburg, Dortmund, Saarbrücken) to let migrants participate in local politics. Yet, this form of consultation remains insufficient to provide real citizen participation. Migrants, regardless of whether they come from an EU or non-EU country, who have resided in a city for a certain length of time, must have the right to actively and passively participate in local elections.
47 That is, migrants who were born in the receiving country and either their parents or grandparents migrated to it.
48 See http://anstiftung.de/ (accessed 29 July 2016).
49 Which turned out in most cases as the starting point for wider social integration (anstiftung & ertomis 2015).
50 Social innovations in local communities via socioeconomic self-organisation can be facilitated by financial support of large-scale enterprises which might also bring in their competences on condition that the projects remain autonomous (Elsen 2007, 76).
51 Speaking in economic terms, if this integration work was not accomplished voluntarily by the community gardens, the local authority would have to pay for social workers.
52 This refers for example to the provision of water and soil, to the use of garden equipment from the local authority, and to the ground itself which should be given for free to the gardeners.
53 This is also enshrined in the Aarhus Convention (UNECE 1998, 522): 'Each Party shall provide for early public participation, when all options are open and effective public participation can take place'.
54 'Not In My Backyard' is 'a social phenomenon ... stand[ing] for a rejection of some-

thing that is generally supported, as soon as it encroaches on the own living environ-ment and personal space' (WBGU 2011, 73).
55 Semi-public enterprises are owned by more than 50 per cent by the city, yet function like private enterprises.
56 Boundary rules are one of the seven rule types defining the institutional setting of an action situation (Ostrom 2005, 186–210). They 'define (1) who is eligible to enter a position, (2) the process that determines which eligible participants may enter (or must enter) positions, and (3) how an individual may leave (or must leave) a posi-tion' (ibid., 194).

References

anstiftung & ertomis. 2015. 'Wie erreichen (Interkulturelle) Gemeinschaftsgärten Flüch-tlinge und AsylbewerberInnen?' http://anstiftung.de/urbane-gaerten/praxisseiten-urbane-gaerten/1750-wie-erreichen-interkulturelle-gemeinschaftsgaerten-fluechtlinge-und-asylbewerberinnen?tmpl=component&print=1&page= [27 August 2016].

Arnstein, Sherry R. 1969. 'A ladder of citizen participation'. *Journal of the American Insti-tute of Planners*, 35(4): 216–24.

Bailey, Peter. 1978. *Leisure and class in Victorian England: Rational recreation and the contest for control 1830–1885*. London: Routledge & Kegan Paul.

Bandura, Albert. 1997. *Self-efficacy: The exercise of control*. New York: W.H. Freeman and Company.

Barca, Stefania and Emanuele Leonardi. 2016. 'Working class communities and ecology: Reframing environmental justice around the Ilva steel plant in Taranto (Apulia, Italy)'. In *Class, inequality and community development*, eds Mae Shaw and Marjorie Mayo, 59–76. Bristol: Policy.

Barnebeck, Stephanie. 2016. 'Socio-ecological transitions in the water system'. In *Cities in transition: Social innovation for Europe's urban sustainability*, eds Thomas Sauer, Cris-tina Garzillo, and Susanne Elsen, 125–57. Abingdon/New York: Routledge.

Barnebeck, Stephanie, Yannick Kalff, and Thomas Sauer. 2016. 'Institutional diversity'. In *Cities in transition: Social innovation for Europe's urban sustainability*, eds Thomas Sauer, Cristina Garzillo, and Susanne Elsen, 192–203. Abingdon/New York: Routledge.

Barthel, Stephan, John Parker, and Henrik Ernstson. 2015. 'Food and green space in cities: A resilience lens on gardens and urban environmental movements'. *Urban Studies*, 52(7): 1321–38.

BBC News. 2015. 'China explosions: The questions people are asking about the Tianjin blasts'. *BBC News*, 17 August. www.bbc.com/news/world-asia-china-33923472 [27 August 2016].

Beck, Ulrich. 1986. *Risikogesellschaft: Auf dem Weg in eine andere Moderne*. Frankfurt am Main: Suhrkamp.

Beck, Ulrich. 1993. *Die Erfindung des Politischen: Zu einer Theorie reflexiver Modernisierung*. Frankfurt am Main: Suhrkamp.

Beck, Ulrich. 1996. 'Weltrisikogesellschaft, Weltöffentlichkeit und globale Subpolitik: Ökologische Fragen im Bezugsrahmen fabrizierter Unsicherheiten'. In *Kölner Zeitschrift für Soziologie und Sozialpsychologie Sonderhefte, Umweltsoziologie*, eds Andreas Diekmann and Carlo J. Jaeger, 119–47. Opladen: Westdeutscher Verlag.

Beck, Ulrich. 2007. *Weltrisikogesellschaft: Auf der Suche nach der verlorenen Sicherheit*. Frankfurt am Main: Suhrkamp.

Beck, Ulrich. 2009. *Risk society: Towards a new modernity*. Theory, culture and society series. London: Sage.

Biesecker, Adelheid and Stefan Kesting. 2003. *Mikroökonomik: Eine Einführung aus sozial-ökologischer Perspektive*. Munich: Oldenbourg Wissenschaftsverlag.

Boonstra, Beitske and Luuk Boelens. 2011. 'Self-organization in urban development: Towards a new perspective on spatial planning'. *Urban Research and Practice*, 4(2): 99–122.

Bourdieu, Pierre. 1983. 'Ökonomisches Kapital, kulturelles Kapital, soziales Kapital'. In *Sonderband 2, Soziale Ungleichheiten. Soziale Welt*, ed. Reinhard Kreckel, 183–98. Göttingen.

Bureau of European Policy Advisers European Commission. 2011. 'Empowering people, driving change: Social innovation in the European Union'. Luxembourg: Publication Office of the European Union. www.google.co.uk/url?sa=t&rct=j&q=&esrc=s&source=web&cd=1&ved=0ahUKEwj815Pt_OLOAhVMKh4KHfeWCCIQFggpMAA&url=http%3A%2F%2Fec.europa.eu%2FDocsRoom%2Fdocuments%2F13402%2Fattachments%2F1%2Ftranslations%2Fen%2Frenditions%2Fnative&usg=AFQjCNF-_xW7coSQF9__INyY7jR5wM7Hzw&bvm=bv.131286987,d.dmo [27 August 2016].

Castells, Manuel. 1983. *The city and the grassroots: A cross-cultural theory of urban social movements*. Berkeley CA, Los Angeles CA: University of California.

Colding, Johan and Stephan Barthel. 2013. 'The potential of "Urban Green Commons" in the resilience building of cities'. *Ecological Economics*, 86: 156–66.

Colding, Johan, Stephan Barthel, Pim Bendt, Robbert Snep, Wim van der Knaap, and Henrik Ernstson. 2013. 'Urban green commons: Insights on urban common property systems'. *Global Environmental Change*, 23: 1039–51.

Crouch, Colin. 2004. *Post-democracy*. Malden MA: Polity.

Davies, Anna and Julie Simon. 2013. 'Engaging citizens in social innovation: A short guide to the research for policy makers and practitioners. A deliverable of the project: "The theoretical, empirical and policy foundations for building social innovation in Europe" (TEPSIE), European Commission – 7th Framework Programme'. http://siresearch.eu/sites/default/files/5.4_final.pdf [8 December 2016].

Diekmann, Andreas and Carlo C. Jaeger. 1996. 'Aufgaben und Perspektiven der Umweltsoziologie'. In *Kölner Zeitschrift für Soziologie und Sozialpsychologie Sonderhefte, Umweltsoziologie*, eds Andreas Diekmann and Carlo J. Jaeger, 11–27. Opladen: Westdeutscher Verlag.

Elsen, Susanne. 2007. *Die Ökonomie des Gemeinwesens: Sozialpolitik und Soziale Arbeit im Kontext von gesellschaftlicher Wertschöpfung und -verteilung*. Weinheim, München: Juventa.

Elsen, Susanne and Judith Schicklinski. 2016. 'Mobilising the citizens for the socio-ecological transition'. In *Cities in transition: Social innovation for Europe's urban sustainability*, eds Thomas Sauer, Cristina Garzillo, and Susanne Elsen, 221–38. Abingdon/New York: Routledge.

Enquete-Kommission 'Zukunft des Bürgerschaftlichen Engagements' des Deutschen Bundestages (Enquete), ed. 2002. *Bericht: Bürgerschaftliches Engagement: auf dem Weg in eine zukunftsfähige Bürgergesellschaft*. Opladen: Leske + Budrich.

European Commission (EC). 2003. 'Common implementation strategy for the water framework directive (2000/60/EC): Public participation in relation to the water framework directive'. Guidance document no. 8, produced by Working Group 2.9 – Public Participation. Luxembourg. www.magrama.gob.es/es/agua/publicaciones/Guia8_tcm7-29013.pdf [27 August 2016].

European Environment Agency (EEA). 2014. EEA reports. Vol. 3. 'Public participation: Contributing to better water management. Experiences from eight case studies across

Europe'. Copenhagen. www.eea.europa.eu/publications/public-participation-contributing-to-better [27 August 2016].

European Parliament and Council of the European Union, ed. 2000. 'Directive 2000/60/EC of the European Parliament and of the Council of 23 October 2000 establishing a framework for community action in the field of water policy'. 327th edn, *Official Journal of the European Communities*. http://eur-lex.europa.eu/resource.html?uri=cellar:5c835afb-2ec6-4577-bdf8-756d3d694eeb.0004.02/DOC_1&format=PDF [27 August 2016].

Fischer-Lescano, Andreas and Kolja Möller. 2011. *Der Kampf um globale soziale Rechte: Zart wäre das Gröbste*. Berlin: Klaus Wagenbach.

Gaskell, S. Martin. 1980. 'Gardens for the working class: Victorian practical pleasure'. *Victorian Studies*, 23(4): 479–501.

German Advisory Council on Global Change (WBGU). 2011. Flagship report. World in transition: A social contract for sustainability. Berlin: WBGU. www.wbgu.de/file admin/templates/dateien/veroeffentlichungen/hauptgutachten/jg2011/wbgu_jg2011_en.pdf [27 August 2016].

Giddens, Anthony. 1984. *The constitution of society: Outline of the theory of structuration*. Cambridge: Polity.

Habermas, Jürgen. 1973. *Legitimationsprobleme im Spätkapitalismus*. Frankfurt am Main: Suhrkamp.

Habermas, Jürgen. 1984. *The theory of communicative action. Volume one: Reason and the rationalisation of society*. Translated by Thomas McCarthy. Boston MA: Beacon (orig. pub. 1981).

Habermas, Jürgen. 1985. *Die Neue Unübersichtlichkeit: Kleine Politische Schriften V*. Frankfurt am Main: Suhrkamp.

Habermas, Jürgen. 1987a. *The philosophical discourse of modernity: Twelve lectures*. Cambridge: Polity in association with Basil Blackwell (orig. pub. 1985).

Habermas, Jürgen. 1987b. *The theory of communicative action. Volume two: Lifeworld and system: A critique of functionalist reason*. Translated by Thomas McCarthy. Boston MA: Beacon (orig. pub. 1981).

Habermas, Jürgen. 1995a. *Theorie des kommunikativen Handelns: Band 2 Zur Kritik der funktionalistischen Vernunft*. Frankfurt am Main: Suhrkamp (orig. pub. 1981).

Habermas, Jürgen. 1995b. *Theorie des kommunikativen Handelns: Band 1 Handlungsrationalität und gesellschaftliche Rationalisierung*. Frankfurt am Main: Suhrkamp (orig. pub. 1981).

Habisch, André. 2002. 'Sondervotum des sachverständigen Mitglieds Prof. Dr. André Habisch: Soziales Kapital, Bürgerschaftliches Engagement und Initiativen regionaler Arbeitsmarkt- und Sozialpolitik'. In *Bericht: Bürgerschaftliches Engagement: auf dem Weg in eine zukunftsfähige Bürgergesellschaft*, ed. Enquete-Kommission 'Zukunft des Bürgerschaftlichen Engagements' des Deutschen Bundestages, 350–6. Opladen: Leske + Budrich.

Häikiö, Liisa. 2012. 'From innovation to convention: Legitimate citizen participation in local governance'. *Local Government Studies*, 38(4): 415–35.

Harvey, David. 2012. *Rebel cities: From the right to the city to the urban revolution*. London: Verso.

Helfrich, Silke. 2014. 'Gemeingüter sind nicht, sie werden gemacht'. In *Commons: Für eine neue Politik jenseits von Markt und Staat*, 2nd edn, ed. Silke Helfrich, 85–91. Bielefeld: transcript. www.boell.de/sites/default/files/2012-04-buch-2012-04-buch-commons.pdf [27 August 2016].

Helfrich, Silke and David Bollier. 2014. 'Commons als transformative Kraft. Zur Einführung'. In *Commons: Für eine neue Politik jenseits von Markt und Staat*, 2nd edn, ed.

Silke Helfrich, 15–23. Bielefeld: transcript. www.boell.de/sites/default/files/2012-04-buch-2012-04-buch-commons.pdf [27 August 2016].

Jackson, Tim. 2009. *Prosperity without growth: Economics for a finite planet.* London: Earthscan.

Kalff, Yannick. 2016. 'Socio-ecological transitions in the energy system: The local government view'. In *Cities in transition: Social innovation for Europe's urban sustainability,* eds Thomas Sauer, Cristina Garzillo, and Susanne Elsen, 59–92. Abingdon/New York: Routledge.

Kemmis, Stephen. 2001. 'Exploring the relevance of critical theory for action research: Emancipatory action research in the footsteps of Jürgen Habermas'. In *Handbook of action research: Participative inquiry and practice,* eds Peter Reason and Hilary Bradbury, 91–102. London, Thousand Oaks CA, New Delhi: Sage.

Lefebvre, Henri. 2009. *Le droit à la ville,* 3rd edn. Paris: Economica-Anthropos (orig. pub. 1968).

Lefebvre, Henry. 1991. *The production of space.* Translated by Donald Nicholson-Smith. Cambridge: Blackwell.

Löw, Martina. 2001. *Raumsoziologie.* Frankfurt am Main: Suhrkamp.

Löw, Martina, Silke Steets, and Sergej Stoetzer. 2008. *Einführung in die Stadt- und Raumsoziologie,* 2nd edn. Opladen, Farmington Hills MI: Budrich.

Meadows, Donella H., Jørgen Randers, and Dennis L. Meadows. 2005. *Limits to growth: The 30-year update,* 3rd edn. London: Earthscan.

Moulaert, Frank. 2000. *Globalization and integrated area development in European cities.* Oxford: Oxford University Press.

Mulgan, Geoff. 2006. 'The process of social innovation'. *Innovations, Technology, Governance, Globalization,* 1(2): 145–62. www.policyinnovations.org/ideas/policy_library/data/TheProcessofSocialInnovation/_res/id=sa_File1/INNOV0102_p145162_mulgan.pdf [27 August 2016].

Naschold, Frieder. 1972. 'Zur Politik und Ökonomie von Planungssystemen'. In *Politische Vierteljahresschrift Sonderheft, Gesellschaftlicher Wandel und politische Innovation,* ed. Deutsche Vereinigung für politische Wissenschaft, 13–53. Opladen: Westdeutscher Verlag.

Nowotny, Helga, Peter Scott, and Michael Gibbons. 2013. *Re-thinking science: Knowledge and the public in an age of uncertainty.* Cambridge: Polity (orig. pub. 2001).

Ostrom, Elinor. 1990. *Governing the commons: The evolution of institutions for collective action.* New York: Cambridge University Press.

Ostrom, Elinor. 2005. *Understanding institutional diversity.* Princeton NJ: Princeton University Press.

Ostrom, Elinor and T. K. Ahn. 2003. 'Introduction'. In *Foundations of social capital,* eds Elinor Ostrom and T. K. Ahn, xi–xxxix. Cheltenham, Northampton MA: Edward Elgar.

Pincetl, Stephanie. 2007. 'Urban parks movement'. In *Encyclopedia of environment and society,* ed. Paul Robbins, 1870–2. Thousand Oaks CA, London, New Delhi, Singapore: Sage.

Polanyi, Karl. 2001. *The great transformation: The political and economic origins of our time,* 2nd edn. Boston MA: Beacon Press (orig. pub. 1944).

Poteete, Amy R., Marco A. Janssen, and Elinor Ostrom. 2010. *Working together: Collective action, the commons, and multiple methods in practice.* Princeton NJ: Princeton University Press.

Purcell, Mark and Shannon K. Tyman. 2015. 'Cultivating food as a right to the city'. *Local Environment: The International Journal of Justice and Sustainability,* 20(10): 1132–47.

Putnam, Robert D. and Kristin A. Goss. 2001. 'Einleitung'. In *Gesellschaft und Gemeinsinn: Sozialkapital im internationalen Vergleich*, ed. Robert Putnam, 15–43. Gütersloh: Bertelsmann Foundation.

Randers, Jørgen, 2012. *2052: A global forecast for the next forty years*. White River Junction VT: Chelsea Green.

Reed, Mark S. 2008. 'Stakeholder participation for environmental management: A literature review'. *Biological Conservation*, 141: 2417–31.

Rifkin, Jeremy. 2004. *The end of work: The decline of the global labor force and the dawn of the post-market era*. New York: Jeremy P. Tarcher/Penguin (orig. pub. 1995).

Roth, Roland. 2002. 'Sondervotum des sachverständigen Mitglieds Prof. Dr. Roland Roth zum Resümee des Teils A: "Bürgergesellschaft als Bezugsrahmen" (A6)'. In *Bericht: Bürgerschaftliches Engagement: auf dem Weg in eine zukunftsfähige Bürgergesellschaft*, ed. Enquete-Kommission 'Zukunft des Bürgerschaftlichen Engagements' des Deutschen Bundestages, 350. Opladen: Leske + Budrich.

Saracini, Nadia. 2011. 'Stolen land stolen future: A report of land grabbing in Camodia'. Association of Word Council of Churches related Development Organisations in Europe. www.aprodev.eu/files/Trade/landgrab_aprodev.pdf [27 August 2016].

Schicklinski, Judith. 2016. 'Socio-ecological transitions in the green spaces resource system'. In *Cities in transition: Social innovation for Europe's urban sustainability*, eds Thomas Sauer, Cristina Garzillo, and Susanne Elsen, 93–124. Abingdon/New York: Routledge.

Schumpeter, Joseph A. 1983. *The theory of economic development: An inquiry into profits, capital, credit, interest, and the business cycle*. New Brunswick: Transaction Books (orig. pub. 1934).

Schumpeter, Joseph A. 2005. *Business cycles: A theoretical, historical, and statistical analysis of the capitalist process*, Volume I. Chevy Chase MD: Bartleby, Mansfield Centre, CT: Martino (orig. pub. 1939).

Seibel, Wolfgang. 1994. *Funktionaler Dilettantismus: Erfolgreich scheiternde Organisationen im 'Dritten Sektor' zwischen Markt und Staat*, 2nd edn. Baden-Baden: Nomos.

Seley, John E. 1983. *Politics of planning series: The politics of public-facility planning*. Lexington MA: Lexington.

Shiva, Vandana. 2013. *Making peace with the earth*. London: Pluto.

United Nations Economic Commission for Europe (UNECE), ed. 1998. Convention on access to information, public participation in decision-making and access to justice in environmental matters. 38I.L.M.517. Vol. 38: International legal material. www.unece.org/fileadmin/DAM/env/pp/documents/cep43e.pdf [27 August 2016].

von Braunmühl, Claudia von. 2010. 'Demokratie, gleichberechtigte Bürgerschaft und Partizipation'. In *Ökologie und Wirtschaftsforschung, Postwachstumsgesellschaft: Konzepte für die Zukunft*, eds Irmi Seidl and Angelika Zahrnt, 189–200. Marburg: Metropolis.

Wright, Michael T., Hella von Unger, and Martina Block. 2010. 'Partizipation der Zielgruppe in der Gesundheitsförderung und Prävention'. In *Prävention und Gesundheitsförderung, Partizipative Qualitätsentwicklung in der Gesundheitsförderung und Prävention*, ed. Michael T. Wright, 35–52. Bern: Huber.

Zapf, Wolfgang. 1989. 'Über soziale Innovationen'. *Soziale Welt*, 40(1–2): 170–83.

7 Reappropriating urban green spaces and urban food production

This chapter deals with the reasons behind the reappropriation of public space and relates it to the topic of urban food production. It continues the analysis of actors, processes, and contributions of citizen-driven activities within the governance of urban green spaces and urban food production across European cities by granting specific insights into the state of self-organisation in the green spaces resource system, clustered into several thematic strands. Movements cannot always clearly be distinguished from each other and might also fall concurrently into more than one category. Section 7.1 links the creation of space to the themes of power, democracy, and public space, while Section 7.2 specifically deals with the disappearance and the loss of public space, very often linked to privatisation tendencies. Section 7.3 looks into the defence of urban green spaces by (re)appropriating them. Section 7.4 deals with the issue of urban food production which can be viewed from various, often interlinked, angles: as one form of productively reappropriating public space, as an element of a multiple activity society, as well as a means to raise awareness for a sustainable global food and agriculture system.

7.1 Power, democracy, and public space

Theory of space starts from conceiving space as a general category, yet in the scope of this thesis the interest specifically lies in public spaces. From an urban sociology perspective, public spaces are the city's figurehead. They do not exist by themselves but are only created by actors out of urban spaces (Klamt 2012, 778; Klamt 2006). Space is a social structure, created by human action, and the process of creating space is subject to power relations (Castells 1983, 311). Constituting space in action is usually a negotiation process between actors with mostly diverging interests. Negotiating power structures is a central component of this process. However, different societal groups do not have equal opportunity to take part in this process of space creation (cf. 6.3.2.2). This is because access to social goods such as knowledge or money as well as the social position are the precondition for determining how to arrange these goods relationally in a place – to create space (Löw 2001, 218). Therefore, socially disadvantaged persons have fewer options to alter and design spaces (ibid., 212). This inequality, paired with the option of different groups creating several spaces in one place (ibid., 64), makes urban spaces particularly prone to becoming conflict sites for societal subgroups' struggle for equality (Löw *et al.* 2008, 65). Social movements can modify urban spatial structures by questioning their meaning and reinterpreting their functions, thus triggering social change by assuming the role of 'agents of urban-spatial transformation' (Castells 1983, 312). The diverse creative actions of urban gardeners who 'plant fruit trees, establish mobile gardens or, as "guerrilla gardeners", throw "seed bombs" into what activists view as badly used open spaces'[1] (Barthel *et al.* 2015, 1329) can be considered as campaigns about the creation of urban space and against predominating power relations.

7.2 Disappearance and loss of public space/privatisation

The commodification and subsequent privatisation of public spaces, resulting in their disappearance, can be considered as a spatial structure, since these processes render spaces 'as wealth a strategic resource in the societal relative strength'[2] (Löw 2001, 217, own translation). For the governance of urban green spaces this means that greater attention is often paid by the local authority to the voice of economic actors in local development options on public spaces and neighbourhoods. The empirical data (cf. 5.3) provides examples of this trend, which manifests itself for example in Istanbul, with the building of mosques with underground shopping malls on urban green spaces. The commodification of spaces reaches its climax, if for example in real estate speculation land is sold to make the most profit possible disregarding the housing needs of less well-off parts of the population (Harvey 2012, 28–9). Privatisation is a process that is very difficult to reverse and the state has few instruments to ensure the sustainable governance of privatised urban green spaces. Their privatisation excludes the financially less well-off from having access to them and decisions about the governance of these spaces are no longer democratically monitored (Elsen 2007, 122, 179).

7.3 (Re)appropriation of public space – defending urban green spaces: self-organisation in reaction to the reduction of urban green spaces for building and infrastructure development

According to Löw (2001, 227, own translation), change in spaces can occur through 'the creation of institutionalised arrangements [as] … events in opposition to the dominant culture which … opens up individual courses of action and can … lead to changes in social structures'.[3] The creation of urban commons through citizen action can be considered as such a change in space, challenging existing power structures and strengthening democratic processes, since grassroots political action is needed to appropriate public spaces (Harvey 2012, 73).[4] Elsen (2007, 160, own translation) points out that the 'conservation or civic appropriation of livelihoods [is] the most important aim of sustainable societies'.[5] Commons do not merely exist but are created when people interact in resource use, thereby creating rules (Bierling-Wagner *et al.* 2013, 10). The multiple crises since 2008 and subsequent austerity policies have aggravated tendencies of commodification and privatisation, also known as 'enclosure'[6] (Helfrich and Bollier 2014, 18).[7] The emerging interest in and increased creation of urban commons result from this, with commoners defending one of the basic principles of commons, which is their 'collective and non-commodified' (Harvey 2012, 73) use. These civil society actions are necessary to counter the commodification and privatisation of public space. Appropriating these spaces, in some cases for food production (cf. 7.4.1), is a means of regaining 'direct democratic controls'[8] (Elsen 2007, 19, own translation) to guarantee their sustainable governance. It is a means of regaining 'control over the city, over the production of its space' (Purcell and Tyman 2015, 4). In this regard urban gardening and agriculture can become part of the right to the city movement, then joining forces with other activists to counter neoliberal city development by asking the basic question in what kind of city one wants to live.

The empirical data reveals forms of protests against the reduction of urban green spaces due to building and infrastructure development. Which possibilities exist for citizens to react to and influence the decreasing availability of urban green spaces (cf. 5.3)? The degree of practised *citizen participation* in the governance of urban green spaces greatly varies across European cities. *Co-decision-making* is rarely found. A respondent from Copenhagen claims that citizens should not only have the option to influence the planning process, but have to have the *feeling of ownership*, the feeling of being responsible themselves for change, with concomitant options to become active. This does not mean that experts' knowledge is not needed anymore. There must be *joint experiments* that need to be scaled up if they work:

> Involvement ... [is] not just about putting people together at a table.... We need to experiment together, we need to test something, evaluate how it works, how to go on, scale up – such experiments with residents of an area, before establishing something bigger.
>
> (Copenhagen, a3, 37)

Actors warn that if the current economic growth path, drastically named 'developers' dictatorship' by one respondent (Lublin, a4, 26), is further pursued, there will be almost no urban green spaces left (Lodz, a4, 23). Life in the city will become unbearable, because the city will become ever denser and this density will spread to the outskirts (Lugano, a4, 30, 56; Strasbourg, a4, 24–6). The city's population will increase, there will not be sufficient public spaces, and the vacancy rate will remain high instead of producing more housing space. Thus, increasing the amount of urban green spaces is seen as the city's biggest challenge (Jihlava, a4, 51; Thessaloniki, a4, 29–31, 52). Where governmental and economic actors unwaveringly cling to the growth path (Strasbourg, a4, 20), making decisions over the heads of citizens, and not granting a sufficient degree of citizen participation, there is the high probability that *tensions and conflicts over the use of space* will emerge and citizens will *self-organise* to protest. If such protest *comes late in the planning phase*, the chances of success are small, as in the case of citizens' protests against construction projects (Lodz, a4, 36). Nevertheless, this section shows that in some cases these *protests*, ranging from small citizens' initiatives at the neighbourhood level to larger city wide social movements, lead to citizen empowerment, a higher degree of citizen participation, and ultimately to political change. However, having partly been institutionalised and subsequently achieving a (partial) implementation of their goals, their intensity might then decrease, as was the case in past movements for example in the Madrid Citizen Movement (Madrid, a4, 66–8; cf. 6.3.1.1).

Citizen groups are formed in every region in reaction to *building and infrastructure development, which reduces green spaces* (Aalborg, a4, 83–7; Lodz, a4, 31–2; Umea, a3). If urban green spaces are threatened, and in some cases even if private green spaces are endangered, this meets resistance, as in the case of allotment-garden renters who feared losing their dearly held gardens (Gothenburg, a4, 63–6) or in the case of protest against big infrastructure projects, for example a planned motorway through the city (Linz a4, 66–8). In Cracow, residents protested against the widening of roads which would have meant tearing down their houses. Furthermore, citizens, sometimes in coalition with NGOs, protest against the logging of trees for construction purposes (Jihlava, a4, 45; Linz, a3, 63–7; Lublin, a1, 23; Timisoara, a4, 157).

Citizens' protests emerge against *non-accessibility* as well as the *commercialisation* of urban green spaces. In Lublin there were protests against the long-term closure of a big public park, and in Glasgow citizens' protests prevented the opening of a park for commercial usage for the hospitality industry (Glasgow, a4, 98). In several parts of Cracow, protests have occurred against the *privatisation* of public land. There were minor protests when a piece of land was sold to a private investor, in this case the church, and was subsequently not accessible for citizens any more (Cracow, a1, 71–5). In one case residents self-organised, with the support of an NGO, against the city's plan to sell pieces of land of a public park to the highest bidder for construction purposes. After their protests and a year-long conflict, a consensus was reached in several meetings. Some spaces were preserved and turned into gardens, resulting in a significant monetary loss for the city's budget, whereas the rest was put up for sale (Cracow, a2, 37–9; a3, 74–6, 81 and a4, 48). All over Istanbul there are smaller or bigger conflicts over accessibility and the reduction of green spaces due to building development that often end in protests, the biggest and most famous one being that of Gezi Park (Istanbul, a4, 48). Conflicts with the local authority emerge (Cracow, a4, 51) because citizens feel that 'every time you need to fight to keep the areas green and to stop building on [them]' (Milan, a3, 55).

Citizens' protest is channelled and 'professionalised' if supported or even originally organised by local NGOs, sometimes also in cooperation with local politicians. Interesting coalitions have been formed in Istanbul, a city suffering greatly from the consequences of persisting economic growth logic, for example the rapid disappearance of urban green spaces for building and infrastructure development. Here, local NGOs collaborate with local district politicians to jointly fight against construction plans on urban green spaces that provide for mosques with underground shopping malls in public parks. This coalition has managed to mobilise numerous residents. The number and quality of NGOs is increasing (Istanbul, a4, 91), and citizens join them to jointly protest against the reduction of urban green spaces. Actions range from demonstrations to court hearings (Istanbul, a1, 23–9, 43 and a4, 48, 74–80; Saarbrücken, a4, 25). In one case, the metropolitan local authority's plan to build a shopping mall was opposed by the district government more than 20 times by *taking proceedings*, yet without success. According to Istanbul's respondents, in most cases citizens' protest is not successful due to existing power structures: 'If you are not ... in a position of power, you can try as hard as you like. You cannot stop the big projects. They crush you' (Istanbul, a1, 39). Apart from going straight to court, NGOs also use the means of *vetoing* decisions, leading to a renewed examination, as in the case of Jihlava, where trees on private land were supposed to be cut. An NGO figured out that the obtained expert opinion was manipulated, and obtained another one which was then submitted at the regional level, saving the trees (Jihlava, a4, 43).

Citizens also self-organise in associations or social movements to *reappropriate* abandoned areas, for example old military fields, by doing urban gardening and agriculture on them, to prevent construction on them and to put pressure on the city to instead develop urban green corridors (Madrid, a4, 62–4, 72). In Spain, this phenomenon has a historical precursor: towards the end of the dictatorship and afterwards, during the transition to a democratic system, citizens' movements mushroomed and claimed urban green spaces (cf. 6.3.1.1), which led to their expansion and to the movements' influence on their governance (Madrid, a4, 36, 57–60).[9] In Greece the value of land has fallen due to the crises, building activity has often been stopped or slowed down, and citizens occupy this land (Thessaloniki, a4, 52).

In some places, initial protest evolves into constructive *collaboration* across sectors and a *higher degree of citizen participation*. In Milan, an association now has a good relationship with the local authority, yet this was only achieved after protest actions (Milan, a4, 54–7). In Lugano, a citizen movement, fighting to obtain sustainable urban planning which safeguards the remaining unbuilt mountains around the city from construction, led to the foundation of an association countering real estate development in the outer city district. It has achieved an institutionalised hearing process for a participated planning procedure, consisting of informative meetings with all stakeholders involved, led by an external facilitator. However, building activity is continuing (Lugano, a4, 18–20, 24, 26, 58–68, 84–6).

Not only civil society, but also *economic* actors try to protect urban green spaces. For example, a company from Larissa is rehabilitating a ditch, transforming it into a park to reach the level of biodiversity that had existed before the area was degraded by grazing and often arbitrary irregular construction (Larissa, a3, 28).

7.4 Urban food production

The urban gardening movement in European cities has attracted attention to using common green spaces for urban food production. In contrast to Europe, in other parts of the world urban food production has never decreased, and has even been expanded. In African cities for example, for a large proportion of the population, food production for self-consumption has always been a means of ensuring food sovereignty. In Cuba, due to the decades-long embargo, the greater Havana area has developed into a metropolis of organic commercial and subsistence food production, with cooperatives playing an important role, feeding the population with fresh fruits and vegetables (Clouse 2014, 21, 24, 41). Urban food production is not a new phenomenon in European cities. For example, some time ago, fruit trees could be found in every French city and town (Strasbourg, a4, 82–3). While the original reason for producing food in cities was to let workers produce fresh food for self-consumption, reasons, motives, and forms of growing food in the city have diversified. In several European cities civil society actors have started food production, either without or in cooperation with the local authority. The interest in producing food in the city is ever-growing, although it is greater in some cities than in others, with generally least action in the East and in Istanbul, where it is, according to a respondent, not the citizens' mentality to grow food in the city (Istanbul, a1, 73). An interviewee from Paris describes its scale in the city as manageable, with some collective gardens existing, but not having developed into a social movement (Paris, a4, 56). A totally different picture presents itself in Leeds, with many initiatives happening recently, whereas before there was not much action either. Now, there is a lot of interest and positive movement (Leeds, a4, 59–60). Also in Linz citizens and citizen groups want to get more involved in urban gardening (Linz, a4, 94–6). Interest is high mainly in dense cities with a low percentage of urban green spaces, where most inhabitants have neither their own garden nor a balcony. This takes the form of interest in allotment gardens as well as in community gardens (Innsbruck, a3, 77; Milan, a3, 59; Saarbrücken, a4, 50). The following three subsections shed light on underlying motives for urban food production in European cities by clustering the empirical data obtained into the four main existing forms of producing food in cities, as proposed by a respondent (Leeds, a4, 97–9). The four types are not hermetically separated from one another, but very often overlap.

7.4.1 The productive reappropriation of public space: the example of community food production for self-consumption

On the one hand increasing urbanisation leads to a reduction in the amount of surface area that can still be used for agriculture. On the other hand industrial agriculture leads to a decrease in soil quality in the long run and thus in lower yield rates (Reganold *et al.* 1987).[10] By deliberately bringing organic food production back into the city, urban gardening and agriculture can raise awareness about these tendencies. With regard to inner-city densification and urban sprawl, urban green spaces might be safeguarded when turned into food production sites. In this respect it is increasingly recognised in academia (Barthel *et al.* 2015; Gasperi *et al.* 2015) to rethink European cities as places to grow food. This cannot be achieved without the active involvement of civil society actors. Joint food production in urban green spaces is one way of influencing the governance of urban green spaces, by asking for a city with a sufficient amount of green spaces for its inhabitants, accessible to everyone (Müller 2014, 269) at no cost. This demand results in immediate concrete action on the spot. Purcell and Tyman point out that urban food production can become part of the 'right to the city' movement, countering privatisation tendencies and claiming the decommodification of space. It can challenge dominant processes of urban space production and use by, instead of passively leaving this process to neoliberal urban developers 'which [value] space predominantly for its exchange value, and prioritises private property rights over other claims' (Purcell and Tyman 2015, 1), becoming active by equally producing and managing space yet with another logic and other motives behind it.

Community food production for self-consumption is centred on social interaction. It is about growing food *together with others* to build a community. It shifts gardening from the private into the public sphere, making it a visible, open, and common activity. In this way, across European cities, *self-organised* community food production creates *urban green commons* (cf. 6.3.1.2). For example, in Copenhagen the initiative 'Copenhagen Food Community' is only one out of many in the city (Copenhagen, a4, 39). In Potsdam a *non-profit association*, undertaking many different sustainability projects, is a major player in the city in the network of community gardens (Potsdam, a4, 12, 21–7, 49, 55–7). Community food production often makes use of *fallow land*. In Strasbourg inhabitants started to plant tomatoes on an urban green space (Strasbourg, a4, 89), and in Aalborg a project to make use of fallow public land was successfully started, with one of the developed initiatives being urban gardening (Aalborg, a4, 61). In Madrid the urban gardens' network was created as a citizens' initiative without support from the city council (Madrid, a3, 59), starting urban gardening for example in the city's biggest park in the heart of the city (Madrid, a4, 45). Most neighbourhood associations operate on *appropriated abandoned urban space*, which is foreseen for building development, in order to do urban gardening (Madrid, a3, 59).[11] In Milan an association has reclaimed an abandoned park, which led to the uncovering of illegal activities taking place there. They have converted parts of the park for allotments and farming (Milan, a4, 52).

In Thessaloniki, due to a lack of action in the governance of urban green spaces on the part of the public authority, there have been several civil society actions to use urban space for food production: 'On the one hand we observe the poor management of the municipality and on the other hand the beautiful self-organised initiatives of civil society' (Thessaloniki, a3, 85). Strong self-organised initiatives have emerged. For example, the first and biggest citizens' *urban agriculture initiative* is called 'Periastikes Kalliergies'[12] (PER.KA) operating on a former military camp (Thessaloniki, a3, 78). It was formed after the concession of this urban space from the district's local authority to the citizen group, in order for it to cultivate vegetables and fruits for self-consumption, with the idea of urban agriculture for subsistence without selling the yield (Thessaloniki, a3, 46). Meanwhile, the initiative has yielded numerous similar sub-initiatives in other parts of the city always on abandoned military camps (ibid.). Particularly the first PER.KA shows a 'unique development in terms of citizen participation' (ibid.). Apart from former military camps, even dumping sites were used to start urban gardening and agriculture. In two cities' dumping sites, there was a citizens' initiative started by a large group of urban farmers, starting to cultivate fruits and vegetables, cleaning, embellishing, and making the spaces available for food production designated for self-production (Thessaloniki, a3, 78, 85). This happened because the ongoing transformation of the former military camp into a composting site undertaken by city employees was suddenly stopped due to the economic crisis and consequent budget problems. The staff was dismissed, and the place turned into an illegal dumping ground (Thessaloniki, a3, 84–5). Here, citizens reacted to the *city's difficulty in governing urban green spaces* by self-organising.

In some cities there is a high degree of *cooperation across sectors*, which expresses itself in *vivid communication* through different channels (Leeds, a4, 86). In Leeds two initiatives were born after activists had contacted the local authority. The first, 'Feed Leeds' tries to encourage community food growing in parks and was connected to all pre-existing food growing initiatives, allotment garden organisations, and other kinds of sustainability groups, to create a *loose but very active local network*. It connects civil society actors and is also in touch with politics (the council) through the creation of an independent committee. It was born when an activist got in touch with a councillor who understood that *stepping back from controlling green spaces and allowing a more democratic use of them* would be beneficial to the city as a whole, while *relieving the public budget*. Anticipating that major budgetary cuts would occur, meaning that the city would not be able to afford to govern urban green spaces as in the past, he believes that by involving citizens, costs can be saved (Leeds, a4, 31–40). This *politician actively supports* the initiative by asking what he can do to improve conditions for it to flourish (Leeds, a4, 86). The second and third initiatives try to carry the idea of growing food in cities into formal educational institutions: there is the 'Leeds Edible School Sustainability Network' which fosters sustainability issues and healthy eating habits in schools, as well as 'Leeds Edible Campus' to also connect research activities to the existing network, by creating a showcase of urban agriculture. Furthermore, new initiatives are emerging, for example the 'Incredible Edible Todmorden Initiative' (Leeds, a4, 31–5) or the 'Meanwood Valley Urban Farm', the first urban farm in Great Britain which is open to schools and families (Leeds, a4, 82–4).

7.4.2 An element of a multiple activity society

Urban gardening and agriculture and the linked issue of new subsistence open up an explicit sociopolitical discourse on which activities are considered to be work. A pluralised conception of work sees urban gardening and agriculture as being part of a myriad of meaningful activities that have the potential of increasing social capital in the local community and thus of fostering local sustainable development (cf. 2.4.4). During the Italian Presidency of the EU Council, a public consultation and subsequent conference on the social economy's role as a 'key driver of economic and social development in Europe' (Italian Government 2014, 1) was conducted. The strategy defines social economy as

> a universe of organisations based on the primacy of people over capital. Their aim is providing goods, services or jobs to their members or to the community at large, with a long-term perspective, with the participation of members-stakeholders in the governance of the organisation, and through the reinvestment of profits in their mission.
>
> (Italian Government 2014, 2)

This definition is compatible with the one given by Moulaert and Ailenei (2005, 2044), who conceptualise the social economy comprehensively as comprising 'a wide family of initiatives and organisational forms – i.e. a hybridisation of market, non-market (redistribution) and non-monetary (reciprocity) economies'. These forms can be clustered into the three '[sub-]concepts of third sector, social economy and solidarity economy' (ibid.; cf. also 2.4.4).[13] As the empirical data (cf. 7.4.2.3), as well as the Havana case (cf. 7.4) show, local social and solidarity economies in the field of urban food production have the potential of creating 'green jobs'. At the moment, urban food production in European cities is still primarily done for subsistence reasons, not selling the yield (cf. 8.3). So, if food is produced for self-consumption or for barter, this can contribute to realising a multiple activity society at the local level. For Paech (cf. 2.4.3.6) urban food production is a major element of a post-growth economy. If gainful employment was halved, there would be more time to engage in the production of local food in the city. Urban modern subsistence in food requires time from those involved and basic knowledge about how to grow food in the city. This type of 'creative subsistence' (Paech 2015, 37, own translation) can create a new balance between conventional consumption behaviour and self-sufficiency options, contributing to leading a modern life 'with less money and production' (ibid., 29, own translation), while also raising environmental awareness as well as keeping and transmitting the knowledge of growing food which has partly already become lost amongst city dwellers (Barthel *et al.* 2015, 1321–2).

7.4.2.1 *The example of private food production for self-consumption*

Private food production for self-consumption is done on private ground and is practised alone or with family members. The majority of city dwellers do not possess
their own garden to grow food in, so they draw on the possibility of renting an
allotment garden either from private owners or from the city. Allotment gardens
have a long tradition in European cities (Leeds, a4, 82–6), especially in former
industrial ones, even if their diffusion varies across regions (less in Southern and
Eastern Europe). Even if becoming less popular from the 1960s onwards due to
economic revival with a corresponding turning away from self-producing
options,[14] they have always continued to exist and have been experiencing an
increased interest since the end of the last millennium. For example, in Dortmund there are more than 120 allotment *associations* (Dortmund, a4, 42). In
Milan, the owner of an inner-city plot started a pilot project renting 60 allotments to families. There are more than 350 families on the waiting list and this
is without ever placing an advertisement (Milan, a3, 59). He is trying to obtain
land from the city to be administered in the form of a *cooperative* in order to
enlarge the already existing allotments. Then everyone interested in producing
food could become a cooperative member by buying a share. By letting a
cooperative care for a piece of inner-city agricultural land, its abandonment will
be prevented and thus it will also be withdrawn from financial building speculation interests, thus *countering land speculation* and *prevailing profit-orientation* in
land use policy (Milan, a3, 37–9, 61). In Potsdam, an association with numerous innovative ideas also manages to put them into practice, with one of them
being the growing of food in their own garden for self-consumption (Potsdam,
a4, 21–7, 49, 55–7). In the same city, there is also a trend of young people
renting an allotment together, thus blurring the boundary between private and
community food production (Potsdam, a3, 220–2 and a4, 41).

7.4.2.2 *New coalitions to take care of urban green spaces*

Another interesting observation in the data has been the emergence of new
forms of cooperation and coalition in some places in order to deal with local
challenges concerning urban green spaces, partly referring to food production
also, which deserve a deeper investigation.

For the majority of cities, communication of actors within and across sectors
is reported, possibly leading to higher levels of cooperation and collaboration
(Copenhagen, a4, 15; Innsbruck, a3, 45), which might in turn lead to a shift in
the constellation of actors in the local action situation. Why do civil society
and economic actors enter the local action situation and gain more influence in
it and how do they interact with more established actors? These questions
cannot be answered without shedding light on the cities' financial situation, as
shown by the empirical examples below.

Problems with the public budget are mentioned in every region and have reached
the state of public poverty in some cities. Especially in cities in which the local

authority has severe difficulties in affording the provision of urban green spaces, new self-organised initiatives have emerged at grassroots level for maintaining and even developing those, thus tackling local challenges and becoming active players in local governance processes. Here, *self-organisation mitigates public poverty*. Where the public budget suffers most, there is a high probability that self-organisation emerges. Civil society actors, sometimes in cooperation with economic actors, become active in the maintenance of urban green spaces. This includes cleaning actions, tree-planting, gardening, and the redesigning of parks (e.g. adding benches, creating spaces for children) (Milan, a4, 102; Naples, a3, 72–6 and a4, 32, 47, 57; Sibiu, a2, 69–71; Thessaloniki, a3, 20–1, 44, 85 and a4, 13).

This trend has been increased in the aftermath of the multiple crises from 2008 onwards, with austerity policies putting high pressure on local public budgets (Rome, a1, 35). Many cities have realised that involving these actors in the governance of urban green spaces can save costs (Milan, a4, 36–8; Naples, a3, 76). Hence, in several European cities, the local authority opts for assigning the care for urban green spaces to associations as well as to private enterprises (*adoption*). 'We are doing the adoption of green areas by citizens. This is also important in this time of scarcity of resources, involving citizens not only in the planning but also in the maintenance which has high costs' (Rome, a1, 35). In Milan, the initiative to give abandoned land to citizens to take care of it came from the local authority (Milan, a3, 68). Citizens can join associations and organise for example the cleaning of parks, while the local authority provides the legal framework for these actions (Madrid, a3, 53–7 and 71; Naples, a3, 74–6 and a4, 51, 57).[15] In Thessaloniki, a private enterprise in cooperation with civil society actors adopts urban green spaces in deprived areas to take care of them, turning them into parks accessible to everyone (Thessaloniki, a3, 20–1).

The aforementioned examples show that *cooperation takes different forms* and can either be *initiated from the top down or from the bottom up*. Spontaneous self-organised initiatives might be taken up and fostered by the local authority. Or, it can be that the local authority provides from the beginning a concrete sphere of activity for citizens and enterprises to become active. And sometimes it is the citizens themselves who have asked to help and support the local authority. 'Citizens … often ask to be able to help with day to day support in their neighbourhood's small green area' (Rome, a1, 35).

However, these new forms of collaboration are in most places *not yet anchored institutionally*. Most projects are still in the trial phase, not having been evaluated yet. They often still *miss clear rules*, for example *responsibilities are not clearly assigned to stakeholders*, so that cooperation does not run smoothly yet. Rosol (2014, 248) found that the precondition for community gardens initiated by the local authority to be successfully governed by citizens is that gardeners can decide themselves on 'how to design and run the gardens', confirming one of Ostrom's design rules (cf. 3.3.1). Another reason why coalitions might not function smoothly are legal obstacles (cf. 9.3), since still 'the field of application for licensing and delegated management systems by the public authorities is a narrow one' (EC 1995, 74). For example in Milan the municipality uses tendering measures to give a small number of allotments to associations. The application requires a lot of time resources from the associations and creates competition between them. In one case, accessibility to urban green spaces was reduced by assigning their care to a golf association that limited access to its members (Milan, a3, 55). In some cities enterprises and associations have to pay for the maintenance costs, for example they acquire equipment at their own cost, when adopting a piece of land, which disadvantages local associations (Naples, a3, 75–6). In Thessaloniki, an initiative of park regeneration was started by two civil society groups together with an economic actor, providing material, volunteers, as well as financial means. The local authority was not able to provide them either with soil, which would have cost around 500 euro, or with professional support such as workers or machines (Thessaloniki, a3, 76). The examples show that civil society actors can support the local authority in green spaces maintenance. However, to ensure their long-term commitment and to achieve stable sustainable results, they must be backed by the local authority. The minimum of assistance is that no financial costs are burdened on the civil society or economic actors who already bring in their non-paid workforce.

> Now there is the possibility to adopt a green space, but why should the associations be responsible for the maintenance costs because the municipality does not manage to have the money? The adoption should be: I control that you do it, because as association I might be interested in adopting a green area, but maybe I cannot substitute you…. It should be you, municipality to do it, and me association that adopted the area to control it…. So, if an association is allowed to participate in the maintenance of the green spaces, to participate, not that it has to do it all alone.
>
> (Naples, a3, 76)

The local authority has to pay for the maintenance costs and provide equipment and soil. Civil society commitment must always remain voluntary and cannot be used as an excuse to cut back public services (cf. 1.1, Chapter 3, and 9.2).

7.4.2.3 *Commercial food production*

The main purpose of *commercial food production* is to sell the food produced with the possibility of *creating green jobs*.[16] Here, the approach of the *social and solidarity economy* comes in (cf. 2.4.4 and 7.4.2; United Nations Inter-Agency Task Force on Social and Solidarity Economy 2014).

Compared with other parts of the world, for example in Cuba (Clouse 2014), commercial urban food production is still almost non-existent in Europe. Thus, the potential of using urban green spaces for commercial food production in the scope of social and solidarity economy initiatives is far from being fully exploited yet. *Cooperatives* in the field of urban food production are only mentioned in two cities, Milan (cf. 7.4.2.1) and Larissa. In Larissa, although 'there are … not many well-organised ... cooperatives and associations in the city, with vision and clear goals' (Larissa, a3, 46), many small innovative civil society initiatives, such as women's cooperatives selling locally produced organic food, exist (Larissa, a4, 89). Such examples of social and solidarity economy often emerge 'as an answer to state and market failure.... The solutions, created under circumstances of need or crisis, open up future prospects for sustainable urban spaces and ideas for a complementary local social policy based on productive options' (Elsen and Schicklinski 2016, 234).

7.4.3 Raising awareness for a sustainable global food and agriculture system

As mentioned in the preceding two subsections, urban food production can raise awareness of the value of land as a common, which often happens in reaction to increasing urbanisation tendencies with concomitant land consumption and the loss of fertile soil through infrastructure and building development. It can also keep and transmit knowledge about growing food and allow people to become engaged in a meaningful work activity, having the potential to evolve into social and solidarity economies. Apart from that it can also open up a discourse about the detrimental consequences of chemical industrial monoculture-based agriculture, about biodiversity, food sovereignty, and trade and food justice in the global context. This is a concrete example of what Beck (2000, 48), following Robertson (1995), calls '*glocalization*'. If local movements take up global concerns, this shows that

> globalization – which seems to be the super-dimension, appearing at the end from outside and overshadowing everything else – can be grasped in the small and concrete, in the spatially particular, in one's own life, in cultural symbols that all bear the signature of the 'glocal'.
>
> (Beck 2000, 49)

When local urban gardening groups inform and educate through actions like seed swapping for global issues such as decreasing biodiversity substantially caused by the market power of a handful of big corporations, the global becomes a local issue. At the same time the local becomes global if these groups become interconnected with others around the world, facilitated by new media. 'Today the ability to realize global potential depends on connections with and between highly decentralized and locally operating groups' (Nowotny *et al.* 2013, 41). In a globalised world 'merging the global with the local' (ibid.), very often local claims are connected to global issues. Local concerns need to be regarded as part of global ones (Robertson 1995, 32–7; Beck 2000, 48–9) and acting locally implies thinking globally.

The Sustainable Development Goals draw the vision of a world 'where food is sufficient, safe, affordable and nutritious' (UNGA 2015, 3), and the second sustainable development goal wants to '*end hunger, achieve food security and improved nutrition and promote sustainable agriculture*' (ibid., 15). Similarly, yet more specifically, the Milan Urban Food Policy Pact (Mayors and representatives of local governments 2015)[17] aims at

> develop[ing] sustainable food systems that are inclusive, resilient, safe and diverse, that provide healthy and affordable food to all people in a human rights-based framework, that minimise waste and conserve biodiversity while adapting to and mitigating impacts of climate change.

Such goals are urgently needed and shall be taken as the starting point and guiding principles to change the current unsustainable global agriculture and food system into a more sustainable and just one.

The disastrous consequences of the global food and agriculture industry and of a liberalised global trade system for the majority of the population in the Global South are outlined below. This is followed by a summary of how a sustainable equitable alternative system looks.

7.4.3.1 Flaws of the current global agricultural and food system

The globalised industrial fossil-fuel-based chemical food and agriculture system generates 40 per cent of global greenhouse gas emissions responsible for climate change (Shiva 2013, 17, 103). Moreover, it has harmed biodiversity, waters, forests, and soils (Meadows *et al.* 2005, 46; Shiva 2013, 14), since it is extremely energy-intensive (Reganold *et al.* 1987, 370; Shiva 2013, 17, 102, 142), makes use of and contaminates almost three-quarters of the Earth's water resources and has ruined three-quarters of agricultural biodiversity (Shiva 2013, 17). This system paired with a liberalised global food and agriculture trade system is environmentally and socially unsustainable. It has not managed to shift the majority of the population in the Global South out of poverty and hunger, but has even had a reverse effect, as Shiva (2013) shows for India, and as will be explained in the rest of this subsection.

It is important to note that the rise in food prices leading to the major food crisis in 2008 and the subsequent one in 2011 (Shiva 2013, 138–9) was not due to rising demand in the Global South, but happened for three main interrelated reasons: first, land in the Global South has increasingly been diverted from growing food for local and regional consumption to growing cash crops for export; second, because, under the trade liberalisation policy of the World Trade Organization, the local and regional food market in the Global South has been more and more threatened by agricultural and food products being imported from industrialised countries; and, third, because the deregulation of the financial economy has led to an increased commodification of food in a first and land in a second step, with concomitant speculation on these two commodities (ibid., 136; cf. remaining paragraphs in this subsection, below).

Referring to the first reason, the diversion of land for growing cash crops is done to grow food for export, yet also increasingly for growing feed, primarily soya, for the globalised meat industry as well as for producing biofuel (ibid., 164–5). Land in the Global South is more and more used to cultivate mono-culture cash crops for export to industrialised countries instead of producing diversified food staples for local consumption (ibid., 199, 220–2). Increasingly cultivated crops for export are not even consumed by humans but either used as fodder or for producing bioenergy.[18]

Currently, global food policy is largely determined by a small number of multinational corporations. They increasingly control seeds[19] which leads to a decreasing range of species and varieties and makes farmers dependent on the global agricultural corporations selling seeds (Organisation für Eine Solidarische Welt (oew) *et al.* 2015). Farmers all over the world are increasingly threatened by seed laws that forbid them to exchange uncertified seeds (Shiva 2013, 21, 165–8). The commodification of nature, including turning food and land into a commodity, as well as the patenting of seeds, has increased in recent decades (ibid., 15–16).

India serves as an example to show how the adoption of an unlimited eco-nomic growth logic in the field of agriculture and food does not lead to local sustainable development but instead aggravates the situation for the majority of the population. In a country where more than half of the population belongs to smallholding farmer families (Singh *et al.* 2002, 3), the government gave in to the pressure of the World Trade Organization, opening up the job-providing agricultural sector to foreign enterprises resulting in an absolute monopoly of a small number of potent corporations (Shiva 2013, 199).

Referring to the second reason, countries of the Global South are also forced by the World Trade Organization to allow imports of food commodities from industrialised countries (ibid., 160). This means for example that the Indian market has been virtually destroyed by inexpensive imports (ibid., 161, 197). Importing agricultural products and food from industrialised countries to the Global South (for example tomatoes, meat, soya), despite destroying local and regional markets, is nevertheless still subsidised, for example by the EU and the US.

Connected to the import of agriculture and food commodities is the entrance of big foreign retailers, destroying the decentralised well-functioning system of small-scale entrepreneurs (ibid., 161, 221) as well as increasing food waste: in the industrial global food system half of the food is wasted due to long-distance transport and large-volume retail (ibid., 17, 137).

The third reason can be explained as follows. Especially in the aftermath of the US sub-prime crisis and the resulting financial crisis, food and land have become strategic assets for investors (ibid., 30, 157–60), promising high profit margins. Turning food into a globally traded commodity was followed by land commodification leading to landgrabbing, not only but primarily in the Global South (ibid., 30, 157–60). This is even more dramatic when knowing that three-quarters of the population of the Global South live from the land they inhabit (ibid., 30). Making the human right to food the subject of financial speculation by turning food and land into commodities increases the poverty and hunger of local people, who are then forced to migrate into the cities (oew *et al.* 2015).

These interrelated reasons show that the food crisis did not appear from nowhere but is a logical and structural consequence from an unjust global trade and food and agriculture system not orientated on the principles of food sovereignty, food democracy, or even fighting hunger but being dominated by and following the profit-maximisation logic of the big food and agricultural corporations (Shiva 2013, 191) which successfully lobby the EU and international organisations such as the World Trade Organization (ibid., 170). It also shows that social and environmental sustainability cannot be separated. Climate change is the consequence of a resource- and energy-intensive and fossil-fuel-based economy (ibid., 101–3) endangering both the environment and human beings. The idea that only an industrial agriculture relying on chemicals and genetically modified organisms in combination with the liberalisation of the global food and agriculture market will make food available and affordable for everyone to end hunger is wrong, because the reasons for the food crisis lie in the way of food production, the distribution of food, and in the ownership of natural capital such as water, seeds, and land (ibid., 137).[20] The liberalisation of the world (financial) economy in general and the global agricultural and food market specifically has not shifted the majority of the population out of poverty and hunger but instead made autonomous food systems dependent (ibid., 196). The number of hungry and poor people in the world has increased for the cited reasons. The combined sum of these reasons has led to falling incomes for local farmers, while food prices still rise. Cynically half of the world's and India's hungry are smallholding farmers (ibid., 129, 136). These farmers are forced to produce for export and to buy overpriced imported products for themselves. The disastrous social and environmental consequences of this system become evident. On the one hand it has already provoked an immense and irreversible biodiversity loss of three-quarters of crop plants (ibid., 9). On the other hand every fourth Indian is hungry, every second child heavily malnourished (ibid., 21), and smallholder farmers impoverished, become indebted, and even commit suicide (ibid., 103, 197).

7.4.3.2 The alternative: a biodiverse just global agriculture and food system

The Sustainable Development Goals, more specifically target 2.3 of the second goal, specifies how hunger can be ended. It foresees to, 'by 2030, double the agricultural productivity and incomes of small-scale food producers, in particular women,[21] indigenous peoples, family farmers, pastoralists and fishers, including through secure and equal access to land, other productive resources and inputs, knowledge, financial services, markets' (UNGA 2015, 15, goal 2, target 2.3). Moreover, target 2.4 foresees to

> ensure sustainable food production systems and implement resilient agricultural practices that increase productivity and production, that help

maintain ecosystems, that strengthen capacity for adaptation to climate change, extreme weather, drought, flooding and other disasters and that progressively improve land and soil quality.

(Ibid., 15, goal 2, target 2.4)

And finally target 2.5 foresees to

maintain the genetic diversity of seeds, cultivated plants and farmed and domesticated animals and their related wild species, including through soundly managed and diversified seed and plant banks at the national, regional and international levels, and promote access to and fair and equitable sharing of benefits arising from the utilization of genetic resources and associated traditional knowledge.

(Ibid., 16, goal 2, target 5.2)

Yet these goals can only be reached if states in the global trade in food and agriculture products 'refrain from promulgating and applying any unilateral economic, financial or trade measures ... that impede the full achievement of economic and social development, particularly in developing countries' (ibid., 8, introduction, 30.).

A biodiverse just global agriculture and food system would let smallholding farmers exchange and sell seeds and provide them with open-pollinated non-hybrid varieties (oew *et al.* 2015). It would be independent from the volatile global food and agriculture market as well as from global corporations' seed monopolies by rebuilding local food systems controlled by the local community (Shiva 2013, 134). It would mean replacing industrial fossil-fuel-based agriculture based on monoculture, chemical fertilisers, herbicides, and pesticides, and increasing genetic engineering by biodiverse small-scale organic farming, which is especially important for securing people's livelihood in the Global South. While conventional industrial agriculture consumes more energy than it generates as food (Shiva 2013, 17), biodiverse small-scale organic farming produces more energy in the form of food than has been used as input (ibid., 102). It also uses ten times less water to achieve the same yield of food as conventional industrial agriculture (ibid., 153). Moreover, it preserves biodiversity, enriches the soil and the diet[22] and mitigates climate change through renouncing synthetic fertilisers[23] and through sequestering carbon in the soil by the buildup of humus (Meadows *et al.* 2005, 274; Shiva 2013, 151–3). It could thus reduce those 40 per cent of greenhouse gas emissions that industrial agriculture has provoked (Shiva 2013, 103). Refuting conventional industrial agriculture's main argument, it even increases the overall output, which means that hunger can be ended by supporting smallholder farmers practising biodiverse organic agriculture (Shiva and Pandey 2006; Shiva and Singh 2012; Shiva 2013, 227–30). This is because in conventional industrial agriculture productivity is measured without counting all inputs, by focusing only on one crop, for example wheat, and by using only one part of it with dumping the rest (Shiva 2013, 228), while biodiverse organic agriculture systems use different crop varieties using all outputs (ibid., 229). India's whole population could be nourished healthily without anyone suffering from hunger if biodiverse organic farming was implemented all over the country (ibid., 131). For the cited reasons, biodiverse organic farming could solve the interrelated climate, food, and water crises (ibid., 154).

Changing production conditions is one side of the coin; the other is raising consumers' awareness to achieve a change in consumer behaviour. With the rise of the food and agriculture industry and concomitant mass consumption of processed food, the role of the 'smart' or 'conscious' consumer, especially in industrialised countries, becomes essential. Such consumers are aware of their personal contribution to achieve better living conditions for people in the Global South and for safeguarding the world's environmental livelihoods.[24] This is about transparency about food ingredients and about the social and environmental production and transport conditions of food. The attentive and conscious handling of food in the Global North can achieve a wider change. It can increase food sovereignty in the Global South. Yet, a personal change in lifestyle and daily consumption patterns[25] seldom happens by itself but must be fostered by information and education about global interrelations in the food and agriculture system (oew *et al.* 2015).

7.4.3.3   *The example of 'pick-it-as-you-walk-past' food production*

In 'help-yourself, urban harvest, free-to-use, or pick-it-as-you-walk-past' (Leeds, a4, 99) production, food is grown by a group of individuals and left to be picked by everyone passing by. This movement wants to *raise awareness of the value of land as a common*, as well as promote discourse around the global issues of *food sovereignty and a more sustainable and equitable global food and agriculture system* (cf. 6.4.3). In Strasbourg, the movement 'Incroyables Comestibles' ('Unbelievable Comestibles', own translation) tries to raise awareness about urban food production by bringing back fruit trees as well as agriculture into the city and to reintroduce native species (Strasbourg, a4, 82–3). In Potsdam the intercultural garden founded by an NGO has created an orchard which is open to everyone (Potsdam, a4, 173). In Saarbrücken the movement 'Saarbrücken – die essbare Stadt' ('Saarbrücken – the edible city', own translation) was founded by some individuals who started to grow vegetables in an urban space without official permission by the local authority, gaining ever more members. It was supported by a local NGO, for example via lecture events, and subsequently also by the city. Meanwhile growing continues on a second spot, this time a private space, with the owner's permission, the church. The movement is judged by a respondent as a successful example of self-organisation, although it has to be seen whether it is more than a temporary trend (Saarbrücken, a4, 69).

Notes

1 Barthel *et al.* (2015); copyright ©2013 by Urban Studies Journal Limited. Reprinted by permission of SAGE Publications, Inc.
2 Löw (2001); reproduced with permission of Palgrave Macmillan.
3 See Note 2.
4 Harvey (2012, 73) gives the example of 'Syntagma Square in Athens, Tahrir Square in Cairo, and the [!] Plaza de Catalunya in Barcelona … [,] public spaces that became an urban commons as people assembled there to express their political views and make demands'.
5 From: Elsen (2007); ©Juventa.
6 Translated and reproduced from Helfrich and Bollier (2014).
7 In the governance of green spaces, enclosure can be defined as 'deprivation of rights of urban dwellers whose parks and public spaces are to an unjustifiable extent misused for commercial purposes' (Helfrich and Bollier 2014, 16, own translation); see Note 2.
8 See Note 5.
9 One of the demands of the Madrid neighbourhood movement was '*more open space, preservation of parks, conservation of tree-lined streets* and general environmental protection' (Castells 1983, 225). For example, the movement achieved the construction of a small urban public garden in a housing area erected by a private developer at the end of the 1960s without any open or green spaces. Also, in the fight over the construction of a shopping centre on the last vacant spot, a compromise was reached and a public park was built on part of the land (ibid., 249–51). Moreover, in another part of the city, the protection of the '*colonias*' (ibid, 256) – residential quarters, single-storey houses with gardens – was stipulated in the Special Master Plan for the Conservation of Madrid instead of tearing them down for building high-storey buildings (ibid.).
10 The long-term study

> compare[d] the long-term effects (since 1948) of organic and conventional farming on selected properties of the same soil. The organically-farmed soil had significantly higher organic matter content, thicker topsoil depth … and less soil erosion than the conventionally-farmed soil…. [So] in the long term, the organic farming system was more effective than the conventional farming system in reducing soil erosion and, therefore, in maintaining soil productivity.
>
> (Reganold *et al.* 1987, 370)

11 The interviews give no hint whether these actions stand in the tradition of the Madrid neighbourhood movement.
12 'Peri-urban agriculture'.
13 According to Moulaert and Ailenei, these forms are often used interchangeably despite their varying connotations in different countries. For a clearer distinction between these three sub-concepts, cf. Moulaert and Ailenei (2005, 2042–6).
14 This refers to the Northern and Western part of Europe, and does not reflect the situation in the countries belonging to the former Soviet Union.
15 Yet, mere cleaning actions are also seen critically by civil society actors. In Sibiu a local NGO organised cleaning actions of urban green spaces, yet later discontinued them saying that the actions were counterproductive, since the people that clean are already aware of its necessity, so practically they clean for people who do not have this awareness, without creating any change in awareness (Sibiu, a4, 54–6).
16 In a joint report by UNEP, ILO, the International Organisation of Employers, and the International Trade Union Confederation 'green jobs [are defined] as positions in agriculture … that contribute substantially to preserving or restoring environmental quality. Specifically, but not exclusively, this includes jobs that help to protect and restore ecosystems and biodiversity' (Renner *et al.* 2008, 35–6).

17 The voluntary memorandum of understanding, launched by Milan's local authority on the occasion of the 2015 Expo 'Feeding the Planet, Energy for Life', was signed by mayors and representatives of local governments from around the world to draw attention to the role of local authorities in promoting sustainable food systems.

18 This switch from food production for human consumption to the use as fuels has been accelerated by the subsidies and energy policy of the US and the EU (Shiva 2013, 163; OEW *et al.* 2015).

19 To do so corporations currently circumvent article 53 on 'Exceptions to patentability' of the European Patent Convention which reads 'European patents shall not be granted in respect of: ... plant or animal varieties or essentially biological processes for the production of plants or animals' (European Patent Office 2013, 112, art. 53) (my Note).

20 Having been promoted as an alternative to the use of chemicals, genetic engineering has instead led to an increased use of herbicides and pesticides (Shiva 2013, 148, 176–8), and has made it possible for enterprises to control seeds (ibid., 129) instead of increasing crop yield (ibid., 190).

21 Ensuring women's access to natural resources such as land and water is extremely important for reaching food sovereignty since they generate more than 50 per cent of global food and more than four-fifths in Africa (Shiva 2013, 90) (my Note).

22 Biodiverse organic farming does not only increase variety in the diet but it also, if it includes millets and pulses, achieves a higher per capita-per acre nutrition value compared to non-organic monocultures (Shiva and Pandey 2006, 8, 13; Shiva and Singh 2012; Shiva 2013, 229–30).

23 This is since nitrogen fertilisers are based on fossil fuels and produce nitrogen oxide which is much more climate-damaging than CO_2 (Shiva 2013, 151).

24 Thought out, such consumers would buy primarily local and regional seasonal non-processed and non-frozen organic food, possibly directly from the producer, complemented by organic fair trade products and reduce their consumption of animal products, primarily in red meat.

25 In this regard it is worthwhile noting that food has become extremely cheap in industrialised countries due to the liberalisation of the global trade system in agricultural and food commodities, disregarding social and environmental externalities. Very cheap products are available at the expense of people in the Global South and environmental damage. In this regard, people in the Global South are double losers. They not only produce food for export cash crops instead for their own food sovereignty but are also faced with high food prices: For example in Vietnam and India more than 50 per cent of one's income is needed to buy food (Shiva 2013, 217).

References

Barthel, Stephan, John Parker, and Henrik Ernstson. 2015. 'Food and green space in cities: A resilience lens on gardens and urban environmental movements'. *Urban Studies*, 52(7): 1321–38.

Beck, Ulrich. 2000. *What is globalization?* Cambridge, Malden MA: Polity.

Bierling-Wagner, Eugen, Verena Fabris, Maria Kemmetmüller, Josef Mauerlechner, Michaela Moser, Judith Pühringer, Robert Rybaczek-Schwarz, Martin Schenk, and Hansjörg Schlechter. 2013. 'Editorial'. In *Was allen gehört: Commons – neue Perspektiven in der Armutsbekämpfung*, ed. Die Armutskonferenz, 8–10. Wien: Verlag des Österreichischen Gewerkschaftsbundes.

Castells, Manuel. 1983. *The city and the grassroots: A cross-cultural theory of urban social movements*. Berkeley CA, Los Angeles CA: University of California Press.

Clouse, Carey. 2014. *Farming Cuba: Urban farming from the ground up*. New York: Princeton Architectural.

Elsen, Susanne. 2007. *Die Ökonomie des Gemeinwesens: Sozialpolitik und Soziale Arbeit im Kontext von gesellschaftlicher Wertschöpfung und -verteilung.* Weinheim, Munich: Juventa.

Elsen, Susanne and Judith Schicklinski. 2016. 'Mobilising the citizens for the socio-ecological transition'. In *Cities in transition: Social innovation for Europe's urban sustainability,* eds Thomas Sauer, Cristina Garzillo, and Susanne Elsen, 221–38. Abingdon/ New York: Routledge.

European Commission (EC). 1995. 'Local development and employment initiatives: An investigation in the European Union'. Internal document SEC 564/95. http:// bookshop.europa.eu/en/local-development-and-employment-initiatives-pbCM899 5082/ [27 August 2016].

European Patent Office (EPO). 2013. European patent convention. http://documents. epo.org/projects/babylon/eponet.nsf/0/00E0CD7FD461C0D5C1257C060050C376/ $File/EPC_15th_edition_2013.pdf [27 August 2016].

Gasperi, D., G. Giorgio Bazzocchi, I. Bertocchi, S. Ramazzotti, and G. Gianquinto. 2015. 'The multifunctional role of urban gardens in the twentieth century: The Bologna case study'. *Acta Horticulturae,* 1093: 91–8.

Harvey, David. 2012. *Rebel cities: From the right to the city to the urban revolution.* London: Verso.

Helfrich, Silke and David Bollier. 2014. 'Commons als transformative Kraft: Zur Einführung'. In *Commons: Für eine neue Politik jenseits von Markt und Staat.* 2nd edn, ed. Silke Helfrich, 15–23. Bielefeld: transcript. www.boell.de/sites/default/files/2012-04-buch-2012-04-buch-commons.pdf [27 August 2016].

Italian Government. 2014. 'Unlocking the potential of the social economy for EU growth: The Rome strategy. Based on the proceedings of the Rome conference, November 17 and 18, 2014'. http://socialeconomyrome.it/files/Rome%20strategy_EN.pdf [27 August 2016].

Klamt, Martin. 2006. 'Raum und Norm: Zum Verhalten und seiner Regulierung in verschiedenen öffentlichen Räumen'. In *Öffentliche Räume – öffentliche Träume: Zur Kontroverse über die Stadt und ihre Gesellschaft,* ed. Claus-Christian Wiegandt, 29–45. Münster: Lit.

Klamt, Martin. 2012. 'Öffentliche Räume'. In *Handbuch Stadtsoziologie,* ed. Frank Eckardt, 775–802. Wiesbaden: VS Verlag für Sozialwissenschaften.

Löw, Martina. 2001. *Raumsoziologie.* Frankfurt am Main: Suhrkamp.

Löw, Martina, Silke Steets, and Sergej Stoetzer. 2008. *Einführung in die Stadt- und Raumsoziologie,* 2nd edn. Opladen, Farmington Hills MI: Budrich.

Mayors and representatives of local governments. 2015. 'Milan urban food policy pact: 15 October 2015'. www.foodpolicymilano.org/wp-content/uploads/2015/10/Milan-Urban-Food-Policy-Pact-EN.pdf [27 August 2016].

Meadows, Donella H., Jørgen Randers, and Dennis L. Meadows. 2005. *Limits to growth: The 30-year update,* 3rd edn. London: Earthscan.

Moulaert, Frank and Oana Ailenei. 2005. 'Social economy, third sector and solidarity relations: A conceptual synthesis from history to present'. *Urban Studies,* 42(11): 2037–54.

Müller, Christa. 2014. 'Reiche Ernte in Gemeinschaftsgärten: Beim Urban Gardening findet der Homo oeconomicus sein Korrektiv'. In *Commons: Für eine neue Politik jenseits von Markt und Staat,* 2nd edn, ed. Silke Helfrich, 267–72. Bielefeld: transcript. www.boell.de/sites/default/files/2012-04-buch-2012-04-buch-commons.pdf [27 August 2016].

Nowotny, Helga, Peter Scott, and Michael Gibbons. 2013. *Re-thinking science: Knowledge and the public in an age of uncertainty*. Cambridge: Polity (orig. pub. 2001).

Organisation für Eine Solidarische Welt/Organizzazione per Un mondo solidare (organisation for a solidary world), Neetwork of South-Tyrolean fair trade stores, Politis, specialised secondary school for tourism and biotechnology Marie Curie Meran, association 'Sortengarten Südtirol' (garden of sorts South Tyrol) and permaculture community garden Guggenber/Ulten, European Academy of Bozen/Bolzano, Arno Teutsch, Cristina Crepaz, and Autonomous Province of Bolzano – department presidium and external relations – office for cabinet affairs (oew). 2015. 'Südtiroler Manifest zur Ernährungssicherheit: "Den Planeten ernähren" – Was wollen, was können, was müssen wir tun'. www.eurac.edu/de/services/meeting/events/PublishingImages/Pages/Tag-der-Entwicklungszusammenarbeit/Manifest.pdf [27 August 2016].

Paech, Niko. 2015. 'Wachstumsdogma zur Postwachstumsökonomie'. In *Die Kunst des Wandels: Ansätze für die ökosoziale Transformation*, eds Susanne Elsen, Günther Reifer, Andreas Wild, and Evelyn Oberleiter, 25–44. Munich: oekom.

Purcell, Mark and Shannon K. Tyman. 2015. 'Cultivating food as a right to the city'. *Local Environment: The International Journal of Justice and Sustainability*, 20(10): 1132–47.

Reganold, John P., Lloyd F. Elliott, and Yvonne L. Unger. 1987. 'Long-term effects of organic and conventional farming on soil erosion'. *Nature*, 330: 370–2.

Renner, Michael, Sean Sweeney, and Jill Kubit. 2008. 'Green jobs: Towards decent work in a sustainable, low-carbon world'. United Nations Environment Programme (UNEP), International Labour Organization (ILO), International Organisation of Employers (IOE), International Trade Union Confederation (ITUC). www.unep.org/PDF/UNEPGreenjobs_report08.pdf [27 August 2016].

Robertson, Ronald. 1995. 'Glocalization: Time-space and homogeneity-heterogeneity'. In *Global modernities*, eds M. Featherstone, S. Lash, and R. Robertson, 25–44. London: Sage.

Rosol, Marit. 2014. 'Community volunteering as neoliberal strategy? Green space production in Berlin'. *Antipode, A Radical Journal of Geography*, 44(1): 239–57.

Shiva, Vandana. 2013. *Making peace with the earth*. London: Pluto.

Shiva, Vandana and Poonam Pandey. 2006. *Biodiversity based organic farming: A new paradigm for food security and food safety*. New Delhi: Navdanya.

Shiva, Vandana and Vaibhav Singh. 2012. *Health per acre: Organic solutions to hunger and malnutrition*. New Delhi: Navdanya.

Singh, R. B., P. Kumar, and T. Woodhead. 2002. 'Smallholder farmers in India: Food security and agricultural policy'. Food and Agriculture Organization of the United Nations Regional Office for Asia and the Pacific. ftp://ftp.fao.org/docrep/fao/005/ac484e/ac484e00.pdf [27 August 2016].

United Nations General Assembly (UNGA). 2015. 'Draft resolution referred to the United Nations summit for the adoption of the post-2015 development agenda by the General Assembly at its sixty-ninth session: Transforming our world: the 2030 Agenda for Sustainable Development'. Seventieth session, Agenda items 15 and 116. www.un.org/ga/search/view_doc.asp?symbol=A/70/L.1&Lang=E [27 August 2016].

United Nations Inter-Agency Task Force on Social and Solidarity Economy (TFSSE). 2014. 'Social and solidarity economy and the challenge of sustainable development: A position paper by the United Nations Inter-Agency Task Force on Social and Solidarity Economy (TFSSE)'. www.unrisd.org/80256B3C005BCCF9/httpNetITFramePDF?ReadForm&parentunid=4FB6A60F1DBA5995C1257D1C003DAA2A&parentdoctype=paper&netitpath=80256B3C005BCCF9/(httpAuxPages)/4FB6A60F1DBA5995C1257D1C003DAA2A/$file/Position%20Paper_TFSSE_Eng.pdf [1 October 2016].

8   Actors' motivations

Keeping in mind the research questions, it seems to be important to pay attention to the micro-level of the individual actor and to carve out respondents'
motivations to commit themselves to sustainability issues in the respective city,
be it in the field of urban food production or elsewhere. Local actors' motivations for committing themselves to sustainability issues in general and for producing food in the city in particular were modelled as the latent variable, which
influences the characteristics of the independent variable (cf. Figure 5.1). It thus
indirectly also impacts the dependent variable. Understanding local actors'
motivations is one key for designing sustainable local policy options. Knowing
them helps to explain behavioural changes in the socio-ecological transition
and can give important insights to the local authority on how best to set incentives to involve all local actors in governance for sustainability as well as how to
keep and possibly even raise their commitment, with the ultimate aim of designing sustainable local policy options. Moreover, since in the following sections
local actors' motivations from different sectors are analysed and juxtaposed, this
might help to develop sector-specific motivation strategies.

8.1 A theoretical model

So far the two main forms of civic activities have been examined at the meso-
level, viewing the emergence of participation and self-organisation as a collective social process, not considering the individual, apart from stressing that
all citizens, including socioeconomically disadvantaged persons, must be
involved. This section now reaches the micro-level, asking about the individual
actors' motivations to become engaged in civic activities in the field of sustainability in general and in the governance of green spaces in particular. Before
approaching this issue from the empirical stance later in the text, it is necessary
to provide a theoretical basis explaining actors' motivations. The thesis primarily takes a sociological lens, shedding light on different forms of social innovation (self-organisation in general, social movements, and citizen participation)
in order to understand how social change in a socio-ecological transition
becomes possible. Every explanation, however, remains incomplete without also
considering the individual actor and specifically his or her motivation to become

active. The need to consider both the social structure and personal agency in order to explain human action is stressed in Bandura's (1997, 6) self-efficacy theory as part of social cognitive learning theory, which links psychological and sociostructural theories:

> Social cognitive theory thus avoids a dualism between individuals and society and between social structure and personal agency.... Human behavior cannot be fully understood solely in terms of either social structural factors or psychological factors.... The self is socially constituted, but, by exercising self-influence, individuals are partial contributors to what they become and do.

Thus, concentrating on the individual, Figures 8.1 and 8.2 give an overview of different theoretical approaches that are helpful to explain actors' motivations for becoming involved in sustainability issues. Taking a philosophical stance, Nussbaum's (1992) capability approach determines ten basic capabilities constituting human life. Taking a psychological perspective, Deci and Ryan's (2000) self-determination theory circumscribes three basic human needs, and Katz's

7 out of 10 basic capabilities (Nussbaum 1992, 222)

'Being able to have good health; to be adequately nourished...'

'Being able to ... have pleasurable experiences'

'Being able to have attachments to things and persons outside ourselves...'

'Being able to form a conception of the good and to engage in critical reflection about the planning of one's own life'

'Being able to live for and with others, to recognize and show concern for other human beings, to engage in various forms of familiar and social interaction'

'Being able to live with concern for and in relation to animals, plants, and the world of nature'

'Being able to laugh, to play, to enjoy recreational activities'

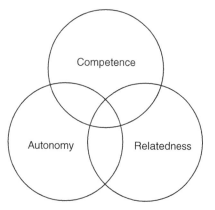

Self-determination theory with three basic needs (Deci and Ryan 2000)

Figure 8.1 An overview of different theoretical approaches to explain actors' motivations for becoming involved in sustainability issues (1).

Source: own.

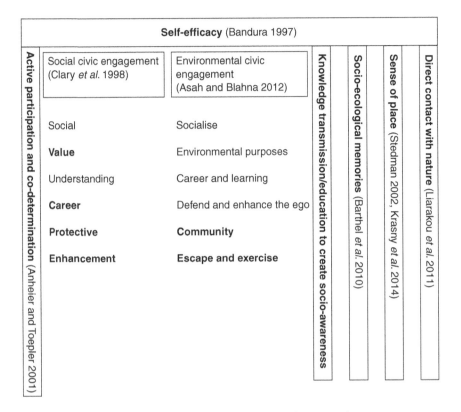

Figure 8.2 An overview of different theoretical approaches to explain actors' motivations for becoming involved in sustainability issue (2).

Source: own.

(1960) likewise needs-based functional approach to the study of attitudes carves
out different functions that are fulfilled for the individual when assuming a
certain attitude.[1] Some explanations of motives for civic engagement in social
(Clary *et al.* 1998) and environmental matters (Stedman 2002; Liarakou *et al.*
2011; Asah and Blahna 2012; Krasny *et al.* 2014) explicitly or implicitly refer to
Katz's functional approach, whereas others do not (Anheier and Toepler 2001;
Barthel *et al.* 2010). The common point of all approaches is that human
behaviour is multi-causal, and thus cannot be explained by a single motive
alone.

The items on Nussbaum's list of ten basic capabilities constituting human life
are not distinct but interconnected, mutually influencing each other (Nussbaum
1992, 222; cf. Figure 8.1).[2] Those relevant to understanding actors' motivations
for becoming active in sustainability matters, including in the governance of
green spaces, are '*being able to have good health; to be adequately nourished*' (ibid.,
222),[3] '*being able to ... have pleasurable experiences*' (ibid.), '*being able to have*

attachments to things and persons outside ourselves' (ibid.), and '*being able to form a conception of the good and to engage in critical reflection about the planning of one's own life*' (ibid.). Also important are '*being able to live for and with others, to recognize and show concern for other human beings, to engage in various forms of familiar and social interaction*' (ibid.), '*being able to live with concern for and in relation to animals, plants, and the world of nature*' (ibid.), and '*being able to laugh, to play, to enjoy recreational activities*' (ibid.). To feel related to nature and animals implies being aware of the fact that humans share with them a single world on which all depend and in which processes are linked and mutually influence each other and which should therefore be respected and taken care of (Nussbaum 1999, 54). This general list is fundamental to understanding actors' motivations for engaging with sustainability and green spaces issues. Items of it reappear under different names and in more specialised form in the approaches presented in the next paragraphs.

According to self-determination theory, 'an understanding of human motivation requires a consideration of innate psychological needs for competence, autonomy and relatedness' (Deci and Ryan 2000, 227).[4] These three basic needs are interrelated in so far as everyone 'plays a necessary part in optimal development so that none can be thwarted or neglected without significant negative consequences' (ibid., 229). Whereas *competence* refers to the need 'to engage optimal challenges and experience mastery or effectance in the physical and social worlds' (ibid., 252), *relatedness* means 'to seek attachments and experience feelings of security, belongingness, and intimacy with others' (ibid.). *Autonomy* refers to the need 'to self-organize and regulate one's own behavior (and avoid heteronomous control), which includes the tendency to work toward inner coherence and integration among regulatory demands and goals' (ibid.), and it also 'means to act volitionally, with a sense of choice' (Deci and Ryan 2008, 15).[5]

Clary and colleagues (1998), in their psychological functional analysis research on community service volunteers' motivations, refers to the classic theories of attitudes (Katz 1960). The functional approach tries to understand which psychological functions for an individual are served by taking a certain attitude and performing a specific action accordingly. Katz (1960, 204) distinguishes

> four functions which attitudes perform for the personality …: the *adjustive function* of satisfying utilitarian needs, the *ego-defensive function* of handling internal conflicts, the *value-expressive function* of maintaining self-identity and of enhancing the self-image, and the *knowledge function* of giving understanding and meaning to the ambiguities of the world about us.[6]

Clary and colleagues build on these four types, finding six functions determining volunteers' motivations and stressing that a person is able to execute a single action simultaneously serving multiple psychological functions (Clary *et al.* 1998, 1517). They isolate a specific *value* function: 'One function that may be served by involvement in volunteer service centers on the opportunities that volunteerism provides for individuals to express values related to altruistic and humanitarian concerns for others' (ibid.). The quite specific *career* function 'is concerned with career related benefits that may be obtained from participation in volunteer work' (ibid., 1518). The *protective* function is about 'protecting the ego from negative features of the self and, in the case of volunteerism, may serve to reduce guilt over being more fortunate than others and to address one's own personal problems' (ibid.). The *enhancement* function points to the idea that

> people use helping as a means of maintaining or enhancing positive affect.... Thus, in contrast to the protective function's concern with eliminating negative aspects surrounding the ego, the enhancement function involves a motivational process that centers on the ego's growth and development and involves positive strivings of the ego.
>
> (Ibid.)

In a way it can thus be regarded as contributing to the 'competence' need. The remaining two functions are not new: *understanding* 'involves the opportunity for volunteerism to permit new learning experiences and the chance to exercise knowledge, skills, and abilities that might otherwise go unpractised' (ibid.), and the *social* function 'reflects motivations concerning relationships with others. Volunteering may offer opportunities to be with one's friends or to engage in an activity viewed favorably by important others' (ibid.).

Motivational functionalism has been applied specifically to environmental volunteering by Asah and Blahna (2012, 473), also finding six different categories of functions. All but one can be assigned to Clary and colleagues' model, yet the naming and clustering are slightly different: Asah and Blahna also determine a social function, calling it *socialise* and a value function, specified as *environmental purposes*. Yet, they neither distinguish between an understanding and career function, fusing it into a *career & learning* function, nor do they distinguish between a protective and enhancement function, merging it into the *defend & enhance the ego* function. They make out two new functions: *community* and *escape & exercise*. The first is a specification that would fall under the value and enhancement functions, to do something for the common good.[7] The second refers to recreation/relaxation out of daily routines and sometimes linked to physical exercise.

Four further dimensions of motivation need to be added to understand environmental civic engagement. *Socio-ecological memories*, as first carved out by Barthel *et al.* (2010) and later by Krasny *et al.* (2014), are 'means by which knowledge, experience and practice about how to manage a local ecosystem and its services is retained in a community, and modified, revived and transmitted through time' (Barthel *et al.* 2010, 256). People feel the need to pass on this collective memory to the next generation. Stedman (2002, 563) defines *sense of place* as 'a collection of symbolic meanings, attachment, and satisfaction with a spatial setting held by an individual or group'. This means that people are attached to this place (Krasny *et al.* 2014, 18) and might take action if they see 'their' place endangered. *Direct contact with nature* is carved out by Liarakou *et al.* (2011, 660) as an important motivation for environmental civic engagement. The fourth dimension is linked to the community function: Anheier and Toepler (2001) determine several groups of motives for civic engagement (not specified to environmental civic engagement). Their whole approach is not presented here since when taking a closer look at the single motives clustered in the groups, it turns out that they can be subsumed in those of Clary and colleagues and also in Asah and Blahna's model apart from the motive of '*active participation and co-determination*'[8] (Enquete 2002, 51, own translation, italics added). This motive expresses the wish to actively participate in, co-determine, and shape political and societal life and thus demands a higher degree of participation than the community function. People become engaged in matters for the common good because they want to actively participate in and co-determine societal and political life and to change societal drawbacks.

Bandura's (1997) self-efficacy theory explains why some people show more resilience than others in pursuing their activities even though encountering severe drawbacks. *Self-efficacy* is one factor why motivation is upheld over time despite severe hindrances. According to Bandura (1997, 3) '*perceived self-efficacy refers to beliefs in one's capabilities to organize and execute the courses of action required to produce given attainments*'. People with a high degree of self-efficacy show a higher degree of perseverance in performing a task (ibid., 160). To link up to the beginning of this section and to the relationship between the individual and society, it should be mentioned that Bandura links the general individual concept of self-efficacy to the collective one of political efficacy. He does this by defining the latter as 'participants' beliefs in their collective capabilities to accomplish social changes through political action' (ibid., 487). Whereas actors with little political efficacy are more easily discouraged by minor hindrances, actors with a high degree of political efficacy believe in a possible change of even the most rigid political system through joint efforts (ibid., 485). The upholding of this sense of efficacy even in cases of severe drawbacks is explained by actors' support from their community (ibid., 523), as well as by their strong belief in their value system, which makes them act against societal conditions that contradict their moral standards. They accept even severe difficulties resulting from their actions because remaining inactive would heavily impair their self-respect (ibid., 489). Here the value and protective functions can be recognised.

8.2 Motivations to commit oneself to sustainability issues

In this section, the interviewees' motivations to deal with sustainability issues in general are presented.[9] One question in the interview directly refers to the respondent's personal motivation to get involved with sustainability issues and another question to the beginning and extent of their involvement.[10] Answers to these two questions often overlap. The time span of dealing with sustainability issues ranges from four to up to 40 years, and more than half of the respondents indicate that they have been involved for more than 12 years. No respondents had difficulties in explaining their involvement in and motivation to deal with local sustainability issues, showing that the chosen interviewees can be truly considered as local experts (Sauer *et al.* 2015, 30–1). Given answers for the motivation can be clustered into seven thematic fields emerging out of the data, keeping in mind that these are not hermetically closed categories but often overlap, most often respondents' answers fall into the category *wish to change something*, followed by *creating awareness*. An equal number of given answers can be clustered into the categories *job-relatedness, personal interest*, and *emotions*, followed by *civil society's corrective power* and *legal framework* (Figure 8.3).

Apart from the categories *job-relatedness* and *legal framework* all the others can be assigned to one predominant motivation category. Motives like striving for wealth, power, or profit accumulation are never mentioned. Although the sample is not representative and governmental actors are underrepresented, it is interesting to note that only one of the governmental actors' answers can be clustered into the category *personal interest*, suggesting that governmental actors tend to deal with sustainability issues because their job requires them to do so and not necessarily out of personal conviction. The categories *wish to change something, emotions*, and *creating awareness* are clearly headed by civil society actors. The category *civil society's corrective power* is exclusively cited by them. The following paragraphs shed light on the respondents' motivation by presenting their answers clustered into subcategories and relating them to the theoretical framework (cf. Figures 8.1, 8.2, and 8.4).

Respondents from the *economic* sector mainly deal with sustainability because it is part of their *job*. This is so because sustainability topics seem to have

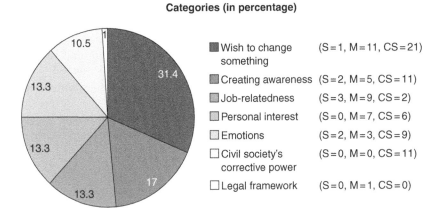

Categories (in percentage)

Figure 8.3 Personal motivation to become involved in sustainability issues.

Source: own.

Notes
N = 55: 7 governmental actors (S), 21 economic actors (M), 27 civil society actors (CS).

become *inevitable* for enterprises. Sustainability issues need to be taken into consideration if a company wants to be successful in the market (Bilbao, a3, 23; Innsbruck, a3, 29; Linz, a3, 17). Also, governmental actors need to deal with sustainability due to its high influence on urban development, having become transversal and tightly linked to the political agenda (Copenhagen, a2, 21). The concept has become so widespread that it is impossible not to take it into consideration (Cracow, a1, 28). Therefore, when asked for their motivation, many respondents cite in first place their *position*, which requires them to deal with sustainability (Cracow, a3, 31; Saarbrücken, a3, 14–18). Two respondents *earn a living* from sustainability issues (Umea, a3, 23; Lublin, a4, 56). This all suggests that the sustainability discourse has been mainstreamed into political and economic discourses and cannot be circumvented easily.

Sometimes the *legal framework* can be an additional motivating factor to become committed to sustainability issues, as in the case of the respondent owning a piece of land in a city for which the land development plan only foresees agricultural use, inducing him to rent allotments to families for food production (Milan, a3, 25). Here, the administrative circumstances are such that they foster sustainable action of individuals, even if these individuals do not yet act out of intrinsic motives.

The *wish to change something* is clearly a motivation factor for *civil society* actors and to a slightly lesser extent also for *economic* actors. Respondents state that they *want to contribute to a more sustainable world* by being active locally (Bilbao, a3, 38; Jihlava, a4, 29–31; Paris, a4, 19). Only civil society actors express the need to *preserve* biodiversity as well as *the livelihoods of future generations* (Dortmund, a4, 22; Lublin, a4, 60; Saarbrücken, a4, 17). They cite for example increasing pollution of the environment and the immense ongoing biodiversity loss (Copenhagen, a3, 22–3; Bilbao, a4, 26). A more energy-efficient and resource-conscious way of living and running the economy to reduce raw material consumption and waste is proposed (Aalborg, a4, 22) to reduce harming the environment. Some see the *survival of humankind* as endangered, if no action is taken. They consider the sustainable development approach the right thing to do and believe that action at lower levels, down to the local level, can supplement global action (Bilbao, a3, 21–7; Lodz, a4, 20–1). Numerous actors explicitly refer to everyone's *individual responsibility* to change behaviour and to become committed to sustainability issues (Bilbao, a3, 22–3; Leeds, a3, 33). Respondents are worried about their carbon footprint and the way the economic system works (Bilbao, a3, 22; Leeds, a4, 29), which can lead to making sustainable choices in their private consumption as well as to following sustainability criteria in their enterprise, such as in building construction or waste recycling (Gothenburg, a3, 14–15), even if it augments costs in the short term (Lugano, a3, 35). Some feel the need to immediately change something (St. Gallen, a4, 9) and therefore inform and remind people of their personal responsibility (Lublin, a4, 60), even knowing that their action might only have small effects (Glasgow, a4, 30–2). This category points to the *value* and *environmental purposes* functions. Respondents have internalised environmental protection as a core value and act accordingly. Referring to the statements about individual responsibility, there is also a reference to the *protective* function. Having acknowledged their individual responsibility, they would feel guilty not to act accordingly.

The *wish to create awareness* is a key motivation factor for *civil society* actors. Some experienced key moments very early in their life that triggered their commitment to sustainability, which illustrates the importance of starting education for sustainability at an early age. For example, one respondent's attention was caught by her primary school teacher during a school trip when the issue of smog hanging above the city was highlighted. This led her to decide to become active in protecting the environment (Larissa, a4, 32). Another chose to work on environmental topics professionally after having done a course on environmental education at primary school (Rome, a1, 21). A third person was pushed into environmental activism by seeing the beauty of a field on the city's fringe area, knowing that its continued existence was under threat due to extreme building development pressure (Lugano, a4, 16–18). These examples show the importance of an individual's capacity of '*being able to live with concern for and in relation to animals, plants, and the world of nature*'[11] (Nussbaum 1992, 222). People who have developed this capacity in early years are more prone to an increased level of awareness towards sustainability issues. The importance of *creating awareness via knowledge transmission and education* is only mentioned by *civil society* and *economic* actors. One respondent points to the fact that his inherent love of nature, which he already felt as a child, was fostered by his parents, and now as an adult he is still learning about concepts to advance sustainability (Copenhagen, a3, 22). The importance of transmitting knowledge to people of all ages is recognised by numerous actors. Children must be educated in environmental matters (Bilbao, a3, 23). Hands-on, close-to-nature activities can be one way of doing this: one respondent rents allotment gardens to make people and especially children understand nature by growing vegetables, so that 'they have to respect the environment in all aspects of the everyday life' (Milan, a3, 23). Respondents feel that they have to inform people about sustainability issues and to remind them of their individual responsibility. They therefore get involved in environmental groups that offer for example open meeting space for joint learning (Bilbao, a4, 23–4; Dortmund, a4, 22; Lublin a4, 60; Potsdam, a4, 53–5). Besides these examples of informal education, some respondents have chosen a more formal way of teaching sustainability issues in educational institutions. The joint idea behind this is to make students deal with the sustainability topic, to internalise it, and ultimately to apply it in their jobs and/or daily life (Lugano, a3, 39–46; Gothenburg, a4, 15; Sibiu, a4, 43–6; St. Gallen, a4, 9). One respondent stresses that technical knowledge is insufficient for advancing sustainability, if it is not combined with people's motivation and desire for a change in behaviour, which can be achieved through information, particularly of an interdisciplinary nature (Copenhagen, a4, 19). These actors actively want to participate in societal life and co-determine it in order to shape it through transmission of their knowledge or through education. This is because they have understood the importance of knowledge for creating awareness and subsequent behavioural changes. Considering that the empirical data highlighted in this paragraph reveals that this is an important motive, falling into *creating awareness* as the second most often cited category, it is deemed necessary to add an additional category of *knowledge transmission/education to create awareness* to the overview of approaches in order to explain actors' motivations for becoming involved in sustainability issues (cf. Figure 8.2).

Personal interest in sustainability issues is a strong motivation factor, yet almost solely for *economic* and *civil society* actors. This interest can sometimes be traced back to childhood (Copenhagen, a3, 22), and numerous actors state that they chose either their study field, profession, work place, or volunteer activity explicitly because it has to do with sustainability issues (Madrid, a3, 23; Thessaloniki, a3, 26; Istanbul, a4, 14–16; Naples, a4, 23). Two respondents emphasise that they chose their profession because it provides them with the opportunity to put personal convictions into professional practice, expressing their wish to have a meaningful profession, one which advances sustainability (Madrid, a3, 23; Linz, a4, 19). Here, we can again recognise the *value* function as well as the *environmental purposes* function.[12]

Emotions primarily motivate *civil society* actors. Two of them cite their *worries* and *fears* about existing threats to the environment, which induce them to become active (Leeds, a4, 29; Lugano a4, 16–22). This points to the *relatedness* need which includes to 'experience feelings of security' (Deci and Ryan 2000, 252), a need that gains importance in a world that has to cope with multiple globalised risks of modernisation, amongst which environmental ones take a big share (Beck 2009, 21–2).

Another respondent feels deep *anger* and *fury* when perceiving that human action is destroying nature. Two respondents manage to transform their negative feelings into proactive commitment, which helps them to cope with the persisting threats. One actor from Copenhagen stated: 'I turn my anger into something constructive. ... I could not resign myself to just be[ing] "pissed". I had to act positively on it' (Copenhagen, a3, 22). The second actor is from Leeds (a4, 108–10). Here the *value*, and the *environmental purposes* function, can be recognised, which is so distinctive that it leads to strong feelings provoking activism. These people have managed to turn their concern for the common good and the state of the ecosystem, as well as their own initial frustration because of it, into a proactive energy instead of falling into a state of resignation. One actor explains his motivation by the sense of obligation to serve his country, which includes becoming engaged in local politics, which encompasses dealing with sustainability issues (Istanbul, a1, 59). Here, the *value* function can equally serve as an explanation. In this case the primary value referred to is *patriotism*, which includes the need to protect one's country's environment. Actors' involvement in the governance of green spaces is often enriching for them personally, since they see themselves in a continuous learning process. Being committed to sustainability issues is personally *satisfying* (Istanbul, a1, 59; Timisoara, a3, 31–9; Leeds, a4, 108–10) and thus is connected to the *enhancement* function. Last but not least, motivation increases when actors experience that their action has an impact, as small as it might be. Knowing that the path to sustainability is arduous, it requires a lot of *stamina* (Copenhagen, a3, 66 and a4, 55). Predominantly civil society actors, when asked for their motivation, cite strong will, self-confidence, positive thinking, patience, and dedication instead of being in a hurry or despair (Leeds, a4, 108–10; Thessaloniki, a4, 62). The work is done, though knowing that in the end perhaps only a small step is achieved and no quick results are produced (Bilbao, a4, 78; Istanbul, a4, 52). Not feeling like the helpless victim at the mercy of ongoing inevitable environmental degradation, but experiencing a state of *self-efficacy* via actively coping with existing sustainability challenges despite drawbacks, seems to be an important motivation factor, primarily for civil society actors. Respondents believe that their actions 'can make a difference' (Milan, a4, 20). They are proud that set goals have been reached despite adverse circumstances, and they ascribe this success to their strong will: 'We have been taught that nothing can stop us! ... Also that whatever the goal was every time, we have managed to achieve it, with more or less effort' (Thessaloniki, a4, 62). These people have experienced that they are capable of acting and reaching set goals. This high degree of self-attribution is closely linked to a positive attitude, which is upheld even if only small results have been achieved. Positive thinking is maintained, as is believing in a constructive collaboration with other local actors from different sectors: 'We can come together constructively' (Istanbul, a4, 56). They prefer to become active and assume responsibility themselves, instead of waiting for others to do so. Speaking with Bandura (1997, 524), they have a high sense of *self-efficacy*, having understood that small actions at the local level are not a drop in the ocean but that

> global effects are the products of local practices. Each person, therefore, has a part to play in the solution. The strategy of 'Think globally, act locally' is an effort to restore people's sense of efficacy that there are many things they can do to make a difference.

Actors are motivated to develop further actions when they see that initiatives succeed and that lots of citizens are also participating in urban activism.

The category *civil society's corrective power* is – not surprisingly – only brought forward by *civil society* actors.[13] For some, *meeting people already involved* was a motivating factor to become active or to accelerate their involvement (Bilbao, a4, 26; Larissa, a4, 32), pointing to the *social* and the *socialise* functions. Commitment can express itself in the form of *protest* movements against unsustainable projects, for example against a gas pipeline in ecologically sensitive areas in the 1980s (Madrid, a4, 27). An actor who defines himself as a naturalist explains his motivation by the fact that he understood that being a naturalist, with the knowledge that the environment needs to be protected, is insufficient in itself, but that *political action* is also required. This means that you have to learn by doing and to also deal with things you had not been interested in before

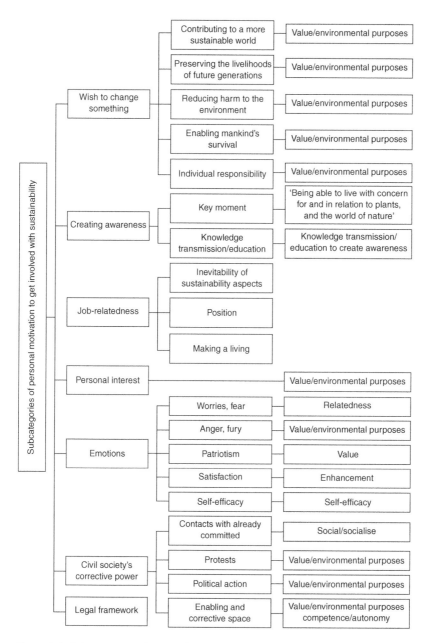

Figure 8.4 Subcategories of personal motivation for becoming involved in sustainability issues.

Source: own.

Notes
N = 55, 7 S, 21 M, 27 CS.

(Strasbourg, a4, 33–5). Here again reference can be made to the *value* and *environmental purposes* function. Another actor clearly states that his civil society commitment gives him the opportunity to do things that are important to him, but which he cannot achieve in his job, since when dealing with sustainability professionally, for example in the governmental or the economic sector, you cannot always follow your preferences: 'Professionally one doesn't always get to do what he/she likes, wants, promoting an idea, while an NGO allows one to think of a project which is atypical' (Sibiu, a4, 53). 'Professionally I do what the market asks for, what must be done and many times I feel the need to do something extra' (Sibiu, a4, 195). Here, apart from referring to his values, which can be explained with the *value* and *environmental purposes* functions, the actor expresses his need for *competence* and *autonomy*. Doing the things one is good at, feeling competent when mastering also challenging tasks, and choosing autonomously which actions to take to reach one's set goals, are needs that some people luckily find satisfied in their job. Some of those for whom this is not the case turn to (environmental) civic engagement to fulfil these needs. The quote also shows that the intermediary sector can be considered an *enabling corrective space* to the state and market. Although no actor explicitly expresses disappointment with state and market institutions, an actor did comment that environmental issues are not sufficiently high-ranking at the national level and that therefore their country lags behind European standards in environmental issues. Thus, it is important to put pressure from below to complement already existing pressure from above, by the EU (Paris, a4, 19). Furthermore, motivation simply evolved because of the lack of sustainability projects locally (Sibiu, a4, 46, 53; Thessaloniki, a4, 27).

8.3 Motivations for producing food in the city

What are the underlying motives for citizens to self-organise in the governance of urban green spaces and to produce food in the city? The quantitative research delivers insights into citizens' motives for the first part of the question and shows that *being self-sufficient in food production* altogether does not yet play a big role. *Beautifying one's neighbourhood* ranges first, followed by *contributing to societal life*, and *creating things*. *Acting independently from local government* and *being self-sufficient in food production* do not represent central motives. The regional distribution does not show significant disparities for the most often cited motive. Yet, *contributing to societal life* and *creating things* are less often cited in Eastern Europe compared to the other regions. The strongest regional discrepancy between the *East* and the other regions concerns *being self-sufficient in food production*, which is no motivation at all in the East (cf. Figure 8.5).

The interview data supports this, since actions around urban food production remain virtually unmentioned in the East in contrast to the other regions. The interviews also show that the trend of community food production for self-consumption is growing, while the more traditional way of producing in allotment gardens is continuing. The *pick-it-as-you-walk-past* movement and

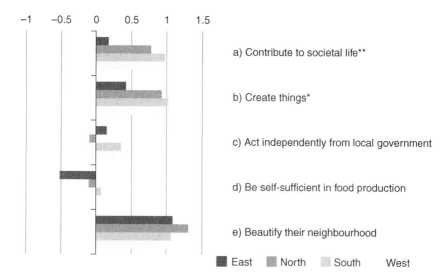

Figure 8.5 Regional differences in citizens' motivations for self-organisation in the governance of urban green spaces.

Source: Schicklinski 2016, 105.

Notes
Scaled from –2: strong disagreement, to 2: strong agreement.
* $p < 0.01$;
** $p < 0.001$.

commercial food production are only starting in a small number of cities. Motives for producing food in the city are diverse, yet often interlinked and also vary according to the four main types of urban food production (cf. 7.4). They are presented in the following paragraphs and linked to the theoretical framework (cf. Figures 8.1, 8.2, and 8.6).

Even if according to the quantitative data, *self-sufficiency in food production* is not a major motive in any region, the qualitative data points to an increasing importance of this motive in the *South*. The topic of being self-sufficient in fresh, healthy food at low costs, especially for citizens with a low economic status, is only raised in this region. Here, *food sovereignty* is becoming an issue again. Using urban green spaces for growing food for self-consumption is a food sovereignty and poverty-combatting strategy with its roots in European nineteenth-century industrial cities (Kropp 2011, 78). It provided workers with the option of growing fresh healthy food for self-consumption since their income did not allow for a well-balanced nutrition (Poole 2006, 9). In the first half of the twentieth century, especially during the Second World War, and still in the first post-war years, giving people partial autonomy for their own food production continued to be of utmost importance for part of the population. For example, in Leeds during the Second World War's Dig for Victory campaign,[14] lots of parks were turned into allotments. Although people were virtually entirely fed by the US convoys, the campaign gave the people power over their own diet, which was psychologically and morally important, apart from the social and health benefits (Leeds, a4, 93–4). In the course of post-war economic growth in the second half of the last century, this function lost its importance. The empirical examples show that, especially after the multiple crises from 2008 onwards and subsequent austerity policies being enforced in several European countries, this function has been reappearing. Urban food production has in some places, but mainly in Southern European cities, again become a means *to mitigate private poverty*. Individuals take the crisis as a starting point to join others in becoming active. Innovative processes can equally be launched by the local authority (cf. also 7.4.2.2). For example, in Milan the local authority continues to follow the idea of giving allotments to families with a lower income (Milan, a3, 47). In Thessaloniki, the local authority plans to increase the number of allotments, which do not have a strong tradition in Greece (Thessaloniki, a3, 79). In Larissa, the local authority initiated a municipal vegetable garden in 2011, which gives citizens with a low or no income the possibility to grow food for self-consumption. The demand is high and the garden has already been expanded (Larissa, a3, 50 and a4, 42): 'The local government has contributed considerably by setting up many new green spaces, apart from the municipal vegetable garden that has been recently established for citizens of low economic status who are unable to purchase food for their household' (Larissa, a4, 42).[15]

Where citizens lack the financial means to purchase fresh healthy food, urban gardening and agriculture can be a means of achieving the basic capability of *'being able to have good health; to be adequately nourished'*[16] (Nussbaum 1992, 222). The act of *creating things* and more specifically of physically *creating something with one's hands* ('You want to get your hands dirty' Copenhagen, a3, 60) points to the *escape and exercise* function, to an activity providing recreation and relaxation, sometimes linked to physical exercise, thus also having a physical component. This aspect is closely linked to the search for a *nature-related activity* (Saarbrücken, a4, 50; Copenhagen, a3, 60). The act of creating takes place outside and in close contact with nature and thus points to the category of *direct contact with nature*. These two interlinked motives are increasingly important for the generation of young city dwellers who spend their working day in front of computer screens and seek to experience nature this way, as a balance to their working activity. Here, gardening can help to slow down and to ground oneself. This well-being element of urban green spaces and especially of jointly growing food in them is slowly also being recognised in urban development. For example in Paris, urban green spaces are seen as possessing 'exceptional potentialities' (Paris, a3, 57) – meaning that they are considered to be valuable meeting places with joint gardening as one possible activity – and are now also being taken into consideration in the planning of social housing.

Citizens want to actively *create urban common space*. They 'would like to create something from scratch, because it is in their immediate environment' (Copenhagen, a4, 39). Behind that stands the desire to have a *common meeting space* which they are able to *identify* with. This refers explicitly to a *physical, nature-related* – thus outdoor – meeting place, posing a counterweight to infinite social networks' virtual meeting options. Citizens beautify their neighbourhood because they are attached to it, it is important to them (*sense of place*). Therefore, they want to *actively participate and co-determine* the design of the area on their doorsteps. The private actor renting allotment gardens to families (cf. 7.4.2.1) does so 'to give back the peri-urban land to families, so that they identify it with the place where to spend free time and where to grow veggies and fruits' (Milan, a3, 21). In Romania, during Ceaușescu's dictatorship, the rural population was forced to move to the city but did not want to give up their habits and traditions of growing food:

> People ... did not give up certain activities, habits, or simple pleasures. They wanted to organise a space close to their hearts, so they arranged those small neighbourhood places: gardens, flowers, plants or fruit trees.... It generates a common place, ... and people adhere to it, because it is their product, one with which they identify, and surely they will take care of it.
>
> (Timisoara, a4, 117)

In more recent times, NGOs have started urban gardening in Cluj and Bucharest, and in Timisoara there is a small group of urban gardeners creating common space for interaction, having been inspired by activities in other countries. The respondent sees the local authority's duty as providing public space for such interaction, underlining the potential of urban green spaces for innovative solutions:

> On the one hand, whoever has a garden is usually very defensive and generates a certain property limit. On the other hand, there are spaces, which are spontaneously generated, and they stand for the human being's capacity to bring forward solutions.
>
> (Timisoara, a4, 119)

The interviews support the quantitative finding that *acting independently from local government* is not a focal motive for citizens' self-organisation. They want to create common space and do not exclude interaction with the local government if it contributes to them achieving their aim. The interviews support the motive of *contributing to societal life*. Growing food together in a group contributes to the capability of '*being able to have attachments to things and persons outside ourselves*'[17] (Nussbaum 1992, 222) as well as generating *social* cohesion benefits (Copenhagen, a3, 60; Leeds, a4, 94). People get the chance to socialise and be with like-minded people. This refers to the *social* or *socialise* category. Jointly growing food helps to build communities and to strengthen social ties, leading to the creation of a *community* spirit. Members that contribute to the community's common good fulfil the *community* function. They feel connected with their community and want to give something back to it.

Community food production is one way of *joint learning for sustainability, via knowledge appreciation and the sharing of knowledge, leading to joint citizens' knowledge production* across generations, cultures, gender, and social positions. Every citizen can play a part in it, and often very diverse knowledge across generations and cultural and geographical backgrounds is shared and spread: 'What are you going to do about these spots on these cabbages?' 'Oh, my grandpa knows something about that' (Leeds, a4, 94). This points to the *understanding* or the *career & learning* category, allowing for diverse learning situations and the building up and transmission of knowledge. In a medium-sized city in Sweden in a housing area with 32 different nationalities, allotment gardens were opened up where people could meet and communicate about growing food. The majority of migrants there come from rural areas and have the knowledge of how to grow food (Gothenburg, a4, 84). Having received only a low level of formal education, here their knowledge in the field of food production is appreciated. They are thus recognised by others, responding to their need for *competence*. As mentioned above, in Romania the rural population that moved into the city retained their *habit and tradition* of growing food. This points to the *socio-ecological memories* category, illustrating people's need to keep on practising the cultivation of fruit and vegetable and to pass on their collective knowledge and memory to the next generation in order to prevent its loss.

Mainly actors involved in the initiation and organisation of urban food production options for citizens mention the aim of knowledge transmission to create awareness for sustainability issues, pointing to the category *knowledge transmission/education to create awareness*. From experiences with urban food production, a lost (if at all ever existing) *relationship with nature* can be rediscovered and *regained* (Strasbourg, a4, 109). One actor describes it as conveying

> 'a feeling for nature' [which] is that you have your own relationship with nature. You know how it feels to walk around in the blueberry bushes.... You have a sense of it, and you can understand how it is and familiarise yourself with it, and one can yearn for it.
>
> (Umea, a3, 82)

By working in and with nature and observing its rhythm and laws, one learns about 'the difference between life and death, for instance when you swat an ant [, or you experience] the pleasure to grow vegetables and eat them' (Paris, a3, 51). Thus, you learn to *respect nature*. This raises awareness of the capability 'being able to live with concern for and in relation to animals, plants, and the world of nature'[18] (Nussbaum 1992, 222). Furthermore, you learn about the *value of food*, noticing, for example, that it is not available all year round. This is one way of making people understand the *origin of food* (Leeds, a4, 97–9) and raise awareness of the need for regional economic cycles, for example in fruit and vegetable production, the importance of gaining independence from the international world market, which could collapse in an oil crisis (Potsdam, a4, 29–31, 173).

This might, in the long term, lay the foundation for *respecting the environment in all aspects of life*.

> Growing food helps educate your children, because they understand what it is, the fertile earth ... that ... produces food.... Yes, it is a new culture, that they bring home from the allotments. Then the families become convinced, that they have to respect the environment in all aspects of everyday life.
>
> (Milan, a3, 21–3)

People active in nature-related activities early in their life, but also later, most probably develop *long-term environmental civic engagement* in the governance of urban green spaces, for example in voluntary land stewardship (Copenhagen, a3, 60) or in another area. This shows that urban gardening and agriculture can be a means of fostering the habitualisation of sustainability commitment by activities that at first glance do not feature a direct link to sustainability issues. These activities, however, are essential since they become embedded in people's 'lifeworld' with the possibility of provoking life-long sensitivity to environmental issues and concomitant action (WBGU 2011, 263) as well as of sensitising for global economic socio-environmental equity issues.[19]

The motive of *knowledge transmission/education to create awareness* also comes to the fore in aspects relating to *education/learning* in the empirical data. If people have created a communication and meeting place such as an urban garden for example, this allows them to socialise, develop ideas, make plans, unfold their creativity, interact, and give their opinion (Milan, a4, 85–7; Potsdam, a4, 43–5). In all these activities, *democratic rules and cooperation* are practised. Furthermore, several empirical examples across the cities show that this can be an *inclusive* process across different *cultures, generations, genders and social positions*, countering cities' ability to alienate and create anonymity as well as its gentrification–segregation tendencies, in order to ultimately contribute to a more inclusive society. Whereas some projects officially foster the integration of migrants, this is an implicit goal of others, often happening by chance. For example, in Milan an association takes care of a small part of a big public park near a school in the most multicultural part of the city, on which it has started urban gardening and farming. Fostering integration is, besides achieving a positive use of the park, the main objective (Milan, a4, 7–9). In Potsdam, some of the urban gardening projects are explicitly intercultural gardens, which work with migrants, schools and kindergartens in the neighbourhood. In Dortmund the traditional allotment garden clubs have adapted their statute, now also providing 'raised beds that can be worked on from the wheelchair or the wheeled walker' (Schicklinski 2015, 312).

The variety of learning options that urban green commons provide via the actors' governance of land are encapsulated by Colding and Barthel (2013, 163). They include 'environmental and ecological learning, ... learning related to social organization, the politics of urban space, social entrepreneurship, as well as ... [for] community empowerment ... and for fostering of democratic values'.

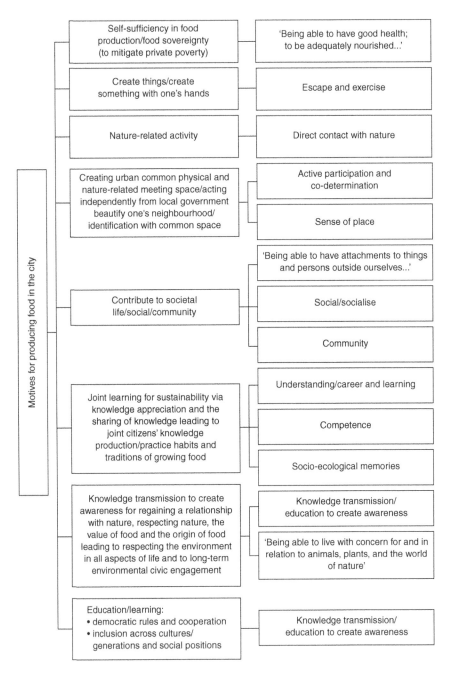

Figure 8.6 Motives for producing food in the city.

Source: own.

Notes
N=55, 7S, 21M, 27 CS

This subsection has shown that there are manifold motives for producing food in the city. It is possible that part of the movement is just a transient trend and might soon vanish. Yet there are clear empirical signs that there is something more profound and longer-lasting in the movement. Its ingredients include anti-modern protest against the rationality of the first modernity as well as protests against second modernity phenomena, for example the destructive parts of glo-balisation as becoming evident in the unjust globalised food and agriculture system. Particularly joint activities relating to urban green spaces can be seen as opening up discourses and providing common ground for the flourishing of ideas, ideas of how to become active in improving, in concrete terms, living conditions locally, while maintaining a global perspective, with topics such as food sovereignty and sustainable agriculture. With reason, the (re)awakened trend of producing food in European cities can be considered the 'beginning of a paradigm shift, which does not only regard nutrition but also the topics of solid-arity, biodiversity, democracy, the active sharing of public space, self-determination and quality of life' (Krobath 2013, 292, own translation). It offers a joint learning field for sustainability, sustainability understood in the social, environmental, and economic dimension, including justice for other world regions and for future generations.

Notes

1 Katz's theory is not shown in Figure 8.1 or 8.2, yet since Clary *et al.* (1998) take his theory as a starting point to develop their model of social civic engagement, it should be acknowledged when investigating actors' motivations.

2 The figure only displays those seven capabilities that are helpful in explaining civic engagement in sustainability issues; for the list of all ten capabilities cf. Nussbaum (1992, 222).

3 Italics added in all direct citations from this source in this paragraph.

4 Deci and Ryan's self-determination theory has been largely recognised to explain motivation as linked to basic needs, replacing older approaches, such as the one of Maslow (1943) who describes a hierarchy of five correlated sets of goals (basic needs), suggesting that the lower needs have to be satisfied before the higher ones evolve (Maslow 1943, 372–85). Yet, he explains that this hierarchy is not static but that 'the most prepotent goal will monopolize consciousness' (ibid., 394), meaning that needs can be co-existing and that the lower ones do not need to be fulfilled 100 per cent before the higher ones can emerge (ibid., 386). The five sets of goals are physio-logical (for example hunger, thirst), safety, love, esteem (to have self-respect and self-esteem which is partly built up by recognition from others and which leads to self-confidence) (ibid., 381–2), and self-actualisation – the wish for self-fulfilment (ibid., 383, 394). He also mentions cognitive needs such as the wish to learn (ibid., 384), yet without classifying them into the hierarchy. The author would like to thank Demis Basso for his hint to self-determination theory.

5 Figure 8.2 is to be read as a continuation of Figure 8.1, starting with Nussbaum, via Deci and Ryan, Clary *et al.*, Asah and Blahna, Barthel *et al.*, Stedman and Krasny *et al.*, Liarakou *et al.*, and Anheier and Toepler to Bandura. The words in capital letters point to motives that were not explicitly given in each time preceding approach. For example Deci and Ryan's relatedness need is implicitly mentioned in four of Nuss-baum's cited capabilities, whereas competence and autonomy are new aspects.

6 Reprinted from Katz (1960), copyright 1960 by Daniel Katz, used with permission from Oxford University Press.
7 Asah and Blahna (2012, 473) group the following constitutive items in it: 'To show my community that I care', 'To feel connected with my community', 'To show that I can make a difference', and 'To give something back to my community'.
8 Enquete-Kommission 'Zukunft des Bürgerschaftlichen Engagements' des Deutschen Bundestages (2002); ©Springer, with permission of Springer.
9 The sample includes answers from politicians, civil servants, economic, and civil society actors (cf. 4.3.2.2).
10 'To what extent are you involved in sustainability issues in [name of city]?' and 'What was your motivation to get involved with sustainability in [name of city]?, 'When did your involvement start?'
11 Italics added.
12 This category can, in a way, be considered as a foundation for the *wish to change something* category. Most people that have developed the wish to change something have in a first step developed a personal interest in sustainability issues.
13 This coincides with a general trend, also becoming evident in the quantitative data on every resource system in the scope of ROCSET, of every sector estimating its own contribution to sustainability higher than the one of the other two.
14 This campaign of the British Ministry of Agriculture started in 1939 (Poole 2006, 156).
15 The case of Greece shows that since the crises of 2008, civil society actors have increasingly and very innovatively become active to achieve food sovereignty themselves (similarly Salzer 2013, 285–6) to counter the situation that many people cannot even afford basic foods any more.
16 Italics added.
17 Italics added.
18 Italics added.
19 No respondent specifically refers to global equity issues of fair trade, corporate seed control, and the functioning of the global industrialised agro- and food system. However, the interview guide's questions on personal involvement and motivation were posed very generally and the focus of the interview was communicated as enquiring on the local socio-ecological transition with reference to urban green spaces. A second round of data collection would be necessary to judge whether the topic of achieving global equity in general and in relation to the agro- and food system specifically is really as little present in actors' minds as it appears to be from their definitions of sustainability and their explanation of personal involvement and motivation.

References

Anheier, Helmut K. and Stefan Toepler. 2001. *Bürgerschaftliches Engagement zur Stärkung der Zivilgesellschaft im internationalen Vergleich: Gutachten für die Enquete-Kommission 'Zukunft des Bürgerschaftlichen Engagements' (KDrs. Nr. 14/153)*. London, Baltimore MD: n.p.

Asah, Stanley T. and Dale J. Blahna. 2012. 'Motivational functionalism and urban conservation stewardship: Implications for volunteer involvement'. *Conservation Letters* (5): 470–7.

Bandura, Albert. 1997. *Self-efficacy: The exercise of control*. New York: W.H. Freeman and Company.

Barthel, Stephan, Carl Folke, and Johan Colding. 2010. 'Socio-ecological memory in urban gardens: Retaining the capacity for management of ecosystem services'. *Global Environmental Change*, 20(2): 255–65.

Beck, Ulrich. 2009. *Risk society: Towards a new modernity.* Theory, culture and society series. London: Sage.

Clary, E. Gil, Robert D. Ridge, Arthur A. Stukas, Mark Snyder, John Copeland, Julie Haugen, and Peter Miene. 1998. 'Understanding and assessing the motivations of volunteers: A functional approach'. *Journal of Personality and Social Psychology*, 74(6): 1516–30.

Colding, Johan and Stephan Barthel. 2013. 'The potential of 'Urban Green Commons' in the resilience building of cities'. *Ecological Economics*, 86: 156–66.

Deci, Edward L. and Richard M. Ryan. 2000. 'The "what" and "why" of goal pursuits: Human needs and the self-determination of behavior'. *Psychological Inquiry*, 11(4): 227–68.

Deci, Edward L. and Richard M. Ryan. 2008. 'Facilitating optimal motivation and psychological well-being across life's domains'. *Canadian Psychology*, 49: 14–23.

Enquete-Kommission 'Zukunft des Bürgerschaftlichen Engagements' des Deutschen Bundestages (Enquete), ed. 2002. *Bericht: Bürgerschaftliches Engagement: auf dem Weg in eine zukunftsfähige Bürgergesellschaft.* Opladen: Leske + Budrich.

German Advisory Council on Global Change (WBGU). 2011. Flagship report. World in transition: A social contract for sustainability. Berlin: WBGU. www.wbgu.de/file admin/templates/dateien/veroeffentlichungen/hauptgutachten/jg2011/wbgu_jg2011_en.pdf [27 August 2016].

Katz, Daniel. 1960. 'The functional approach to the study of attitudes'. *Public Opinion Quarterly*, 24(2): 163–204.

Krasny, Marianne E., Sarah R. Crestol, Keith G. Tidball, and Richard C. Stedman. 2014. 'New York City's oyster gardeners: Memories and meanings as motivations for volunteer environmental stewardship'. *Landscape and Urban Planning* (132): 16–25.

Krobath, Peter A. 2013. 'Wir geben euch Geld, damit ihr gut produzieren könnt'. In *Was allen gehört: Commons – neue Perspektiven in der Armutsbekämpfung,* ed. Die Armutskonferenz, 292–3. Wien: Verlag des Österreichischen Gewerkschaftsbundes.

Kropp, Cordula. 2011. 'Gärtner(n) ohne Grenzen: Eine neue Politik des 'Sowohl-als-auch' urbaner Gärten.' In *Urban gardening: Über die Rückkehr der Gärten in die Stadt,* 4th edn, ed. Christa Müller, 76–87. Munich: oekom.

Liarakou, Georgia, Eleni Kostelou, and Costas Gavrilakis. 2011. 'Environmental volunteers: Factors influencing their involvement in environmental action'. *Environmental Education Research*, 17(5): 651–73.

Maslow, Abraham. H. 1943. 'A theory of human motivation'. *Psychological Review*, 50: 370–96.

Nussbaum, Martha C. 1992. 'Human functioning and social justice: In defense of Aristotelian essentialism'. *Political Theory*, 20(2): 202–46.

Nussbaum, Martha C. 1999. *Gerechtigkeit oder Das gute Leben.* Edited by Herline Pauer-Studer, translated from American English by Ilse Utz. Frankfurt am Main: Suhrkamp.

Poole, Steve. 2006. *The allotment chronicles: A social history of allotment gardening.* The nostalgia collection. Kettering: Silver Link.

Salzer, Irmi. 2013. 'Gutes Essen für alle! Keine Ernährungssouveränität ohne Commons'. In *Was allen gehört: Commons – neue Perspektiven in der Armutsbekämpfung,* ed. Die Armutskonferenz, 279–87. Wien: Verlag des Österreichischen Gewerkschaftsbundes.

Sauer, Thomas, Stephanie Barnebeck, Yannick Kalff, and Judith Schicklinski. 2015. 'The role of cities in the socio-ecological transition of Europe (ROCSET)'. Area/Work Package 501.4. WWWforEurope Working Paper no 93. www.foreurope.eu/index.php?id=766&tx_sevenpack_pi1[search][rule]=AND&tx_sevenpack_pi1[search][sep]=space

&tx_sevenpack_pi1[show_abstracts]=0&tx_sevenpack_pi1[show_keywords]=0&tx_
sevenpack_pi1[year]=2015&tx_sevenpack_pi1[show_uid]=133&cHash=56521872d5a
40c1d525ba75da5c6b23d#c133 [27 August 2016].

Schicklinski, Judith. 2015. 'Germany: Dortmund'. In 'WWWforEurope, Annex to MS94:
Compilation of case study reports. A compendium of case study reports from 40 cities
in 14 European countries'. Work Package 501 MS94: 'Final draft report'. 94th edn, eds
Cristina Garzillo and Peter Ulrich, 304–16. www.foreurope.eu/fileadmin/documents/pdf/
Workingpapers/WWWforEurope_WPS_no094_MS94_Annex.pdf [27 August 2016].

Schicklinski, Judith. 2016. 'Socio-ecological transitions in the green spaces resource
system'. In *Cities in transition: Social innovation for Europe's urban sustainability*, eds
Thomas Sauer, Cristina Garzillo, and Susanne Elsen, 93–124. Abingdon/New York:
Routledge.

Stedman, Richard C. 2002. 'Toward a social psychology of place: Predicting behavior
from place-based cognitions, attitude, and identity'. *Environment and Behavior*, 34(5):
561–81.

9 Proposing an innovative policy framework as resulting from identified barriers and conducive conditions for citizen participation, self-organisation, and the socio-ecological transition

Chapters 5–8 presented a descriptive analysis and a discussion of the empirical results relating them to the theoretical framework given. This analysis and discussion is continued in this chapter with regard to the five identified intervening variables. Based on this, a policy framework is proposed that facilitates and fosters civil society's transition-driving role by allowing for and fostering innovative solutions in the governance of urban green spaces to drive the socio-ecological transition of European cities. Thus, the empirical findings are related back to the research questions and hypotheses.

This chapter attempts to explain, by analysing the intervening variables (cf. Figure 5.1), why in some cities civil society is more developed and the socio-ecological transition is more advanced than in others. Institutional conditions are identified under which 'best practice' examples have evolved which are presented to prepare replicability elsewhere.

The evolvement of citizen participation and self-organisation can either be hindered or supported and even accelerated. Barriers are reported from all regions and can mostly be cross-checked by identifying their opposite under the cited conducive condition. To examine both, barriers and conducive conditions, the quantitative data gives important overall indications, whereas more specific points are brought to light by the qualitative data. When examining the variables for successful self-organisation and citizen participation it is noticeable that most of them are identical with the ones referred to for the successful socio-ecological transition, suggesting that the latter is closely connected to self-organisation and citizen participation. This supports the hypothesis underlying this thesis that a socio-ecological transition in the green spaces resource system in European cities is not feasible without the strong participation and self-organisation of civil society actors.

Results are presented around the five major intervening variables that either directly influence the socio-ecological transition in the green spaces resource system or indirectly by being conducive or hindering to self-organisation and citizen participation (Figure 5.1).

Three of these variables correspond to structural obstacles already mentioned in a 20-year-old document of the European Commission (1995, 23–5). The document carves out the main barriers and conducive conditions for the emergence of local development and employment initiatives which, when confronting them with the empirical qualitative data, have also proven to be variables influencing the emergence of self-organisation and citizen participation in the governance of urban green spaces (Elsen and Schicklinski 2016, 236). The report notes the existence of structural obstacles such as financial, legal, and institutional ones, which correspond in this thesis to *financial means, legal framework*, and *functioning of local authority*. Apart from *financial means*, which is not a variable in Ostrom's framework, all four other intervening variables are found in her framework (cf. 5.1, 3.3.1): *local decision-making autonomy* falls under GS6a 'collective-choice rules' (Sauer 2012, 155), *legal framework* belongs to GS7 'constitutional rules', *functioning of local authority* can be assigned to GS1 'government organizations', and *learning and social capital building in the local arena* is a composition of U6 'norms/social capital' and U7 'knowledge of SES/mental models' (Ostrom 2007, 15183) with reference to the importance of a local arena for conflict resolution.

9.1 Local decision-making autonomy

9.1.1 Empirical results

This subsection examines the influence of local decision-making autonomy on self-organisation and citizen participation in the governance of urban green spaces and tries to answer the question whether local decision-making autonomy matters for the socio-ecological transition.

In the governance of urban green spaces the local authority has a high level of autonomy, compared to the energy and water systems (Barnebeck *et al.* 2016, 196–7). According to both qualitative and quantitative data, across cities the local level is perceived as best suited for governing the green spaces resource system. As the quantitative data shows, the level of *local decision-making autonomy* in investing, planning, and regulating green spaces is high but not very high on average according to respondents from all sectors. There are no differences between the regions as a whole, but between the countries of the regions, showing that the degree of autonomy granted to the local level differs across countries. The quantitative data illustrates three points. First, the availability of green spaces is influenced by several factors amongst which the *national regulatory framework* is not important, while *local regulations* tend to be important. Second, the most often cited factors improving green spaces are the *availability of unbuilt land, local building codes and sectoral plans, local political commitment*, the *capacity of the local government*, and *citizen empowerment*. Third, most actors see more support for sustainable governance of urban green spaces coming from European and national policies than from local ones. This tendency is most distinct amongst civil society actors. Only in the North does local policy play a bigger role than the national one, which could be ascribed to municipalities' high level of autonomy there. This third statement seems at first sight contradicting to the preceding two from which it can be discerned that the green spaces resource system is mostly influenced by local factors. Possibly, actors associate political support more with funding options than with the legal framework. Furthermore, according to all sectors, the local government is the most important actor in *defining rules on use and access to urban green spaces* in the governance of urban green spaces. Local associations and civil society groups as well as other local actors have medium influence, whereas the existing local cooperative initiatives are of low importance. For *ensuring the availability of high-quality green spaces*, according to all sectors, the local level of the city is most relevant, followed by the district level, while the subnational, national, and EU level are of medium to low importance.

Also the interviews support the conclusion that local decision-making autonomy matters for self-organisation and citizen participation and the socio-ecological transition in the green spaces resource system. If the degree of *local autonomy* is too small, as for example in a centralised system where the municipal council has little power, citizen participation is discouraged (Larissa, a3, 79). Most actors estimate local autonomy as *conducive* to the transition, considering it to be necessary to *formulate local policies according to local goals, needs, and interests* for achieving sustainability (Copenhagen, a2, 90–2; Istanbul, a1, 81 and a4, 67–72; Sibiu, a2, 185–8; Thessaloniki, a4, 86). This is because the local authority is *most aware of the city's existing problems*. In lots of places it is stressed that local autonomy is essential, since the local authority knows best the citizens' needs in order to develop a corresponding policy (Bilbao, a3, 123–5; Larissa, a3, 79; Thessaloniki, a4, 86). This underlines the importance of the local level in a system of polycentric governance for the socio-ecological transition.

In Istanbul *missing local autonomy*[1] is seen as a major obstacle to achieving sustainability. Due to a highly centralised system, the central government has to approve all projects at the city level. This responsibility is not shared with either the regional or the local level, leading to *minimal local autonomy* (Istanbul, a1, 41, 77). Thus, sustainability plans conceived at the local level can easily be thwarted by the national level (Istanbul, a1, 13, 17). The district level is the politically and financially weakest unit of all government levels, also for decisions directly concerning the governance of urban green spaces in the respective city district – 'They tie your hands with laws and regulations' (Istanbul, a1, 66). Yet, due to the small size of a lot of urban green spaces, this resource system especially lends itself to being governed also on the lowest level. For example, the district level could organise maintenance in collaboration with civil society actors, for example volunteers, associations, and schools, while responsibility for bigger urban green spaces as well as for street greening and other general issues would remain with the city level. Indeed, the option of involving civil society actors in the maintenance of green spaces to save costs is already practised in several cities (cf. 7.4.2.2).

Referring to the influence of local decision-making autonomy on self-organisation and citizen participation, a regression analysis uncovered relationships between local preconditions and the emergence of new institutional arrangements by identifying factors influencing self-organisation capabilities. As shown in Table 9.1, on the one hand a high level of local government autonomy in improving and expanding as well as in investing in green spaces is beneficial to the *commonness of civil society groups*. The same holds true for a high degree of leadership of the local authority in ensuring the availability and quality of green spaces.[2] On the other hand if the capacity of the local government in providing financial and human resources is high, this makes the commonness of civil society groups less probable. The same holds true for a satisfactory level of monitoring of local land quality, pollution, and biodiversity. From this it can be concluded that a high degree of local autonomy combined with a high degree of leadership of the local authority provides the right framework conditions for civil society groups to enter the stage. If the local administration is then capable of providing a satisfactory level of monitoring, closely linked to its capacity of financial and human resources, civil society groups become less involved than in cities in which public authorities have problems in ensuring a satisfactory level of governance of urban green spaces.

Several empirical examples show that a high degree of *local autonomy* is generally conducive to citizen involvement and to the advancement of the socio-ecological transition, provided that it goes along with a shift of financial resources from higher government levels to local ones. For example, Danish

Table 9.1 Influence of various variables on civil society groups' existence

Civil society groups in the green spaces resource system are common in the city	Coefficient	Standard error
Availability and satisfactory access to public green spaces in general	0.417	0.270
Involvement of local civil society actors in the governance of urban green spaces***	1.221	0.324
Local government's autonomy in improving/expanding green spaces***	0.741	0.272
Capacity of the local government (financial capacity and human resources)*	−0.620	0.335
Leadership of local government administration in ensuring availability and quality of green spaces**	0.641	0.248
Monitoring of local land quality, pollution, and biodiversity is satisfactory*	−0.433	0.238
Autonomy of the local government in investing in green spaces***	0.724	0.274
Local government and civil society groups closely collaborate in governing green spaces***	1.336	0.299

Source: adapted from Schicklinski 2016, 108.

Notes
Ordered logistic regression, 128 observations, p-value = 0.000; Pseudo R^2 = 0.3815, Log likelihood = −117.92 (control variables: city and sector).
* $p < 0.05$;
** $p < 0.01$;
*** $p < 0.001$.

local authorities are amongst those with the highest degree of local autonomy granted with a very high level of responsibility in relation to management and economics from higher government levels. Therefore, the commitments local authorities have towards the national government and the EU are also bigger than elsewhere. They are however subjected to strict rules which leaves a wide scope for *autonomous governance*. Municipalities showed little interest in experiments of running an even more autonomous local governance, proving their satisfaction with the flexibility of the current framework, which allows them to 'produce a form of self-government within the framework' (Copenhagen, a2, 88). 'The municipality is a strong player. [It is] the counterpart of parliament.... It is a good division of power' (Copenhagen, a3, 70). The local authority governs urban green spaces and can take important decisions independently, setting priorities in agenda and budget (Copenhagen, a4, 59–61). In Copenhagen the administration is, with 45,000 employees, the city's largest employer, with as many as 180 people working exclusively on the environment, bundling expert knowledge from many different disciplines. Thus, having the authority and the human and financial resources to be innovative, the economy follows suit (Copenhagen, a2, 90–2). Operating in a clear set legal framework, local authorities are granted a wide scope of autonomous governance with a concomitant high degree of responsibility and human and financial resources to try out innovative options.

Local autonomy is also understood in the sense of having a *direct communication channel from the city to the EU's institutions* for not wasting time and opportunities due to an intermediary body for European project planning (Rome, a1, 80).

Generally, a high degree of *local autonomy* is seen everywhere as a transition factor apart from by a minority of actors who depict *local autonomy* as being *hindering* to the socio-ecological transition. They deplore the excessive autonomy of the local government in the governance of urban green spaces, which can also be *misused* by local actors or lead to piecemeal planning when regional coordination might be required. For example, if the national and regional urban planning laws leave a lot of room for manoeuvre for local governments, this can be misused to the detriment of sustainability, with municipalities opting for profit and turning urban green spaces into construction sites (Milan, a3, 64). In Switzerland, some actors regard the high level of local autonomy as hindering since federalism with a high degree of local autonomy concedes much power to the local government, with each municipality levying its own taxes and making its own rules. Planning and collaboration on the regional (canton) level is deemed necessary by some actors to avoid a *fragmentation* of the territory (Lugano, a3, 26–7, 135–6 and a4, 78).

9.1.2 Policy implications

Despite living in a globalised world, sustainability issues, especially in the governance of urban green spaces, have a *local focus* due to the nature of the resource system and its governance. The governance of urban green spaces, though embedded in a system of multilevel governance, is mainly determined by local factors and steered locally. To local issues local solutions must and can be found, incorporating the innovative force of civil society and economic actors. Policy measures have to be tailor-made to local conditions, since start-up and framework conditions vary greatly across European regions. *Local autonomy* in a decentralised system is generally more apt to support the socio-ecological transition than little or no autonomy granted by centralised systems (Meadows *et al.* 2005, 274). This is because local autonomy allows the decision-making for public policies to be undertaken 'by those authorities which are closest to the citizen' (Council of Europe 1985, article 4, paragraph 3). Politically granted local autonomy has to run parallel to *financial autonomy* (cf. 9.2). This means that the principle of connexity needs to be respected. A high level of local autonomy could be misused for the self-interests of local politicians and administrative authorities unless there is a strong civil society control in the form of high-level citizen participation (cf. 10.1), as well as a *clear enforcing legal framework* in place (cf. 9.3).

Due to the complexity and interrelatedness of sustainability issues, a local approach needs to be embedded in a system of *polycentric governance* (cf. 3.5), and *coherence* between local, regional, national, and EU policies must be created. The European and national policy context and legal frameworks need to set guidelines but leave a wide scope for local governance. Nevertheless, for some issues regional collaboration is also required. For example, in the elaboration of a regional development plan, planning at the regional level is necessary and must include goal-setting in a way that cities cannot play one off against the other (Dortmund, a4, 96; Lugano, a3, 26–7). The necessity of applying the subsidiarity principle, thus conceding room for manoeuvre to the local and regional level, was already stressed in the 1970s by de Rougement (1977, 348), proponent of European integration, who argued for a 'Europe of Regions' manifesting itself in a high degree of federalisation and a regional–local interplay of self-governance. 'The local level enables widespread, synergetic, and participatory solutions and can be a laboratory for politics of possibilities from below' (Elsen and Schicklinski 2016, 238). 'These bottom-up policies and top-down structures have to be interlinked as enabling and supporting conditions' (ibid., 229). Following Ostrom (2009, 227–8), for polycentric governance to succeed, social capital is essential. Regarding citizens as pivotal actors and involving them accordingly as well as establishing networks between actors across different levels, sectors, and areas of society seems to be both the prerequisite for social capital to evolve and its consequence (cf. 9.4).

9.2 Financial means

9.2.1 Empirical results

Closely linked to the issue of local autonomy is the one of financial means. A *tight local budget* in general and for urban green spaces in particular is in all regions the most often cited economic challenge (Glasgow, a4, 54; Madrid, a3, 77; Sibiu, a3, 35–7). This forces actors to find ways of decreasing costs and of finding new funding sources to keep up maintenance. In all regions but the North, *construction development pressure* is seen as a danger to existing urban green spaces. Partly resulting from a tight local budget, this pressure sometimes takes the form of excessive building speculation, which reduces housing space for real needs and provokes urban sprawl (Naples, a4, 26; Lodz, a4, 23; Lugano, a4, 27–8; Timisoara, a4, 54). Apart from the legal framework limiting local autonomy by prescribing a more centralised system (cf. 9.3), local autonomy is influenced and can be limited by specific interest groups and private investors willing or not to invest their money in the city. Due to a desolate budget situation, cities often depend on such investments (Linz, a3, 73; Potsdam, a3, 182). This highlights the situation reported from cities in all regions, claiming that political local autonomy, in the sense of being legally authorised to decide independently on the governance of urban green spaces, exists in theory. However, in practice it is highly limited by the *lack of financial means* needed to implement policies (Leeds, a3, 80–6; Naples, a4, 59–64; Saarbrücken, a3, 52–4; Sibiu, a2, 130–1, a3, 56–7, 99 and a4, 176–7). *Political actors' dependency* on *economic actors* might also reduce their will to opt for participatory measures. Particularly in times of scarce public resources, lobbyists' and investors' voices might count more than citizens' will, neglecting participatory measures or disregarding their outcomes in the end (Gothenburg, a3, 88). Also, since *organising participatory procedures* is difficult and *requires time and resources* (Copenhagen, a2, 80–5 and a3, 66; Linz, a4, 82–4; Lugano, a3, 153; Strasbourg, a4, 94–106), there is an increased risk that funds to implement citizen participation and to allow for and support self-organisation will be cut, especially in times of tight budgets (Saarbrücken, a4, 68, 73; Thessaloniki, a4, 72).

The Danish example (cf. 9.1) shows that the principle of subsidiarity, of which a high degree of local autonomy is part, must go hand in hand with the application of the principle of connexity. If tasks are handed down to the local level without providing the financial resources to fulfil them, local authorities see themselves forced to further reduce public spending to a minimum. Then, they often do not shrink back from more drastic options like selling public land to private (foreign) investors, so that even basic public services such as the maintenance of urban green spaces cannot be sustained any more. This aggravates the already severe situation of local public budgets, especially in countries such as Greece and Italy, where the room for manoeuvre for local authorities was already radically curtailed by drastic demands for budget cuts. This virtual decrease in local autonomy stems from extremely tight local budgets and the EU's post-crisis austerity policies pushing the central government to financially control municipalities even more (Thessaloniki, a3, 84 and a4, 67–72). Cities face problems covering even the operating expenses for maintenance, and often are not able to support civil society and economic initiatives. A comparative situation is reported from Italy and Romania, where the legal framework allows for local autonomy, yet in Italy the threat 'to be out of the stability pact'

(Naples, a4, 64) reduces public spending to a minimum, not leaving room for action at the local level. In Sibiu, despite being chronically understaffed in the administration, the city cannot hire due to its current budgetary position (Sibiu, a2, 131). Cash-strapped cities have to find economic maintenance options or new funding sources or have to generate income at all costs (Leeds, a3, 86). Thus, cities opt for building on the last urban green spaces, which are offered to wealthy private persons (Saarbrücken, a4, 62) or sell big sections of their agricultural land to foreign investors, often without the general public even noticing (Potsdam, a3, 192). In Madrid, within the last five years the budget for the maintenance of urban green spaces has been cut by almost 40 per cent, and the quality could only be upheld because of the knowledge and creativity of the city's employees caring for green spaces. If the budget decreases further, quality will suffer (Madrid, a3, 27–9, 45–7, 61, 69).

In Poland less than 20 per cent of cities' budgets stems from direct local taxes. The rest comes from national taxes redistributed to the regions and cities. Already stretched city budgets have additionally been burdened by tasks shifted from the national to the local level – for example on education – without providing the equivalent funding (Cracow, a1, 87). This disregards the *principle of connexity* (cf. 2.4.4). The situation is not only severe in Eastern Europe. Insufficient implementation of the connexity principle is also criticised by Rietzler (2014, 1–2). She states that municipalities report a clear depletion stemming from a sinking public investment ratio that leads to an investment bottleneck.[3] In order to avoid future follow-up costs, higher tax revenues are suggested. They could be generated on the one hand by the taxation of high incomes and assets, with municipalities receiving an adequate share of them and on the other hand by a better financial support for municipalities, especially for financially weak ones.

The situation described above implies that investments in local urban green spaces often highly depend on external funds (Lublin, a1, 35; Sibiu, a2, 131 and a3, 101–3). Attempts have been made to match each urban green spaces project with national or EU funding programmes (Larissa, a4, 75). The findings on the higher dependence on EU financial resources in the East and South are supported by the quantitative data, which show only one regional difference in the relevance of different government levels in ensuring the availability of green spaces. The East and the South attribute a medium relevance to the EU level, whereas the West and the North only see a low relevance (cf. Figure 9.1). Even if public funding schemes still tend to provide short-term instead of long-term support (EC 1995, 23), the existence of public and private *funding* schemes, for example from foundations, but very importantly also from the EU, is decisive (Copenhagen, a3, 37; Milan, a4, 98; Sibiu, a4, 89–91; Timisoara, a3, 76–8). Especially EU *funding schemes* seem to be, in spite of their complexity, a functioning instrument to drive the transition at the local level. In order to receive EU funds, sustainability criteria must be met. This can be the trigger to elaborate a local sustainability strategy. European funds, accessible also for local civil society actors, for example small associations, help to raise people's

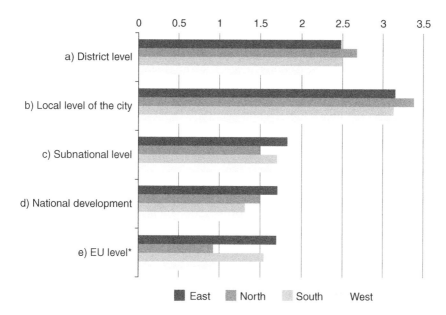

Figure 9.1 Regional differences in the relevance of different government levels in ensuring the availability of urban green spaces.

Source: Schicklinski 2016, 121.

Notes
Scaled from 0: none, to 4: very high.
* *p* < 0.001.

sustainability awareness, since they enable networking, learning from others, and the sharing and spreading of good practices. Some European funds are also accessible for local civil society actors, such as small associations. Individuals and institutions with the *knowledge* of how to successfully apply for funding, for example from the EU, are of key importance here. The 'crisis' and subsequent austerity politics have aggravated cities' *financial situation* and intensified their dependency on EU funds (Naples, a4, 19, 59–64). There is a great need for building up knowledge of writing EU project proposals to attract funds (Naples, a4, 79).

9.2.2 Policy implications

The German Advisory Council on Global Change points out that city departments that are essential to achieve the socio-ecological transition, for example those working on biodiversity conservation, climate protection, and sustainable urban planning, are still neglected in terms of financial allocations and standing compared to departments dealing with the problems of the first modernity, in charge of 'policy areas dedicated to the historic core problems of industrial and welfare societies' (WBGU 2011, 192). Especially in times of difficult financial situations for local authorities, the proportion of the city budget for the governance of urban green spaces is quickly cut, and local authorities try to reduce the costs involved with the maintenance of urban green spaces to a minimum. Technical solutions are to plant solely endemic flora, minimise water consumption, and avoid pesticides, to follow the simple rule that plants need the basics of air, water, and light to grow (Thessaloniki, a3, 67–8). Apart from this, there is a visible tendency to involve citizens as well as private enterprises in the governance of urban green spaces. This is a desirable tendency per se. Following the principles of *participatory local governance and urban development*, citizens and economic actors alike should be involved. Yet, at this point it must be emphasised that this should not lead to letting local governments off the hook for the governance of urban green spaces. In all cities studied, responsibility for the governance of urban green spaces remains with the local authority on whose will for cooperation self-organised actors are highly dependent to scale up successful bottom-up actions. The *coordination role* of local stakeholders is even more demanding when citizens are involved, because when new players enter the action situation, interaction and cooperation need to be structured and institutionalised.[4] The activities of civil society in this field always need to remain voluntary. Socially innovative forms of self-organisation can complement and advance existing governance of urban green spaces while at the same time also providing numerous ecological, social, and even economic benefits. Yet, they cannot solely constitute the governance of urban green spaces, nor can 'social innovation ... be ... a substitute to current social policies' (Bureau of European Policy Advisers European Commission 2011, 41) by assuming tasks inherent to the welfare state. This risk of an 'emerging ... (problematic) policy agenda for "outsourcing" traditional welfare state functions to community groups' (Seyfang and Smith 2007, 587) should be kept in mind. The danger of using civil society actors for the goals of neoliberal urban development has been described in critical urban research (e.g. Wolch 1990; Mayer 2006; Rosol 2014) and must not be underestimated. In this regard, Rosol's work specifically concentrates on urban gardening activities. She describes these between the poles of creating urban commons, thus a more just, ecological, and inclusive city and its functionalisation by the local authority for neoliberal city development. For the case of Berlin she reveals the involvement of civil society actors in urban governance as 'seemingly "soft" strategies' (2014, 239) which are less obvious at first sight than the '"classical" neoliberal strategies such as privatization, re-regulation and liberalization in the transformation of cities' (ibid.).

If civil society activities support welfare state functions, they must get the appropriate funding to do so and can then be a valuable complement to state welfare structures, as also suggested by an actor from Milan: 'These initiatives ... have great potentiality' (Milan, a4, 36). 'The retired person that has the allotment does not need social services. People that have social ties do not need the municipality's support. So, if the municipality supports the associations, the associations support them' (Milan, a4, 38). Involving civil society actors in welfare state functions must remain an option, a choice. If it leads to a cutback in welfare, it is practically a drawback in the European welfare discourse, which is also stressed by Gorz (1988, 211). It is in this area of tension between the 'lifeworld' and the 'system' (cf. 6.2.2) that urban (green spaces) governance based on self-organised civil society gaining more influence in interaction with the local authority can function successfully. 'Lifeworld' and 'system' have their eligibility, are necessary for a functioning local community, depend on, and can supplement each other (Gorz 1988, 198–9; 1997, 177).

Financial questions are tightly linked to the kind of time perspective taken. Solutions must be embedded in a *long-term perspective*. Rules (as expressed in the legal framework from the local to the EU level) (cf. 9.3) need to be modelled more around *long-term sustainability outcomes* instead of following the short-term logic of mere economic growth (Meadows *et al.* 2005, 274) and offering solutions that seem to be cheaper at first sight, yet in sum are not due to their social and environmental externalities and future costs (cf. 2.4.2). This must be done by setting corresponding financial and fiscal incentives. Meadows *et al.* (2005, 259) propose to '*extend the planning horizon* … [by] develop[ing] the incentives, the tools, and the procedures required for the media, the market, and elections to report, respect, and be responsible for issues that unfold over decades'. Instead of following a sector-specific logic and a short-term perspective, public funding must provide long-term support for integrative and holistic local and regional development in order to achieve a *long-term planning security* of support programmes. Political decisions on sustainability must be made *less dependent on election periods and economic actors*. These constraints currently still make political decision-makers avoid socio-environmental priorities.

9.3 Legal framework

9.3.1 *Empirical results*

When asked specifically about *rules and policy instruments* that are supporting, missing, or need to be changed in order to achieve a socio-ecological transition locally, interviewees most often mention the existing *legal framework* as obstructing. This can be due to its *complexity* and *complicatedness*. It can be bureaucratic and even chaotic. Often it is not clear which government level is responsible for a specific action. For example in Greece the decentralisation *Kallikratis* reform programme of 2010 (Kalff 2016, 84–5) even increased this lack of clarity about the competent jurisdiction and responsibility (Thessaloniki, a3, 38–9). It can also be that EU regulations are interpreted differently at the national level than intended in Brussels, and thus the final national law is complicated (Jihlava, a3, 66).

On the one hand an *ineffective, thus too flexible or even missing – or not enforced – legal framework* can be hindering. It can be too general and abstract (Timişoara, a4, 124), or the national legal framework concerning construction can be too permissive, making it difficult to protect urban green spaces (Cracow, a2, 33). This can mean that regional and national laws do not prevent the consumption of the territory (Milan, a3, 27, 39) or that the local legal framework for tree-cutting and replacement might not be strict enough without a local law protecting trees, meaning that tree-cutting – also in private areas – is possible without replacing them elsewhere (Linz, a4, 76). If the value of nature is further disregarded in legal texts, urban green spaces will continuously be considered as relatively insignificant. This is for example the case where penalties for the removal of trees were removed in an amendment to the national Environmental Act and where the urban green spaces category has not been incorporated as public purpose into the law on spatial planning (Lodz, a4, 58). The rules around the release of building permits is a central regulating instrument, with the potential to reduce building activity (Linz, a3, 59; Sibiu, a2, 36). If *rules* are *too permissive* or not applied properly, construction activity is not curtailed. For example, when building permits are easily handed out (Lublin, a4, 28), citizens are tempted to reduce even their own private green spaces to make money, as for example in the case of Lugano, where owners of old villas with large gardens tore them down to replace them with tightly packed new buildings (Lugano, a4, 60). In other cases, private persons receive a building permit after having built illegally (Istanbul, a1, 39). Where urban planning law at the national and regional level leaves too much room for manoeuvre to the local authority, city government can end up choosing to sell land to private investors instead of preserving urban green spaces (Milan, a3, 64). If the *legal framework* is *incomplete*, for example not defining well what falls into the category of urban green spaces and what their different values are, these spaces are less protected (Timisoara, a4, 64–70). The lack of a land development plan facilitates building on environmentally sensitive areas that are not foreseen for urban development (Lublin, a4, 26), and even where such a plan exists it might not have been updated, and therefore all urban green spaces that are not covered by it are threatened (Lodz, a4, 23). An example from the past comes from Romania, where in the 1990s there was no legislation on construction, leading to uncontrolled building activity (Sibiu, a2, 57–63).

Here, actors from all regions stress the importance of a *strong national and EU legal framework*, for example in the field of nature protection or building development, which forces the local level to abide by it (Copenhagen, a3, 80; St. Gallen, a4, 10–11). European directives which have to be implemented down to the local level are helpful, for example in forcing the local authority to introduce a register for urban green spaces. Therefore, according to many actors, stricter environmental *legislation* on the national/EU level with more solid and clearer rules is needed, whose non-compliance at the local level is also consistently sanctioned (Lugano, a4, 99; Madrid, a3, 92, 95–6; Timisoara, a3, 167–71 and a4, 183–5). For example, if the city has to comply with federal law in the field of nature protection and building development (Saarbrücken, a4, 31), if the national environmental law prescribes the amount of surface of green spaces according to the number of inhabitants (Sibiu, a2, 56–61), or if a clear regional environmental framework exists (Bilbao, a3, 40–4), this can foster the transition. Primarily, in the East, an overly permissive EU legal framework, not sufficiently forcing either the national or the local level to reach sustainability goals in the green spaces resource system, is deplored (Lodz, a4, 57; Timisoara, a4, 74–6). Furthermore, the national and EU level can set financial and fiscal incentives to force local authorities to act more sustainably, for example by predetermining the goals concerning land consumption, land taxes, etc. (Madrid, a4, 40; Paris, a4, 19; Saarbrücken, a4, 90–1; Timisoara, a4, 72). Regarding projects of the EU, it is suggested setting stricter citizen participation requirements instead of just having citizen participation indicators (Naples, a3, 28). In this regard Turkey's halt in the EU accession process is regretted by civil society, since working towards EU accession would have meant working towards compliance with the EU's legal framework, which would have advanced sustainability (Istanbul, a4, 101–3).

On the other hand, an overly *inflexible legal framework* can hinder civil society's activities instead of providing a regulative supportive frame for small-scale experiments. The EC (1995, 24) finds that 'legal systems often appear to militate against new initiatives' and that 'most projects, when innovative, tend to clash with the inflexibility of existing legal instruments' (ibid., 74). This is confirmed by the empirical data. National and regional laws might not leave manoeuvring room for local actors due to the local level having the least power (Istanbul, a1, 61). The framework can be too general and abstract (Timisoara, a4, 124). The EU's legal framework might not be flexible enough to be adapted to local conditions. For example, the EU's legal framework for organic agriculture needs to be adjusted or local exceptions have to be made, since, for example in North Sweden, organic greenhouse cultivation of vegetables is not possible without additional artificial light which is not permitted by the current framework (Gothenburg, a4, 104–7).

Innovative bottom-up solutions might meet legal obstacles, for example by the prohibition of selling food produced in urban gardens in schools (Gothenburg, a4, 90–2). In Milan, the Agriculture South Park was built by the region 25 years ago. However, the land can only be used for conventional agriculture, not for example for urban gardening or allotment gardens (Milan, a3, 41). The legal framework should be supportive of small-scale experiments of self-organisation and citizen participation. Yet, often innovative ideas cannot be implemented because of an inflexible Public Procurement Law setting as primary criterion the price (Lublin, a1, 54), thus accepting only the cheapest solution. Innovative potential should also be a criterion to receive funds. One actor puts it this way:

> There must be clear and transparent criteria, because these are public funds…. There must be such a vision. Some space must be given and the possibility to assess the whole concept, perhaps innovative, perhaps going beyond the framework, to make it possible. So there are not such typical technocratic rules that do not allow us to spread our wings.
>
> (Lublin, a1, 54)

9.3.2 Policy implications

Urban green spaces are essential for a city's sustainability in ecological, social, and economic terms. Nonetheless, they are increasingly threatened by urban development pressure. A *clear restrictive legal framework* to protect their preservation and possible extension is needed, as well as a legal framework facilitating citizen participation and self-organisation in their governance. In that respect, the German Advisory Council on Global Change (2011, 203) states that

> legislative, executive and judicative [!] must create or extend the regulatory framework required to empower the economy, science and the civil society to use their resources and apply their capabilities to developing, implementing and using measures such as ... the redesigning of urban spaces, and changes in land use.

To arrive at a sustainable regional food production system, trade policy as well as public procurement needs to be revised, for example to improve market access for smallholder farmers (cf. 9.4.2.4). Both must

> facilitat[e] food supply from short chains linking cities to secure a supply of healthy food, while also facilitating job access, fair production conditions and sustainable production for the most vulnerable producers and consumers, thereby using the potential of public procurement to help realize the right to food for all.
>
> (Mayors and representative of local governments 2015)

Helfrich and Bollier (2014, 22, own translation) specifically stress that 'laws, institutions and ... politics ... [must] facilitate commoning'.[5] By 'integrat[ing] the various "bottom-up" approaches in a comprehensive innovation scenario' (WBGU 2011, 264), existing dynamic self-organisation is fostered. For sustainable governance of urban green spaces and especially with regard to the creation of an urban food policy (cf. 9.4.2.4), the legal framework needs to be changed. Since land in Europe is a scarce resource, the legal framework needs to

> protect and enable secure access and tenure to land for sustainable food production in urban and peri-urban areas, including land for community gardeners and smallholder producers, for example through land banks or community land trusts; provide access to municipal land for local agricultural production and promote integration with land use and city development plans and programmes.
>
> (Mayors and representative of local governments 2015)

A recent concrete example of such a progressive change in the legal framework in the direction of sustainable governance of urban green spaces in connection with urban food production can be found in the Italian region of Lombardy where the regional authority enacted a law to foster urban gardening and agriculture due to its ecological, social, and economic benefits and its capacity to draw attention to the value of local production and to contribute to environmental education, including biodiversity and food issues (Regional Council Lombardy 2015). Article 1, paragraph 1 reads:

> The region fosters the realisation of didactic, peri-urban social, urban, and collective gardens to spread the culture of the green and of agriculture, to sensitise the families and the pupils for the importance of a healthy and balanced nutrition, to disseminate techniques of sustainable agriculture, to revalue abandoned areas, to promote social affiliation as well as the development of small food self-sufficiencies for families.

Thus, the law fosters urban gardening and agricultural activities that are done in the city or in the suburbs on urban green spaces and distinguishes four types of gardens: 'didactic gardens' are mostly located on the premises of schools and aim at educating pupils on environmental and food issues. They are explicitly asked to foster school–community interaction ('The projects provide for moments of participation and collaboration with the families of the pupils which are involved in local associations' (ibid., article 4, paragraph 3, own translation)). The focus of 'peri-urban social gardens' is to use agricultural areas at the city's fringes to achieve social integration of elderly and socially weak people by giving them the option to grow food for self-consumption. The 'urban social gardens' follow the same aim as the previous group, yet additionally they are recognised as 'innovative elements of the urban contemporary landscape' (ibid., article 2, paragraph 1, own translation) which contribute to the reactivation of abandoned and underused lots. Both types are directly assigned by the local authority to elderly or socially weak residents who have applied for them. Lastly, 'collective gardens' which are governed by associations, specifically stress the social aspect of gardening in a group which provides joint learning opportunities for those who are interested in gardening, yet lack the knowledge to do so since they have never had a garden. With regard to the last three types of gardens, the local authority is asked to prepare an inventory of all surface areas appropriate to urban gardening and agricultural activities and to realise gardening projects on them.

Responsibility for a garden project can either be taken by the local authority, by an educational institution, or by a nature conservation authority. For these institutions to receive funding from the region, projects need to apply sustainable agriculture measures such as water-saving, composting, and soil fertility conservation measures and work without chemical fertilisers. The three cited institutions can then set their own rules for the governance of the garden and concede it for free to individuals or civil society associations for growing food for self-consumption. The three institutions also have the right to draw on the knowledge of gardening professionals to assist the individuals or associations in their gardening activities. In order to foster the cultivation of endemic species, the proponents of a gardening project can ask the region to deliver to them for free, via the regional authority for agriculture and forestry, a starting package of fruit, vegetable, and flower seeds typical for the Lombardy region. Moreover, the region organises, in collaboration with the authority for agriculture and forestry and with the professional association, the competition 'Gli Orti di Lombardia' (The Gardens in Lombardy, own translation) to award the most significative projects. This is an encouraging example of regional legislation apt to contribute to sustainable governance of urban green spaces, to the mitigation of private poverty, and to environmental education in general and education on biodiversity and food issues in particular.

9.4 Functioning of the local authority

9.4.1 Empirical results

Institutional barriers in politics and administration become evident in all regions. Whereas a low *turnover rate*, meaning politicians staying in power for a very long time, can hinder the transition (Paris, a4, 52), a high turn-over rate, with politicians changing too fast to establish a constructive relationship between civil society and politics (Glasgow, a4, 44), can be equally problematic. Actors from all sectors report *administrative procedures* that are complicated and inefficient, suffering from a high degree of bureaucracy (Naples, a3, 91), for example in budgetary procedures. They are also seen as being non-transparent and non-informative (Bilbao, a4, 43, 46), for example in the process of allocating allotment gardens (Milan, a3, 45, 67–70). City administration is often not perceived as proactive but as hindering (Madrid, a4, 70), also because it is often a very large institution with *insufficient interdisciplinary cross-sector communication and cooperation* capacities (Strasbourg, a4, 52, 74), sometimes due to being headed by different political parties. This can produce contradictory sector policies (Glasgow, a4, 46–8) and even weaken the whole city (Copenhagen, a2, 103–6). For example, environmental protection and municipal policies can be consistent with the general strategy in terms of environmental protection, yet the urban development policy by the City Planning Office might not contain a reference to urban green spaces. Equally, the responsibility for trees might be split between three different departments, yet there is no collaboration between them, even if officials are fully aware of this (Lodz, a4, 25, 30, 59). To civil society actors it is often unclear which department deals with what issue (Glasgow, a4, 44–8), which makes it difficult to identify the right contact person. According to the cited actors, a more uniform structure of administration with one resource being handled by one department could be a concrete solution here.

The continuing predominance of the sector-specific logic of public administration contrasts with civil society's *holistic and integrative approach* to concrete local problems (Elsen and Schicklinski 2016, 236). Ideas coming from civil society actors are not sufficiently valued and taken up by the local authority. For example in Lodz, civil society actors organised workshops for civil servants on the 'improvement of green areas' management in the city or on sustainable development in general' (Lodz, a4, 30), which were not attended by decision-makers themselves but by their representatives. To overcome the above-mentioned logic, citizen participation and multidisciplinarity must find their way into local governance since they are essential in not leaving out important aspects in policy-making (Timisoara, a4, 130–1). This also means acknowledging and making use of *citizens' local expert knowledge* (Copenhagen, a3, 62–4 and a4, 53; Saarbrücken, a4, 69, 72). A Polish actor points out that the local authority can profit from civil society's input, if the latter makes constructive propositions on what and how things can be improved, by analysing which barriers exist and trying to remove them. He advises against an open confrontation with the local authority, since arguing about a lack of financial resources and pointing to a lack of professionalism of civil servants and politicians is a simplification. Civil servants are subject to institutional constraints and are lacking good examples of how to solve problems differently (Lodz, a4, 40). Good examples to break up this sector-specific logic and to come to a multidisciplinary approach preventing important aspects being missed out, and thus approximating civil society's logic, come from Denmark. In Aalborg a sustainability department has been created which coordinates and promotes the policy strategy on sustainability. The idea is to mainstream sustainability issues into all sector policy plans, keeping them as cross-sectoral as possible and developing cross-sector strategies (Aalborg, a4, 15–16). In Copenhagen, administrative staff has understood that innovative integral thinking is needed, in contrast to not looking across the boundaries of one's own profession (Copenhagen, a4, 22): 'You have to work across traditional silos, sectors, and professional barriers.... There are overlapping communications between departments and professional fields, some interesting opportunities that can create value on several levels' (Copenhagen, a3, 14).

In many cities there is the will to let citizens participate, which is even prescribed by law. Yet, there is a *lack of concrete policy tools* (Bilbao, a3, 58; Madrid, a4, 85–91; Rome, a1, 78). There is no institutionalised regular mechanism of citizen participation, for example via a regularly meeting council (Bilbao, a4, 40–7; Milan, a4, 77–83). Instead, citizens are involved case by case. In cases where there are concrete policy tools, it is possible that citizens *are not well informed* about options to participate (Bilbao, a3, 104; Cracow, a4, 74–7; Milan, a4, 79–81; Sibiu, a3, 89–91 and a4, 115). Lacking political will to apply citizen participation also has to do with *political actors' dependency* on *election votes*. Policy-makers want to be in control since in the end they are responsible for the political decisions taken (Copenhagen, a2, 80). Participatory procedures take time (Copenhagen, a2, 81 and a3, 66) and contain the risk of prolonging decision-making (Linz, a4, 84; Strasbourg, a4, 104). Therefore, they do not easily give up a command-driven control.

Missing or obstructing policy instruments are cited. Ongoing land consumption is not sufficiently countered because of the lack of applying appropriate policy instruments. Bringing the local authority and universities closer together is missing in most cities but would be very important also for the planning of urban green spaces (Rome, a1, 78). Insufficient steering tools are often the reason for only single strategies followed by piecemeal actions without a sustainability drive and an overarching sustainability vision for the city behind it (Larissa, a3, 45; Leeds, a3, 39–41; Lodz, a3, 47; Potsdam, a3, 88; Thessaloniki, a4, 21, 35). Yet, an overall concept can only emerge with a clear political will behind it. A lack of urban planning can also stem from a desolate financial situation, as is the case in cities having suffered severe mismanagement, sometimes linked to the misappropriation of public funds in the past (Larissa, a3, 32). Creating a local developing strategy is even more important in times of crisis when overarching national strategies on sustainability development are often missing and financial resources are very much limited. The 'crisis' has aggravated the tendency of always awarding public project tenders to the lowest bidder, going along with decreased quality and sustainability criteria (Thessaloniki, a3, 50). Investing into oversized expensive prestige projects, mostly in the field of building and traffic infrastructure construction, is seen as counterproductive to sustainability, also in an intergenerational sense, leaving the next generations with high debts (Saarbrücken, a4, 86).

Supporting policy instruments are equally stated: strategies at the local and the regional level are a good starting point (Aalborg, a4, 108), such as a master plan on biodiversity (Paris, a3, 59). Citizens need to be involved in the planning process from the beginning, 'in consultations, dialogue meetings, [or] coordinating groups' (Umea, a3, 126). Yet, making plans is relatively easy compared to afterwards implementing them, due to diverging interests and arising conflicts (Aalborg, a4, 29–32). An existing *implementation gap* is reported from every region (Lodz, a4, 25–7; Bilbao, a4, 79; Istanbul, a4, 62, 99–101; Timisoara, a4, 32, 169), yet can be tackled by policy tools adapted to the respective local context. Different examples of such successful tools are given: political decisions can be liable to a 'sustainability check' (Saarbrücken, a4, 83) which asks politicians to expose sustainability impacts of the planned measures. 'Gothenburg municipality invent[ed] an environmental management system called Environmental Diploma' (Gothenburg, a4, 44) for small and medium enterprises, which was so successful locally that it is now enshrined in national law. Furthermore, the 'no net loss' tool can be applied in land use planning (cf. 5.2.2), demanding ecological compensation measures in cases of building in urban green spaces. However, the principle has not become obligatory in national law yet (Umea, a3, 72, 132). The last three examples show how 'rules [can be] used as tools to change the structure of action situations' (Ostrom 2005, 68) by actors at the local level to drive the socio-ecological transition. If all these tools became part of legislation, entering the legal system of the respective country, compliance with them could be claimed by actors and could be enforced via sanctions.

Moreover, interviewees suggest *additional policy instruments that could be developed*. They stress the necessity of policy instruments underlining more the link between today's investments and their positive future effects (St. Gallen, a4, 10) to reveal their superiority to cheaper versions in the long run by also uncovering the latter's social and environmental externalities. Instead of going into oversize prestige projects, funding should be invested into key lighthouse projects that enhance the city as a whole, promoting social, environmental, and economic aspects (Saarbrücken, a3, 70). Civil society actors suggest the monitoring and the evaluation of policy-making by citizens, asking for a combination of a top-down organisation plan for sustainability with an interactive bottom-up citizen-led control system, so that the local authority takes the citizens' needs into account (Thessaloniki, a4, 86).

Urban planning is often *criticised* for either not having been in existence at all, as not having worked well, or as having failed totally (Istanbul, a4, 12; Larissa, a3, 18; Lugano, a4, 34; Milan, a4, 67–71; Strasbourg, a4, 36). Bad *city governance* can lead to de facto inability in coping with numerous challenges in urban planning, not following any sustainability vision (Istanbul, a4, 12; Milan, a4, 26). Where only housing units have been built without also providing the concomitant transport, leisure, and economic infrastructure, cities later face additional costs for maintenance and connection (Cracow, a3, 23; Larissa, a3, 34). Some cities have never followed a specific urban green space policy, leading to a situation in which almost no urban green spaces are left (Lugano, a4, 50–2). What's more, climate change has not yet been taken into consideration sufficiently in urban planning (Dortmund, a4, 30). A removal of urban green spaces and ongoing soil sealing has a detrimental influence on the city's microclimate, as they exacerbate the urban heat island effect (Strasbourg, a4, 24–5, 58, 77–82; Potsdam, a3, 18, 22). However, in a situation with generally rising temperatures in Europe due to climate change, these tendencies become increasingly critical and are detrimental to building a more *climate-resilient city*.

Conducive *institutional conditions* emerge if public institutions are supportive. Having internalised the added value of citizen participation and self-organisation, they act accordingly, supporting citizens. This means that they have a *transparent* way of working with *clear institutionalised communication and information channels* to citizens (Lugano, a3, 125; Naples, a4, 93), as well as from citizens to the local authority (cf. also 9.5). This confirms the need for 'information rules [which] affect the level of information available to participants ... [and which must] relate to the set of all possible channels connecting all participants in a situation' (Ostrom 2005, 206). Clear communication also means that when participatory tools are employed, administration has to break the technical language down into a *language easily understandable* by citizens, instead of using a *complicated* technical *vocabulary* (Bilbao, a4, 75).

9.4.2 Policy implications

The set *goal of the governance of urban green spaces* must be to prevent the further reduction of green spaces and to possibly regain lost ones. This refers to inner-city urban green spaces but also to the city's fringe area. The concept of the 'green compact city' (EC 2010, 28) means to counter urban sprawl, while at the same time maintaining or even increasing the amount of urban green spaces. In this sense, an actor proposes to effectively improve the urban microclimate by greening all terraces and roofs, which can only succeed if the public sector participates (Thessaloniki, a3, 24). Also, all urban planners must be aware of the value of the relationship between humans and nature. People working in the maintenance of green spaces and scientists like ecologists and naturalists are more likely to be aware of this value, while some urban planners might still consider urban green spaces solely as empty abandoned spaces (Paris, a3, 49). In this regard, a report from the EC (1995, 73) notices the beginning of a change in thinking in urban regeneration.

> The need to redevelop former industrial areas ... and the growing interest of urban populations in 'green' areas ... have led many towns to change their approach to open, public areas: these are no longer seen as empty spaces but as community areas.

The report also points out an 'employment creation potential linked with the development or upgrading of urban public areas ... [for example in] the maintenance of public areas' (ibid.). Although it only mentions public–private partnerships, this changed approach can be a starting point to also involve civil society actors more in job creation (cf. 10.1).

For the socio-ecological transition to succeed in the governance of urban green spaces, the functioning of the local authority must be aligned towards five major necessary components of the local policy framework, which will be presented in the following subsections. These are *achieving participatory local governance, recognising urban green spaces as commons and adjusting the governance of urban green spaces accordingly, achieving cross-sectoral interactive networked governance, creating a local urban food policy,* and *achieving integrated local and regional socio-ecological-economic development.*

9.4.2.1 Achieving participatory local governance

The socio-ecological transition in the green spaces resource system can only be achieved if the majority of citizens are taken along in this process, in other words if options for self-organisation and citizen participation in the governance of urban green spaces exist. *Sustainability concerns everyone,* since everyone is dependent on the Earth's environment and its natural resources. By implication this means that everyone has the right to participate as much as possible in the city's transition path. Sustainability is *not an expert topic.* Particularly the governance of urban green spaces lends itself to the involvement of all stakeholders, as it deals with a tangible topic that is mostly governed at the local level and in which ideas can be tried out and implemented quite quickly and cost-efficiently compared to other resource systems. Nevertheless, also in the governance of urban green spaces the complexity and abstractness of sustainability issues need to be reduced. Issues need to be presented to citizens in an easily understandable language, and concrete options for civic engagement need to be pointed out and proposed.

To bring about a change towards more sustainable governance of urban green spaces, the (local) policy framework must facilitate civil society initiatives, meeting citizens on equal footing. In well-run cities that are skilled at planning (Copenhagen, a4, 30), the chances for successful citizen participation are higher and the local government can more easily ensure that *participatory procedures are professionally applied*, not leaving (legal) loopholes for the misuse of citizen participation on the side of citizens or politicians, which have been reported from every region. The three empirical findings of the need to involve citizens at the earliest possible moment with real power to influence the outcome of the decision-making process, the highest possible degree of transparency, and the use of independent mediators in the event of conflict are also cited by the German Advisory Council on Global Change (2011, 211, 279) as essential criteria for successful citizen participation. When participatory tools are applied only late in the planning process or their outcomes are ultimately not taken into consideration, or if individuals and associations try to get through particular interests, citizen participation misses its aim (Cracow, a1, 51–2; Gothenburg, a4, 68).

According to several actors, there is an increasing understanding that urban green spaces are an important asset for cities, yielding numerous ecological, social as well as economic benefits, making a strong argument for their preservation (Bilbao, a4, 77; Potsdam, a3, 164). However, in practice urban green spaces are still exposed to high development pressure. In this situation *they can best be protected if citizens have recognised their value* and identify with these common urban green spaces. *Involving citizens in the governance of urban green spaces* by supporting citizen participation and providing space for self-organisation can be an effective way of raising citizens' consciousness of their value and can trigger further civic engagement, also in other fields. Nevertheless, a lack of citizen participation tools is reported from several cities (Rome, a1, 78). Involving citizens more strongly is necessary since *progress in the socio-ecological transition can only be made with a citizen perspective*, certainly not with a sector perspective. This is also recognised by two of the recently published Sustainable Development Goals which intend to, 'by 2030, enhance inclusive and sustainable urbanization and capacity for participatory, integrated and sustainable human settlement planning and management in all countries' (UNGA 2015, 22, goal 11, paragraph 3) as well as to 'ensure responsive, inclusive, participatory and representative decision-making at all levels' (ibid., 26, goal 16, paragraph 7).

In a study on policing in several urban neighbourhoods in Indianapolis, Ostrom delivered two main findings. First, collaboration between citizens and the local authority leads to a better quality of public policies. Yet, second, a non-esteeming attitude of the local authority towards civic engagement entails a decreasing willingness among citizens to care about community issues. 'Human services could not be effectively produced by official agencies alone. Citizens are an important coproducer. If they are treated as unimportant and irrelevant, they reduce their efforts substantially' (Ostrom 2010, 10). Therefore, the local authority needs to know what matters to citizens and needs to have them as well as economic actors on their side (Copenhagen, a2, 100). Consequently, more powerful participatory tools are demanded, up to the point of giving citizens a veto power on decisions. It is deemed necessary to surpass the state of mere consultation, for example on how resources are consumed, to increase the transparency of the political process and to let citizens control political actors (Naples, a4, 15–19). This implies for example to pass from consultation to citizens' budgets, referenda, and civic audits in order to reach out to all citizens and not only those organised in associations. Other action would be to strengthen neighbourhood associations and also to install consultative committees on district municipalities, as well as consult citizens in the street and via NGOs (Bilbao, a4, 98; Istanbul, a1, 81; Lugano, a3, 153; Naples, a3, 91 and a4, 87–93; Saarbrücken, a4, 88). This should continue to the point of demanding that citizen participation must become obligatory in urban development projects (Copenhagen, a3, 37). Advanced technology development facilitates the use of participatory tools. Citizens should be allowed to vote via phone/internet on 'decisions that directly influence a specific sphere of life' (Lodz, a3, 59). Where citizen participation is already practised, it can be improved and shifted to higher levels, as the case of Naples with three concrete examples reveals. First, the city's department for citizen participation needs to gain more power since at the moment the committees are just round tables elaborating a proposition, which the counsellor does not have to bring in front of the council to be adopted or not (Naples, a3, 91). Second, citizen participation tools (for example committees) should also be introduced at the district level (Naples, a4, 86–93). Third, more powerful participatory tools such as referenda and civic audits[6] should be introduced to hold the city accountable, as 'the Committees are there only to give opinions. The civic audit instead would keep the municipality accountable' (Naples, a4, 87–93). Giving citizens a veto power on decisions, for example on how resources are consumed, serves to control politics and increases the transparency of the political process. Also more space for self-organisation is demanded. For example, an economic actor from Larissa wants the municipality to give citizens' initiatives the right to organise environmental and cultural events in the city's green spaces.

> There are several cultural groups with increased activity, related to the green areas of the city at some level. For example, they could be hired to create artistic works in the parks. The city's artists, I believe, would accept this offer, even with a small fee, in order to show their works to the public.
>
> (Larissa, a3, 67)

The empirical examples show that various forms of *citizen participation* and *self-organisation* are manifestations of social innovation. By pursuing social, environmental, and economic objectives, they can contribute to the socio-ecological transition. Therefore, favourable political and administrative framework conditions have to be created. The empirical data in combination with theoretical approaches reveals the kind of policy framework that is needed for constructive collaboration between the local authority, economic actors, and citizens, enabling innovative solutions in the governance of urban green spaces, urban food production, and participatory urban development.

The local authority must allow for, give room to, and encourage civil society action to unfold, for example by providing meeting space. The concrete possibility for citizens to take on responsibility for the common good (for example in the governance of urban green spaces) must be offered. Respondents would consider civil society actors to be able to overcome the city's challenges if the local authority *allowed citizens to take action more* and if political and economic actors invested in the activities coming from the citizens (Milan, a4, 36–8). For example, 'these ugly images that physically and aesthetically pollute the environment (abandoned, derelict buildings, spaces filled with useless objects, clay plots and brown fields, etc.)' (Thessaloniki, a4, 22) could be reduced by numerous small actions spreading across the city, such as turning abandoned fields into green spaces and demolishing derelict buildings. This can even relieve the public budget, however cannot be an excuse to further cut the green spaces budget, which is already one of the first to be cut in times of scarce public resources due to its low status in municipal planning (Umea, a3, 68; cf. also 9.2). Especially in the field of urban food production (cf. 7.4.1), innovative ideas have evolved that could be developed further as social and solidarity economy options (cf. 9.4.2.5).

A command-driven governance approach has already partly been abandoned where the city allows associations and enterprises to care for urban green spaces. Yet, existing collaboration needs to be improved, as shown in the example of the adoption of urban green spaces in Naples. Associations and enterprises caring for urban green spaces should not be left alone with the maintenance task (cf. 10.1). The local government must set the legal framework, coordinate, and support actors with equipment and soil. This way civil society and economic actors can bring in innovative ideas: 'Maybe you – municipality – have an old employee that takes care of this and uses old techniques, and me – association – I can tell you new stuff' (Naples, a3, 76). This way the city would still save costs, since the work is done by volunteers. Last, but not least, responsibility for taking care of green spaces can also be partly shifted to the renters of properties, obliging them to take care of the public green spaces around the property (Lodz, a4, 53).

9.4.2.2 Recognising urban green spaces as commons and adjusting the governance of urban green spaces accordingly

Gorz (1997, 162) describes how a policy of urban regeneration can foster self-organised activities, not regarding them as a stopgap but as an inherent part of sustainable local development (cf. 9.4.2.5). His accentuation of the importance of self-organised activities is shared by numerous other scholars. According to Harvey (2012, 88) 'the role of the commons in city formation and in urban politics' has to be understood and politically acknowledged. Ostrom's interdisciplinary empirical work has revealed that a sustainable governance of commons is possible if actors cooperate and certain rules are followed (cf. 3.3.1). The governance of urban green spaces should make use of this wealth of experience. This means that options must exist for urban green spaces to be turned into urban commons via citizen action. *The governance of urban green spaces, guided by the urban green commons concept*, entails cross-sectoral collaboration, demanding that the state must

> supply more and more in the way of public goods for public purposes, along with the self-organization of whole populations to appropriate, use, and supplement those goods in ways that extend and enhance the qualities of the non-commodified reproductive and environmental commons.
>
> (Harvey 2012, 87–8)

Considering urban green spaces as commons is not only about advocating the reversal of privatisation trends but entails an increase in power of action for civil society actors in gaining 'political steering, control and socioeconomic safeguarding of access'[7] (Elsen 2007, 23, own translation). 'Policy makers and planners should stimulate the self-emergence of different types of UGCs, and support their evolvement in urban areas through creating institutional space' (Colding and Barthel 2013, 163). In practical terms this could mean conferring the right to govern green spaces to citizens (Colding *et al.* 2013, 11).

9.4.2.3 Achieving interactive governance

A sustainable society can only be achieved via cooperation (Biesecker and Kesting 2003, 191–2), and for effective climate change mitigation and adaptation measures 'improving institutions as well as coordination and cooperation in governance' (IPCC 2015, 26) are necessary. Defining aims and taking decisions must be a *transparent process* from the beginning of the policy cycle. Citizen participation tools control whether this is the case. In general, *participatory local governance* must become standard.[8] This is not a new claim. De Rougement (1977, 272) already asked in the 1970s to consistently apply the subsidiarity principle and to practise participatory local governance. The local level lends itself perfectly to practise citizen participation (ibid., 267), which confers both freedom and responsibility to citizens (ibid., 303), and to achieve a renewal of democracy from below. He (ibid., 217) pleads for a new local governance style which is marked by communication and transparency.

A change in this direction is already visible, as Beck (2009, 199) remarks: 'The rational-choice, hierarchical means-end model of politics … is being displaced by theories that emphasize consultation, interaction, negotiation, network'. 'A conscious policy would allow and facilitate the influence of civil society to unfold' (Elsen and Schicklinski 2016, 230). It would facilitate the generation of social capital by fostering sector-spanning collaboration between different local actors which would then lead to increased civic engagement in various spheres of activity. Where this is successful, local partnerships can be built that solve local problems (Roth 2000, 353–4). Also Sustainable Development Goal 17, paragraph 17 (UNGA 2015, 28) demands to 'encourage and promote effective public, public-private and civil society partnerships, building on the experience and resourcing strategies of partnerships'. If political actors are successful in setting the right framework conditions for building such partnerships, they can even become transition drivers, interacting with other actors from a proactive administration, economy, and civil society (Aalborg, a4, 43). Urban social innovation can be launched by bottom-up actors, yet can also be initiated by governmental actors, by the local authority in power. Meadows *et al.* (2005, 273) underline the importance of 'leaders who are honest, respectful, intelligent, humble, and more interested in doing their jobs than in keeping their jobs, more interested in serving society than in winning elections'. For example, the mayor of Sibiu is described as dedicatedly driving forward sustainability issues. The initiation of networks by political or administrative actors can stabilise the collaboration between heterogeneous local stakeholders and make the emergence of social innovative projects more probable. For example, in Jihlava, the mayor pursues an 'enlightened approach of city government … [having] created a heterogeneous team of visionaries' (Jihlava, a3, 39) which takes decisions and actions. The team consists of locals but also of people who are not from the city. Some of them had no experience in governing a city, for example knowing about budget allocation, so 'they were not limited by the financially limited thoughts and could come up with interesting ideas' (ibid.). Others were not politicians and therefore not dependent on re-election, so they were not forced to fulfil pre-election promises.

'Facilitating intermediary actors are necessary to initiate processes of development and change' (Elsen and Schicklinski 2016, 236). The transition is often driven by committed *change agents* from all sectors who have first adopted changing and newly evolving norms and significantly pushed for their manifestation in rules. This is the case with the highly motivated innovative experts working as civil servants in the local administration, who are little bound by bureaucracy and have a sufficient budget. Here, successful norm-adoption has led to higher levels of trust and cooperation between stakeholders and to vivid institutionalised interaction processes. This also helps to break the *sector specific rationality* that many local authorities still abide to, which has to be replaced by following *cross-sector inter- and transdisciplinary strategies* to overcome an existing implementation gap. Examples of urban innovation initiated from within the local authority come from Copenhagen and Saarbrücken. In Copenhagen there is a palpable feeling of entrepreneurship in the local authority. Civil servants are very motivated and even passionate about their work, and they are given resources and the allowance and space to realise their innovative ideas:

> It is easier to be an employee in the City of Copenhagen than in other
> municipalities in the world. That is less bureaucratic – that you have a free
> space as a civil servant in Copenhagen. There are better options for 'entre-
> preneurship' in the municipality.... There are some really good innovative
> people ... who are really passionate about what they do, and they are
> allowed to do so.
>
> (Copenhagen, a3, 52)

In Saarbrücken, a civil society actor underlines the creativity of the head of the
green spaces department in promoting sustainability aspects in the maintenance
of green spaces with fewer resources (Saarbrücken, a4, 66).

The approach of *'interactive governance'*, as conceptualised this millennium by
Kooiman and Bavinck (2013, 11) 'responds to ever growing diversity, dynamics
and complexity' (ibid.), demanding an involvement of all actors in a network
structure which implies their interaction as a basic principle of the approach. Its
assets are described by an actor from Copenhagen (a3, 16) who states that via
interdisciplinary networks and venues that allow for politicians and citizens to
interact and to develop ideas and find solutions, mutual inspiration takes place
and synergies are discovered. Creating such a facilitating political culture has
been tried for example in Freiburg[9] with the foundation of a sustainability
council in 2006 which is composed of lay experts from the local Agenda 21
movement, de facto experts for specific topics, administrative experts in certain
specialist subjects from the local government, and members of the city council.
This council for example elaborated in a participatory process the local sustainability goals. Traits of this type of networked governance also become visible in
Leeds. There is a high degree of cross-sector cooperation around the topic of
urban food production. Numerous activities are going on in cooperation with
the local authority, schools, the university, and civil society and economic
actors. This is partly thanks to well-informed leading figures from civil society
that are good networkers implementing innovative ideas. For example, initiatives were started after an activist had contacted the counsellor who then realised that interacting actors from different realms can bring benefits to the city.
Now, all actors are connected in a very vivid loose local network, and via the
creation of an independent committee, contact to the local authority is institutionalised. The example of Leeds comes closest to the claim made in the Milan
Urban Food Policy Pact (Mayors and representatives of local governments
2015) that the local authority needs to *'identify, map and evaluate local initiatives*
and civil society food movements in order to transform "best practices" into relevant programmes and policies, with the support of local research or academic
institutions'. The approach of interactive governance conceives governance as
an interplay between the realms of state, market, and civil society (Kooiman
and Bavinck 2013, 9, 13) and in this sense it is also close to the approach of

> urban entrepreneurialism [which is a] pattern of behaviour within urban
> governance that mixes together state powers (local, metropolitan, regional,

national, or supranational) with a wide array of organizational forms in civil society (chambers of commerce, unions, churches, educational and research institutions, community groups, NGOs, and so on) and private interests (corporate and individual) to form coalitions to promote or manage urban or regional development of one sort or another.

(Harvey 2012, 100)

Incipient stages of interactive governance of urban green spaces are found in several cities, where, often out of financial needs, the local authority opts for assigning the care for urban green spaces to associations as well as to private enterprises. Despite not working perfectly yet and containing the risk of functionalising civil society actors for neoliberal urban development strategies, it is one example of the collaboration of local actors across sector boundaries to find, via a joint learning process, innovative solutions to local shared problems (for example Milan, Madrid, Naples, Rome, Thessaloniki).

Interactive governance allows the local system's *increased complexity* stemming from the multiplication of actors entering the action situation to be dealt with. Pressure can be built up from civil society actors, triggering a change in the local action situation 'while again being changed by it' (Elsen and Schicklinski 2016, 227). In Lugano, citizens fight to safeguard remaining unspoilt mountains around the city from construction. They achieved an institutionalised hearing process for a participated planning procedure consisting of informative meetings with all stakeholders involved which is led by an external facilitator. In Copenhagen, high pressure from NGOs on the local authority led to the official involvement of civil society actors in local politics, for example in committees.

> In these cases, actors have provoked institutional changes by entering the action arena.[10] They now interact with other actors already present in the arena according to newly created or re-negotiated rules which retroact and alter in turn their initial behaviour.
>
> (Ibid., 228)

A larger number and a greater diversity of actors increase the conflict potential, for example in rule definition around fallow land or permanent rights of use (cf. 6.3.2.5). This demands 'high-level skills on the part of the citizens and governments in the arts of nonviolent conflict resolution' (Meadows *et al.* 2005, 274). In this situation it is the local authority's task to provide a policy framework allowing for constructive interaction of all actors and to coordinate the process of rule setting and conflict regulation.

Since social innovation is *not bound to a specific sector* and can equally emerge in the civil society, governmental, or the economic sector, cross-sector *collaboration* is essential. A high degree of collaboration by local actors creates an atmosphere of *mutual trust* and is beneficial to the transition (cf. 3.3.2). Instead of considering socially innovative civil society actors who challenge routines of politics and administration by following their own rationality as a threat or a disturbing factor, the local authority should recognise their potential to contribute to the joint goal of the socio-ecological transition. Citizen participation is an indispensable complement to top-down policy-making. Policy-making must be monitored and evaluated by citizens. With such a combination of a top-down organisation plan for sustainability with an interactive bottom-up citizen-led control system, the local authority can best take citizens' needs into account while pursuing the goal of the socio-ecological transition. Action situations for all local actors to meet need to be opened up and must be permanently anchored institutionally in order to allow for a *regular exchange of information* and to provide spaces for conflict management. Here, the local authority's *coordination* role is demanded.[11] Thought out, real citizen participation means to *collaborate on an equal footing*. To engage with a more democratic way of city governance is worthwhile, since cities that manage to include a wide range of stakeholders in local governance seem to be more advanced in the transition. Collaboration with science should also be sought. Scientific and non-scientific actors have to collaborate on an equal footing to solve local problems, highlighting 'the significance of cooperative knowledge production with local people' (Elsen and Schicklinski 2016, 237) and contributing to the 'decentralization of … scientific expertise' (Meadows *et al.* 2005, 274).

9.4.2.4 *Creating a sustainable regional food policy*

With a rising urbanisation trend, ongoing climate change, and a persistent unsustainable and unjust global food and agriculture system, cities are urged to question the way they are provided for with food and water and to devise a sustainable regional food policy guaranteeing access to healthy sustainable food for every citizen:

> *Noting current food systems are being challenged* to provide permanent and reliable access to adequate, safe, local, diversified, fair, healthy and nutrient rich food for all; and that the task of feeding cities will face multiple constraints posed by inter alia, unbalanced distribution and access, environmental degradation, resource scarcity and climate change, unsustainable production and consumption patterns, and food loss and waste.
>
> (Mayors and representatives of local governments 2015)

This cannot be achieved without redesigning urban–rural linkages, thus improving collaboration at the regional level. Sustainable Development Goal 11, paragraph a (UNGA 2015, 22) asks for 'positive economic, social and environmental links between urban, peri-urban and rural areas by strengthening national and regional development planning'. In concrete terms this means arriving at a

> *holistic and integrated land use planning and management* in collaboration with both urban and rural authorities … by combining landscape features, for

example with risk-minimizing strategies to enhance opportunities for agro-ecological production, conservation of biodiversity and farmland ... [and] climate change adaptation.

(Mayors and representatives of local governments 2015)

Urban–rural linkages must be strengthened by fostering sustainable organic urban and peri-urban agriculture and by integrating it into urban and regional planning. A central cornerstone of a sustainable just regional food policy is to support smallholder farmers, since they

> play a key role in feeding cities ... by helping to maintain resilient, equit-able, culturally appropriate food systems; ... reorienting food systems and value chains for sustainable diets is a means to reconnect consumers with both rural and urban producers.

(Ibid.)

Small-scale organic regional food production can be supported and strengthened by the local authority by providing services such as 'technical training and fin-ancial assistance (credit, technology, food safety, market access, etc.) to build a[n] economically viable food system with inputs such as compost from food waste, grey water from post-consumer use, and energy from waste, etc.' (ibid.).

Up to absolute urban food sovereignty can be achieved by a combination of strengthening urban and peri-urban agriculture. Short sustainable food chains and rural–urban linkages are created by supporting 'producer organisations, producer-to-consumer networks and platforms, and ... civil society-led social and solidarity economy initiatives and alternative market systems' (ibid.). Cities can become 'edible' by various measures: urban green spaces can be released for maintenance including food production to a diversity of civil society actors such as private persons, social cooperatives, or educational institutions (Regional Council Lombardy 2015). When new buildings are planned or old ones refur-bished, the possibility of creating green roofs, balconies, terraces, and com-munity gardens shall be kept in mind. Where urban green spaces have already been sealed or where the soil might be contaminated, mobile raised beds can be installed. Also on private ground, for example in enterprises, as well as on public ground belonging to buildings of the city, urban gardening can be started by employees (oew *et al.* 2015) and possibly be opened to all citizens. To achieve 'a socially inclusive and a rights-based approach in urban food policy' (Mayors and representatives of local governments 2015), it must be recognised '*that civil society and the private sector have major roles to play* in feeding cities, bringing experience, innovation and campaigns for more sustainable food systems' (ibid.). In order to foster and institutionally anchor the creation of a sustainable, just regional food policy and ongoing experiments in the governance of urban green spaces, the Milan Urban Food Policy Pact proposes the 'appointment of a food policy advisor' and the 'development of a multi-stakeholder platform or food council'. Furthermore, *urban gardening and agriculture need to become an urban planning goal*, following lighthouse projects such as the concept 'Essbare Stadt' ('Edible City', own translation) in the German town of Andernach, where the city's concept for urban green spaces includes the transformation of flower beds into vegetable and fruit plantations (Potsdam, a4, 168–71). Another encouraging example, albeit currently remaining in the state of a project idea, is the spatial concept for urban agriculture and metropolitan food policy *Agropolis München* (Agropolis Munich, own translation). An interdisciplinary group of architects, landscape architects, and urban planners conceived a project that makes sustainable food production, distribution, and consumption basic constituents of urban development. This group pursues three interconnected main goals: 'sustainable production of healthy food, … qualification measures and jobs as well as scope for existing knowledge and interest (for example of the elderly, unemployed, immigrants)…, … [and] the creation of conscience and transparency for food and its production' (Schröder *et al.* 2010, 12, own translation).

9.4.2.5 *Achieving integrated local and regional socio-ecological-economic development*

Under the heading 'Tools for the Transition to Sustainability', Meadows *et al.* (2005, 274) cite 'an economy that is a means, not an end, one that serves the welfare of the environment, rather than vice versa' and further demands a 'decentralization of economic power' (ibid.). Enlarging this thinking by the social dimension and keeping in mind the Paris Agreement (article 7, paragraph 9, clause (e)) suggesting 'build[ing] the resilience of socioeconomic and ecological systems, including through economic diversification and sustainable management of natural resources' (UNFCCC 2015, 24), one arrives at social and solidarity economy as a tool to foster integrated local and regional socio-ecological-economic development (cf. 2.4.4). In fact, the Milan Urban Food Pact (Mayors and representatives of local governments 2015) deems it necessary to

> *encourage and support social and solidarity economy activities*, paying special attention to food-related activities that support sustainable livelihoods for marginalized populations at different levels of the food chain and facilitate access to safe and healthy foods in both urban and rural areas.

It also recognises '*the informal sector's contribution* to urban food systems (in terms of food supply, job creation, promotion of local diets and environment management)' (ibid.). The local authority must '*promote networks and support grassroots activities* (such as community gardens, community food kitchens, social pantries, etc.) that create social inclusion and provide food to marginalized individuals' (ibid.).

> Examples for investing in the capacities of the silent majority [, not yet specifically in the area of food production, yet in the broader field of the

governance of urban green spaces,] come from Saarbrücken where the community work offices are very active and supported by the local government. The community association 'Menschen für Malstadt' ('People for Malstadt', author's translation) promotes citizens' initiatives in cooperation with the district's community work office and runs another project in cooperation with the department of green spaces to commonly improve existing open green spaces. In another district, the community work office is supported by a non-governmental organisation and subsidised amongst others by the city, enabling it to run several projects in the field of community work, sustainability and community enterprises.

(Elsen and Schicklinski 2016, 232)

Social and solidarity economy activities in the green spaces resource system, including (peri-)urban food production, have the potential to become the means of a social policy which, if based on the following eight basic principles elaborated by Elsen (2007, 55–6, own translation), is apt to drive integrated local and regional socio-ecological-economic development:

1 It defends the social and environmental vital interests and puts them before property interests.
2 It enables socioproductive participation through self-organised and common activities....
3 The social is an integral component of socioeconomic solutions. Social problems are not considered to be and treated as external to the economy.
4 Public duties are organised effectively and synergetically in plural and democratic forms – e.g. in multi-stakeholder enterprises.
5 Local social policy uses material resources and social capital in a socioproductive manner, generates and manages material resources and social capital.
6 It opens up learning options and possibility spaces for experimenting with new approaches of societal problem solving, also and specifically where people live in exclusion....
7 It is geared to a plural economy serving the satisfaction of human needs and respecting ecological boundaries. It needs the possibility to independently generate resources by acting in the market and in non-market-compliant economies for social objectives.
8 Against the backdrop of mass unemployment the relief of the concerned people from blackmailing economic deprivations through a guaranteed basic cover and from the degrading constraint to work as service in return for transfer moneys is necessary. The partial decoupling of gainful employment and income is the basis for the formation of new socially embedded economies.[12]

9.5 Learning and social capital building in the local arena

9.5.1 Empirical results

As evolving from the qualitative data, learning processes and the building of social capital have proven to be important intervening variables (cf. Figure 5.1). This subsection gives examples of advanced and less advanced processes of learning and social capital building.

Mental models are considered as a challenge in all sectors and regions. It is deplored that 'a relationship with nature ... has somehow been lost' (Paris, a3, 44–9), especially with urban dwellers, and that a lot of politicians are not aware of the necessity of education to understand the need for the socio-ecological transition (Paris, a3, 50–3). Apart from that, some cities report a conservative mentality in the administration: '"It cannot be done.", ... "That is the way it should be.", or "The developer knows better what is good for people"' (Lublin, a4, 24).

Several actors stress the importance of *political will* and courage with the local authority as preconditions for promoting the sustainability cause (Aalborg, a4, 43; Bilbao, a3, 38; Leeds, a4, 59; Saarbrücken, a4, 29) and for allowing citizen participation and giving room to self-organised initiatives. The local authority must have the sincere intention of involving citizens, being convinced of the value of citizens' input in the long term (Aalborg, a4, 43), thus *recognising citizen participation and self-organisation as a constituent part of democracy*. In reality, however, participatory tools might be used just because they are required by law without influencing further policy outcomes (Copenhagen, a3, 37, 62–4; Istanbul, a4, 62; Lodz, a4, 13; Paris, a4, 66). They might only be drawn on if they fit the political planning process and might only be suggested at a late stage (Cracow, a4, 75; Saarbrücken, a4, 55). If true will is missing, self-organisation might still emerge in forms of protest against established structures but never in collaboration with the local authority (Bilbao, a4, 41–7; Istanbul, a1, 81 and a4, 56, 62–4; Lublin, a4, 24; Madrid, a4, 70, 85; Saarbrücken, a4, 68; Thessaloniki, a3, 33). Little democracy beyond voting exists where the *local government* is *indifferent* towards self-organised initiatives (Thessaloniki, a4, 72–4). They may even be regarded as a disturbing factor (Naples, a3, 76) in political and administrative routines. According to this respondent, associations that want to take care of a public green space and that would even shoulder the costs of this are only allowed to do so because of the city's desolate financial situation (ibid.). In Timisoara the socially innovative idea of putting up green roofs which came from civil society actors was not taken up by the local authority, even though the structure of the socialist buildings, with several floors, lent itself to the installation of green roofs. Civil society actors even invited economic experts from Germany to present a viable green roof solution to the local authority (Timisoara, a4, 43–7). In the same city, although suffering from a serious lack of green infrastructure, the city's most biodiverse urban green space next to the river was sealed and built on without leaving an ecological corridor, disregarding the knowledge about its ecological importance provided by an NGO

(Timisoara, a4, 30, 99–100). The extreme case of *political oppression* ranging from hindering the operation of NGOs to physical violence during demonstrations was only reported from Istanbul (a4, 74–80). Lacking political will can stem from the fact that the local authority is *not yet used to applying citizen participation tools* and is *afraid of being criticised* by citizens (Lugano, a3, 110–13, 117, 119–20), or they *do not trust citizens* to be able to decide for the common good, insinuating that they only care for their own interest (Lugano, a4, 68). This shows that they are not used to the idea of citizens becoming active in common good matters beyond their voting right (Strasbourg, a4, 94–8, 101–4).

Lack of trust on the side of citizens is reported from every region but the West (Cracow, a4, 23–5; Glasgow, a4, 79–82; Lodz, a3, 120–6). It can be due to the secret, sometimes illegal, dealings between the public and the private sector with concomitant exercise of influence experienced by citizens (Milan, a3, 84). As a result, people can end up refraining from joining associations and ceasing to care about the common good (Milan a3, 57 and a4, 26). Citizens might not trust association leaders any more if they have experience of them being led by personal interests in the past (Larissa, a3, 73–5). They may also have experience of political scandals at higher levels as well as an inefficient legal system (Jihlava, a4, 81). It is also possible that existing participatory tools have been badly managed by the local authority so that citizens are tired of them (Bilbao, a4, 43). Citizens that mistrust local leaders do not participate, because they do not believe that their voice matters in the end (Glasgow, a4, 78–80). Several actors deplore *citizens' indifference* towards citizen participation and self-organisation. They say that citizens are not interested in the common good or in public matters and believe that only a minority of citizens is active, while the majority is not interested and at most complain (Larissa, a3, 62 and a4, 63–7; Milan, a4, 81; Paris, a3, 33; Sibiu, a3, 124–6 and a4, 77; Strasbourg, a4, 96–100). This can be due to a *lack of civic education* (Thessaloniki, a3, 61–5). Yet, a *lack of time* for voluntary work due to gainful employment and the fast pace of society is also mentioned as a reason for citizens' non-participation (Bilbao, a3, 104; Strasbourg, a4, 100). 'Maybe the citizens should get more involved, fight for more causes, but for the moment they fight for survival, and this is a problem which takes up all their time for the time being' (Sibiu, a3, 91). Historic reasons for citizens rejecting participation are invoked in the East, saying that they associate it with 'old-time communist social activism' (Lublin, a4, 50).

The *will to collaborate* must exist between actors within and across all sectors. Where no collaboration, possibly on an equal footing, exists (Milan, a3, 45 and a4, 77–83), public authorities do not *recognise that citizen participation and self-organisation are the constituent part of democracy*. A minority of actors claim that cooperation between civil society actors and the local authority does not exist at all. They deplore that there are no common projects between administration and civil society and that there is no response from the government to civil society actors' propositions or that it only happens due to a personal relationship with government employees (Sibiu, a4, 191–4). This is often the case if a general lack of organisation and knowledge is noted with the local authority, stemming from understaffing due to financial hardship or position assignment along clientelistic 'criteria'. In Cracow, 'a committee for public dialogue was … treated … as a necessary evil' (Cracow, a4, 51) by civil servants, and some civil society organisations were rather aggressive, leading to conflicts rigidifying (Cracow, a4, 51). Several actors stress that communication and collaboration between actors across sectors, but also within one sector, still has to improve (Cracow, a4, 31; Larissa, a4, 89; Strasbourg, a4, 71–5). In other cases it had existed until differing interests produced conflicts and the relationship broke down, leading to a halting Agenda 21 process (Bilbao, a4, 45–7; Saarbrücken, a3, 28; Rome, a1, 33–5). In Madrid, there is collaboration between environmental groups and left-wing political actors. However, environmentalists have not yet gained 'a political institutional space' (Madrid, a4, 42).

Depending on the level of citizen participation, citizen participation can be influenced by *aggregation rules*, which are one of the seven rule types defining the institutional setting of an action situation (Ostrom 2005, 186–210). 'Aggregation rules determine whether a decision of a single participant or multiple participants is needed prior to an action at a node in a decision process' (Ostrom 2005, 202). Through citizen participation and self-organisation, the number of actors increases since *new actors are entering the local action situation* and become involved in the decision-making process. This requires more sophisticated *coordination*. To achieve a fruitful collaboration between civil society, economy, and the local authority, *rights and duties of each party*, for example of public authorities, citizens, or associations, *need to be* clearly *defined*. Otherwise, civil society actors do not understand which tasks are delegated to them. This means that *rules* have to be established. These defined rules need to be controlled because there is always the risk of people taking advantage of their power (Rome, a1, 48–9). *Conflicts* emerge when stakeholders' power position risks being threatened by newly incoming actors. Thus, in a first step existing local power structures need to be analysed and understood. In a second step, ways of involving potential stakeholders in rule finding without bypassing present stakeholders must be found. In this process the local authority's task is to offer an institutionalised transparent meeting and discussion platform and to coordinate this process. Citizen participation procedures cannot be improvised but follow certain criteria. Clear rules as well as training for political and administrative staff on these are necessary in order to enable the local authority to handle this increased complexity.

A high level of *cooperation* is expressed in *regular institutionalised collaboration* between civil society representatives and the local authority. Collaboration can be direct or indirect. For example, regarding citizen participation in decisions about urban green spaces, citizens can participate directly in town councils which are open to everyone. Indirectly, they can be represented in a city's green council by a member of a citizens' association. Often different civil society actors collaborate, for example an NGO supporting citizens' initiatives to join forces and to increase chances of success (Copenhagen, a4, 63; Lugano, a4, 46;

Saarbrücken, a4, 71–3). A high degree of cross-sector cooperation can manifest itself for example in numerous activities in the field of urban food production in cooperation with the local authority, schools and universities (Leeds, a4, 31–6). The local authority along with the economy should invest into the potential, the activities, and ideas coming from civil society actors by creating a social dialogue. It should take place regularly in an institutionalised form. The examples of forms of collaboration that have not yet been institutionalised (cf. 7.4.2.2) illustrate the need for a local policy framework that *provides and supports a local arena* for evolving initiatives where experiments and errors can be made and joint learning takes place.

Often actors lament *a missing goal and strategy*. Where a future *joint strategy* exists, there is also a *culture of sustainability*, meaning that the need for it is clear to everyone and that everyone identifies with it as a goal. The socio-ecological transition can be 'driven by learning and norm-adopting individuals … [who are] capable of (1) developing critical levels of trust …, (2) developing … cooperation …, and (3) realising the net benefits of this cooperation' (Sauer 2016, 47). In the interviews, the majority of actors are quite specific about what they have learnt and what should be improved regarding sustainability issues in the city in general and the green spaces resource system in particular. The transition is seen as a mutual *continuous learning process* in the day-to-day work of all participating stakeholders, often leading to new innovative solutions (Madrid, a3, 63). These emerging solutions then have to be tested to determine whether they work locally with all stakeholders participating before being scaled up. Local good practice examples should be made visible and then also be spread (Paris, a3, 61; Timisoara, a4, 156–7). This is helped by *networking*, for example via participation in EU projects, which promotes the learning process across cities, groups, and individuals (Potsdam, a4, 167).

The local authority must guarantee that 'citizen participation and … self-organisation … [lead] to better and sustainable results in all planning and development processes' (Elsen and Schicklinski 2016, 236). One important factor required for this to be achieved is to *involve citizens from the beginning* of the planning process, as stressed by actors from all sectors (Aalborg, a4, 83–7; Copenhagen, a2, 61; Cracow, a4, 75–7; Lugano, a3, 121–5; Saarbrücken, a4, 54–9; Umea, a3, 126). If this is not done and citizens are confronted with a fait accompli, they might show resistance and protest at a later stage of the planning process (Lugano, a3, 125). What is known is more easily accepted and appreciated. A second factor is the necessity to *involve a wide range of actors* in the participatory procedure to make sure that not only the views of the best-organised group with the best lobbying capabilities, such as associations, are taken into account, with the rest remaining unheard (Copenhagen, a2, 94; Gothenburg, a4, 68; Milan, a4, 108). Attention must be paid to minimise the 'participation paradox' (Seley 1983, 20; cf. 6.3.2.4). Experience has shown that successful involvement is achieved by undertaking activities that cater to different groups of people, otherwise only those who are already committed come (Copenhagen, a3, 66; Leeds, a4, 19).

To achieve *real participatory urban governance*, powerful citizen participation tools should be applied (Bilbao, a4, 98; Istanbul, a1, 81; Lugano, a3, 153; Madrid, a4, 96). This means for example to shift from consultation to citizens budgets, referenda, and civic audits to reach all citizens, apart from those organised in associations (Naples, a3, 91 and a4, 93). Advanced technological development facilitates these steps (Lodz, a3, 59).

Awareness about the benefits of citizen participation and self-organisation and the necessity of the socio-ecological transition must be raised via *information* and *education* campaigns. It is about activating bottom-up action and reaching those who are not yet aware, through a process of communication (Larissa, a4, 41–2; Naples, a4, 32; Strasbourg, a4, 94–106). Perhaps these awareness-raising processes can be more successfully achieved in cities that are following a rigorous growth logic, despite pre-existing immense socio-environmental problems, since the social and environmental issues related to economic growth are most evident in these cities. If citizens want to participate, and are politically aware, it makes it easy for NGOs to gather support (Istanbul, a1, 43 and a4, 64). Raising citizens' interest to participate and self-organise is also easier with *concrete practical issues*, directly related to their neighbourhood, than with more abstract planning procedures (Lublin, a4, 36). Local activities of good practice in urban green spaces must be made visible (Timisoara, a4, 156–63), also with the help of *media*. It has to communicate ongoing activities and sensitise citizens. At the moment it does not sufficiently support the sustainability topic. This, however, is important due to the existence of *lobbying against sustainability*, which keeps it socially accepted to be unsustainable (Leeds, a4, 50). This makes it difficult to change public opinion, also because the deniers misuse science to draw a less alarming picture (Leeds, a4, 50, 53). Still, an attempt should be made to change public opinion by introducing 'small doable things' (Leeds, a4, 50) and reporting on those.

Cities most advanced in the transition have adopted a multidisciplinary sustainability approach to avoid missing out important aspects, and they operate in a process of *collaboration* and *compromise-finding* (Innsbruck, a3, 45; Linz, a3, 37; Rome, a1, 31), comprising a high degree of citizen participation from the beginning of the process. It is coordinated by a proactive local authority that jointly elaborates a *long-term strategy* for sustainability with all local stakeholders involved. Concrete options for citizen participation exist and are pointed out. The local authority can *encourage* and *facilitate* self-organisation, for example by coordinating volunteers' involvement and by supporting emerging initiatives financially and by providing space, material, and soil. Such cities run innovative projects with citizens' involvement that are then carried out on a voluntary basis, or they take up and support ideas emerging from self-organised citizens' groups. They foster the *innovative force* of civil society actors, as demanded by one of these actors:

> All the human potentiality, many are working on environment issues. People are very active. The city could give an important contribution.

So what we are lacking now is the political will and the economic part, because the people in Milan are really impressive on this topic. In this park we have an ethical purchasing group. We have fair trade groups, ... because people want to think outside the political boxes and think about the social aspects.

(Milan, a4, 36)

Successful examples have emerged out of *collective learning processes* in which changing and new rules have been internalised. To prevent misunderstandings and manage conflicts in a complex system of a multitude of actors, the local government needs to provide an *institutionalised transparent meeting and discussion platform* and coordinate the process. The basis for this is *political will*. Political actors can even be transition drivers, then interacting with other actors from a proactive administration, economy, and civil society stay the course (Aalborg, a4, 43–5). Not surprisingly, the 'lack of a clear political will to make sustainable development principle number one' (Lodz, a4, 29) is mentioned as a *failure factor* (similarly Leeds, a3, 39–41). *Networking* between stakeholders is facilitated by an *innovative committed administration* which then carries the political decisions out (Larissa, a3, 39–41; Rome, a1, 31; Timisoara, a3, 60).

9.5.2 Policy implications

A *joint understanding and vision* of the socio-ecological transition is the basis for action in the direction of sustainable city development and can only be created if all societal actors are involved in this process. 'A sustainable world can never be fully realised until it is widely envisioned. The vision must be built up by many people before it is complete and compelling' (Meadows *et al.* 2005, 273). The transition must be perceived as a *common collective undertaking* by all stakeholders to develop a culture of sustainability, meaning that the need for it is clear to everyone and that everyone identifies with it as a goal. A local sustainability vision oriented on the social values cited by Meadows *et al.* (2005, 273) – 'sustainability, efficiency, sufficiency, equity, beauty, and community' – provides a sense in life that goes beyond 'the accumulation of material things' (Meadows *et al.* 2005, 274). It does not come out of the blue and cannot be presupposed from the actors. Where it is not yet in existence, it must be created. For this, spaces for self-organisation and citizen participation must be provided since they offer joint learning opportunities and increase the possibility that striving for sustainability becomes the common goal. In the complex and by no means conflict-free process of interactive governance, such an overarching vision is absolutely necessary to bring actors together and to reunite them in the event of differing interests, reminding them of their mutual vision and goal. These are then operationalised in an overarching strategy and into specific goals, plans, and steering tools. Again, this process does not happen top-down but is negotiated in a participatory way by all actors. Another important factor is that sustainability must have a positive *forward-looking connotation* oriented on actors' potential, strength, and successes instead of focusing on weaknesses and failings. Here, the local authority can learn from civil society actors' motivations, creative ideas, and positive spirit.

A *common understanding* of sustainability transition for green spaces is evolving across sectors in several cities. This 'new way of thinking city' (Copenhagen, a4, 15) includes developing *joint, transdisciplinary strategies* as well as *institutional changes*, such as setting up a sustainability department. Roots for this are a *change of awareness and attitude*. In a Swedish city, the community started down this road in the 1990s already. This evolved into a large movement leading to the ongoing vivid implementation phase involving political and technical solutions as well as *constructive conflicts* (Gothenburg, a4, 21–3).

Sustainability cannot be enacted from above, but can only be achieved in a mutual continuous learning process in the day-to-day work of all participating stakeholders, often leading to new innovative solutions. In such a *wide societal learning process for active citizenship, education* and *life-long learning* is crucial in raising awareness and changing mentality, especially in creating a discourse about the relationship of economic growth and quality of life. The complex challenges and the tight time frame of the socio-ecological transition require lifelong learning at the organisational and individual level specifically in the field of transdisciplinary thinking in systems (Meadows *et al.* 2005, 259–60, 274; WBGU 2011, 21–5, 321). Cities that manage to create, provide, cultivate, and develop further formal and informal learning opportunities for citizens, administrative staff, policy-makers, and actors from the economic and the science sector can be described as 'learning cities'. Such opportunities include options for hands-on learning in concrete situations with a visible outcome *to improve citizens' agency* for the transition. Room and support must be given to *joint participatory experiments* that are evaluated after implementation. If they work, they can be scaled up. The one-size-fits-all solution does not exist, but a plurality of instruments is used which is tested incrementally. Sustainability must become a compulsory integrative part of the kindergarten/school/university and professional training *curricula*. *Networking*, for example by participating in EU projects, promotes the learning process across cities, groups, and individuals and allows for trans-regional learning processes. Here, the media plays a decisive role. Its task must be to 'inform governments and the public as continuously and promptly about environmental and social conditions as about economic conditions' (Meadows *et al.* 2005, 259).

Notes

1 Some respondents from big cities refer the term 'local autonomy' to the city level but also use it for the lower district level, wishing this level to receive more power from the city level (respondents from Istanbul, Rome, Naples).
2 The correlation between the variables 'Involvement of local civil society actors in urban green spaces governance' and 'Civil society groups in the green spaces resource system are common in the city' was proven to be significant. Both variables indicate different situations. Whereas the dependent variable refers to self-organisation which

can emerge with or without cooperation with the local authority, the other variable relates to citizen participation, thus implying as precondition an interaction between civil society and the local authority.

3 Rietzler's analysis focuses on Germany, yet other countries of the EU face equal problems.

4 Parts of this coordination task could be 'outsourced' to NGOs closely collaborating with the local authority as suggested by a Danish actor, for example for the local coordination of upscaling small-scale projects (Copenhagen, a4, 75).

5 Translated and reproduced from Helfrich and Bollier (2014).

6 In a civic audit a group of actors from different backgrounds organises an investigation on a specific field of city governance trying to identify the governance problem. To this end the local authority has to deliver information and is accountable to the group.

7 From: Elsen (2007); ©Juventa.

8 One of the most famous and successful examples of citizens' co-decision-making to implement urban sustainability projects can be found in the pioneering Brazilian city of Curitiba (Harvey 2012, 111).

9 Generally, the data from Freiburg was not drawn on for this study since the research focus there was not on green spaces (cf. 4.3.1.2). Yet, since Freiburg can be considered a 'best case' for some institutional changes in local governance for reaching the socio-ecological transition, it is mentioned here.

10 The term corresponds to the one of 'action situation' used in this book (my Note).

11 This stands in opposition to Lefebvre's (2009, 94) idea of *'autogestion'* – self-government which, thought through to the end, would make the state redundant (Purcell and Tymann 2014, 12).

12 See Note 7.

References

Barnebeck, Stephanie, Yannick Kalff, and Thomas Sauer. 2016. 'Institutional diversity'. In *Cities in transition: Social innovation for Europe's urban sustainability*, eds Thomas Sauer, Cristina Garzillo, and Susanne Elsen, 192–203. Abingdon/New York: Routledge.

Beck, Ulrich. 1986. *Risikogesellschaft: Auf dem Weg in eine andere Moderne*. Frankfurt am Main: Suhrkamp.

Beck, Ulrich. 2009. *Risk society: Towards a new modernity*. Theory, culture and society series. London: Sage.

Biesecker, Adelheid and Stefan Kesting. 2003. *Mikroökonomik: Eine Einführung aus sozial-ökologischer Perspektive*. München: Oldenbourg Wissenschaftsverlag.

Bureau of European Policy Advisers European Commission. 2011. 'Empowering people, driving change: Social innovation in the European Union'. Luxembourg: Publication Office of the European Union. www.google.co.uk/url?sa=t&rct=j&q=&esrc=s&source =web&cd=1&ved=0ahUKEwj815Pt_OLOAhVMKh4KHfcWCCIQFggpMAA&url =http%3A%2F%2Fec.europa.eu%2FDocsRoom%2Fdocuments%2F13402%2F attachments%2F1%2Ftranslations%2Fen%2Frenditions%2Fnative&usg=AFQjCNF-_ xW7coSQF9__INyY7jR5wM7Hzw&bvm=bv.131286987,d.dmo [27 August 2016].

Colding, Johan and Stephan Barthel. 2013. 'The potential of "Urban Green Commons" in the resilience building of cities'. *Ecological Economics*, 86: 156–66.

Colding, Johan, Stephan Barthel, Pim Bendt, Robbert Snep, Wim van der Knaap, and Henrik Ernstson. 2013. 'Urban green commons: Insights on urban common property systems'. *Global Environmental Change*, 23: 1039–51.

Council of Europe. 1985. 'European charter of local self-government'. http://conventions. coe.int/treaty/en/treaties/html/122.htm [28 August 2016].

de Rougement, Denis. 1977. *L'Avenir est notre affaire*. Paris: Stock.

Elsen, Susanne. 2007. *Die Ökonomie des Gemeinwesens: Sozialpolitik und Soziale Arbeit im Kontext von gesellschaftlicher Wertschöpfung und -verteilung*. Weinheim, Munich: Juventa.

Elsen, Susanne and Judith Schicklinski. 2016. 'Mobilising the citizens for the socio-ecological transition'. In *Cities in transition: Social innovation for Europe's urban sustainability*, eds Thomas Sauer, Cristina Garzillo, and Susanne Elsen, 221–38. Abingdon/ New York: Routledge.

European Commission (EC). 1995. 'Local development and employment initiatives: An investigation in the European Union'. Internal document SEC 564/95. http:// bookshop.europa.eu/en/local-development-and-employment-initiatives-pbCM899 5082/ [27 August 2016].

European Commission (EC). 2010. 'World and European sustainable cities: Insights from EU research'. Publications Office of the European Union, EUR 24353. https://ec. europa.eu/research/social-sciences/pdf/policy_reviews/sustainable-cities-report_en.pdf [28 August 2016].

German Advisory Council on Global Change (WBGU). 2011. Flagship report. World in transition: A social contract for sustainability. Berlin: WBGU. www.wbgu.de/file admin/templates/dateien/veroeffentlichungen/hauptgutachten/jg2011/wbgu_jg2011_ en.pdf [27 August 2016].

Gorz, André. 1988. *Métamorphoses du travail: Quête du sens: critique de la raison économique*. Paris: Galilée.

Gorz, André. 1997. *Misères du présent, richesse du possible*. Paris: Galilée.

Harvey, David. 2012. *Rebel cities: From the right to the city to the urban revolution*. London: Verso.

Helfrich, Silke and David Bollier. 2014. 'Commons als transformative Kraft: Zur Ein-führung'. In *Commons: Für eine neue Politik jenseits von Markt und Staat*, 2nd edn, ed. Silke Helfrich, 15–23. Bielefeld: transcript. www.boell.de/sites/default/files/2012-04-buch-2012-04-buch-commons.pdf [27 August 2016].

Intergovernmental Panel on Climate Change (IPCC), ed. 2015. *Climate change 2014: Synthesis report. Contribution of Working Groups I, II and III to the fifth assessment report of the Intergovernmental Panel on Climate Change*. Geneva. www.ipcc.ch/report/ar5/syr/ [27 August 2016].

Kalff, Yannick. 2016. 'Socio-ecological transitions in the energy system: The local gov-ernment view'. In *Cities in transition: Social innovation for Europe's urban sustainability*, eds Thomas Sauer, Cristina Garzillo, and Susanne Elsen, 59–92. Abingdon/New York: Routledge.

Kooiman, Jan and Maarten Bavinck. 2013. 'Theorizing governability: The interactive governance perspective'. In *Governability of fisheries and aquaculture: Theory and applica-tions*, eds Maarten Bavinck, Ratana Chuenpagdee, Svein Jentoft, and Jan Kooiman, 9–30. Dortrecht: Springer Science and Business Media.

Lefebvre, Henri. 2009. *Le droit à la ville*, 3rd edn. Paris: Economica-Anthropos (orig. pub. 1968).

Mayer, Margit. 2006. 'Manuel Castells' the city and the grassroots'. *International Journal of Urban and Regional Research*, 30(1): 202–6.

Mayors and representatives of local governments. 2015. 'Milan urban food policy pact: 15 October 2015'. www.foodpolicymilano.org/wp-content/uploads/2015/10/Milan-Urban-Food-Policy-Pact-EN.pdf [28 August 2016].

Meadows, Donella H., Jørgen Randers, and Dennis L. Meadows. 2005. *Limits to growth: The 30-year update*, 3rd edn. London: Earthscan.

Organisation für Eine Solidarische Welt/Organizzazione per Un mondo solidare (organisation for a solidary world), Neetwork of South-Tyrolean fair trade stores, Politis, specialised secondary school for tourism and biotechnology Marie Curie Meran, association 'Sortengarten Südtirol' (garden of sorts South Tyrol) & permaculture community garden Guggenber/Ulten, European Academy of Bozen/Bolzano, Arno Teutsch, Cristina Crepaz, and Autonomous Province of Bolzano – department presidium and external relations – office for cabinet affairs (oew). 2015. 'Südtiroler Manifest zur Ernährungssicherheit: "Den Planeten ernähren" – Was wollen, was können, was müssen wir tun'. www.eurac.edu/de/services/meeting/events/PublishingImages/Pages/Tag-der-Entwicklungszusammenarbeit/Manifest.pdf [27 August 2016].

Ostrom, Elinor. 2005. *Understanding institutional diversity*. Princeton NJ: Princeton University Press.

Ostrom, Elinor. 2007. 'A diagnostic approach for going beyond panaceas'. *Proceedings of the National Academy of Sciences*, 104(39): 15181–7. www.pnas.org/content/104/39/15181.full.pdf [28 August 2016].

Ostrom, Elinor. 2009. 'Gemeingütermanagement: Perspektiven für bürgerschaftliches Engagement'. In *Wem gehört die Welt? Zur Wiederentdeckung der Gemeingüter*, eds Silke Helfrich and Heinrich-Böll-Stiftung, 218–28. Munich: oekom. www.boell.de/sites/default/files/assets/boell.de/images/download_de/economysocial/Netzausgabe_Wem_gehoert_die_Welt.pdf [28 August 2016].

Ostrom, Elinor. 2010. 'A long polycentric journey'. *Annual Review of Political Science*, (13): 1–23.

Purcell, Mark and Shannon K. Tyman. 2015. 'Cultivating food as a right to the city'. *Local Environment: The International Journal of Justice and Sustainability*, 20(10): 1132–47.

Regional Council Lombardy. 2015. *Legge Regionale 1 luglio 2015, n. 18 Gli orti di Lombardia. Disposizioni in materia di orti didattici, sociali periurbani, urbani e collettivi.*

Rietzler, Katja. 2014. 'Anhaltender Verfall der Infrastruktur: Die Lösung muss bei den Kommunen ansetzen'. Macroeconomic Policy Institute, report 94. www.boeckler.de/pdf/p_imk_report_94_2014.pdf [28 August 2016].

Rosol, Marit. 2014. 'Community volunteering as neoliberal strategy? Green space production in Berlin'. *Antipode, A Radical Journal of Geography*, 44(1): 239–57.

Roth, Roland. 2000. 'Bürgerschaftliches Engagement: Formen, Bedingungen, Perspektiven'. In *Bürgerschaftliches Engagement und Nonprofit-Sektor, Engagierte Bürgerschaft: Traditionen und Perspektiven*, eds Annette Zimmer and Stefan Nährlich, 25–48. Opladen: Leske + Budrich.

Sauer, Thomas. 2012. 'Elemente einer kontextuellen Ökonomie der Nachhaltigkeit: Der Beitrag Elinor Ostroms'. In *Ökonomie der Nachhaltigkeit: Grundlagen, Indikatoren, Strategien*, ed. Thomas Sauer, 135–60. Marburg: Metropolis.

Sauer, Thomas. 2016. 'Patterns of change: A general model of socio-ecological transition'. In *Cities in transition: Social innovation for Europe's urban sustainability*, eds Thomas Sauer, Cristina Garzillo, and Susanne Elsen, 39–58. Abingdon/New York: Routledge.

Schicklinski, Judith. 2016. 'Socio-ecological transitions in the green spaces resource system'. In *Cities in transition: Social innovation for Europe's urban sustainability*, eds Thomas Sauer, Cristina Garzillo, and Susanne Elsen, 93–124. Abingdon/New York: Routledge.

Schröder, Jörg, Tobias Baldauf, Margot Deerenberg, Florian Otto, and Kerstin Hartig (Weigert). 2010. 'Open scale, young & local ideas, München, 2009, Interdisziplinärer Ideenwettbewerb, Agropolis-München-Magazin: Die Wiederentdeckung des Erntens im urbanen Alltag'. Zur Eröffnung der Weltausstellung in Mailand ein Heft über den Münchener Beitrag zu 'Feeding the planet – energy for life'; mit einem Bericht über das neue Freiham und die Viktualientram. Munich: Lehrstuhl für Planen und Bauen im Ländlichen Raum, Technical University Munich.

Seyfang, Gill and Adrian Smith. 2007. 'Grassroots innovations for sustainable development: Towards a new research and policy agenda'. *Environmental Politics*, 16(4): 584–603.

United Nations Framework Convention on Climate Change (UNFCCC). 2015. 'Adoption of the Paris Agreement: Conference of the Parties, Twenty-first session, Paris, 30 November to 11 December 2015; Agenda item 4(b), Durban Platform for Enhanced Action (decision 1/CP.17), Adoption of a protocol, another legal instrument, or an agreed outcome with legal force under the Convention applicable to all Parties'. FCCC/CP/2015/L.9. https://unfccc.int/resource/docs/2015/cop21/eng/l09r01.pdf [27 August 2016].

United Nations General Assembly (UNGA). 2015. 'Draft resolution referred to the United Nations summit for the adoption of the post-2015 development agenda by the General Assembly at its sixty-ninth session: Transforming our world: the 2030 Agenda for Sustainable Development'. Seventieth session Agenda items 15 and 116. www.un.org/ga/search/view_doc.asp?symbol=A/70/L.1&Lang=E [27 August 2016].

Wolch, Jennifer R. 1990. *The shadow state: Government and voluntary sector in transition*. New York: The foundation center.

10 Steps to post-growth European cities

10.1 Civil society's role in the governance of urban green spaces in European cities

The empirical data presented in Chapter 5 suggests that civil society actors can make a difference in the governance of urban green spaces and thus that they are conducive to the socio-ecological transition, and even more so if a supporting policy framework is in place (cf. Chapter 9). Focusing on the independent variable, this section depicts civil society actors' role in the governance of urban green spaces in European cities as it currently is and as it could be, taking into consideration the post-growth discourse in order to finally and comprehensively answer the research questions.

Indications of the *transformative role of civil society* come from every region (Copenhagen, a4, 39; Lodz, a4, 32–6; Lugano, a4, 46; Thessaloniki, a3, 42–4 and a4, 13–15). Civil society becomes active next to established structures, sometimes in the form of protests against them, or activities emerge in cooperation with the local authority, depending on the specific political framework given (cf. Chapter 9). Some examples that were not mentioned in the text so far of how citizen groups contribute to maintaining existing green spaces, keeping them available and accessible for all, sometimes expanding them as well as ensuring their biodiversity and their diversity of uses for local needs, are given below:

- In Germany civil society actors have been influential for a comparatively long time. For example in Dortmund, for 30 years the nature conservation associations have been very active players in the designation of conservation areas, in landscape planning, and in the naturalisation of rivers, for example in the project 'Emscher-Umbau' (conversion of the Emscher, own translation) (Dortmund, a4, 28).
- In Sibiu an apartment-owner association has jointly decided to install a green terrace roof on top of their building with their own funds (Sibiu, a2, 103–13).
- Two of the most creative and innovative examples of civil society action come from Greece. In Thessaloniki civil society actors reacted to the city's

problems with the initiative 'Thessaloniki in a different way' (Thessaloniki, a3, 20, 76). It was created to promote a different image of the city by initiating and conducting actions around cultural, architectural, social, and environmental issues, bringing forward creative ideas and innovative proposals. It is supported by hundreds of volunteers often solving city problems such as the case of the regeneration of the harbour and a forest. In Larissa numerous innovative initiatives are conducted by a large NGO. It has organised lectures and conferences on sustainability issues, has conducted a youth exchange between Larissa and a Turkish city on climate change issues, as well as undertaken research on a nearby Natura 2000 area,[1] which succeeded in raising citizens' awareness of protecting it. Last, but not least, it has conducted seminars for farmers and scientists in the field of agriculture, more specifically on the analysis of fertilisers and pesticides, with the double goal of protecting both human health and the environment (Larissa, a4, 14–17, 48).

Citizen participation helps to achieve sustainability aims. In terms of the *quality of the outcome*, the results of participatory processes are considered to be better than those achieved in top-down procedures without citizen participation, since the probability is higher that local needs have been taken into account (Linz, a4, 84; Naples, a3, 28). 'A citizen aware and informed is always the best ally for an administration that wants to pursue certain objectives such as sustainability' (Rome, a1, 55). Even if citizens have not had their ideas taken on board, participatory processes *increase the acceptance of political decisions*, as citizens have the feeling they have been listened to, and thus taken seriously (Copenhagen, a4, 53).

The co-governance of commons fosters civic environmental education, underlines their value, and the necessity to safeguard them (Rome, a1, 54–5) and is thus an important step in the process of turning urban green spaces into *commons*. As expressed by an actor from Rome: '[What] helps a lot, also concerning the education to common goods, … is the perception that this is a common good, not that it belongs to nobody but that everyone takes care of it' (Rome, a1, 35). The more deeply people are involved, the more content they are with the result and the more they use the city, identifying with it and its urban space (Copenhagen, a2, 80). Participating in the care for urban green spaces creates a *feeling of ownership and responsibility* and lets citizens become active beyond their voting right (Copenhagen, a3, 37; Naples, a4, 23–4; Potsdam, a4, 195; Rome, a1, 35). The governance by local associations can become the centre of *community building* with urban green spaces becoming a meeting point for all citizens of the neighbourhood, thus promoting integration (Milan, a4, 48–52).

Self-organised activities can particularly serve a *corrective function for state or market weaknesses and failures*. In a Romanian case a landscape architects' association and students generated rapid economic solutions for the maintenance of some smaller urban green spaces in neighbourhoods with some support of the local authority (Timisoara, a4, 85–7). One of these was the creation of the first Romanian park for blind people. The association attracted funds and also cooperated with the Romanian association of sightless people (Timisoara, a4, 39–42). Where associations or enterprises assume the maintenance of urban green spaces, they can *prevent them from becoming dumping sites* and stop *private actors' building activities* emerging, as mentioned by a respondent from Naples:

> It is exactly here that the citizens need to be, because the private actor relies on the fact that the citizen does not care, and it has been for 30 years that the citizen is not interested in common goods, so the private actors can enter. Pretending that they are improving the area, they might even tell you: 'We have done the parking spaces. We solved the problem of the abandoned park'. So with the excuse to improve, here concrete and there concrete.
>
> (a4, 49)

Civil society actors even manage to *create green jobs* (cf. 7.4.2.3), as in the case of a big Greek NGO that has created a social work programme in four peripheries, one of them in Larissa. Here almost 300 young unemployed people work in the environmental and urban green spaces field (Larissa, a4, 15). Yet, altogether the research only revealed a small number of cooperatives in the field of urban food production (cf. 7.4.2.3) and none in the field of the maintenance of urban green spaces besides food production. Here, the potential is still far from being exploited in Europe. Ideas and good practices could be taken from successful examples outside Europe (for example Cuba, cf. Clouse 2014).

Regarding civil society–science interaction, civil society knowledge is in most places still an untapped resource. The empirical data reveals that universities and other research institutes are increasingly drawn on for their expertise by decision-makers in the sustainability discourse. However, very few examples could be found that equally *involve citizens' lay expert knowledge* and connect it to the 'official' one.[2] This constitutes an untapped opportunity since innovative and realistic solutions to local problems cannot emerge without taking into consideration the knowledge of the persons concerned.

Looking at the data, it seems that social innovation emerges mainly in civil society. Yet, there are also empirical examples showing that *social innovation* can emerge in all societal sectors – it is *not sector-bound*. Even if

> administrations in political bureaucracies and commercial corporations spontaneously rely on the familiar, and on the benefit expectations of the old path ... [also] a greater willingness to take risks ..., [is an] everyday [aspect] of corporate decisions and generational change. Contrary to the convenient preconception, administrations are institutions continuously undergoing a learning process.
>
> (WBGU 2011, 191)

Examples of social innovation emerging in local administration or politics are given in Chapter 9. Furthermore, social innovation also emerges in the economic sector. For example, a company has tried to deliver innovative solutions to contribute to the transformation from an industrial city to a post-industrial one, collaborating with the local authority (Bilbao, a3, 38). Another company is active in promoting urban biodiversity projects and has made urban gardening part of its planning goal, trying to foster mainly urban gardening projects because of the social function they provide (Paris, a3, 24). A third economic actor suggests the transformation of all former military camps into urban green spaces and to link a nearby forest to the city in order to increase the accessibility and availability of urban green spaces (Thessaloniki, a3, 82). In Lugano two landscape architects were informed about sustainable innovative approaches at their landscape architecture school, as part of their university studies, stressing the possible innovative force of science (Lugano, a3, 125–8). The emergence of social innovation in any sector can be fostered through education (cf. 9.5). In Lodz it is lamented that the current method of teaching fosters schematic thinking instead of critical thinking or 'thinking outside the box' (Lodz, a3, 112). This can lead to a lack of innovative thought when 'people get very entrenched in how they are going to do things and it is very difficult politically for those things to shift' (Leeds, a3, 109).

10.2 Conclusion

The socio-ecological transition will only succeed if action is taken at all levels – from global to local. At the global level, the German Advisory Council on Global Change (2011, 13) advises institutional changes. These are to upgrade UN Habitat[3] into a 'World Commission on Low-Carbon Urban Planning' (ibid.), to install a 'UN Specialised Agency for sustainable urbanisation' (ibid.), and to substitute the United Nations Environment Programme with a 'newly established UN specialised agency on the environment with far reaching authority' (ibid., 314). Strengthening global institutions to drive sustainable urbanisation would facilitate and accelerate the process of building low-carbon cities locally in a post-growth society. Being aware of the importance of polycentric governance, this research focused on the local level and contributed to a better understanding of what kind of lifestyles and conflicts are to be expected on the way to *achieving low-carbon post-growth European cities* (ibid., 336) by analysing current trends in the governance of green spaces across these cities. It dealt with the question of how, in the face of global threats like climate change and biodiversity loss, the socio-ecological transition in the green spaces resource system of European cities can be realised and examined civil society's role in this process.

One of this research's underlying hypotheses was that achieving sustainable land use is crucial for the socio-ecological transition in Europe and that especially the governance of the green spaces resource system in European cities plays an important part in this process due to increasing urbanisation and due to the multiple functions urban green spaces provide. The key assumption was that the transition is unimaginable without the participation and self-organisation of socially innovative bottom-up actors. It elaborated on the local conditions and the extent to which civil society can be a transition driver. Current civil society's contribution to the transition in the form of self-organisation and citizen participation was described and conditions for a local policy framework allowing for innovative solutions in the governance of urban green spaces were outlined. The conditions conducive to the emergence and the unfolding of bottom-up initiatives in the design and the preservation of urban green spaces were depicted. Reasons for failure or success of local transition processes were identified and analysed by looking both at the green spaces resource system and connected social structures to better understand how they interact.

The green spaces resource system is, more than for example the energy and water systems, determined by local factors, yet not exclusively, as the influence of EU and national environmental regulations on the governance of urban green spaces shows. Self-organisation and citizen participation emerges more easily and occurs more often in the green spaces resource system than in other resource systems. This is due to a comparatively high degree of local autonomy in this field and to the tangibility of urban green spaces. They are visibly situated in the citizens' living environment, and attempts to reduce them immediately affect their daily quality of life. It is also easier for citizens' associations to gather support for concrete issues, such as the protection of an urban green space, than for lobbying for the more complicated logic of self-sufficiency in the energy system or the introduction of an integrated water cycle.

Self-organised and cooperative forms of the governance of urban green spaces emerge, greatly differing in terms of numbers, proportions, duration, and growth rates according to different urban contexts. The continuing and increasing pressure on urban green spaces has made the local level a field of civil society action. Citizens have become increasingly aware of the importance of urban green spaces and are reacting to the trend of land consumption for building and infrastructure development, of commodification and privatisation tendencies. They protest against the disappearance of urban green spaces and become active in their maintenance, sometimes by growing food in them. These forms of self-organisation to reclaim and reappropriate urban green spaces in order to look after them can be considered a process of urban green commons creation. By changing existing urban spatial structures and creating new ones, prevailing power structures are challenged and democratic processes strengthened. Civil society's diverse, often creative actions, can be considered as fights about the creation of urban space against incumbent power relations and opens up a public discourse about the use of urban space. In this way, citizens become aware that they can influence the governance of urban green spaces and thus take part in designing their city, possibly calling for more citizen participation and self-organisation options also in other policy fields. In some places initial protest has evolved into constructive collaboration across sectors and a higher degree of citizen participation.

In this sense, green spaces in European cities can be considered laboratories of social innovation in which *solutions counting on the innovation force of bottom-up actors* in some places in interaction with open-minded representatives of the state and market sector are evolving to tackle local challenges. The examples of participation and self-organisation from cities across Europe show that people are able to cooperate, to organise, and to take on responsibility for urban green spaces, while also introducing new practices that support the transition. They contribute to the maintenance of these spaces which are available and accessible for all and possibly being expanded whilst ensuring biodiversity and allowing diverse use for local needs at the same time. Thus, they are becoming active players in local governance processes. In some cities civil society actors have fought for their influence, whereas in others it has been granted to them by the local authority, steered from above. Whereas in the majority of cities these are still niche projects, in a minority they have become important players in the governance of urban green spaces, meeting the local authority on an equal footing and cooperating with a wide range of actors.

Urban food production is one example of urban green commons being governed by local actors. The reawakened interest in producing food in cities shows that citizens want to actively participate in the creation of urban common space. A motive often stated for participating in growing food in the city is the wish to have a common outdoor nature-related meeting space to be able to identify with. Jointly growing food in cities provides a variety of learning options for sustainability. From these experiences a 'lost' relationship with nature can be rediscovered and regained, which might lay the foundation for respecting the environment in all aspects of life as well as developing long-term environmental civic engagement. Furthermore, democratic rules and cooperation are practices across different cultures, generations, genders, and social positions, countering the alienation and gentrification–segregation tendencies of cities, in order to ultimately contribute to a more inclusive society. These joint activities open up discourses and common space for ideas of how to become active in improving in concrete terms living conditions locally, while also bearing the global perspective in mind. They can raise awareness of the value of land as a common and for rethinking cities as food production sites. Knowledge of growing food is transmitted and issues like food sovereignty, sustainable agriculture, and the value of food, also linked to the topic of food waste and the need for local and organic food, are raised.

The data revealed that self-sufficiency in food production is of increasing importance, especially in Southern Europe, in order to mitigate private poverty. Food sovereignty, especially for citizens of a lower economic status, has become an issue, particularly in the aftermath of the multiple crises from 2008 onwards. The research brought to light existing civil society activities in the maintenance of urban green spaces in general and in (peri-)urban food production in particular. Both have the potential of being further developed as social policy options into social and solidarity economies in order to contribute to integrated local and regional socio-ecological-economic development. This raises further research questions of how the numerous bottom-up initiatives already in existence in this field can be advanced in this direction. Especially the potential of *using urban green spaces productively for food production in the scope of social and solidarity economy initiatives* is still far from being fully exploited. Another aspect that deserves further research is the revealed existing *processes of local cooperative knowledge production in the field of the governance of urban green spaces between civil society and scientific actors* in some cities which are a second cornerstone to designing sustainable local policy options. These two identified tendencies open up further research needs to better understand the functioning of a post-growth society in European cities and civil society's role in it.

One of this research's aims was to direct the attention of researchers and policy-makers to civil society's role and potential in initiating, contributing to, and sustaining processes of transition across European cities in order to create improved framework conditions for their involvement. Civil society action is accelerated by *advantageous framework conditions*, for example highly motivated innovative experts working as civil servants in the local administration who are little bound by bureaucracy and have a sufficient budget. Cities advanced in the transition run innovative projects with citizens' involvement that are then carried on, on a voluntary basis, or they take up and support ideas emerging from self-organised citizens' groups. These successful examples have emerged out of *collective learning processes* in which changing and new rules have been internalised. These processes are very often driven by committed key persons from all sectors that have first adopted changing and newly evolving norms and significantly pushed for their manifestation in rules. Here, successful norm adoption has led to higher levels of trust and cooperation between stakeholders and to vivid institutionalised interaction processes with the joint goal of the socio-ecological transition.

It cannot be judged yet whether self-organised and cooperative governance of urban green spaces yields better results in terms of a better internalisation of related social and environmental externalities, meaning higher levels of equity, sustainability, and efficiency, than market- or government-based provisions. This is because on the one hand many bottom-up activities have only started recently, and more time is needed to evaluate their impact. On the other hand it is sometimes difficult to attribute successful outcomes to a specific sector. Indeed, local actors operate in the governmental, economic, and civil society realm of society. Although the socio-ecological transition is not feasible without realising and incorporating civil society's innovative potential, social innovation is not bound to the civil society sector but can equally emerge in the governmental and economic sector. Very often, it is collaboration across sectors that allows initiatives to succeed. Also, numerous actors at the local level take double or even triple roles, being present and active in more than one sector,[4] thus complying with Ostrom's thoughts on the benefits of *institutional diversity*. Yet, in all cities, responsibility for the governance of urban green spaces remains with the local authority on whose will for cooperation self-organised actors are highly dependent to scale up successful bottom-up actions.

Cities most advanced in the transition draw on the potential of civil society actors by opening up two-way information channels and by providing concrete options for citizens to participate in local governance processes as well as spaces and support for self-organisation [, recognising public green spaces as urban green commons]. With such a cross-sectoral interactive networked governance style, the possibility of incorporating all actors' knowledge for jointly advancing the sustainability cause in a process of constant, not conflict-free, negotiation of interests is highest.

(Elsen and Schicklinski 2016, 238)

Under such conditions citizen participation and self-organisation in the governance of urban green spaces can unfold and drive the transition to a post-growth society. Yet, the process of involving civil society actors in the governance of green spaces is also to be considered as a tightrope walk between the creation of urban green commons and a functionalisation of civil society actors for neoliberal urban development strategies with concomitant further drawbacks in public budgets. The inherent risk of the latter cannot be denied and civil society actors must be aware of it and self-confidently raise the issue in the negotiation process with the local authority in the case of such tendencies.

Giving space to self-organisation and proposing citizen participation can be tiring and often more exhausting than a mere top-down approach. Yet, local authorities should not refrain from drawing on the potential of including citizens' force, will, and innovation spirit and in times of tight local budgets might not even have another option. It is mainly the task of the local level to allow these spaces of self-organisation and citizen participation, yet regional, national, and EU politics have to provide adequate legal framework conditions to facilitate civic engagement.

The data features that the *logic of economic growth*, accepting its social and environmental externalities, still determines the legal framework as well as most local actors' decisions. Rules – expressed in the legal framework from the local to the EU level – are still not sufficiently modelled around sustainability outcomes, meaning taking into consideration long-term social and environmental externalities with a concomitant shift in incentives. The persistence of the economic growth logic manifests itself in ongoing *soil sealing* and continuing *urban sprawl* due to infrastructure and building development pressure. Swimming against this tide is possible, as numerous examples from across Europe show, yet requires not only awareness and stamina on the individual level but also a joint vision, political will, a supporting legal framework setting the right financial and fiscal incentives, as well as a certain degree of local autonomy. Otherwise, short-term profit interests will continuously determine actors' choices, be it for the mere need of closing holes in strapped public budgets or for securing jobs.

The data shows that mere state and market solutions for the problems of ecological resilience and further ecological and social outcomes of the green spaces resource system are not sufficient and meet significant obstacles in times of scarce public resources. Here, diverse forms of self-organised and cooperative governance of urban green spaces which voluntarily take on important functions that were previously provided by governmental or market actors become important. A counter-power from below emerges here with the potential to surpass its current niche status. Most often it originates in civil society but is then also carried into the economic and political sectors, thus being institutionalised, depending on whether political, social, and economic framework conditions are conducive or hindering.

Especially in the governance of green spaces, with a resource system in which high profit rates are expected from the privatisation of public land, a strong legal framework is necessary to prevent these tendencies, allowing an exit from the economic growth logic and the provision of *growth-neutral land use* within European cities. It seems that this ultimate goal can only be reached with the strengthening of participation and self-organised capabilities in order to create a counterweight from below to a binary state and market logic of commodification.

Notes

1 The Council Directive 92/43/EEC of 21 May 1992 on the conservation of natural habitats and of wild fauna and flora obliges each member state to 'contribute to the creation of Natura 2000' (Council of the European Union 1992, 6, article 3, paragraph 2), which is 'a coherent European ecological network of special areas of conservation' (ibid., 6, article 3, paragraph 1).
2 This could be partly due to the research design (cf. 4.3.1) which did not explicitly inquire about civil society–science interaction.
3 The United Nations programme for human settlements.
4 For example the head of the green spaces department of a German city, who also writes scientific articles, holds lectures and is an active member of the NGO Friends of the Earth Germany.

References

Council of the European Union. 1992. 'Council directive 92/43/EEC of 21 May 1992 on the conservation of natural habitats and of wild fauna and flora'. *Official Journal of the European Communities*. http://eur-lex.europa.eu/legal-content/EN/TXT/PDF/?uri=CELEX:31992L0043&from=en [28 August 2016].

Clouse, Carey. 2014. *Farming Cuba: Urban farming from the ground up*. New York: Princeton Architectural.

Elsen, Susanne and Judith Schicklinski. 2016. 'Mobilising the citizens for the socio-ecological transition'. In *Cities in transition: Social innovation for Europe's urban sustainability*, eds Thomas Sauer, Cristina Garzillo, and Susanne Elsen, 221–38. Abingdon/New York: Routledge.

German Advisory Council on Global Change (WBGU). 2011. Flagship report. World in transition: A social contract for sustainability. Berlin: WBGU. www.wbgu.de/fileadmin/templates/dateien/veroeffentlichungen/hauptgutachten/jg2011/wbgu_jg2011_en.pdf [27 August 2016].

Index

Page numbers in *italics* denote tables, those in **bold** denote figures